MAGGIE

*An Intimate Portrait
of a Woman in Power*

CHRIS OGDEN

SIMON AND SCHUSTER
NEW YORK • LONDON • TORONTO
SYDNEY • TOKYO • SINGAPORE

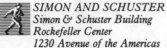 SIMON AND SCHUSTER
Simon & Schuster Building
Rockefeller Center
1230 Avenue of the Americas
New York, New York 10020

Copyright © 1990 by Christopher Ogden
Designed by Edith Fowler
Manufactured in the United States of America

10 9 8 7 6 5 4 3 2 1

Library of Congress Cataloging in Publication Data

Ogden, Chris.
    Maggie : an intimate portrait of a woman in power / Chris Ogden.
        p.   cm.
    Includes bibliographical references.
    1. Thatcher, Margaret.   2. Prime ministers—Great Britain—
Biography.   3. Women in politics—Great Britain—History—20th
century.   4. Great Britain—Politics and government—1979—
I. Title.
DA591.T47037   1990
941.085'8'092—dc20
[B]   90-9480
ISBN 0-671-66760-2   CIP

To Deedy, Margaret, and Michael

Contents

Introduction

I THOUGHT ABOUT writing this book as I watched Margaret Thatcher storm to her third victory in 1987. In a departure from what might have been expected of a conservative British prime minister, she launched her campaign from the Kremlin, eyeball to intellect with Mikhail Gorbachev. For three days, their aggressive jousting crackled. She emerged glowing. Then, back in Britain she capitalized on her surge in popularity by calling an election for another five-year term. Many mornings during that four-week political campaign, I attended her daily news conferences at Conservative party headquarters. Many cabinet members would flank Thatcher, but they sat almost mute, sometimes quavering if she turned to them. She answered everything; she seemed to know everything.

When she chalked up a huge 101-seat margin in the House of Commons that June, she was ensured her place in history, the first prime minister since the 1820s to be elected to three consecutive terms. More important, winning meant her revolution would continue past the decade mark. She was at the absolute peak of her power. She dominated the agenda and her political opposition at home. Overseas, she was helping out Ronald Reagan one day, doing business with Gorbachev the next, all the while defining Britain's role in Europe, in the West, in the world. Other leaders looked liked midgets by comparison. At that moment, over incredible odds, she was the strongest, most powerful woman in the world. Britain was back on the map as Thatcher's Britain. She had managed a remarkable turnaround.

The country had been nearly bankrupt in 1975 when she hijacked her Conservative party. A worried World Bank was sniffing around the Bank of England. Edward Heath, the party leader and former prime minister, had lost two elections the previous year to the socialist Labor party. The Conservative party's squires and grandees huddled in their all-male Pall Mall clubs over claret- and port-soaked lunches, wringing their hands. Something had to be done. But, oh woe, what? Tougher industrial competition loomed from the continent and Asia. Wallet-rattling taxation and a feather-bedded trade union force that preferred masochistic strikes to work shunted investors elsewhere. Some of the nation's best thinkers were streaming out of Britain for more challenging and lucrative work elsewhere.

Britain was the "sick man of Europe," the butt of political lampoonists. Strikes were "the British disease." The nation was on skid row, addicted to big government. Britain had hit bottom. Unlike the United States, France, and the Soviet and Chinese communist giants, Britain had not experienced a reordering revolution in the modern era. Real revolution was the last thing traditional Conservatives wanted, and the socialists had no intention of allowing a diminution of state control. Both had done little more than make small adjustments as the country plunged.

Among Conservatives, Thatcher was an oddball, a virtual outcast among the stodgy Tories. Once a party of privilege, of landed gentry and solid middle-class managers, the Tories were the ultimate old boys, networked and confident. Thatcher came from the bottom of the middle class in a nation where class counts, particularly in the corridors of power. Making it to the top of the Conservative party was in many ways tougher than becoming prime minister.

She was a woman in a society still dominated by men. She was also a ferociously hard worker in a culture that had never prided itself on sweat equity, especially at the top, and a smasher of institutions in a nation that clings to rites and traditions and is notoriously impervious to change.

Hers has been the real life political equivalent of a Horatio Alger hero's fictional rise from rags to riches. Unlike India's Indira Gandhi, Pakistan's Benazir Bhutto, or Corazon Aquino of the Philippines, this woman didn't make it through family connections. Only Golda Meir, prime minister of a young Israel, shared anything like Thatcher's uphill struggle from grocer's daughter in what's been called "the most boring town in England" to become the most dominant political figure in peacetime Britain this century.

She did it by arriving in 10 Downing Street in 1979 with a vision and the backbone to put it in place. The vision was a Britain without socialism, where free enterprise flourished, a Britain that was proud again. She tackled the goals with the fervor of an evangelical mission. A modern medievalist, Thatcher seeks solutions the way knight crusaders sought the Holy Grail. To her, political battles are fundamental, between the forces of light and dark, good and evil, individuals and the state. To her, the infidels were Communists and socialists, enemies of hard work and enterprise, those who threatened freedom. Her rebel force would drive these unbelievers from the field.

No one has been spared in this crusade, an effort marked by constant battles against sometimes towering odds. Overseas, she fought a war with such unabashed vigor that her defense chief called her "the toughest man we've got." At home, she bludgeoned the nation's most difficult union into submission after a year-long, bloody brawl. Inside her cabinet, she butchered weak or less committed ministers and decapitated rivals to emerge transformed from drone to queen bee. Each step of the way, she battled deep-rooted national inertia.

When Thatcher won her third time, I had been writing about her for two years. I had traveled with her in Britain and overseas, had interviewed her, had seen her deal with heads of state and watched her perform in the House of Commons. Her dominance was breathtaking. She was a terrific book subject, but plenty of books, some quite distinguished, had been written about her or were under way. After investigating, however, I discovered that almost all were written by British authors primarily for British audiences.

Yet Thatcher's impact has extended far beyond Britain. She is a larger-than-life global character, the only major leader who endured throughout the entire decade of the eighties. Her uncompromising feelings about Europe compelled continental leaders to pay Britain the kind of attention that Charles de Gaulle coerced for France. Moscow and Beijing courted Thatcher. Black Africa first reviled, then grew to respect her. The Arab world sought her involvement in the Middle East peace process. The Commonwealth battled her over South Africa. Argentina fought her over the Falklands, making her a household name in South America and proving the sobriquet "Iron Lady" to be no misnomer.

Her impact on the United States, and America's on her, has been unparalleled. Thatcher is not just another intellectual Atlanticist. From her early years during World War II to her most recent visits to George Bush at Camp David, Thatcher has admired almost everything about the United States except its budget deficit. Her Yankee identification is an important part of her psyche. Like most so-called Little Englanders, she distrusts continental Europeans. Dogged American determination excites her. She likes the can-do spirit of self-made men. And Americans like her. During the last American presidential campaign, candidates raced to show that they "knew" Thatcher, hoping some of the identification would rub off.

Thatcher was formed by and still remains loyal to the same values that motivate most Americans: self-reliance, hard work, practical financial simplicity. Her appreciation of Ronald Reagan's conservatism and his ability to rally what she considered a confused United States created one of the most extraordinary political relationships this century. Reagan was the chief executive officer of the West during most of the decade, but Thatcher was his chief operating officer, keeping the president on track and the Alliance from backsliding. Until the arrival of Gorbachev, no other foreign leader had anything remotely approaching Thatcher's influence on the United States during the 1980s.

Despite that, despite the significance of her links to the last four U.S. presidents, despite her enormous popularity in the United States, despite her public infatuation with American values, no American in years had written a book about the Thatcher phenomenon. No American, free of the burden of sentiment about class distinctions, had tried to define what happened in Britain to make Maggie not only the most powerful woman in the world, but one of the most powerful leaders, period. This American journalist, a former Moscow and White House correspondent, decided to try, bolstered by some British experiences that predated this latest 1985 to 1989 assignment.

As a child, I had spent the better part of 1952 in Britain. My father, a newspaper editor on a writing sabbatical, took me to Downing Street to wave at Prime Minister Winston Churchill. There wasn't much else to cheer then. Postwar rationing remained in effect. There was little fuel; our rental flat was always cold. Bomb debris littered the country. An outbreak of hoof-and-mouth disease meant all milk had to be boiled. Clean air legislation didn't exist and thick, dank clouds of fog and smoke often choked London. Thatcher was a twenty-seven-year-old newlywed who lived in my neighborhood. I didn't know it at the time, nor would it have mattered if I had. What did strike me at seven was postwar Britain's grimness. "England stinked," I told my parents on arriving in France later that year. Thatcher came of age during those bleak years and the atmosphere I remember helped shape her determination.

From 1970 to 1972, I was back in Britain reporting for United Press International. Prime Minister Harold Wilson's Labor government fell to Heath's Tories soon after my arrival and Margaret Thatcher was installed as education secretary. In no time, she was being pilloried as "Thatcher, milk snatcher," the meanest woman in Britain. Those also were tough years for Britain. Government was ineffectual. Violence ripped through Northern Ireland and trade unions ruled the country. Rationing had ended, but endemic strikes made life miserable. At the UPI offices off Fleet Street, we worked by candlelight when power cuts blacked out London. Newspapers printed tips on how to keep warm without heating. The situation deteriorated so badly that Heath later put public employees on a three-day work week. There was no money in the Treasury for more. The economy was headed for disaster.

By my return in 1985, six years into Thatcher's crusade, Britain was a different place—vibrant, proud, productive. It was not an unqualified success story. The Thatcher tide has not raised all Britain's boats. Social services, the education system, and the weakest segments of society have suffered under her rigid, self-help approach to government. Many Britons rightly fault Thatcher for running a revolution that has left too many casualties along the roadside. She is unpopular with intellectuals who hate her toughness, her single-minded zeal, and her schoolmarmish nagging. Her critics niggle that she hasn't done it all on her own. She's been helped by worldwide economic growth throughout much of the 1980s. A sweeping privatization program—"selling off the family jewels" was how former Prime Minister Harold Macmillan described it—and revenues from North Sea oil made the British economy artificially good. That's all true. Those developments helped. They were surgical tools that Thatcher used to operate on her patient.

It is also true that at the beginning of the 1990s, Thatcher may well be past her prime. In a fast-changing world with key new players, she faces big and serious problems. Her trademark toughness, once her greatest strength, could become a crippling weakness if Thatcher can't show sufficient flexibility to adapt to new political terrain.

With a worldwide economic slowdown taking shape, the British economy has turned rocky again. Thatcher has also hurt herself at home by antagonizing, more than usual, her fellow Tories. Her chief challenger, the Labor party, seems to be getting its act together after years of internal dissension. The collapse of the centrist Alliance party means that Thatcher no longer faces a divided opposition.

Her friend Ronald Reagan has retired from power, and George Bush, who is far more comfortable than Reagan dealing directly with François Mitterrand of France, West Germany's Helmut Kohl, or for that matter, Mikhail Gorbachev, doesn't rely on her as much. Her cautions against lessening NATO's vigilance despite the collapse of the Soviet bloc, however appropriate, sound dated. Her reluctance to push ahead with the political and economic integration of Europe has isolated her among the Allies and made her appear obstructionist, a brake on the high revving engine on the continent.

These are major problems for Thatcher, deeper, tougher, more strategic than the many she's already solved. She's been in big political trouble before, at odds with everyone, infuriating friends, and trailing political enemies in polls by double-digit percentages only to recover in dramatic fashion. In 1981, she seemed incapable of pulling out of a slump, but did thanks to the Falklands; five years later, she was close to being counted out again, but confounded the skeptics. However, this time Thatcher's troubles are worse. Looking like yesterday's woman instead of tomorrow's is the biggest challenge she's faced. Few rule out her capacity to recover, but if Thatcher doesn't change, she may not get the fourth term she wants to win in 1991 or 1992.

Whether she wins it or not matters a lot to her but in the long view is almost irrelevant. The point is that, past her prime or still the best man they've got, Thatcher has already changed Britain. She has given the grand old lady the monumental kick in the pants she needed. She's given Britons new options, including the sometimes uncomfortable awareness that their only limits now are self-imposed. She has restored pride and signposted the way to prosperity, no little accomplishment in a country which has long believed that the creation of wealth was simply too materialistic, too showy, too American. Thatcher understood that the failure to create wealth, the failure to stimulate productivity, investment, and talent meant the demise of Britain.

That prospect of ruin was no idle possibility. Britain was a terminal patient. But Thatcher proved herself to be precisely what the country needed, the right person at the right moment with the right prescription. Others had tried pills and bandages. Thatcher knew that only radical surgery had a chance of working. By the time she arrived, the rot and decay had set in.

CHAPTER ONE

The Inheritance

THE BATTLE OF BRITAIN in 1940 may have been, in Churchill's words, the nation's "finest hour," but until Margaret Thatcher, the rest of the twentieth century was a long downhill slide. When Thatcher took over in 1979, the country boasted the world's greatest English-speaking actors, its best tennis tournament, and the greenest grass anywhere. After that, top quality dropped off fast. The 1960s offered a brief spasm of fresh inspiration that uplifted the nation's spirits and obscured the depth of the rot. By the 1970s, the pop music crown had reverted to the United States and fashion cues were coming once again from France and Italy. Design prizes went to Japan. Germany opened up an ever wider economic lead. In pre-Diana Britain, even the royal family was insipid.

Contrast the gloomy postwar years with the late nineteenth century, when the British Empire, at the height of its influence, controlled 20 percent of the globe. By her Diamond Jubilee in 1897, the sixtieth year of her sixty-three-year reign, Queen Victoria ruled 450 million people, a quarter of the world's population and more subjects than the combined empires of Russia, France, Germany, and Portugal.[1] Britain, slightly smaller than Oregon, controlled 11 million square miles of territory, more than triple the size of the Roman Empire at its height. The Royal Navy, with 61 battleships— 330 ships and nearly 100,000 sailors in all—dominated global sea-lanes, while hundreds of merchant vessels carrying 45 percent of the world's cargoes collected natural resources from the corners of the empire to drive the factories of the Midlands where the Industrial Revolution first took off.

Britain's economic might equaled its political reach. By the turn of the century, Britain controlled a fifth of all world trade, which was based on the pound sterling; three-quarters of the world's investments were channeled through The City, London's financial district.

Britain—Great Britain then—appeared omnipotent, unchallengeable, but its very dominance made it a target for jealous rivals. At sea, Germany's Kaiser Wilhelm struggled to overcome Britain's primacy in blue-water warships. In North Africa, France chipped away at British colonial might. In southern Africa, Brits battled Boers, the descendants of German-Dutch colonizers. Russia threatened British boundaries in Persia and Afghanistan. Across the Atlantic, the United States' Industrial Revolution, which began much later than Britain's, was in full swing, feeding a surge in American growth. The railroad boom led to a growth burst in the U.S. coal, iron, and steel industries, while development of mass production techniques, such as Henry Ford's assembly line, sent America's manufacturing strength soaring. The invention of the wireless and telephone expanded markets and increased the competitive pressure on Britain.

For years there has been debate over whether economic stress and competitive market forces alone would have brought down the empire. Some economists have argued that Britain's huge overseas investment—by 1914, 43 percent of all overseas investment was British—meant less capital at home, lower domestic investment, and weak productivity. Others have said that diversification was underway and that Britain might well have adjusted and preserved its dominance if only peace had continued.

But a 1914 assassination in the Balkans changed everything, particularly the global economy and, by direct implication, Britain's control. Four years later, when World War I was over, Britain was left devastated. The empire had lost three million subjects, including 962,661 citizens in Britain alone. Another two million had been wounded, some so grievously that they ended up wards of the state for the rest of their lives.[2] The island kingdom had lost more than 15 percent of its assets. It owed $11 billion to European allies and $5 billion to the United States, which the war had transformed into a leading economic power. Along with La Belle Epoque, the old international economic order was over.

Britain, though, had "won." France had been invaded and suffered nearly twice as many casualties. Germany had been decimated and disarmed, its naval might sunk. The Austro-Hungarian Empire lay fractured into statelets. The Russian Empire lost chunks of western territory, then suffered revolution and civil war. The United States emerged from World War I as the real winner. The United States entered late, in 1917, and suffered 116,000 deaths, but was otherwise physically untouched by the war. In 1913, the United States was a debtor nation, nearly $4 billion in the red; by 1919, it was a solid creditor, in the black for almost the same amount. Japan had also made sharp inroads in Asia during the war, cutting sharply into Britain's economic dominance. While Britain was fighting, Japan was selling as fast as it could in China, the East Indies, and India, all traditional imperial markets. As demand increased for the new-age fuels, gas and oil, interest in British coal dropped. Britain's shipping advantage was also undercut; the war had produced a glut of ships. In that lucrative and competitive field, Britain also watched its leadership slip away.

Clambering back was difficult. Having lost overseas assets and facing war debts and a depleted treasury without the trade surplus it had traditionally enjoyed, Britain had to tighten its belt. But too nostalgic, too hopeful that the prewar situation could be retrieved, Britain did not want to. It wanted the good old days, with London back on the pedestal reserved for the world's leading banker. In the early 1920s, as the United States poured billions of investment dollars into Europe, ill-founded confidence returned to Britain. In 1925, the year Margaret Thatcher was born, Britain's new chancellor of the exchequer, Winston Churchill, put the country back on the gold standard, valuing the pound sterling at $4.85. Churchill harbored some doubts about the move but said later that if he had not acted, the world would have gone to gold on the basis of the dollar rather than the sterling rate. The decision had been more emotional than rational. The pound was too high, particularly compared with the dollar and French franc, which were backed by stronger gold reserves. Britain was trying to lead the world the way it had before the war, but without the reserves to back it up.

The decision exemplified a serious problem. Britain needed tough, decisive leadership between the wars, but got reminiscence instead. Horrified by the brutality of the war, the pendulum of behavior reverted to mellow docility. After the horror of the teens, British ruling life in the 1920s and 1930s was gentle and orderly. Romantic idealism flowered. Energy and driving zeal, the kind that Nelson and Wellington once typified and that Margaret Thatcher

would try to reinject into the nation a half-century later, were discouraged. "Duty and chivalry are of more account than ambition
and self-seeking," explained a Colonial Office training manual of
the period.[3] Style and upbringing mattered more than competition.
Unfortunately for Britain, the rest of the civilized world felt differently. Rivals had spotted Britain's ripe softness and were behaving ambitiously indeed. "In applying the qualities of gentleness,
trustfulness, altruism and a strict regard for moral conduct to a
sphere of human activity where cunning, cynicism, opportunism,
trickery, and force, all in the service of national self-interest, still
held sway, the twentieth-century British stood disarmed and
blinded by their own virtues," said Correlli Barnett in *The Collapse
of British Power*.[4]

No one typified these years more completely than Stanley Baldwin, the Conservative prime minister when Margaret Thatcher was
born. Kindly, patient, and old-style virtuous, Baldwin hated anything that smacked of confrontation. His favorite mood was "one
of a sunset calm and nostalgia, in which the British nation, like an
old couple in retirement, enjoying the peaceful ending of the day,
contemplated some sweep of English landscape and harkened to
the distant church bells."[5] Baldwin felt life was to be savored and
enjoyed, a wonderful sentiment in the mid-1920s, when it appeared
that world economies were settling back onto a fairly even keel.
But appearances were deceiving. After the Wall Street crash in
October 1929, contemplating landscapes was an ill-afforded pastime. America's recession spread, and the strain began to show all
over the world.

James Ramsay MacDonald, Britain's first Labor prime minister briefly in 1924, returned to Downing Street in 1929, succeeding
Baldwin. A pacifist who fantasized about ridding the world of weaponry, MacDonald was baffled by the Depression. He tried to minimize the effects on Britons by keeping interest rates low and social
services high. The combination savaged the Treasury balance and
led to a then staggering deficit of $500 million. Business confidence
plummeted, and when Britain tried to get help from American
banks, the loans depended on MacDonald's success in putting the
nation's financial house in order. Cutting the deficit meant cutting
expenditures, anathema to a Labor government, and by the time
MacDonald got around to passing the cuts it was too late anyway.
In 1931, Britain abandoned the gold standard and slapped on high
protectionist tariffs; its economic system was collapsing.[6]

Political dangers mounted throughout the 1930s. Japan invaded Manchuria in 1931. Two years later, Hitler began rearming Germany. Italian dictator Benito Mussolini invaded Ethiopia in 1935, while in Spain, civil war raged. The United States, buffered by 3,000 miles of Atlantic Ocean, had retrenched and passed the Neutrality Act of 1935 to avoid the ties that had helped drag it into World War I. Britain was no more anxious to get involved, but with an English Channel only 21 miles wide, it lacked the luxury of geographic disinterest.

Plagued still by the memory of what it had endured in World War I, Britain wanted to hang on to what it had without fighting. "Left or Right, everybody was for the quiet life," Sir Robert Vansittart, permanent undersecretary of the Foreign Office, wrote in the early 1930s.[7] Top Foreign Office and Civil Service mandarins might have been more middle class in the 1930s than their predecessors, but they were no less idealistic and romantic.

In the pre-Victorian era, Britain's leaders had been tough, ruthless strategists, skeptical and suspicious, ready for a fight with swords, pistols, or fists. In the United States, Franklin Roosevelt was rallying Americans with fireside chats. When an MP suggested to Churchill that MacDonald or Baldwin follow FDR's lead, Churchill snorted that "if they did, the fire would go out."[8]

Consensus politicians, usually with strong religious sensitivities, this generation of leaders believed that British authority had flourished in part because it had high moral grounding. With the notable exception of Churchill, their between-the-wars strategy seemed based on the idea that compromise was the best way out of almost any tough situation. This amiable, misguided assumption governed Britain's relations with the world's other key players. As Correlli Barnett noted, at that time "the British approach to diplomacy was rather like their approach to sex: romantically remote from the distressing biological crudities."

More than two hundred years earlier, Thomas Hobbes had written, accurately, that "covenants without swords are but words." After the savagery of World War I, however, the notion of exercising power had become an alien, almost immoral concept in Britain. Britain did not want to rearm even if it could have afforded to. By 1935, when Thatcher was ten, the country's military strength had withered. The Royal Navy was stretched too thin to defend Britain's still far-flung interests. The combination of limited military capability and a national desire to maintain peace and avoid crisis led

Britain to adopt a policy of appeasement, buying off potential enemies by negotiating nonaggression pacts instead of fighting.

Neville Chamberlain, who became prime minister in 1937, became appeasement's most enthusiastic proponent, and the consequences were disastrous. Underestimating Hitler's long-range goals and hoping to keep him pinned down fighting Stalin in the East, Chamberlain believed he could negotiate with the Nazi leader, but he was deluded. After Hitler moved into Austria in 1938, Chamberlain flew to Munich to sign an agreement giving Germany half of Czechoslovakia in return for a pledge that the Nazis stop there. The upper-class Englishman who led a still-substantial empire was pleading with the former house painter and ex-corporal, whose nation had been shattered only twenty years before, to allow Britain to maintain its serenity. Hitler made the deal with a smile, and Chamberlain returned home to proclaim in tragic error, "I believe it is peace for our time." Outside 10 Downing Street, delighted crowds sang, "For he's a jolly good fellow." Soon after, Hitler took the rest of Czechoslovakia and invaded Poland as well. With Chamberlain's treaty in shreds, Britain declared war on September 3, 1939.

Margaret Thatcher was a schoolgirl, six weeks shy of her fourteenth birthday, when Britain went to war. Every evening after school, she lingered in her father's grocery store beneath the family apartment to listen to customers talk about the war. A constant topic was speculation over when the United States would join in. In the First World War, Woodrow Wilson had tried earnestly to maintain neutrality. But Franklin Roosevelt, who swept to a landslide reelection in 1936, had no such inhibitions. When Britain abandoned appeasement as formal government policy, no one applauded more heartily than FDR.

After the Low Countries and France fell in 1940, Chamberlain resigned and was succeeded by Winston Churchill. Supported by a scant handful of MPs, Churchill had opposed appeasement from the start. As streams of influential Britons, including Edward VIII and former Prime Minister David Lloyd George, visited Berlin during the middle 1930s to meet and praise Hitler, Churchill stood alone in warning against the Nazis' multibillion-dollar rearmament program. A prophet without honor at the time, he was branded a warmonger. Prophetically, he had called Parliament's endorsement of the Munich agreement "a total and unmitigated defeat." As for

Chamberlain, Churchill said, "In the depths of that dusty soul, there is nothing but abject surrender."

Being a superior political analyst was not Churchill's sole advantage over his predecessor. Few, if any, leaders this century had more personal charisma than Churchill, who rallied Britain with his extraordinary rhetorical powers. On taking over the leadership of the Conservatives and the prime ministership, he gave a rousing promise: "I have nothing to offer but blood, toil, tears, and sweat. You ask what is our policy? I will say it is to wage war . . . with all the strength that God has given us. That is our policy."

Churchill also knew that the war could not be won without the help of the United States. The U.S. economic challenge to Britain in the 1920s and its political isolationism in the 1930s had made Chamberlain skeptical of America's intentions and its commitment as an ally. "It is always best and safest," he once said, "to count on nothing from the Americans except words."[9] Churchill, however, had close personal ties to the United States. He had visited often, and his mother, Jennie, was American. His personal relationship with Roosevelt, though they often disagreed, became one of the closest between two heads of government and one of history's most significant. According to David Dimbleby, Churchill sent messages to Roosevelt every thirty-six hours, on average, from 1940 to 1945. "No lover," said Churchill later, "ever studied the whims of his mistress as I did those of President Roosevelt."[10]

The "special relationship" developed once the United States entered the war and grew until Germany surrendered in May 1945, a month after the death of Roosevelt, whom Churchill called "the greatest friend we have ever known." Then, as now, the "special relationship" was a two-way street, mutually beneficial. A strong Britain meant a stronger America, as it does today.

Although Britain had been enormously valiant in the field and had again "won" the war with the help of the United States, winning disguised reality. Britain was so battered that its postwar prospects were as bad as the losers'. The cost was worse than World War I— there was almost nothing left at home. For the second time in thirty years, Britain's economy had been destroyed by war. Bombarded and blitzed by the Luftwaffe, city centers were leveled and left strewn with rubble. The national debt had tripled during the six war years. To finance the struggle, the country had sold its most lucrative prewar investments, increased short-term overseas borrowing, and watched domestic disinvestment skyrocket. Overall, the war cost Britain 25 percent of its national wealth.[11] The bombing had stopped, but otherwise, peace seemed little different from war. Victory failed to produce the spoils. Even the limited goods being produced were largely reserved for export to help out the depleted Treasury. Unrequited hopes bred cynicism and dismay.

The national landscape was bleak. Four million men and women moved back into civilian life, creating a housing and employment nightmare. Families crowded into dark, poorly heated tenements, and thousands of squatters took over homes. Coal fires cast a dark pall over city centers. Basic staples, including food and clothing, were hard to find, and a sense of deprivation pervaded the nation. There was little gasoline for car trips and tight restrictions on exporting currency, which meant no overseas holidays. Recovery, if it were to come at all, would take a long time. Indeed, rationing—of meat, eggs, sugar, and stockings—remained in effect another decade.

Thatcher came of age in these lean years. The effects on her were practical, not theoretical. Her powerful belief in freedom of choice, a central tenet of her revolution, had its roots in the war. Lack of choice was all too real when families stood in line outside stores and "registered with the butcher" to get food. Deprivation was palpable and would have a personal as well as philosophical impact. Having grown up with a ration book in her hand, she admitted in later life that she hoarded a tinned supply of food necessities. "No credit" was the policy of her father's grocery store, so paying one's way in good times and bad was a norm she would bring to government. The war also taught her that Britain's economic and military weakness after the first world war abetted Germany's aggression and led directly to the second. Thatcher discussed that lesson at home, studied it in school, and became convinced that only strength, not weakness, could deter aggression.

After World War I, the victorious Prime Minister Lloyd George was reelected. But after World War II, Churchill, who personified Britain and indomitable will, was crushed by an electorate which believed that Labor party leader Clement Attlee would give them a better life. Churchill was stunned. His wife Clementine tried to ease the pain. "It may well be a blessing in disguise," she told him. "At the moment, it seems quite effectively disguised," he snorted.[12]

The rest of the world was amazed, but there had been hints

at home that election was not a sure thing for Churchill. In 1944, while Thatcher was studying at Oxford, an Oxford Union debate resulted in a Conservative defeat on the issue that "this house is satisfied with the [Conservative Churchill] government's proposals for preventing unemployment and want." Another debate that year, on the proposition that "it is in the public interest that after the war monopolies should be publicly owned and controlled," which was Labor party policy, carried by a vote of 213 to 95.

The landslide election swing to Labor went well beyond the personalities of Churchill and Attlee. In 1918, Britain had looked back to what it had known before the war. In 1945, there was no going back. The boys were home with broader horizons. The war had turned out to be the greatest social leveler in modern history. Class barriers had tumbled on the battlefield and continued to topple at home, affecting everything from housing to education and taxation. Everywhere, old-style Conservative ideologies were breaking down. Socialism offered new appeal. A more than century-old doctrine in Britain, first discussed in the 1830s by enlightened industrialist Robert Owen, socialism had evolved throughout the nineteenth century with the progression of industrialism and into the twentieth the devastation of the two wars.

With an almost religious appeal to the masses, socialists claimed to be true democratizers who could deliver justice and equity to societies corrupted by the monied, property-owning upper classes. The movement promised that enlightened socialist states would reengineer society to give citizens a fairer deal. There was a ready audience for such a pledge. The industrial age and inequities of capitalism had heightened social tensions and contributed mightily to the outbreak of war. Mass unemployment of the 1930s, brought on by the Great Depression, plus the scourge of inflation, particularly in Germany, had exacerbated already deep-seated feelings of class hatred. Nazism was one perversion of socialism; Stalin's communism another. The idealistic notion that the state would, in egalitarian fashion, take care of the needs of the people by controlling the distribution of income and property had great appeal. Intellectually, communism was fashionable in the 1930s. W. H. Auden, Christopher Isherwood, and Stephen Spender were members of the Communist party of Great Britain. Three hundred students belonged to Oxford's October Club, a Communist organization, while hundreds more signed on at Cambridge. The United States had its own share of dupes. Edmund Wilson called the Soviet

Union "the moral top of the world, where the light never really goes out." Lincoln Steffens returned from Russia and said, "I have been over into the future and it works."[13]

Stalin's victory in 1945 gave communism additional credibility. By the end of the war, Central and Eastern Europe were controlled by Communists. In Asia, Mao Tse-tung's Communists triumphed in 1949 over the rightist forces of Chiang Kai-shek. "Even in highly democratic societies," wrote Zbigniew Brzezinski, "the notion of state action as the best means for promoting economic well-being and social justice became the dominant outlook."[14]

Because of the war, there had been no British election since 1935 and thus no solid indication of the domestic political mood of the country. The Beveridge Commission of 1942 had given a clue in its call for a social security system. Sir William Beveridge's report on "social insurance and allied services" urged public protection of all "from the cradle to the grave" and outlined a "national minimum" of guaranteed income.[15] The report was seminal and even some key Tories recognized that reform was necessary and the party must update its social views. But Parliament only "welcomed" and did not endorse the commission's findings. Opinion polls showed the country wanted the program, but Churchill could not implement any of the proposals during the war and, despite demands by the Labor party that he act right away, put off considering the report until it was over.

Attlee, who served as leader of the House of Commons in Churchill's coalition government, had kept up the Labor party's organization during the war and reminded the electorate that there would be an alternative when the war ended. In 1941, the party published a record of its wartime social legislation; the following year, Attlee issued "The Old World and the New Society," a set of postwar proposals that the Conservatives never tried to counter.

The Labor party leader had campaigned on a pledge to transform Britain from a tottering capitalist state into a "socialist commonwealth." His program for the future was not only grounded intellectually, but a version had even been tested by the Soviet Union and seemed to work. Attlee was no bomb thrower; nor was he even a working-class Laborite but the son of a wealthy lawyer and an Oxford graduate. An aloof, middle-class politician with a first-class brain, Attlee was one of the best-educated members of his party. Like many middle- and upper-class intellectuals, he was a convert to socialism, switching from conservatism before World

War I, after working for years as a settlement house social worker in Stepney, in London's dismal, not long post-Dickensian, East End.

Attlee was a full-fledged socialist, but his intention was not to replace the old order completely. He wanted to reform it intelligently. He had no intention of seizing personal private property. He liked his middle-class standards and wanted everyone to share them. Society was to be leveled up, not broken down. As Attlee saw it, in the postwar years everyone should be given basic necessities—a minimum standard of living, protection against unemployment, and free health care. Government provided that to servicemen. Why, he asked, should government treat its citizens differently when they weren't fighting a war? To carry out his plan, he set about creating a welfare state, controlling resources and manufacturing by nationalizing utilities and industries.

His proposals offered what Britons said they wanted, but for a country with almost no financial resources, the whole idealistic proposition was highly risky. It had been only five years since Churchill set hearts racing and scalps tingling with his "finest hour" tribute and only two months since the celebration of Germany's defeat, but when Attlee took over in July 1945, those celebrations were already ancient history. Now the challenge was to survive the postwar.

Scarcely a week had passed after Japan's surrender in August when President Harry Truman canceled the Lend-Lease program under which Britain had been loaned supplies and merchant ships to carry them. Generous terms—by American standards—were established for British repayment, but the speed of the decision and the quick demand for interest payments stunned the country and caused resentment. The shock of more expenses with an already empty Treasury forced Britain to reconsider its situation.

The Bretton Woods Agreement of 1944 made the gold-convertible dollar the official standard of global trade and thus the world's dominant currency. A year later, the Labor party took over with a record postwar majority in Parliament and began to implement Attlee's nationalization program. The Bank of England, the coal industry, telecommunications, civil aviation—all came under government control in 1946. Over the next two years, electricity, trains, airplanes, canals, highways, gas, iron, and steel were brought under the government's wing. Nationalization fulfilled a campaign pledge, but the welfare legislation of 1946, based on Beveridge's dramatic proposals four years earlier, was the more historic initiative.

The comprehensive welfare legislation, revolutionary in Britain, provided everyone with free health care, unemployment insurance, and a minimum standard of living. There was nearly full employment after the war, but the memories of unemployment in the 1930s were fresh. Before the war, whole sectors of the work force were not covered by employment programs. Those who were insured regularly saw benefits run out. When that happened, families were subjected to a hated "means test," in which inspectors came to the home to examine the family's finances. Those unfortunates who failed the test, or who were not covered, often wound up destitute and stripped of dignity in the workhouse, a Victorian relic. Effective insurance against illness did not exist. Only workers with good health records had health insurance. Dependents were not covered. Hospitals charged what the market would bear, reducing the treatment for those with limited means. Old age pensions existed, but many pensioners either did not qualify for coverage or were skimpily protected. Neither maternity nor death benefits existed.

The introduction of the National Health Service caused an almost audible sigh of relief in the country. "It made the most incredible difference to the mentality of the less well off," said author Alan Sillitoe, "probably the greatest single factor this century in creating a new pride in the English working class."[16]

Housing was in desperate need of attention. Nearly a half-million homes were lost during the war, with another three and a half million damaged. The terrible prewar standard of housing made it worse. Frustration over slum life was endemic. Black jokes circulated that the Luftwaffe bombing had, but for the casualties, performed a service in leveling entire areas. More than a million homes were built during Attlee's term, no easy accomplishment given the shortage of workmen and supplies.[17] The material that was available and affordable looked just that—cheap and temporary.

There were widespread expectations that education would also undergo extensive reform after the war. Attlee, with his leveling-up approach, should have been the perfect leader to reform a system as imbalanced as the "separate but equal" Jim Crow schools of the American South. There was no better time to attack elitism in the system and chip away at the class barrier by integrating state and private schools. But Attlee, himself the product of private schools, never tackled education.

Overseas, the wartime alliance was breaking up. Roosevelt was dead, Churchill was out of office, and Stalin had new goals. As U.S. troops streamed home from Europe—three million soldiers pulled out between 1945 and 1947—the unchallenged Soviet leader was consolidating his grip on Eastern Europe. In February 1945, Roosevelt, Churchill, and Stalin had met in Yalta, in the Soviet Crimea, to plan the end of World War II. Their agreement, however, had the effect of sanctioning Soviet dominance over Eastern Europe because it failed to compel Stalin to withdraw his occupying Red Army. By now the Yalta agreement was utterly in tatters, ignored by the Soviets, who took advantage of Western disarray to install puppet governments in Bulgaria, Poland, and Romania.

The United States was in no mood to return to Europe to counter the Soviets; Britain was too weak. Just as he had been the solitary British voice to challenge the appeasement policy a decade before, it was left to an out-of-office Churchill to draw attention to Soviet expansionism. In March 1946, on a private trip to Fulton, Missouri, with President Harry Truman, Churchill pulled as hard as he could on the alarm bells. "From Stettin in the Baltic to Trieste in the Adriatic, an Iron Curtain has descended across the Continent," he told a Westminster College audience. Truman agreed, but most Americans had lost interest in Europe. Soviet threat notwithstanding, there was little enthusiasm for racing back to man the barricades.

Communist parties began to prosper in Italy and France. The Attlee government, with profound economic problems at the most basic bread and butter level, was a ripe target for infiltration. Communists spread influence throughout the Civil Service and labor union movement, ultimately leading to purges. By the time the Korean War broke out in 1950, anticommunist fears were at full throttle. The Cold War turned chillier.

There had been virtually no industrial development in Britain from 1939 to 1945 and the country was operating with old plants and equipment. Industrial undermanning was rampant. Many of the youngest and strongest workers were mobilized in 1940 and were only gradually demobbed. The coal industry was among those hit hardest by lack of manpower. The gap between consumption and production of coal in January 1947 was 300,000 tons a week.[18] The fuel crisis coincided with the worst winter of the century.

Blizzards and subfreezing temperatures savaged the country. Power was rationed. Britain came to the brink of collapse. With no quick relief, rationing became even more stringent. In November 1948, the bacon allowance was cut in half—to one ounce a week. By 1949, four years after the war ended, per capita food consumption was still below what it had been a decade earlier.[19] That same year, the bottom fell out of the pound. In September, the currency was devalued by 30 percent, from $4.03 to $2.80. Its life style teetering and prospects grim, Britain was forced to keep retrenching, pulling back further overseas.

Margaret Thatcher, who wore her coat inside buildings to ward off the cold, felt the economic pinch. The shelves of her father's grocery were picked clean. A proud nationalist, she hated seeing her country like this.

Palestine was surrendered. Financial aid to Greece and Turkey, necessary to hold off encroaching communism, was abandoned. India, the jewel in the crown of empire, plus Pakistan, Ceylon, and Burma, were all granted independence in 1947 and early 1948.

The late 1940s were exceedingly hard years and took their toll on Attlee. Truman once called the Labor party prime minister "a modest man," which prompted Churchill to riposte that "he has much to be modest about." Churchill, not atypically, was unfair. The achievements of the small man with the bushy mustache were more radical than modest. Attlee largely decolonized the empire, restructured industry, and instituted a welfare system that would, for a while, be the model for Europe if not the world. He established a new defense policy, which, by granting the United States the right to station nuclear weapons on her soil, ended any remaining doubt that Britain could defend herself without the United States. Politically, he made the Labor party, for the first time, a full-fledged alternative to the Conservatives, who had dominated, sometimes in coalition with Liberals, governance throughout the century.

Attlee filled a perceived postwar need that the state take over an unprecedented amount of responsibility that had always been the provenance of individuals. By doing so, however, he all but destroyed British corporate and personal initiative. Accountability was diluted. Incentive was eliminated. Maintaining a large state superstructure and subsidizing inefficiency meant less money was available for industrial development. The deficiency would compound Britain's recovery difficulties from the 1950s through the 1970s. Maintaining the fiction that Britain remained a European military power also diverted resources that could have been better spent on training, retooling, and plant reconstruction.

Union demands also began rising at the time, locking poorly trained managements into agreements that guaranteed low productivity. Economically, the world was booming in the postwar years— everywhere but Britain. France, Germany, Italy, Japan, and Austria all enjoyed high growth. By the years 1948–1950, world industrial production was growing at 13 percent annually, three times the rate in Britain,[20] where the pace of work has long been leisurely. The seeds of Britain's postwar decline had been sown before the war. But Attlee's socialism, maintained for the most part by his successors until Thatcher, enlarged the problem that Maggie would eventually attack.

The Conservatives did not roll over after their 1945 defeat, the party's first major loss in forty years. Strong corrective measures were called for and Churchill knew it. Seeing voters growing comfortable with a mix of socialism and capitalism, the Tories moved in search of common ground. Churchill asked R. A. Butler to chair a policy review as the basis for the party's reconstruction. Butler, later chancellor of the exchequer, produced broad, vague charters— to allow Churchill room to maneuver—on industry, agriculture, the empire, the role of women. His aim, said Butler, was to provide "a painless but permanent facelift for the party."[21] The Tories promised government on the basis of "humanized capitalism" and "enterprise without selfishness."

By 1950, changing demographics were working in favor of the Conservatives. The old working class was fragmenting and the middle class expanding. Industry was in sharp decline, but small businesses, run by more conservative businessmen, were sprouting up all over Britain. The war had also splintered the servant culture. Bereft of help in the cities, the middle class fled cities to the new, politically more centrist suburbs.[22]

Churchill installed Lord Woolton, the wartime minister of food and a legendary organizer and salesman, as Tory chairman. His instructions, like Butler's, were to modernize the party so it could take advantage of the new demographics. One of Woolton's first goals was to get a broader Tory representation in Parliament. Beefing up local constituency organizations, paying local party representatives better, and downgrading the importance of the personal wealth of candidates all helped. Until this time, a candidate's promise to pay his own way was a major factor in his selection. As

Woolton pointed out, the old process limited the party's choice of candidates to "half a percent of the population."[23] Indeed, almost every Tory MP had been educated at private school.

The change was more than technical. If the party were to survive, like Britain itself, the Tories had to adapt and appeal to workers, the man in the street who felt it was his turn, and new small businessmen as well as the middle and upper classes. Another of Woolton's successes was beefing up the Young Conservatives movement. The Tories had long been considered an old man's party, a geriatric and patrician collection of politicians who governed, it was felt, with a sense of divine right. Woolton undertook a concerted campaign to expand the party's base and rejuvenate its membership. One of the first new recruits, a callow fifteen-year-old, was Norman Tebbit, a far from traditional Conservative who forty years later would be chairman of the Tory party.

The moves would open up the party to a whole new breed of Tory, including Margaret Thatcher. An extraordinary leader, she was no freak, but a product of her environment with the same grim inheritance of her generation. A child of austerity, she knew the frugal deprivation of the Depression years and the uncertainty of war and its cost. Bred to be a new-era politician by a father consumed by politics, she understood how a leader like Churchill, who was willing to take unpopular stances, could change history. Thatcher is a determined nationalist who hates the thought of Britain falling apart. With none of the guilt or confused sentimentality about consensus or the doubts of her political forebears, Thatcher is also a throwback to an earlier era of conviction politicians. Inspired by a special crusading sense of mission, they built Great Britain. She would rebuild it.

CHAPTER TWO

Grocer's Daughter

SHE LIKES TELLING how she lives over the store at 10 Downing Street. After all, over the store was where it all began.

Today's apartment, on the top floor of the prime minister's official residence, is minuscule, a fraction the size of the White House family quarters. The entire complex could fit inside Queen Elizabeth's Buckingham Palace throne room. Most of Number 10, the 250-year-old Georgian brick building only 400 yards from the Houses of Parliament, is devoted to offices and reception rooms, all exquisitely refurbished in 1988. But the residence on the top floor, including the tiny kitchen where Thatcher has been known to whip up postmidnight dinners for top aides working late, is modestly decorated at the Thatchers' own expense.

However unpretentious, the current apartment is far more luxurious than the spartan front room over the grocery store at One North Parade Road in Grantham. The flat where Margaret Hilda Roberts was born just before 9 A.M. on October 13, 1925, had no hot water; no running water at all. Once a week, there were baths with hot water carried to a tub behind the shop. A bowl and pitcher stood on the washstand in each of the two bedrooms. For most of Margaret's childhood, there was no indoor bathroom either. The toilet was a backyard outhouse. To get to the living room, the family trekked through a bedroom. Outside, there was no garden, no grass. There was no place for a child's pet, so none was ever allowed.

The house was like Grantham itself: simple, basic, austere. For centuries, Grantham has been a quiet market town, rarely a destination, almost always a stopover on the way to somewhere else.

In the 1920s, North Parade was part of the main road to Scotland and a busy thoroughfare. Traffic noise from cars and the clip-clopping of horsedrawn delivery drays filtered into the three-story corner house along with the chuffing of steam engines from the railway yard four blocks away. There were some impressive houses on the street, but the Robertses' was not one of them.

Now, as then, the town is charmless and lackluster. Tucked between the coal fields of Nottingham and the pastoral glories of the Vale of Belvoir, Grantham is surrounded by rolling farmlands and villages of buff-gray stone. It has little character of its own. The population is older, for the most part, recessive and unadventurous, and visitors often comment on the sense of time warp here. London is only 100 miles south, but Grantham attitudes, residents concede, trail the capital by about forty years. Almost everyone with ambition gets out of Grantham quickly and rarely returns. Margaret Thatcher was no exception.

Isaac Newton went to school in Grantham. Oliver Cromwell began his crusade to take over England by seizing the town from the royalists. Little has changed in Grantham since those heady days in the early 1600s. By the 1930s, when Margaret Roberts was growing up, Grantham was winding down. The town had been losing steam for nearly a century, since the coach trade started to fade out in the mid-nineteenth century. During Margaret Roberts's childhood, Grantham was a tight, conservative community of waning significance. Its population, nearly static at about 25,000, was dominated by a small group of civic-minded businessmen.

Alfred Roberts was among them. The eldest of seven children, Roberts, who grew up in Northamptonshire, would probably have been a fourth generation shoemaker if bad eyesight had not ruled out leather finishwork. He had no time to linger over the choice of other alternatives. Forced to leave school at twelve to help support his family, he moved to Grantham, where he had been promised a job apprenticing in a grocery store. Nine years later, when Britain entered World War I, Alf went with a friend to enlist. The friend was accepted, but Alf's bad eyesight betrayed him again. He failed the sight test.

Frustrated at missing the war, he returned to the grocery, but Alf Roberts was neither bitter nor a quitter. Diligent and determined, Alf knuckled down to make something of himself. He "got on with it," which is how he taught his daughter to respond to disappointment. Alf got on with his job, putting in long hours at the grocery. He also became a regular at the Grantham Library, devouring books. If he'd had more education, he said wistfully, he would have liked to have become a teacher or school principal.

A deadly serious man, the grocer's assistant was a loner and a grind. He never developed a sense of humor and neither would his daughter. Some said that he drove himself so hard at work because of a chip on his shoulder about his lack of formal education, but his Methodist upbringing was part of the equation, too. When he wasn't at work or reading, Roberts went to church; as a young man, he attended Wesley's Methodist Chapel in south Grantham twice every Sunday. There, at services one week, he met Beatrice Stephenson, a seamstress. Her parents, Daniel and Phoebe, had even less status than Alf—and their financial prospects were dimmer. But they weren't idle or lazy. Daniel was a cloakroom attendant; he manned the lost property office at the railway station. Until she married, Phoebe had worked as a factory machinist.

Daughter Beatrice, plain as dry toast, wore her hair drawn primly back in a bun. She looked like the farmer's daughter in Grant Wood's *American Gothic*. Young Alf, on the other hand, was striking. Tall at 6'2", he had a shock of blond-white hair like spun cotton candy that caused some customers to call him "Sugar." Slender with fine bone structure, he had narrow but bright blue eyes, which peered out through thick glasses. He cut a fairly imposing figure and was far handsomer than Beatrice. Some old-time Grantham residents say that Alf grew to enjoy flirting with customers in later years. But there is no evidence that his attentions were more than superior salesmanship. Years later, his daughter would also relish, innocently, flirtatious give-and-take.

Both Beatrice and Alf were hard workers and fanatic savers. Scrimping and faithfully contributing their joint savings, they decided by 1917 that they had enough. They would get married and buy the small grocery store with the post office attached on the corner of North Parade. They planned the purchase meticulously. There was room in the apartment for two children, but they knew they would have to delay having a family until they could afford one. The little money they had left after buying and stocking the store went for dark mahogany furniture, all purchased at auction. If Beatrice had become pregnant at the beginning of their marriage, all their plans for the future would have gone awry. Severely pragmatic and highly disciplined, they were careful to make sure that didn't happen.

It was four years before Muriel was born, and another well-planned four before Margaret followed in 1925. Throughout their childhoods the girls were never close. Muriel, like her mother, was quiet and withdrawn, a homebody with no overwhelming passion to better herself. Eventually, she would marry a farmer whose proposal Margaret had rejected.

Margaret, on the other hand, took after her father, who doted on her and, sensing her drive and intelligence, became determined to mold her. She would have the education he was denied, and not at the Church of England school behind the grocery either. Alf Roberts's daughter would not attend any Church of England school. He would have enrolled her at Methodist School had it not closed in 1927. So, in 1930, Margaret began at Hunting Tower Elementary, a surprisingly modern and well-equipped county school. Hunting Tower was a mile away from the Robertses' house, on the other side of the railway tracks, but that didn't stop Alf—or Margaret. At the age of five, rain or shine, walking with her nine-year-old sister, Margaret Roberts made the trek four times a day, including a round trip home for lunch.

"She was bright, studious, and serious even as a five-year-old," said John Foster, who sat at the next desk.[1] The teachers at the seven-classroom school spotted this, too, and put her in a class with students almost a year older, a distinction that might have unnerved some children. But not Margaret, who seemed immune to childhood insecurities. Scrupulously well-behaved, she was allowed to sit at the back, annoying some girls who thought her a goody-goody. She quickly developed a reputation as a know-it-all, constantly shooting her hand up in the air to answer questions. "She so wanted to please her father," said Foster. "She always came top of her class and never needed telling anything twice." According to a family friend, John Guile, Alf "did a good deal to push her in school and in her career and she was quite willing to be pushed." She worked hard at everything—like a diligent adult—with little time to spare. She started piano lessons at five. Practicing faithfully, she eventually became an accompanist at church. Her older sister could never keep up with her. "She was four years younger, but always about three lesson books ahead of me," Muriel sighed.[2]

From the start, Margaret had a strong streak of confidence. At nine, she won a poetry recital competition. Deputy Headmistress Winifred Wright congratulated her. "You were lucky, Margaret."

"I was not lucky," Margaret snapped. "I deserved it."[3]

There was not much fun at home. The Depression had hit and times were hard. Both parents worked a grinding twelve hours a day, six days a week. When homework was finished, the girls toiled in the grocery, measuring out sugar from sacks, tea from imported canisters, and butter from huge blocks. They also learned to stock shelves and help with customers. Saturdays, Margaret walked the neighborhood with her father, taking orders and making deliveries.

Alf lectured the girls to try to improve themselves when they weren't working. On Thursdays, early close day at the grocery, he took them to university extension course lectures on current affairs. If he couldn't make it, Margaret was expected to go anyway. She would take notes and brief him on the material he missed. Every Saturday, she went to the library and brought home books—a current affairs or biography for her father, a novel for her mother, and at least one book for herself, often a Kipling, her favorite author. Anytime anyone famous, anyone who could teach them something, came to Grantham, the Robertses were there.

The Victorian virtues that would guide Margaret Thatcher's political life were nurtured in the North Parade Road house. "My father's view was that life was a serious matter. His maxim was that you did not sit idle," Margaret once explained. "Life was the parable of the ten talents. If you had an ability, it was a heinous sin merely to dig it into the ground. It was your duty to better your lot through your own efforts, through competing."[4]

Dinner table conversations became mini-seminars: the causes of the Depression; Stanley Baldwin's government; the rise of Hitler and Mussolini; what was happening in the war. Margaret was the only one at school who knew where the RAF was bombing. Asked how, she explained that "anytime a bombing raid is mentioned on the wireless, we get the atlas out and mark the location."[5] Alf seemed to know everything. "Once I asked him what was this thing called the 'fiduciary issue'? He knew. The gold standard? He knew," she recalled. As far as she was concerned, he knew everything. She idolized him.[6]

Her mother was different, and Margaret had little time for her. Beatrice, a solid, 1930s mother, was never university material. A talented dressmaker, she was, among other things, a professional tailoress before marrying. She made all the girls' clothes and taught them sewing and needlework. She baked twice a week—Thursdays and Sundays—and the girls delivered leftover pies, cakes, and cookies to the elderly and poor or sick neighbors. Beatrice also schooled

them in other, practical homemaking skills. Forty years later, as
Tory party leader, Margaret could still paint and wallpaper a
room—and even enjoy it.

Yet Margaret was never really a homebody. From the time she
was young it was apparent that she wasn't interested in cooking,
puttering around the house, or, for that matter, mothering. She
was, she realized, much different from Beatrice, not embarrassed
by her mother's lack of education as much as she was disappointed
in her lack of interest in self-improvement and other important
issues, like politics. Beatrice never participated in the evening political bull sessions downstairs in the store, where Margaret lingered
and listened. "She was probably upstairs making us a dress," her
daughter said a half-century later. "She did the household things."[7]
Thatcher has described her mother as "a Martha rather than a
Mary," a New Testament reference (Luke 10; John 11) to the two
sisters of Lazarus whom Christ visited. Martha was the bustling
homemaker; Mary the thoughtful one.

"I loved my mother dearly," Thatcher once said, "but after I
was fifteen, we had nothing more to say to each other."[8] As the
years went by, Thatcher not only had little to say to Beatrice; she
had little to say about her. Until she became leader of the Conservative party in 1975, neither Beatrice nor Alf was mentioned in
her *Who's Who* listing. In 1976, she began listing herself as the
daughter of Alfred Roberts, whose influence she repeatedly em-
phasizes. She rarely mentions her mother and has not listed her.

The relationship, or lack of one, with her mother has prompted
endless speculation on the part of British biographers. One writer
even concluded that Margaret hated her mother. According to that
analysis, her toughness as prime minister stemmed from their early
battles.[9] There is no evidence for such a conclusion, but such allegations did prompt Muriel, who rarely says anything good or bad
about her sister, to speak up. "It's true our father was the greatest
influence," she said. "He was the head of the household with all
that implied in those days. But my mother was not completely
dominated by him. My mother looked after the home; my father
looked after the rest of life. She ran a good home."[10]

Until they left home, the girls' lives outside school and the
store centered on the Finkin Street Methodist Church, where Alf
was a lay preacher. His devotion to Methodism went beyond the
church door. For years, he kept St. Thomas à Kempis's *The Imi-
tation of Christ* by his bedside, and he attempted to apply strict

church principles to all facets of his life. When Alf served on the town council, he insisted that Grantham's parks, swimming pool, and tennis courts be closed on Sundays. He relaxed his opposition only under pressure during World War II, when other councilors convinced him that while his own family might not care about relaxing, plenty of servicemen at the local RAF base did.

Sundays meant nonstop religious activity. The girls went to Sunday school at 10 A.M., church service with their parents at 11 A.M., afternoon Sunday school, where Margaret played the piano, at 2:30 P.M., and vespers at 6 P.M. Alf was so strict he would not even permit Sunday newspapers in the house. The only work allowed was cooking and doing the shop's accounts because there was no other time to do them. Sunday meant no movies, no cardplaying, no games at all.

The Robertses' restricted life style was tough on a child, even an old-fashioned girl from an old-fashioned town in an old-fashioned era, but the routine never seemed to bother Alf's younger daughter. Many of her classmates made fun of Margaret, whose behavior, so rigid and serious, made her seem so much older than her years. She became an outsider, immune to the lure of frivolities. Contemporaries found her too difficult and hard-going. She knew everyone, but had few friends to invite home after school. She had homework to do anyway, and she wasn't the sort of person to let less diligent classmates copy it.

Alf made a decent living. The Robertses' grocery was one of the most expensive in Grantham. But they remained utterly frugal. Not until 1935, when Margaret was ten, did Alf buy the family's first radio. The day it arrived, she raced home from school and spent the evening huddled over it. There was a long wait before the next thrill; the Robertses did not buy a car—a used Ford— until after the war, when Margaret had nearly completed university. Money was for saving. "Never be in anyone's debt," was a regular Alf Roberts saying.

Growing up, Margaret had an allowance of tuppence, about 10 U.S. cents, a week, which eventually climbed to sixpence, or 30 cents. Any extra money, a birthday present, or reward for good grades, went into a savings account. Spending money on anything trivial, anything fun like the movies or a soda fountain, was frowned upon. She loved to go out but rarely did. Decades later, she recalled with photographic precision a family bus day-trip to Nottingham to see a Ginger Rogers and Fred Astaire film, including the name of the organist—Sandy Macpherson—at the theater. "I loved every minute of that day," she reminisced.

By ten, she was rushing downstairs after her homework to sit on the counter next to the bacon slicer and listen in on the political conversations. Many of them concerned the election that year, which returned Stanley Baldwin to Downing Street. In Grantham, the Robertses were, of course, heavily involved, working for Victor Warrender, a Conservative candidate for Parliament, who won easily. Margaret was a messenger, running between committee room and polling station and checking off names of voters. When Warrender came around to thank the volunteers, she was thrilled and talked about it for days. That was when she first realized that "politics was in my bloodstream."

The following year, she moved from Hunting Tower Elementary to the Kesteven and Grantham Girls School, a tuition-paying prep school that cost the equivalent of $65 a year. Alf could afford it, but insisted she take the scholarship test in case he died and she needed financial help.

She excelled academically, finishing first in her class of thirty-two. In fact, she came out on top every year she was at Kesteven, except her last, when she finished second. She was an academic grind, but her concentration, which was exceptional, helped. Once, after a violent thunderstorm broke out during an exam, some of the girls began to chat about the ferocity of the storm. "What storm?" asked Margaret. Classmates said she was frequently bossy, but Margaret seemed unaware of it. She tried hard to fit in, and after lunch at home, she always returned to school with some treat to pass around.

She was also a pretty good athlete. At eleven, she was the youngest girl on the Kesteven field hockey team. Later on, she became the starting center half and was finally selected vice-captain. But she did not play for mere pleasure; competition and winning were what thrilled her. Later, when she discovered that politics provided the same kind of excitement, she gave up all interest in sport except for a few family winter skiing trips.

Public speaking was another early interest. "She could use words correctly at a far earlier age than most of her school friends," said Margaret Goodrich, a lifelong friend. Margaret Roberts joined the Kesteven debating society and took elocution lessons outside class. "One simply must talk properly," she told her father when she asked him to pay for them. He agreed, but once her classmates noted her new accent, they started calling her "Snobby Roberts."

From childhood, when she began performing in church biblical plays, Thatcher was fascinated by acting. At Kesteven, she joined the dramatic society and acted in many of the productions, loving the glamour, which was in short supply at home, but enjoying the sense of being center stage, the focus of attention, most of all. She briefly considered becoming an actress, but rejected the thought as too impractical. She has long understood the theatricality of roles. As prime minister, she has not been a great speaker, but she has repeatedly demonstrated an acute awareness of presentation. She takes pains over camera angles, backdrops, even the kind of chair she sits in, replacing those she finds unsuitable. She has a deft sense of timing and a natural instinct for positioning on stage. At meetings, she frequently maneuvers others around like a set director.

As a very young girl, even her piano recitals featured grandiose theatricality and gestures worthy of Liberace. Sometimes her head would almost touch the keys. Then she would arch back, flinging one arm then the other dramatically behind her head.[11] The other children would grimace and giggle; this was an irritating classmate. When mothers asked their daughters, "Why can't you be more like Margaret Roberts?" the girls would burst into laughter.[12]

There was less laughter once Britain entered World War II in September 1939. Margaret was a child of thirteen when it began; a young adult, just shy of twenty, when it ended. The war had a profound impact on her as it did on all Britons who lived through the Dunkirk evacuation, blackouts, the Blitz, the Battle of Britain, German U-boats offshore, and the fears of an all-out Nazi invasion. For a relatively unknown provincial town, Grantham was hard hit by German bombers. During World War I, Grantham had a healthy tank manufacturing industry. It died between the wars, but when the second war broke out, Grantham went back to its old business of producing weapons. That, plus the presence of several RAF bases in the neighborhood and the town's location on the main north-south car and rail routes made Grantham a prime target. For a while, more bombs per capita fell on Grantham than any other British city.[13]

In anticipation of Luftwaffe bombing throughout Britain, more than one million women and children were evacuated from London, scattering to homes around the countryside. One group of nine evacuees lived for a while with the Churchills at Chartwell, Winston's country home in Kent.[14] The Robertses also took in a guest when the parents of a German penpal of Muriel's wrote to ask a favor. Edith, seventeen, was Jewish and lived in Vienna, where Muriel contacted her as part of a school assignment. As Hitler's Wehrmacht thundered toward the Austrian capital in the 1938 Anschluss, Edith's parents wondered whether the Robertses could take Edith in. Alf immediately agreed. Edith arrived with horror stories about the Nazis. Margaret sat engrossed for hours, listening agog and appalled. The experience gave her a far greater awareness of the war and what it meant than others her age.

In October 1939, when Margaret had just turned fourteen and before Grantham came under attack, Kesteven began sharing its classrooms with the Camden High School for Girls, which had been evacuated from London. Margaret and her classmates studied mornings; the Camden girls took over in the afternoon, when the local girls were sent home. When bombs started dropping on Grantham, the Camden girls were transferred to Uppingham. One raid almost wiped out the school. A German bomber, evading flak, flew low toward the school and, swooping over the hockey field, dropped a trail of bombs that stopped just short of the main building. In August 1940, at the start of the three-month Battle of Britain, Germany hurled nearly 1,400 bombers and 1,000 Messerschmitt fighters against fewer than 900 British Spitfires and Hurricanes. The RAF's victory prompted Churchill to say, "Never in the field of human conflict was so much owed by so many to so few." The Blitz, which began in September and lasted until spring 1941, cost some 30,000 British lives in London alone, but Britain never flinched.

Blackout rules went into effect and gas masks were distributed. Two air raid shelters were built on the campus, and the Kesteven girls went to work raising money, filling sandbags, helping with the harvesting, and attending propaganda films. At home, the store had no basement, so whenever the air raid sirens went off, the family hid under the dining room table. Before crawling under, Margaret usually grabbed her homework.[15] Alf read everything he could about the war, Germany, the Axis, the Alliance, and U.S. intentions and passed on what he learned at the dinner table. The Robertses and Edith also clustered around the radio, listening to Churchill's speeches.

They sat transfixed listening to the reports of the late May 1940 evacuation of France at Dunkirk, where hundreds of boats evacuated 350,000 Allied troops, some neck deep in water, while the

Luftwaffe bombed and strafed the beach. On June 4, the day the evacuation ended, Margaret shivered as she heard Churchill rally his countrymen. "We shall go on to the end," he pledged. "We shall fight in France, we shall fight on the seas and oceans. We shall defend our island whatever the cost may be; we shall fight on the beaches; we shall fight on the landing grounds; we shall fight in the fields and in the streets; we shall fight in the hills. We shall never surrender." When Paris fell ten days later, Britons stoically prepared for the worst.

Alf, who had become Grantham's youngest alderman in 1936, was named the city's food officer and supervised the local rationing of foodstuffs. Midway through the war, in 1943, he became mayor, ensuring that the Robertses were even more heavily involved in the war effort. Alf's role, Churchill's spine-tinglers, and Edith's stories began turning Margaret from a strong nationalist to an out-and-out jingoist.

Throughout her mid-teen years, there were no boys in Margaret's life. Grantham was filled with soldiers from nearby RAF bases, but they were absolutely off limits. Kesteven girls weren't allowed to walk home from school with boys from the local prep, Isaac Newton's The King School, let alone with soldiers. Margaret could not have cared less about such restrictions, but she was more interested in boys than she let on. Always busy studying or helping in the store, she never went to school dances, or to movies with boys, although some of her Kesteven classmates dated and went dancing on Saturday nights. "It sounded very nice and I would have liked to have gone," she said wistfully,[16] "but my sister and I didn't go dancing." For Margaret, going to Catlin's cafe for a sundae was a big deal, but even then boys were not involved. Old for her years in most respects, Margaret was a late developer when it came to the opposite sex.

Muriel left home to study physiotherapy, and when Kesteven graduation approached, Margaret started making her own plans. Influenced by Kipling, she thought about joining the Civil Service to work in India, but Dorothy Gillies, her Kesteven headmistress, tried to talk her out of it. The service accepted few women, and an India posting was exceptionally difficult. "Those sound like good reasons for trying," Margaret responded, but she decided to pursue a science major in university instead. There were several reasons behind her interest in science. She had done well in biology and math and was particularly fond of her chemistry teacher, Katie

Kay. Another, she said, was that "We thought then that there were no problems that could not be resolved by science." But there were more pragmatic ingredients in her planning. In wartime Britain, where Depression memories were also all too fresh, she knew that science skills would always guarantee her a job. Finally, few young women studied chemistry at university compared with liberal arts. She had a much better chance of being accepted at a top university as a science major.

Uncharacteristically, she began having second thoughts almost immediately. At sixteen, with memories of the Warrender campaign still vivid, she got involved in another campaign. This time her candidate, Sir Arthur Longmore, lost, but her political juices got heated up again.

Alf, a part-time justice of the peace as well as alderman, encouraged her. He took Margaret, the son he never had, around the Grantham courthouse, where the structured arguments, legal briefs, and courtroom theatricality all mesmerized her. One day, during a lunch with Alf and lawyer Norman Winning, she complained that her chemistry major was a mistake. Now she wanted to be a lawyer, but had gone too far down the science road. She had made a terrible error and felt trapped.

Nonsense, said Winning, who held a physics degree himself. Science would help, not hurt. Carry on with the chemistry, he advised, get a degree, then study law. The combination would provide a real sense of discipline and would make it easier to enter a lucrative field like patent law. The advice was a huge relief. Years later, she would declare, "That talk with Mr. Winning was really crucial."[17]

When her friend Margaret Goodrich was accepted at Oxford in 1941, sixteen-year-old Margaret was determined to follow suit as quickly as she could.[18] Miss Gillies, the headmistress, tried to convince her to reconsider; she thought Margaret was trying to go too far too fast. Hold off a year, maybe even two, Miss Gillies recommended. Margaret was furious. Storming out of the meeting in a rage, her face scarlet, she told Goodrich that Gillies was "trying to thwart my ambition." But Gillies was doing nothing of the kind. She acknowledged that Margaret Roberts was one of Kesteven's outstanding students, but she felt that more time in secondary school would round her off socially and remove some of her school-marmishness. Gillies felt that Margaret—overly ambitious, pushed too hard by her father—was too young to apply. It was all true.

But Margaret had made up her mind and was beginning her preparations. Kesteven did not offer Latin, required by Oxford, so she took outside tutoring, cramming a four-year language course into one year. At seventeen, she took the Oxford entrance exam and was delighted to earn top grades in Latin. Satisfaction notwithstanding, she nursed a grudge against Miss Gillies for years. In 1960, nearly twenty years later, Margaret—already in Parliament—returned to Kesteven as an honored guest for an "Old Girls" reunion. Miss Gillies, retired by then and elderly, spoke and in the course of her address, misused a Latin phrase. Thatcher followed her to the podium and pointedly corrected her old headmistress. Her schoolmates were appalled.[19] Indeed, for all her success, spitefulness is a trait she has never completely eliminated.

With her Latin examination behind her, Margaret applied to Somerville College, one of Oxford's oldest women's colleges, as well as Nottingham, a state university, and Bedford College, part of the University of London. The backups accepted her, but Somerville put her on a waiting list, a bitter disappointment. For the first time, she had not gotten something she had worked for.

Margaret decided to return to Kesteven, feeling the worse because Miss Gillies had been right, she *had* been overreaching. Yet only days into the term, just after she was named a house captain and co-head girl, the school's highest honor, the headmistress summoned her. Somerville had a cancellation. Margaret never looked back, packing two bags and heading for the railway station. She had been lucky. A wartime ruling earlier that year decreed that only those under eighteen by November 1 were eligible for four years of school. Students over eighteen were eligible for two years only. With her birthday on October 13, Margaret had qualified for the full four years by scarcely a fortnight.[20]

If she had not been accepted at Oxford, Margaret Roberts would almost certainly still have become a politician. Through Alf, politics was in her blood. But the prime minister's office would have been a steeper climb. For 700 years, the road to power and influence in Britain has begun in the lecture halls, seminar rooms, and quadrangles of Oxford and Cambridge universities. Collectively, the two ancient campuses are known as Oxbridge. They are more than mere schools: attendance at either signifies an unparalleled level of social and intellectual credibility. For generations in Britain, if you did not attend either Oxford or Cambridge, it was next to impossible to enter the ranks of the elite. In the United

States, the equivalent would be Yale, Harvard, Stanford, and the University of Chicago rolled into two. From around the world, the best and brightest flocked to Oxbridge, returning home to run cabinet ministries, corporations, or the nations themselves.

The two campuses have been a fertile spawning ground for politicians. Of Britain's forty-seven prime ministers, twenty-three have been educated at one or the other of the two; thirteen were produced by Christ Church alone, one of Oxford's thirty-four colleges. With the exception of Indira Gandhi, who attended Somerville eight years earlier, Oxbridge had produced male politicians almost exclusively until Margaret Roberts arrived—and she considered not staying. She hated Oxford at first. Unlike Cambridge, which is close to Grantham and which offers idyllic, sylvan gardens along the "Backs," which border the River Cam, Oxford is a busy commercial city. "An edgy and exhausting place," the writer Jan Morris calls it. "Few cities have been more loved, loathed and celebrated." For an unsophisticated suburban girl, not yet eighteen, Oxford was the far side of the moon.

There were 75 first-year women at Somerville. Margaret was one of 803 Oxford women and 1,813 men, the latter down nearly 1,000 since the war began. She was painfully homesick. "Living at home, you never know what it's like to be lonely," she once said of this time. She turned shy, particularly when she was teased about her shrill Lincolnshire accent. (Endless elocution lessons have failed to stop detractors from singling out her voice for criticism. "She sounds as though she is about to tell you your favorite pet has died," said one.)

Unlike many of her fellow students who had come from exclusive Oxbridge feeder schools, she knew almost no one and kept to herself. Socially inept, awkward, and totally lost with men, she was badgered by the other girls. Her references to "Daddy, the Mayor" didn't help. Nor did her frank admissions about aiming for big things. Her ambition was boundless; her candor, guileless.

Wartime activities helped pull her into the Oxford scene. Just as it dominated the nation, the war was a constant shadow over Oxford. Six members of the eight-man crew in the 1939 Oxford-Cambridge boat race, the last before the war interrupted the series, died in the war. No bombs ever fell on Oxford. Some historians say that was because Hitler planned to make the town his occupation headquarters, and the university prepared as if he might show up

at anytime. Somerville was transformed. Blast walls were constructed around the college's main entrances. Two large water tanks
for firefighting were installed. The women dug up the quadrangle
lawn to grow food, part of the "Dig for Victory" effort. Margaret
took her turn on fire watch brigade and worked at the local armed
forces canteen, handing out cookies and coffee to servicemen. Like
the rest of Britain, Oxford also felt the pinch of war. There was
little money for physical upkeep. More important, books were in
short supply. Every morning, lines snaked outside the libraries
waiting for the 9 A.M. opening; by 9:05 A.M., all the seats inside
were full. Few worn-out books could be replaced, and when new
books did surface, they were snapped up instantly. When fuel con-
servation measures went into effect and heating was cut back, students sat through lectures in their overcoats.

Although the Nazis never got to Oxford, the Americans did.
From 1943 to 1945, the city crawled with American servicemen.
The Clarendon Hotel was turned over completely to U.S. forces,
while the Mitre pub was invariably packed with Americans, Ca-
nadians, and Australians. Residents said they were more likely to
meet American soldiers on the streets of Oxford than British troops.
Margaret met Americans at the canteen and liked their fresh-
scrubbed confidence, contrasted with some of the blasé, world-
weariness she saw in their British counterparts. She got around on
a bicycle, and U.S. soldiers riding by in jeeps and trucks frequently
waved and made her smile.

Her studies, though, particularly chemistry, with its rigorous
schedule, kept Margaret more isolated than most of her women
contemporaries who studied liberal arts. Classes did not start until
9 A.M., but she began rising at 6:30 A.M. to study, a habit that
endures in Downing Street. She spent most mornings and afternoons closeted in laboratories, attended lectures from 5 to 7 P.M.,
and came home after dark to eat alone, often only some toast or an
egg.

Despite the early wobbles, the demands of Somerville began
to ease the loneliness, and the college started to exert its influence
on the grocer's daughter. Founded in 1879, Somerville was new for
Oxford. That meant it lacked some of the archaic traditions of the
other colleges, the oldest of which was founded in 1249. Somerville's
nondenominational aspect also had an impact. That meant, wrote
a Somerville historian, "that the college has recruited from no spe-

cial section, no one creed, class or social connection." Since she came from the bottom half of the class system, that worked to Margaret's advantage.

Somerville was serious, but then and now determinedly unpretentious. A current catalog notes only that certain Somervillians "have distinguished themselves in both academic and public life," noting, without naming them, that two prime ministers came from its ranks.

Margaret set no records academically. "Nobody thought anything of her," said Dame Janet Vaughan, a distinguished researcher who was Somerville's principal.[21] "She was a perfectly good second-class chemist. None of us ever thought that she would go very far."[22] Her tutor was Dorothy Hodgkin, a brilliant crystallographer who won the Nobel Prize in chemistry in 1964 and was the first woman since Florence Nightingale to win the Order of Merit, an honor society of only twenty-four members picked personally by the Monarch. Hodgkin agreed with Vaughan. If Margaret Roberts was going to make a mark, it was not going to be as a chemist. "One could always rely on her to produce a sensible, well-read essay, and yet there was something that some people had that she hadn't quite got," Hodgkin said. "I don't believe she had a particularly profound interest in chemistry."[23]

What she did have was a profound interest in politics, and the interest was becoming an absorption. Luckily, Somerville's free-wheeling, left-wing political tradition guaranteed plenty of attention for the conservative Miss Roberts. She stood out in the sea of Labor party supporters. But she remained a pain in the neck, a borderline offensive ideologue who could speak of little else save politics. Even at eighteen or nineteen, her political discussions were crushing offensives rather than dialogues. The political jugular was always her goal. Janet Vaughan tried to avoid Margaret. "If I had amusing, interesting people staying with me, I would never have thought really of asking Margaret Roberts because she wasn't very interesting to talk to," she said. "We used to argue about politics, but she was so set in steel."[24]

The nuances of political concepts did not interest Margaret. Obstinacy, resoluteness, and doggedness defined her approach from the outset. She infuriated critics of conservatism by refusing to acknowledge that any opposing argument had merit. Her tone was crusading, delivered with the messianic zeal, if not the rhetorical flourish, of a latter-day television evangelist. Once she got rolling, even her friends could not tolerate her single-mindedness. Politics and study became her only topics of conversation. She started sounding like a broken record. "Too concerned with only two things," Margaret Goodrich lamented with a sigh.[25]

She could have blunted some of the edge with a well-timed smile and a quip, but Margaret simply could not do it. Smiling and quipping were not natural legacies of the Robertses' household. Over the years, her most ardent supporters would constantly press her to relax, lighten up. She always found it difficult, almost impossible. Margaret could not tell jokes, an odd failing for most successful politicians, and did not enjoy or understand most of them. Field Marshal Lord Brammall, the chief of her General Staff, once said that if a joke were an integral part of a briefing, "we'd tell her a joke was coming and explain it." A blank stare or a startled "Oh" was the usual response.[26] Once, in the early 1970s, she returned to Oxford to speak at a "gaudy," a light evening devoted to amusing speeches. She was neither amused nor amusing. "Hello Somervillians and taxpayers," she began, launching into a discourse on tax law. The audience squirmed; some walked out.[27]

She joined the Oxford University Conservative Association because she could not get into the more famous Oxford Union, center of the campus debating societies. There was nothing personal about denying her entry. Founded in 1823, the union did not open its doors to any women until 1963. (Benazir Bhutto, later the prime minister of Pakistan, was elected president of the Oxford Union in 1976.) In 1944, during Margaret's second year, a union motion to admit women was defeated 127 to 24. Sexism was, not surprisingly, well entrenched at Oxford. Indeed, up into the 1920s, women had been required to take exams in segregated seats hidden behind special screens. Not until 1945 was a woman named a full professor.

The general political bias at Oxford during the war was left-wing, reflecting the increasing inclination of the nation. But that didn't bother Margaret. Alf had constantly warned her against being a follower, and Margaret never minded swimming against the current. She liked the competitive challenge and she believed in conservatism. But she also knew what she was doing; there was something icily calculating about her that she could not always conceal. Nina Bawden, a member of the rival Labor party club, remembers Roberts as a "plump, neat, solemn girl of nineteen" and recalls the future prime minister's reaction to her defense of Labor. "Margaret smiled, her pretty China doll smile. Of course, she admitted, the Labor club was more 'fashionable'—a deadly word that immediately reduced my pretensions—but that in a way suited her purposes," said Bawden. "Unlike me, she was not 'playing at politics.' She meant to get into Parliament and there was more chance of her being 'noticed' in the Conservative club if only because most of its members were dull and stodgy."[28]

But not all its members. At the end of her second year, Margaret fell in love with the son of an earl. The romance was her first and she found it difficult to stop talking about him, despite teasing by the other girls. They were jealous, and some also felt that Margaret, already difficult, would be unbearable if she netted a lord. Their fears were unrealized. The young man took her home to meet his family, but his mother did not approve of the grocer's daughter. Soon after, she was dumped.[29] After that, she socialized in groups.

Margaret was midway through Oxford when the war ended in 1945. She had followed avidly all the news of the D day invasion the previous June and watched the reports in fascination as tens of thousands of American troops charged across Omaha Beach and kept flooding into Europe. The U.S. army and navy had grown to three times the size of Britain's by the end of the war. The wrapup was rapidly turning into an American show, and Margaret sympathized with Churchill, who was determined to participate fully in the peacemaking alongside the Americans and Soviets.[30] Forty years later, as prime minister, she too labored to ensure Britain had a role in negotiations between the superpowers.

Joy in Britain at the end of the war was short-lived as Britons learned there would be no quick recovery. For a while, the situation worsened. Bread, which had not been rationed during the war, was restricted after the peace. Medicine and vitamins were in short supply: there were widespread outbreaks of boils and scurvy. The Oxford crew had weighed an average of 180 pounds a man before the war; for their first postwar race the oarsmen, including a stroke who had been held in German prison camp for three years, averaged 154 pounds. Men, older and more experienced, began streaming back to campus in the autumn of 1945. The Rhodes Scholarship program, halted in 1939, resumed, matching the regular thirty-two scholarships with another thirty-two for those who had seen war service. The pace of campus life intensified and with it Margaret's own activities.

Almost immediately, Winston Churchill called the first elections in a decade to replace the predominantly Conservative wartime

coalition government. Through OUCA, the Conservative association, Margaret became thoroughly involved. At the time, Oxford
sent three MPs to Westminster—two from the university, elected
by graduates, and one from town. Margaret showed no interest in
the university slots. That was not "real" politics as far as she was
concerned. The race for the city of Oxford, traditionally a "safe"
Tory seat, drew her instead.

There the battle was between Quintin Hogg, a Tory aristocrat,
and Frank Pakenham, a Roman Catholic Labor party intellectual.
Hogg would win and became one of Britain's most distinguished
postwar politicians, joining Thatcher's cabinet as lord chancellor,
Britain's top judge. Pakenham, a delightful eccentric, later inherited
a peerage as Lord Longford. A determined anti-Thatcherite, he
became better known as an antipornography and prisoners' rights
campaigner and the patriarch of the Pakenham/Longford literary
clan, the first family of British letters, which included such members
as his wife, biographer Elizabeth Longford, daughters Antonia
Fraser and novelist Rachel Billington, son Thomas Pakenham, and
son-in-law playwright Harold Pinter.

Margaret worked for Hogg, spending days door-knocking,
handing out campaign literature, and giving, and enjoying, her first
political speeches. The Tories were favored to win the 1945 election.
They held a massive majority going into the polling. Party leader
Churchill had just led them to victory over Germany, and the Tories
controlled 432 seats in what was then a 615-seat Parliament.

The result, of course, was one of the biggest upsets in modern
political history. Churchill and his Conservatives were not merely
beaten. They were crushed, losing more than half their seats. In
the new 640-seat Parliament, increased to represent a larger population, the Tories controlled only 213 seats, compared with 393
held by Clement Attlee's Labor party. The Tories had missed the
mood of the country, which wanted to see a more forward-looking
government more willing to take care of the welfare of its citizens.

If the left-leaning Oxford students were not dismayed, Margaret was dumbfounded. "We were all absolutely shaken. To me
it seemed utterly unbelievable that the nation could have rejected
Winston after everything he had done." It was, she said, "fantastic,
unbelievable."[31]

Margaret Thatcher would devote her political career to dismantling Attlee's "welfare state," but Margaret Roberts benefited
from one of Attlee's first acts: his decision to increase the pay of

MPs from £600 to £1,000 a year, then the equivalent of nearly $5,000, a living wage for someone with no other means of support. "From that moment on," she said, "it became possible to think in terms of a political career."[32] Soon after, she was at a dinner party, staying late to have coffee and help with the dishes. "I was having a fierce argument with one of the boys when someone interrupted to say, 'Of course, Margaret, you will go in for politics, won't you?' I stopped dead. Suddenly, it was crystallized for me. I knew." She had been thinking about it, so she hesitated only slightly before answering. "Yes," she responded, then added even more enthusiastically, "I ought to be an MP."[33]

First she had to finish school, get a job, and get situated.

After the war, Oxford became more intensely political. Labor's victory ironically contributed to a resurgence of interest in conservatism on campus, boosted by an influx of new students who had seen war service and a sense that conservatism needed reforming. In 1945, OUCA enrolled its thousandth member. A year later, membership had leaped to 1,750 and the association boasted a new leader: Margaret Roberts, the first woman president. Few were surprised by her victory. No one worked harder for the party or the association. Being the only woman on the otherwise all-male board never bothered her. Just as she would bestride her cabinet as prime minister, she had little difficulty dominating the men at the association.

She coauthored OUCA's official assessment of the Tory defeat. "Conservative policy has come to mean, in the eyes of the public, little more than a series of administrative solutions to particular problems co-related in certain fields by a few unreasoning prejudices and the selfish interests of the monied classes. If this extremely damaging view is to be refuted, it is essential that the relation between overall policy and the various solutions be shown and that the latter be demonstrably free from any suspicion of compromise between national and sectional interests."

It was obvious she was not a writer, but what was significant about the paper was its tone: the palpable sense of purpose. Her assessment, however awkward, marked the first time she tried to define her political philosophy. She was not radical. Most of her fellow OUCA members remember her as a centrist Conservative during her leadership years. She had, however, been expanding her reading and her thinking. In 1945, she consumed *The Road to Serfdom*, an apocalyptic tract by Friedrich von Hayek, an Austrian professor at the London School of Economics, who argued that any widening of socialist state power, led inevitably to tyranny, including the Nazi model.

She also joined a study group on Methodism, but found Oxford's brand of the religion "much more formal than anything I had been used to."[34] She dropped Methodism and began attending services at St. Mary's, the Anglican church. Skeptics later questioned her conversion. The Church of England is the church of choice for ranking Conservatives and only half-jokingly referred to as the Tory party at prayer. But she vigorously denied any suggestion that she changed religions for political advantage adding, incorrectly, "Church doesn't make the slightest bit of difference at all" in British politics.[35]

The OUCA, with its meetings, speeches, and evenings for hosting visiting Tory politicians, consumed a great deal of Margaret's time, and she was already on a schedule that allowed a bare minimum of rest—bed at 2 or 3 A.M., up at 6:30 A.M. Her studies suffered. "Her heart was always elsewhere," said tutor Vaughan. Her senior thesis, on X-ray crystallography, was acceptable. But she had trouble with the final exam and finished with a second-class bachelor of science degree in chemistry. It was a solid pass, but without distinction. Studying more might not have made all that much difference. "Firsts" at Oxford require a touch of brilliance. Margaret Roberts was a solid student, academically superior, but not intellectually brilliant. The results were nothing to be embarrassed about, but she was. Slightly. She had only herself to blame, though, she admitted. She had spent too much time on politics to get a first.

As she graduated in 1947, she recalled the meeting with her father and Norman Winning about going on to study law. She had not changed her mind. Chemistry was not going to get her where she wanted to go, she told classmates. But it could pay the bills in the meantime. After leaving Oxford, she used her chemistry degree to get a job with British Xylonite Plastics (BX), one of the country's oldest plastic firms. She went immediately to work for £350, about $1,600 a year, as a research chemist, about £50 or $225 less than men received for the same job. Two other Oxford girls hired by BX rented an apartment, but Margaret wasn't interested in sharing. She not only preferred being alone, but pragmatically, she wanted someone to cook her meals. So she rented a room in the home of recently widowed Enid McAuley and rode a bus to the factory.

Instantly it was clear she did not fit in. Her job, to help develop a special adhesive, often took her out of the lab and onto the shop floor, exclusively a male domain. The freshly minted graduate, a product of single-sex schools with no experience with men, let alone tough laborers, was lost. They expected to be called by their first name. She could not bring herself to do that. She insisted on Mister and a surname. Her affected upper-class accent and starchy primness rankled. The men started calling her "Duchess." At office parties, the other two new women joined in the festivities while Margaret sat by herself and left early. When she spoke at all about anything other than her work, it was always politics, delivered in unrelenting fashion. When she wasn't looking, the men gave the Duchess the finger. Margaret hated the job. She longed for weekends when she would pull on her one black dress and head for a Colchester Conservative party gathering.[36]

A chance meeting in 1948 put her onto the next rung. That autumn, she was invited to represent the Oxford Graduates Conservative Association at the party's annual conference, the most important fixture on the political calendar. Held by each of Britain's parties over four or five days from early September to mid-October, the conferences display the wares of each party as they prepare for the national election. They also give party officials a chance to preen and strut, to try out policies and themes, and to mix socially. An important part of the exercise is talent-spotting. Young activists are given a chance to speak so panjandrums can winnow potential up-and-comers to work in the trenches or even compete for a seat in the House of Commons.

The conference to which Margaret was invited was held at Llandudno on the wind-lashed north coast of Wales. Among the Tory faithful gathered was John Grant, director of Blackwell's, a big Oxford bookstore, who knew her well, and John Miller, chairman of the Conservative party in Dartford, a heavily industrial, Labor party stronghold east of London. During a lunchbreak, Margaret and the two men left the smoke-filled conference hall and strolled down an ocean pier for some air.

"I hear you're trying to find a candidate," Grant said to Miller. The local party chief was looking for cannon fodder to fight for the Conservatives at the next election in Dartford. In 1945, the Tories had been crushed in the district, called a constituency. There was every reason to believe the same thing would happen again. But a challenger had to be found and it did not matter where. In Britain, unlike the United States, MPs frequently have no ties to a constituency unless they have been representing it a long time. Some own no home there, but visit frequently, holding "surgeries" where they listen to voters' concerns. Some do not even regularly stay the night in their constituencies.

"Yes, we need a very able young man," Miller responded. "It's a tough constituency."

"Would you not consider an able young woman?" Grant asked.

"Oh, no," Miller said without hesitation. "Completely unsuitable. Not that kind of area at all. Dartford's an industrial seat."

Grant persisted. "Don't turn her down out of hand. At least meet her. She's young, only twenty-three. And for a difficult seat like Dartford, a woman might be just the right thing. Would you consider her?"

Miller paused. "Well, she can apply."

Nodding over at Margaret, Grant said it was she whom he had in mind. Miller summoned Dartford's women's chairman, who took one look at her and repeated his advice, "Just apply."

"Until then, I hadn't really thought of applying (anywhere) at all," said Margaret. "But that was how I came to."[37]

There were twenty-six other applicants for the right to run what would almost certainly be a losing campaign. All were men, none from Dartford. Four local businessmen had been approached to contest the seat; all had declined. But the futility of contesting a safe Labor seat did not daunt Margaret. She was excited and pumped up by the prospect of campaigning. She sailed through her presentation, carefully memorized and delivered without a note. Knowing her stuff was only part of it. She felt as though she belonged. She enjoyed canvassing and was more comfortable talking up the Tories with voters than she had been with classmates. In a political setting, she almost glowed. The panel was impressed.

"It was obvious she had a marvelous brain," said Margaret Phillimore, a member of the Dartford Conservative Association. "She was very poised, even for twenty-three, but human, likeable, and good company." Raymond Woolcott, also on the selection committee, came home and gushed to his wife about a candidate who was "beautiful, well dressed, and knew what she was talking about."[38] He thought she'd be fine to throw up against Norman Dodds, the popular Labor party incumbent. The rest of the committee agreed. In February 1949, they selected Margaret, who became the youngest parliamentary candidate in Britain, for an election whose precise date was not known, but which had to be held not later than July 1950.

On February 28, she was presented to Dartford's full Tory constituency for formal adoption. With Alf sitting beside her, applauding, she spoke on a theme close to his heart and hers, one she would return to always: the need for tax cuts to provide incentives. The committee vote went twenty to one in her favor. A collection for campaign expenditures raised 37 pounds 13 shillings, the equivalent of about $170. She was on her way.

First, there was time to celebrate at a reception which followed the adoption meeting. Margaret circulated easily, but like Cinderella at the ball, she kept an eye on the clock. Nagging away in her businesslike mind was a practical question. The party was running late; she couldn't run off. But how was she ever going to get the forty-five miles back to Colchester in time for work at BX in the morning? After she mentioned her concern to John Miller, the party chairman checked around and came back with a solution. One of the guests was driving back to London. He'd be glad to take her to Liverpool Street station near Trafalgar Square for the late train to Colchester. His name was Denis Thatcher.

Tall, trim, and athletic-looking despite his glasses, Denis was director of his family's paint firm. He had once run for office himself, but his bid for a county seat in Kent in southeast England had been unsuccessful. He was also a former army major who had served in France and Italy during the war, even receiving an MBE, a not insignificant citation. Single and, at thirty-three, ten years older than Margaret, Denis was dashing. He loved to drive his Jaguar fast and did so that night on the road back to London. [39] Margaret had to ask him to slow down. She liked talking to him, though. He was comfortable and direct discussing politics and particularly knowledgeable about business and economics. They even found they shared a taste in big band music. There were, however, no romantic twinges. Asked later if meeting Denis had been a case of love at first sight, she exclaimed, "Certainly not!"[40]

Being tapped for the election was the excuse she had been waiting for to quit British Xylonite Plastics. But she had to find a new position. There were no decent jobs for her in Dartford, but she did find one closer than Colchester, in Hammersmith, West London, at J. Lyons, a food conglomerate where she tested fillings for sponge cakes and worked on an artificial ice cream. Anxious to start campaigning, she moved to Dartford, again opting for a boardinghouse. It hardly mattered where she lived. She was rarely there.

She commuted to London daily on the 7:10 A.M train, faithfully reading the *Times* or *Daily Telegraph*, a newspaper so conservative it was commonly called the *Daily Torygraph*. Taking the 6:08 P.M. train home, she ran in for a quick bite and was back on the street by 8 P.M. for meetings and endless canvassing. She had no car or money for taxis and local public transportation was poor. Still, she accepted every invitation, and volunteers took turns ferrying her around.

Ray Woolcott, one of her early boosters and the local ward chairman, often drove her. One night late, he escorted her to her room where she pointed to a tin of sardines on the counter and said, "That's my dinner." When he got home, he described the scene to his wife Lucy. "I was scandalized," she said. "There she was, working sixteen hours a day and coming home to a plate of sardines." They decided to ask Margaret to move into their house. They had three bedrooms, but no children, so two were unused. She stayed eighteen months and, said Lucy, "she was, of course, the perfect guest."[41]

After her constituency meeting, Margaret would get home at 10:30 or 11 P.M., make a cup of coffee, sit in the study in front of a fire, and write letters and review papers until 1 or 2 A.M. Invariably, she was up by 6 A.M. and left the house at 6:35 A.M. for the train. The routine was exhausting. She admitted she was doing too much. Most of the time, she simply tried to put the pain out of her mind and get on with it, another discipline that has endured. "Sometimes it was too much, but the great secret of life is turning 90 percent of it into habit," she discovered. "That way you just keep turning it over."

Some nights, she'd stand in Lucy's kitchen after midnight, heat up a steam iron, and press her black velvet evening dress for the next night's meeting. She took great care of the few clothes she had. She was starting to date sporadically and was becoming increasingly conscious of her appearance. Her complexion was always good, but she was slightly chubby. She ate little and worked hard, but like many postwar Britons loved scarce sweets and had trouble resisting Lucy Woolcott's chocolate cookies.

By the time she moved to Dartford, men were still unimportant. She had plenty of pent-up passion, but for politics, not sex. She had no time to get involved, nor did she need to. Her sex life was nonexistent, but that was fine. She was a virgin, but not at all bothered about the fact. She went out occasionally. One fellow sent her orchids. Willie Cullen, a Scottish farmer she met at a dance, took her out several times and eventually proposed marriage. She declined. Soon after, he started dating Muriel and proposed to her. Muriel said yes and they moved to a farm in Kent.

Denis Thatcher occasionally scooped Margaret up in his Jag for a meeting or dinner. But it was far from a hot and heavy romance. Margaret was concentrating solely on the ticking electoral clock. The government's five-year term would end in July 1950, and Attlee would have to call an election by then, although in practice he could call one anytime he thought his chance of winning was best.

That finally happened in February 1950. Margaret had been organizing for a year. Her own prospects remained bleak, but there had been other local election results around the country showing swings to the Tories. So despite the Dartford tradition of voting for the Labor party, she was optimistic. "If you're not an optimist when you're young," she said, "you'll never be one."[42]

The Conservatives' national game plan was to attack Attlee for destroying the economy. "Free the people from the yoke of Socialism," barked Churchill, campaigning to recapture Downing Street. With the election set for February 23, Margaret took to the streets in bitter winter cold, campaigning vigorously on the one theme that would dominate her political life. The election was a choice between two ways of life: "One leads inevitably to slavery; the other, to freedom," she exhorted. "Vote right to keep what's left," was another popular aphorism. Repeatedly, she used a metaphor borrowed from her father to characterize Britons under Labor party rule. "A caged bird has social security. It has food and warmth. But what good is all that if it has not the freedom to fly out and live its own life?"[43]

As the youngest woman candidate, Margaret drew flocks of journalists to Dartford to watch her campaign, across the heavily industrial district. She had a natural, almost innate, sense of publicity and knew from the outset how to play to photographers and journalists. She did not have to be cajoled into posing in a white lab smock amid her beakers and test tubes. She suggested it. She never turned down an invitation unless it meant she had to leave work at Lyons early or arrive late. She refused to do either.

She stood outside factory gates for shift changes, strode into every shop and talked to every business meeting she could. The press cast her as indefatigable and plucky, but also exceptionally intense, a hard case. According to reporter Robert Muller, "she was fearless at meetings and pleasant, but cool to meet; blinkered, determined, ambitious."

For all her intensity, she got along surprisingly well with her Labor party opponent Norman Dodds. She took pains not to attack him personally, saving her ammunition for his party. She dispatched young volunteers to his appearances to take verbatim notes, so she could quickly respond to what he was saying. Dodds, on the other hand, who had won handily in 1945 and was confident of victory, campaigned leisurely and treated Margaret with avuncular charm. Grinning warmly, he promised to take her to lunch in Parliament when the campaign was over, which he did.

The Tories lost, but they had hacked Attlee's parliamentary majority from 146 seats to 5. The Conservative surge helped Margaret, but she had made her own mark as well. She cut Dodds's majority by nearly one-third—from more than 19,000 to 13,000—partly by doubling the turnout of Dartford Tories.

The local Conservative association was delighted with her showing. It was clear there would be another election soon. Attlee would have trouble hanging on in the House of Commons with such a small majority. Dartford quickly readopted her and gave her a brooch in appreciation. Nationally, the Tory leadership also noticed her performance. At a women's party rally that summer in London's elaborate Albert Hall, she was asked to introduce Winston Churchill, and she made the most of the brief encounter. It was one of the few times she ever met him, but years later, when she was in Downing Street herself, she would repeatedly refer to "Winston" in her speeches. Tory grandees would grimace and exclaim that she was being overfamiliar. "He'd be spinning in his grave hearing her try to sound like his best friend," snorted one. That did not put her off. She cited him whenever she could, and the new Tory faithful, her Tories, cheered the mentions until they were hoarse.

Attlee's government lurched on for only another eighteen months until October 1951, when a second general election was held. In the meantime, Margaret had moved out of the Woolcotts' and away from Dartford to her own apartment in Pimlico, near the Thames in central London.

Denis Thatcher was still taking her out. The early 1950s were grim, however, with little money around and ration cards for food, clothing, and gasoline still in use. Thick smog from countless peat fires choked city centers, particularly London. "They were rather dark days without much gay life about," Margaret recalled.[44] Nor was there much passion in her relationship with Denis, who was more interested in her than she in him. But there was a growing mutual appreciation, and they did have enough in common for Margaret to consider the relationship logically and analytically, if not romantically.

"He was in the paint and chemicals business, and I was a chemist," she remarked matter-of-factly. The extent to which there was any other chemistry between them was less clear. "He was on the financial side; I was interested in economics. We were both interested in politics. We had a lot in common."[45] Denis offered more. He was in love. He perked her up after the February loss and helped her get ready for her next shot, in October 1951.

That was a more desultory campaign. It followed so quickly that neither Margaret nor the voters could muster much enthusiasm. She canvassed Dartford again, but it wasn't the same. She no longer lived there. Getting there each day was difficult. Plus she knew all too well that there was no way she could overturn Dodds's 13,000-vote lead. In the year and a half since the last election he hadn't put a foot wrong.

Also, for the first time since Oxford, she was distracted. Denis had returned from a trip to France in September, just after the election was announced. He proposed and she accepted. Quickly they checked with Dartford chairman Miller for advice. Should they announce their engagement or wait until after the election? Miller advised waiting. Turning twenty-six during the campaign, she was asked if she had any marriage plans. Accurately, if only for the moment, she responded that she had "no time to spare for marriage."

When the votes came in, Margaret had cut Dodds's majority by another 1,000, nothing great, but nothing to be ashamed of either. However, the Conservatives won. Attlee was out and, at the age of seventy-seven, a querulous, cantankerous Churchill was back in Number 10 Downing Street. It was time to celebrate. In Dartford, after Margaret thanked her workers who were celebrating the national victory even as they accepted her defeat, there was one more bit of news. Denis took over the podium to announce that he would marry their candidate.

CHAPTER THREE

Wife and Mother

████████

MARGARET ROBERTS was ready at twenty-six to get married, and despite his appearance as a carefree bachelor content to zoom around in his Jaguar, Denis Thatcher was too. It would not be the last time that appearance and reality conflicted in Denis. There has always been more to Denis Thatcher than his image suggested. Throughout her public life, Denis has been portrayed in Britain as a likable, gin-swigging buffoon. He is likable and he does enjoy his gin, sometimes too much, but he has been no buffoon. Indeed, for all her ability and strengths, there is a powerful likelihood that without Denis Thatcher, Margaret Roberts would not have become prime minister. Long-time friends and associates insist that Denis is the best thing to have happened to Margaret. "She never would have made it without him," said one friend, a strong, but not uncritical, admirer. "He has provided her a financial safety net; more important, he has humanized her. Without Denis, she would have been intolerable." He has been, for her, the perfect consort.

A moderately wealthy businessman, dedicated to supporting a driven wife, Denis Thatcher has backed Margaret every step of the way—financially and emotionally. He was the catalyst behind her break from Grantham and her past. He helped make it possible for her to get a law degree. He paid for a live-in nanny and the children's boarding school, giving her even more freedom. He provided the financial means for her to enter and pursue politics without distractions. "Denis's money got me on my way," she concedes without apology.[1] As her principal cheerleader and provocateur in private, he has also kept her on her way. She knows what she has in Denis and appreciates him. He is there to pick her up, along with the bills. He dusts her off and lets her get on with it. She is hardly gushy about him. Their marriage was based "on common interest," she says, adding practically, "it's better to start that way because it endures." But since then, she adds, softening, their relationship has evolved into "a great love story, the gold thread" that has made the rest of her successes possible.

A decade older, Denis has brought his wife stability. In many ways, including his businessman's conservatism, he has been an extension of the father she idolized. Suffering none of the hang-ups that sometimes afflict men with famous wives, Denis has been her closest friend and strongest supporter, proud of her yet content with himself. She knows he has sacrificed privacy, freedom, and any semblance of a normal, married life for her. As long as he stays healthy, she will press on. The only scenario in which colleagues see her volunteering to leave office early would be if Denis were struck with an incapacitating illness. "She'd give it up for him," says a political colleague of thirty years. "She knows what he's given up for her."

It took Denis and Margaret two years to get to the altar after their first meeting. He admits to being smitten early—even if she wasn't. "What caught my eye were the same qualities as now," he said twenty-five years later when she became party leader. "She was beautiful, very kind and thoughtful. Who could meet Margaret without being completely slain by her personality and intellectual brilliance?"[2] Now, after nearly forty years of marriage, his enthusiasm remains undiminished. No one understands Margaret as well as Denis. He works well with her—and knows when to leave her alone. He calms her down when she gets excited, which is often. "When I'm in a state," she admitted shortly after becoming prime minister, "I have no one to turn to except Denis. He puts his arm round me and says, 'Darling, you sound just like Harold Wilson.' And then I always laugh."[3]

A dutiful, but unobtrusive public partner—"a pace behind her, old chap," he explains with a smile—Denis plays a more traditional role in private. He is a skillful host at private gatherings. Guests who do not know him well and are used to her are amazed to see Denis controlling the conversation at dinner parties while the prime minister listens quietly. When discussions take an embarrassing turn, he rescues her with an abrupt, "Time to go, darling." He is the only one who orders her around. Once, late at night, spotting her talking politics and drinking whiskey in her study with aides, he bustled in in a robe and grabbed her. "Come, woman. It's 2:30 A.M.; you know you'll be up at 6." She stood up and trailed meekly behind him. At other times, Denis has been known to rise after dinner with the women and troop good-naturedly to another room while Margaret stays at the table with the men.

On other occasions, like public receptions when Denis has had too much to drink, Margaret gets irritated and exasperated. She avoids showing her feelings, ignoring him instead, keeping her distance, working the opposite end of the room and only rarely giving the impression of dodging him. In more private circumstances, she bears with it when he comes home "kneeless," as she calls it. One weekend, she invited several friends to Chequers, the prime minister's official country residence, for a dinner to mark Denis's birthday. He forgot about it, stayed late at the golf club, and came home wobbly. Unperturbed, Thatcher sat him down, shoveled three servings of suet pudding into him, and sent him off to bed.

They get along so well because they both keep busy with their interests. They also share the same uncompromising political conservatism. Denis agrees with her core beliefs, but is farther to the right. "I don't pretend I'm anything but an honest-to-God right-winger," he once admitted.[4] He likes South Africa, a favorite golfing destination, so much that his public enthusiasm for the apartheid state has had to be toned down. He is equally vocal on the subject of socialism, which he hates in all forms. Denis staunchly backs management over trade unionists, whom he calls "Luddites," and misses few opportunities to trumpet his charge that the BBC is in the hands of "the Bolshies." He has expressed near contempt for foreigners. Asked once whether he had ever been anywhere outside Britain that he liked, he thought a moment before responding, "Dallas."

"I sometimes have to exercise a bit more tact than he might do," the prime minister once admitted. "But if now and then his views differ from mine, so what? They add to the spice of life. I think people adore him and I do too." Actually, though Denis never hesitates to advance right-wing positions to his wife, he is careful to keep his mouth shut in public, though it sometimes requires almost superhuman effort. For all his natural candor, he is the soul of discretion when it matters, and he has never seriously embarrassed the prime minister. Since his wife was elected party leader in 1975, Denis's only interviews have been with his journalist daughter, Carol. "So long as I keep the lowest possible profile, neither write nor say anything, I avoid getting into trouble," he says with a grin.

Personally, the two Thatchers are very different. She calls him "D" or "D.T." in private, "Denis" in public. He has a panoply of references for her, ranging from "Margaret" in groups, to "woman," "Thatcher," "lovey," or "the Boss." They share few friends. She has little time for his golfing cronies; he has little interest in her political coterie. Denis has been known to practice his putting on the lawn at Chequers while she meets inside with her cabinet. He loves holidays and will get away without her, driving himself to the airport, whenever he can; she hates vacations and will use almost any excuse to avoid them or to return early to work. He feels cramped at Number 10; she prefers it to anywhere else in the world. Denis smokes; she does not nor does she like anyone smoking around her. Denis is also a sports fanatic, but sports bore her.

Denis is a world-class male chauvinist married to the supreme symbol of female equality. She is audacious, sometimes too bold. Denis sounds bold, or at least blunt, in his private speech, but with his corporate background, he is by nature more cautious. Out of the public eye, they speak their mind to each other without rancor. "You may think me wrong, Margaret, but—" She breaks in suddenly, "You are wrong, Denis." The age difference, however, has never bothered her. Since grade school she has been more comfortable with older people.

Because she is so busy, Denis frequently goes his own way. For years, the demands of his job took him away as he worked to support the family. "People have often said, 'You do so much for Margaret in politics.' It's a beautiful theory, but it's not really true," he said. "I've had a wife and two kids to keep and my job comes first."[5] Now, he leaves for either business or, more often, for amusement. When he is gone, she gets lonesome. "I can get on with it when I am alone, but there is an emptiness there, sometimes," she conceded.[6]

Denis retired with a parting gift of a Rolls-Royce from full-time business in 1975, the year Thatcher became leader of the Conservatives, but he retained a number of corporate directorships. Unlike Margaret, who is a loner, he is, as the British say, "very clubbable" and likes to hang out, wearing his regimental or club ties, drinking gin with pals at places like Lord's Taverners or the Dulwich and Sydenham Golf Club. Asked at a boozy men's gathering what he actually did all day, Denis joked, "When I'm not paralytic, I like to play golf." A left-hander, he has a twenty-two handicap, but can play to a fourteen, meaning he can win the wagers.[7] He tries to get out on the golf course twice a week, sometimes with Willie Whitelaw, but more often with Bill Deedes, former editor of the *Daily Telegraph* and a friend since the 1950s. Denis's passion has, biographer Hugo Young pointed out, given Thatcher an influential philosophical link to every nineteenth hole in Britain.

When the going gets particularly rough, Denis makes a point of staying around to lend a shoulder and a sympathetic ear. During the Falklands War, for example, when British soldiers were dying and the prime minister was upset and tense, he scarcely left her side. He knew she needed support and was there to sit with her into the night when she poured out anxiety for "the boys." It is the same on the campaign trail, where Denis is a fixture, shilling, nodding, applauding, and forever interjecting "Hear, Hear" at the right moment. But if he can avoid a public function, he will. He hates short, overnight working trips and will almost always leave the prime minister to do those on her own. He'll also pass up longer jaunts if they're not the kind of place he likes. He passed up one of her most famous visits, to Moscow to see Mikhail Gorbachev in 1987, so he did not have to be hosted for five days by the dogmatic Raisa. "Pinkos," he tells friends, are not his type.

In private, he can turn the air blue with an expletive, but in public it is more likely to be old lines of soldier-speak that litter Denis's comments. "Better put that question to the GOC" (general officer commanding) means ask the P.M. "Moving PDQ" is a favorite. "Another cockup" is how he characterized the failure of an African meeting to take place on schedule. "Bugger me, Margaret, if anyone else could make a speech like that," he cried out at a lunch for Greek Prime Minister Andreas Papandreou after Mrs. Thatcher had neatly summarized several millennia of Greek history in a toast. "Oh, sorry," he added, noticing the wife of the Archbishop of Canterbury next to him. "I forgot you were there."[8] On another occasion, when asked if he and the prime minister had separate bank accounts, he replied, "God yes, and separate beds, too."

Ripe for caricature, Denis has been the subject of a popular

West End play, *Anyone for Denis*, which was based on a hilarious and still long-running spoof correspondence between Denis and a golfing chum in the fortnightly, satirical magazine *Private Eye*. The "Dear Bill" feature portrays him as a common type, middle-class, archconservative Englishman, a modern-day, braying Major, if not a full Colonel Blimp.

The lampoon is accurate, but incomplete. Denis is a shrewd consort who has managed to offer strong support without meddling, while remaining his own man. Privately, he knows it is far better to be considered a silly ass than a meddlesome, behind-the-scenes guru. Because of the comic persona he helped perpetuate, he has been able to make an impact without being censured, unlike Nancy Reagan and Rosalynn Carter.

He has not had as much influence on Thatcher as either of those strong-willed spouses, but he had more clout than has ever been clearly delineated. The prime minister trusts his judgment about situations and his gut instincts about people. He passes them on with no sugar coating. Denis is considerably more perceptive than she about sizing up people, particularly the men around her. Maggie has frequently mistaken charm for talent; Denis is less easily fooled. "Sometimes she does not like what he tells her, but she knows he is totally on her side," said Whitelaw, the former deputy prime minister who has known the Thatchers for years.[9]

Denis's business experience added some sophistication to the strict monetarist instincts she picked up in Alf's grocery. Her natural tendency was to avoid any kind of debt, including charge accounts. Denis did not mind her paying cash for personal purchases, but he taught her that debt was sometimes necessary for a company, and a country, to grow. His undiminished enthusiasm for the private sector mirrors her own, as does his loathing for big government. Critics maintain that his "empire mentality" fans the prime minister's foreign prejudices. He has given her an earful on South Africa, but she has her own reasons for refusing to impose sanctions—she is convinced they don't work—and has not needed bolstering from Denis. Generally, though, foreign policy has never been Denis's strength. He once told an American how lucky he was to have George Bush as vice president in case anything happened to Ronald Reagan. "Just imagine if that awful Carter had been assassinated," Denis exclaimed, confusing administrations. "You would have had a real crook as president, that Spiro Agnew."[10]

• • •

Despite the unquestioned success of their marriage, when the Thatchers first announced their engagement in 1951, some of Margaret's friends were astonished. No one believed she had a serious boyfriend. She never talked about dating. "She rather produced Denis out of a hat," said Margaret Phillimore. "She was so occupied with politics and her job that she didn't seem to have time for a boyfriend." Nonetheless, six weeks after the engagement announcement, they were married. In between, she took him to Grantham to meet her parents, and Denis brought her home to meet his mother and sister. Both visits were awkward. Denis's mother asked whether Margaret intended to give up her political career after her second failure at Dartford. Absolutely not, she replied. Up went the backs of the elder Thatchers, who already had concerns about their son marrying a shopkeeper's daughter. In Grantham, there was another delicate obstacle: Denis was Anglican and, worse, he was divorced, no mean hurdle for a strict Methodist family. Despite attending Anglican services at Oxford, Margaret had never advertised her drift from Methodism, particularly to Alf, nor had she formally broken from the church.

Denis was more solidly middle-class than Margaret. Born in London in 1915, he grew up in comfort, holidaying summers on the south coast and playing golf with his father. At eight, as is traditional among middle- and upper-class English boys, he was sent off to boarding school, Mill Hill, a second echelon, minor prep. He never attended university but went straight into the Royal Artillery. During the war, Denis served in France and Sicily, rose to the rank of major, and was mentioned in dispatches. When the war ended, he didn't want to leave the army. A locker-room man, Denis enjoyed the camaraderie and team spirit of the military. But he was forced to leave when his father died shortly after Armistice and he was called to run the family business, Atlas Preservatives. His grandfather, a farmer, had discovered and marketed a sheep dip and weed killer, and Denis's father had expanded the firm into chemicals and paints. Denis settled in as the plant's managing director.

He looked relaxed, but his personal life was in turmoil. In 1942 he had married another Margaret. "It was a typical wartime romance," he said later. "We knew each other only a few months and then I was posted overseas until the end of the war. We were never able to live together. It ended because I was away and I can't blame her." The divorce in 1946 was amicable. There were no children, and two years later the first Margaret Thatcher remarried. She and Denis never see each other and the two Margarets have never met.

The second Mrs. Thatcher had difficulty dealing with the prior marriage. She found it painfully embarrassing and, after wrestling with the subject for a while, decided to treat it as if it had never taken place. It took her twenty-five years to acknowledge publicly that Denis had been married before. She did it then only when pressed by journalists taking a closer look once she became party leader. It was the first her children, who were then twenty-three years old, had heard of it, and they were startled by the news. To the press, she offered a Victorian explanation: "One didn't keep it a secret he'd been married before," she said with arch primness. "One just didn't talk about a thing like that." She would not entertain further questions on the subject.[11]

They married on a bitterly cold, foggy December 13, 1951, in a Methodist service at Wesley's Chapel in East London. Only fifty guests were invited to see Alf give his treasured daughter away. In the front row were Beatrice, Muriel, and her husband William Cullen. On Denis's side of the aisle sat his widowed mother and his sister Joy, who has her brother's humor and direct approach. They both thought Denis could have done better. No one except Alf doubted that Margaret was marrying up, but Margaret ignored anyone bold or rude enough to allude to the social gap.

Handel's "Water Music," Clarke's "Trumpet Voluntary," and Bach's "Jesu, Joy of Man's Desiring" were her musical selections. Because of Denis's previous marriage, Margaret did not wear white, surprising some guests who did not know the reason. Instead, she made a fashion statement, the first of many that would propel her climb from deep dowdy to the international best-dressed lists. Her wedding dress, deliberately theatrical, was a long, flamboyant velvet, an exact copy of one worn by the Duchess of Devonshire in a famous eighteenth-century painting by portraitist Sir Joshua Reynolds. A brilliant sapphire blue, complete with matching hat and ostrich feather—she loves hats—the dress was, not accidentally, the Tory party's official color. Ever practical, she turned it into a dinner dress after the wedding and "wore it for a long time afterwards."[12] The Thatchers honeymooned in Portugal, Madeira, and

Paris, combining pleasure with business for Denis. The trip was her first abroad.

Returning to London after three weeks, still their longest vacation together, they moved into Denis's place, a small, rented sixth-floor apartment on Flood Street in Chelsea. The neighborhood remained their home for many of the twenty-eight years before Downing Street. Once married, Margaret no longer had to support herself, so she quit work at J. Lyons, dropped out of politics, and went to law school to become a barrister. The course took two years, at the end of which, after two exams, she would be "called to the bar." She would then spend a third year clerking for a senior barrister, as did all prospective barristers, helping prepare cases and accompanying him, togged out in wigs and gowns, to court.

In the midst of her studies, a year after the wedding, Margaret learned she was pregnant. She knew that a child would change her life, but she did not want birth to keep her from politics. She had no idea what it would be like trying to be a mother as well as a wife and politician, but the idea of women playing more than one role had recently been on her mind. Only months before, King George VI had died and was succeeded by his daughter Elizabeth, who was six months younger than Margaret. A strong monarchist, Margaret was elated by the prospects of a woman on the throne. Elizabeth was the first female monarch since Victoria's reign ended in 1901 and only the second since Queen Anne died in 1714. Margaret was curious enough about what the change might mean for women in public life that she wrote an article headlined "Wake Up Women" for the now defunct *Sunday Graphic* newspaper.

"Women can—and must—play a leading part in the creation of a glorious Elizabethan era," she wrote. Women who abandoned careers to bring up children sold themselves and their families short, she insisted. Women could work both inside and outside the home without disruption. "The idea that the family suffers is, I believe, quite mistaken." There should be no limits on women, especially not in politics, no matter what their family situation. "Should a woman arise equal to the task, I say let her have an equal chance with the men for the leading cabinet posts. Why not a woman Chancellor—or a Foreign Secretary?"[13] There was a reason she did not mention prime minister. That, she felt, was not a realistic proposition in her lifetime. Alf was delighted with the article; all that training to think and act independently, without limitations, was bearing fruit. Beatrice's reaction to what was essentially a formal repudiation of her kind of motherhood has not been discussed.

Pregnancy did not slow Margaret down. In addition to her law studies, she became a full-time housewife for the first time, cooking and decorating. Up at 6 A.M., she'd whip up eggs and bacon for Denis before he drove to work. At night she cooked solid English fare, roasts and chops—basic, hearty, and not very time-consuming. Painting and wallpapering were her favorite ways to relax. Whenever she felt tired from the law books, she'd pull on tentlike painter's overalls and start stripping and sandpapering walls and trim. It was therapy, a change of pace, but she took it seriously. She always wanted it done right. Slapping paint around amateurishly was never her style. When Downing Street was being redecorated in 1988, she stopped to speak to Carla Powell, a friend and the wife of her private secretary Charles Powell, who was stippling a wall with paint. "Watch the drips," Thatcher admonished. "You run the country, I'll take care of the painting," Carla retorted. Thatcher burst into laughter.

Margaret passed the first bar exam in May 1953 when she was five months pregnant. In August, seven weeks ahead of schedule, she gave birth to twins in Princess Beatrice Hospital in Chelsea. The multiple birth was a complete surprise. Amniocentesis and scans were not available then, and she had no idea she was carrying more than one child. Labor was long and hard until finally, her doctors decided on a caesarian delivery. A boy was born first; two minutes later, a girl appeared. Each weighed only four pounds. The Thatchers had no names picked out, later deciding on Mark and Carol, not in honor of anyone in particular. "We just wanted simple names that couldn't be shortened," she said.[14] "We didn't like nicknames."

Denis was nowhere to be found that Saturday. Margaret was not officially due until October, and he had gone to an international cricket match between England and Australia. Afterward, he and friends had adjourned to a pub to celebrate; England had won "The Ashes." There was no way to contact him when her contractions started. She made her way to the hospital and endured labor alone. "*Do* I remember," she recalled later. "We couldn't find my husband anywhere. He had mooched off."[15] There was mock anger in her recollection, but some genuine resentment lay behind the sentiment. It would have been nicer had he helped her to the hospital and waited, even though he would not have been present for the actual births. But he was not there at all and still she had succeeded on her own. She did not love Denis any less, but it did reinforce a growing idea that there was little she could not do by herself.

Two weeks in hospital forced Thatcher to think what she would do next. Talking about combining a career and motherhood was one thing; doing it was another, especially with two babies. She knew that infant twins were enough to keep most women busy and tired. But she was worried that her mind would turn to mush if she didn't continue her career. Images of her mother Beatrice raising her and Muriel flashed through her mind. "I was concerned, particularly with two, that I might be tempted to spend all my time on the household and looking after them and not continue to read or use my mind or experience. I felt I must really use the rest of me as well."[16]

"I remember lying there and thinking, if I don't now that I'm in hospital, actually fill in the entrance form for the final of the law, I may never go back to it. But if I fill in the entrance form now, pride will not let me fail. And so I did. That was really an effort of will."[17] Four months later, she took the final and passed. No one was prouder than Denis: "Bar intermediate in May; twins in August and Bar finals in December. I'd like to meet another woman who can equal that record."[18] She had been highly efficient, a boy and girl born at the same time. "She got it right on the first attempt," a friend said with admiration. "She didn't have to think about getting interrupted again." True, but any mention of "efficiency" in the production of her children not surprisingly elicits a thundercloud scowl from Thatcher. She did not, however, ever have plans to have more children.

She decided not to stand for office again while the children were young. Lawyering was something else. Working at the bar meant regular daytime hours while still logging valuable preparation for the inevitable return to politics—once the twins were in boarding school. In the meantime, she pointed out that, as preemies, "they were small and needed a lot of looking after." Like any new mother, she was nervous at first. "I worried all the time. Of course, 90 percent of the time, you worry about things that don't happen, but still you worry." Late night campaign hours never exhausted her, but the twins did. "I began to wonder whether I would ever get a decent night's sleep again," she lamented, echoing the sentiments of mothers the world around. She never breast-fed them, but gave them bottles morning and night. When they got older, she always left on a night light. "There's no point trying to make them get used to the dark. Most children are afraid of the dark."[19]

The apartment, smaller than the one in Grantham, was cramped, but was rent-controlled and cost a mere $18 a week. They did not want to move if they could avoid it. For a while, all four lived in the same room until luck intervened and the apartment next door became vacant. Denis rented it, broke through the wall, put in a door, and installed the twins and a nanny in the next room, which Margaret decorated in pinks and blues. She dressed the twins immaculately, often identically in outfits cut and stitched by Beatrice, the former professional dressmaker. Alf and she came to London occasionally to see the grandchildren. Alf, loosening up as he aged, unceremoniously sprawled on the floor to play with them. Margaret and Denis rarely returned to Grantham; the town bored her and reminded her of a difficult, nearly friendless youth. Nor did they see much of Denis's family; Margaret was not very comfortable with them.

Denis made good money at Atlas, but he was almost as frugal as Alf. Nothing was wasted by the thrifty Thatchers. When the children eventually moved into separate rooms, Margaret turned their nursery curtains into winter coat linings.[20] The children were all-consuming at first, but Thatcher was eager to get back to work. "They do become the center of your life." she said of the children. "And yet, I knew that I had something else to give."[21]

Her chemistry background had helped sharpen her already powerful memory for detail, so she decided to concentrate on tax law, a particularly male preserve within an already male profession. She got off to an inauspicious start. To her own and everyone else's surprise, the barrister to whom she apprenticed declined to hire her after her six-month tryout. Thatcher was dismayed. She had not been brilliant, but she had worked hard. Laboring on tax relief schemes and foreign tax legislation, she frequently brought home reams of revenue figures so Denis, more comfortable with balance sheets than she, could help with the figures. Her co-workers blamed Margaret's dismissal on the unpredictability of their boss, not her work. She had been treated shabbily, Thatcher concluded. She was bitter, but wasted no time on recriminations. She quickly found another job and worked as a full-time tax barrister for the next five years.

Politics was still on her mind. She thought constantly about how best to get back into public life, making it clear she would drop tax law in an instant if the right opening came along. Although she had originally planned not to stand for office until the twins went away to school, Margaret couldn't stick to that plan. She could not stop looking for a constituency, trying to get on a by-election ballot, the vote to replace an MP who either dies or steps down between national elections. She tried all over London and surrounding areas, determined to find a constituency within daily commuting range so she could minimize her time away from the children.

The twins were only a year old when she sought selection for the Orpington seat in North Kent. Turned down, she nearly made it at Beckenham; next came Ashford, Maidstone, and Hemel Hempstead. Oxford also turned her down. Selection committees told her they were impressed with her qualifications and intelligence, but questioned whether a young wife with babies would not be better off staying home. She was incensed.

Complicating her tryouts was confusion over where the family would live. The rent on their Chelsea apartment was scheduled to jump in 1958, and the Thatchers had to decide whether to stay and pay the higher fee or buy somewhere else. But buying made no sense until Thatcher was selected somewhere. That she would not be picked or that she would stop looking for a seat never occurred to her.

Finally, the government's decision to cut back rent controls forced the Thatchers' hand. They left Chelsea and bought a four-bedroom house on nearly an acre of land in Kent, due south of London. No sooner had they concluded the deal than the Finchley seat, due north of London, became available. Unlike some constituencies, Finchley was sensitive about their candidate living at least near the district. To be considered as replacement for the retiring Tory who had held the seat for more than twenty years, a candidate had to be under forty and live less than forty miles away. Margaret was thirty-three; the Farnborough house was thirty-five miles away. And by this time, Thatcher had become a professional applicant. She went to selection meetings the way actors auditioned. She had her routine down cold.

The beauty of Finchley was that it was close to Westminster and a safe Tory seat. The Tories had outpolled Labor by more than 12,000 votes in the last election. The trouble was that nearly 200 candidates applied for the seat. A written test cut the field to twenty-two. Thatcher's presentation moved her into the final round of four, the only women. According to the *Finchley Press*'s coverage, her talk was impressive. "Speaking without notes, stabbing home points with expressive hands, Mrs. Thatcher launched fluently into a clear-cut appraisal of the (post-Suez) Middle East situation, weighed up Russia's propagandistic moves with the skill of a housewife measuring the ingredients in a familiar recipe, pinpointed Nasser as the fly in the mixing bowl, switched swiftly to Britain's domestic problems (showing a keen grasp of wage and trade union issues), then swept her breathless audience into a confident preview of Conservatism's dazzling future."[22]

Finchley wanted a candidate with lots of energy. The members were worried about an upsurge of sympathy in the constituency for the Liberal party and were looking for a lively candidate to combat it. When asked what she would do, Thatcher replied, "I will let the people know what Conservatism is about and I will lead the troops into battle." That was just what Finchley wanted to hear. She was chosen. "It may seem like hindsight," said council member John Tiplady, "but when we interviewed the candidates, we asked ourselves, 'Is this a future prime minister?' Margaret clearly was and everybody thought so."

Denis didn't learn that his wife was back in politics until two days after the decision. In South Africa on business, he read in a London paper that Margaret had been picked for a safe seat; she was an odds-on favorite for a place in Parliament when the next election was called. Although she had spent four years trying to get picked for a seat, she had actually, if unintentionally, kept her pledge not to return to politics full time while the twins were babies. They were five that year 1958, the beginning of the end of their contact with her.

By the time they reached five, they had not seen much of her, but once she was elected to Parliament, they would scarcely see her at all. Throughout the mid-1950s while they were toddlers, she was busy as a lawyer and never home weekdays anyway. Living in Farnborough, she commuted daily to London either by train with her men neighbors or in a battered old Vauxhall. Denis drove to work in the opposite direction in a company car with vanity plates DT1.

The twins were fixtures in the neighborhood, always out in the street or playing with other kids. But Margaret was rarely seen. She made the children breakfast; at 5:30 P.M., she was out the office door like a shot to get home before the children went to bed. But once she got into Parliament in 1959, she was rarely home except in the early morning. "It wasn't exactly sparkling at that hour," said Mark, "but at least we all found out each other's plans for the day." She called the children regularly at 6 P.M. from the Commons to say goodnight, but according to colleagues, rarely if ever mentioned them to anyone at work.

Until they left for boarding school, the twins were raised mostly by a nanny, a warm and outgoing older woman named Abby who was more mother than Thatcher. Abby and the children hugged and loved one another with the kind of warmth neither child got often from its parents. Abby's role was hardly unique. Nannies have been raising children of well-to-do Britons since the mid-nineteenth century, when the Industrial Revolution increased the numbers of the wealthy and produced a new servant class from those who used to work on farms. The custom has endured, although on a dramatically reduced scale, since the war.

After nanny, it's off to sex-segregated boarding school, another concept perfected by middle- and upper-class Britons to ensure, well before puberty, the insulation of parents from their children. Sex segregation has been a historic tradition in many cultures. In Britain, however, children are sent away much earlier, at only seven or eight years old. Sociologists have lists of reasons for the nanny/boarding school practice ranging from the Victorian belief that children were "little defective adults, sodden with original sin" which had to be squeezed out by rigid disciplines[23] to the custom of parking children in boarding schools in Britain rather than bringing them to the outposts of empire where education was dodgy. But there is another, unscientific reason: Britons, by nature, are generally cool toward children. Elsewhere in Europe, children are rarely separated from parents at such an early age. On the continent, only brittle Austria, another former seat of empire, prefers its children seen but not heard.

Although the Thatchers were not that different from many other middle-class Britons in their basic hands-off attitude, there were other reasons they spent so little time with the twins. Denis was, at thirty-eight, already much older than the average first-time father. A veteran rugby referee, he loved sports and, on occasion, threw cricket and rugby balls in the backyard with Mark. Still, running around after children was not a favorite Denis pastime. Nor was it for Margaret. She had grown up quickly and, encouraged by her own behavior, had always been treated as a little adult. Surrounded by older people, she had never been all that comfortable with others her age. She hardly knew what it was like to be treated as a child. Now, she preferred to work. She had no intention of being a homebody like Beatrice.

Abby's warmth was in sharp contrast to Denis and Margaret's temperaments. Denis loves a good time but has a short fuse and can be very standoffish. Margaret also has a temper and can be highly emotional, as cabinet ministers who have felt the lash of her tongue testify. For the most part, however, she seldom loosens control of her feelings and was rarely demonstrative toward the children. Even when showing affection she is reserved. And when she is cold, she can be icy. Her father, no Mr. Warmth, called her chilly reserve her only significant failing. "Margaret is 99.5 percent perfect," he once said during her early campaigning years. "The other point .05 percent is that she could be a little warmer."[24] Thatcher laughs when she hears the "perfect" comment, but admits that she has always kept a tight rein on her emotions. "Self-control is something we were taught," she said.[25] "We were not a very demonstrative family."

When she was around, Thatcher was anything but a relaxed, laid-back mother. She referred to the children as "dear" or by name. She stuck to her intention never to call them by a nickname and never lapsed into sweet familiarisms. Taking her cue from her own childhood, she allowed no pets in the house. She did not play games or run off with the twins on a lark, but, like Alf, stressed culture, making sure they had music lessons. Because there had been no dancing when Margaret was growing up, she was determined that they have dance lessons. They were also dutifully trotted around London to the theater and opera. Because their mother still remembered it as a treat, they often went to the movies. But the twins also had absentee parents in a way that Margaret never did.

Her own strict upbringing and unrelieved pragmatism made Margaret an awkwardly compulsive mother. Once, when the twins were away at school and she felt particularly driven, she tore into their toy boxes, determined to clean them up. Out went piles of long-treasured toys simply because she was convinced they were no longer used and the twins were tired of them. It never occurred to her to ask the children first if they minded. Nor did it cross her mind to ask them to cull the collections themselves. There was a job to be done and she was trying to help. The episode was typical Thatcher: she made up her mind and did it—working hard, on her own, but not pausing to consider all the consequences. When the

twins returned and discovered what she had done, they were devastated.[26]

It was not all bleak. The family used to spend three weeks in
August at the beach on the Isle of Wight. Mark and Carol loved
the beach, picnicking in the sand and sometimes bouncing offshore
in a speedboat rented by Denis, who loved to go fast on water as
well as land. The beach was always a struggle for Thatcher. She
hated sunbathing. "I turn red and peel," she confessed. "I've never
managed brown legs in my life."[27] But neither was she a stick-in-
the-mud. She'd help organize dress-up competitions for the kids.
One creation, an Egyptian mummy which involved wrapping a child
in endless yards of bandages, was an easy winner. When the twins
were seven, Mark came down with chicken pox and the Isle of
Wight trip was scrubbed and replaced by two weeks of Christmas
skiing in Switzerland. Everyone had such a good time, they repeated
the trip for the next five years. Family pictures at the time show
Thatcher fashionably togged out in dark glasses and a black-and-
white knit sweater, gamely smiling at the top of the Lenzerheide
slope.

She was easier on her children than Alf had been on her and
Muriel. Perhaps because she was home so infrequently, she was
never a particularly strict disciplinarian. In Parliament, she endorsed caning recalcitrant children in school. But she never lifted
a hand against her own children, though by most accounts Mark
could have used more discipline. An almost hyperactive child, he
frequently got into mischief. "We weren't brought up very strictly,"
Mark said years later. "If I did the things she expected of me and
behaved in a reasonably civilized fashion, it was fairly easy going.
If I misbehaved or did something idiotic, then it was trouble, just
as it would be with any mum."[28] She never indulged the twins with
lots of toys, clothes, or a hefty allowance. She is generous to those
in need, mostly with support, but with money when she feels it
necessary. As an MP, she has on more than one occasion sent money
or food anonymously to constituents. Generally, however, like her
parents and Denis, she is frugal.

When she was a child, Thatcher rarely had other children over
to her house. There were several reasons. One was that she was
bossy and not much fun; she didn't have many friends. Another
problem was her father's economies. Because of his watchful eye
on the purse strings, she never felt she had much to offer in the
way of games, treats, or meals. And despite his crack about Mar-

garet's chilliness, Alf also had a reputation for being pretty cool to children. All the things that made North Parade a mecca for political discussion conspired against it becoming an attractive place for youngsters. Thatcher was sensitive to the need for her own children to have more playmates than she had. She encouraged them to have friends over and made a point of having them invite kids whose parents were having marital problems. That kind of subtle, understated kindness is one of Thatcher's best qualities, a humaneness that shows up time and again in her political life but rarely comes across in public.

Later, Denis felt strongly that Mark should go to boarding school. Thatcher, who had lived at home until she went to Oxford, was less anxious to see the twins leave so early. But she realized that neither she nor Denis was home much. Another reason to send Mark off was the twins themselves; they did not get along at all. Margaret once called them "mortal enemies." "They are very, very different," she said. Mark, the elder twin, was difficult. Carol was kinder, gentler, and more withdrawn. Boarding school would give them, their parents believed, a constant environment, regular schedules, and some distance from one another. At eight, the same age his father had left home, Mark was sent off to Belmont, a feeder for Denis's old school, but he did not follow Denis to Mill Hill. Instead, Mark went to Harrow, founded in 1571 and one of Britain's most ancient and respected schools. Two years later, at ten, Carol went off to Queenswood, a school not on the same level as Harrow, although Carol was by far the better student.

Mark never did well in school. He studied little at Harrow and never went to university. He joined a firm of accountants but repeatedly failed the qualifying exam to become an accountant and later drifted into a series of motor racing jobs that proved as unsuccessful as accounting. He kept crashing.

Not surprisingly, both children have had problems living in their mother's shadow and in dealing with her fame, but they have dealt with them in different ways. Mark has long been his mother's favorite. Handsome, lean, and well dressed, once a bit of a playboy, his appearance pleases Thatcher, who has always doted on him. "I'm more like my mum," he has said. People who know him disagree. They say he is more like his father—interested in good times, sport, fast cars—but not as nice as Denis. "He's a very spoiled and arrogant boy who trades on his mother's position," said one of Thatcher's closest associates. Adds another, a personal friend of the family who has high respect for the parents: "There is no other way to put it: Mark is a total ass. He has always traded on his family name. Money is very important to him, fancy clothes, flashy cars. But if you cannot do something for him, he won't give you the time of day." "That odious son" is how another member of the Thatcher inner circle describes Mark.

In 1982, Mark became lost while racing in a trans-Sahara rally and disappeared for six days. Thatcher was distraught. Fearing him dead, she wept frequently, including on television. Denis was dispatched to Morocco to join the search party. When Mark reappeared, a young lady in tow, the prime minister was exhilarated. Denis was pleased he was safe, but livid at his son's insouciance and failure to recognize the trouble he had caused, including putting the armed forces of several countries on alert to search for him. He chewed out his son. In the late 1980s, Mark moved to the United States and settled in Texas, where he has repeatedly infuriated the British Embassy and State Department with petty demands and complaints. He returned to Britain periodically and in 1987 asked Bernard Ingham, Thatcher's press secretary, what he could best do to help his mother's third campaign. "Leave the country," the blunt Ingham responded. Mark did. That same year, he married the pretty blond daughter of a Dallas car dealer, and together they produced, in 1989, the prime minister's first grandchild.

Thatcher is blind when it comes to Mark, blaming herself for his behavior. Denis, on the other hand, is wise to his son and was cool to him for years. "He was as critical of his son as anyone would be of a son like Mark," explained a Denis intimate. When a media campaign against both of them raised questions about their business connections, however, Denis pulled Mark back under his wing in a gesture of solidarity against the "reptiles"—the press. From that moment on, right or wrong, Denis decided to back his son.

While Mark used his mother's name, Carol tried hard for years to live independently and bypass her family connections. A friendly woman with a sense of humor, she specifically asked her mother not to use any influence when she began studying law—at her mother's suggestion. Thatcher's politics had focused attention on Carol at school, and she was desperate to avoid the limelight, never more so than when the Fleet Street press was scrutinizing her love life. Anxious for privacy when Thatcher became Conservative party leader, Carol moved as far from London as she could, to Australia, where she worked as a cattle station hand, a newspaper reporter, and, finally, a talk show hostess. "If Carol ever saw a string that could be pulled, she'd run a mile rather than pull it," her mother said proudly.[29]

Carol returned to Britain to help in the 1983 campaign and stayed. Her determination to avoid pulling strings suffered a hiccup when she was hired by the *Daily Telegraph*, then edited by her father's golfing chum Bill Deedes. She worked hard and, while no superstar, held her own. Few colleagues held her name against her. When the *Telegraph* was sold in 1986, a new editor was named and Carol was fired. "The prime minister went thermonuclear," was how one aide described her rage. After fifty faithful years as a *Telegraph* reader, Thatcher switched to the *Independent*.

Thatcher claims to be proud of Carol, but the fact that she is a sweet woman who tries, far harder than Mark, has not been enough for her mother. Thatcher is totally success-oriented, but her daughter has been less than successful in some areas her mother considers important. Carol graduated from university and passed her law exams but never practiced law. In her late thirties, she is now a free-lance journalist. Carol has been unlucky in love. For a while she dated Jonathan Aitken, a Conservative MP, but he dropped her, very publicly, and no great new romance looms on the horizon. "She suffers by being her mother's daughter," explains another friend, whereas "Mark exists by being his mother's son." Thatcher worries about her daughter. She is concerned that Carol, for all her efforts to please her, simply doesn't have her life together. She would like to see her daughter thinner, trendier, more sophisticated, with a successful boyfriend or husband.

Few children of famous parents have found life easy. That has been true for many British political families, including the Baldwins, Churchills, and Macmillans. Mark and Carol have not been spared. Most friends of the family point to Thatcher's political schedule as the obvious culprit that sabotaged a normal home life, but that is simplistic and unfair. Denis is equally guilty. He not only missed their birth, but was repeatedly absent during their childhood. Nor did Margaret's absences tempt Denis to become more of a house-husband. Even when he was not traveling, Denis frequently drove home from Atlas at 8 or 9 P.M., after Abby had put the children to bed. Denis was in his fifties when the twins, away at school, entered their teens. Except for introducing Mark to golf, he has been no more involved with the children's upbringing than the far busier prime minister. His devotion has, by the accounts of most friends, always been focused more on his wife than his children.

Thatcher's first concentration is work, and from the twins' earliest days she too was often gone or distracted by work at home. She tried to keep in touch in her own way, but without much of a childhood herself, she has never understood children. In later years, she made trips, albeit infrequently, to Texas to see Mark and has been known to leave home in the middle of the night to meet Carol at a train station, then stay up talking with her nearly to dawn. There's no question about how she feels about her children. A fiercely protective mother, she loves them dearly and, in public, speaks of them with enormous pride. Privately, say those close to her, she carries a heavy guilt complex for not being there for the twins when they needed her. She would not trade the hours she spent in the Commons late at night or the weekends in her constituency, but she does regret not having done more with Mark and Carol. For all her toughness, she is highly sensitive and well aware that her workaholism and political success have come at a price that has contributed to their difficulties. "She is an unbelievably successful politician," says one of her closest friends, "but an unsuccessful mother and she knows it."

CHAPTER FOUR

Into Parliament

WHEN PRIME MINISTER Harold Macmillan called the 1959 election, no politician was more eager than Margaret Thatcher. The moment he dropped the flag, she threw herself full tilt into her third campaign—the first she had a chance to win. Arriving in the 5½-square-mile constituency each morning shortly after 8 A.M., she campaigned until after dark. Her technique was simple—talk to everyone; don't miss anything. She visited shops, senior citizen homes, offices, schools, and even union halls, where usually only Labor party politicians showed up.

Her speed, efficiency, and knowledge bowled over most of her Finchley constituents. She also displayed a graceful charm that most people who do not know her are surprised to discover. A quarter-century later, she would use a more flirtatious variation of the same charm to captivate such opposites as Ronald Reagan and Mikhail Gorbachev. In the 1959 campaign she could whip in and out of a house in less than ten minutes, swallow a cup of tea, and leave the family thinking she had dropped by for a leisurely visit that spanned the afternoon. With shopkeepers, she could rattle off food prices and discuss their problems from the informed perspective of a grocer's daughter. They never forgot her empathy. She never forgot their names—or anything else about them. Even by politician standards, she has always been exceptional for remembering, without notes, personal details. Although it was her first race in Finchley, she had been working the constituency for a year, ever since her selection as the Tory candidate. She was not only calling constituents by name, but making references to details like a car accident in which a constituent's cousin had broken a leg or someone's granddaughter who had been born in Florida.

Finchley was tailor-made for Thatcher. Its middle-aged to elderly electorate consisted mainly of self-made homeowners who lived on clean, suburban streets. Their homes were neat and well maintained, but not posh. Many heads of households were small businessmen. There were almost no blacks, Asians, nonwhites, or immigrants among the 67,000 residents in the days when Thatcher launched her first campaign. There was, however, a significant Jewish community, nearly a quarter of the constituency, and Thatcher struck a strong bond with them. She shared many of their values: belief in self-education, self-help, hard work, and suitable reward. Later, Jewish MPs would be among her most influential advisers. Five joined her cabinet, more than have served any other prime minister. (On her sixtieth birthday, the Finchley Friends of Israel planted sixty trees in her honor on the Golan Heights.)[1]

By election day, October 8, 1959, Thatcher had canvassed Finchley more thoroughly than anyone ever before—and all on her own. Because the seat was considered easy pickings, the party organization had not been much help. But when the votes were counted, even the locals were impressed with her showing. There was a high, 81 percent turnout, but even with two other candidates in the race, Thatcher won more than half the vote and a huge majority of 16,260, more than 3,500 votes over her predecessor's margin. It was the first of many times that a divided opposition would contribute to a big Thatcher victory. Five days short of her thirty-fourth birthday she was off to Westminster and the House of Commons, where she would become the youngest member of Parliament. But first, there was one bit of business. The election had taken place, as usual, on a Thursday. By the following Monday, 700 party workers had received handwritten thank you notes, a practice she has followed ever since.

Nationally, the Conservatives won a landslide, their third successive win, and increased their margin in the House of Commons from 58 to 100 seats. The 1950s had been all-Tory, but the 1959 capstone victory was deceptive. There had been political stability, but it masked rot. Churchill contributed to the charade. After defeating Attlee in 1951, Churchill had finally retired in 1955 at the age of eighty-one. The old lion's return engagement had only lasted three and a half years, and he had been ailing most of the time.

His return and other events throughout the decade obscured

the nation's continued downward slide. Britain detonated its first atomic bomb in 1952, the same year the British Overseas Airway Corporation (BOAC) put the world's first commercial jet into service. In 1953 Edmund Hillary became the first man to climb Mount Everest, the world's highest peak. Hillary was a New Zealander, but Commonwealth ties were strong and he was quickly adopted as a veritable cousin. Also in 1953, Princess Elizabeth was crowned Queen and Churchill won the Nobel Prize for literature; in 1954 Roger Bannister became the first man to run the mile in less than four minutes.[2] These were uplifting and exciting events that allowed Britons to maintain the illusion that theirs remained an exceptional nation, destined to retain a special, global role. But they were deluded, and their faith was based on superficialities and self-deceptive pride.

The 1956 Suez fiasco stripped away the veneer to reveal the unrepaired cracks in the foundation. Britain was humiliated when it tried to recapture the canal it had built and controlled with France from its opening in 1869 until Gamal Abdel Nasser nationalized the passageway in July 1956. Almost immediately, Churchill's successor Anthony Eden decided to recapture the canal by force with the help of France and Israel. The October invasion, however, earned worldwide opprobrium, including that of President Dwight Eisenhower, who thought Eden had lost his mind. Britain was forced to withdraw in one of its most humiliating setbacks ever, jolting Britons, who were forced to realize that Britain's vaunted authority was a sham. Armies that had patrolled the empire and won World War II suddenly could not mount a surgical strike on ill-equipped Egypt.

The debacle caused a financial earthquake and a run on sterling that demonstrated the frailty of the economy and proved that the nation remained at the mercy of creditors. Diplomacy was a shambles. Britain, which had prided itself on a highly developed sense of international morality and a sensitive, rational approach to issues, had been caught in the act as a short-sighted conniver. In less than a month, the country passed over the cusp, its final eclipse as a power ignominiously obvious.

Eden, sick from a botched gallbladder operation, resigned within weeks of the troop pullout, and in January 1957 Harold Macmillan took over the Tory party and became prime minister. Macmillan was an ironic choice. He had been one of the leading proponents of the Suez invasion. But as Eden's chancellor of the exchequer, Macmillan was also one of the first to comprehend the devastating financial impact of the ill-considered raid. After watching the pounding of the economy and the storm of international criticism, he had executed a neat U-turn and advocated a quick retreat so the country could cut its losses. His rival for the leadership, R. A. "Rab" Butler, another former chancellor, was passed over for being too cautious to lead a party trying to reach out to cope with social change.

When he took over from Eden, Macmillan hardly seemed the right choice for a fresh approach. He looked more like a holdover from another age. Peter Jenkins, one of Britain's foremost political commentators, recalled him as a "ridiculous figure." Macmillan's first public words on assuming office only weeks after the Suez humiliation were: "So do not let us have any more defeatist talk of second class powers and dreadful things to come. Britain has been great, is great and will stay great provided we close our ranks and get on with the job." "We hooted with laughter at this," said Jenkins. "Both at the ludicrous sentiments and the languid, upper-class la-di-da drawl in which they were expressed."[3]

It was an odd attitude, but then Macmillan was a peculiar politician. A complex character, his moods ranged from tortured, questioning introversion to elegant ebullience. Both a modern politician and a neo-Edwardian relic, his very personality reflected a nation torn between eras. Born in 1894, the upper middle-class son of a publisher whose company still bears the family name, Macmillan was educated at the cream of British private schools, Eton and Balliol College, Oxford. He had all the tickets. His commission as a Grenadier Guards captain guaranteed his entree to any upper-class drawing room, and his four wounds from World War I gave him hero status. Despite his injuries, Macmillan loved the military and was contemptuous of colleagues who were not veterans. After the war, posted to Canada, he served as aide de camp to the governor general, the Duke of Devonshire, and fell in love with his daughter Dorothy, whom he married in 1920. The wealthy and well-connected family introduced him to the top levels of the aristocracy, the world of country estates, shooting parties, and debutante balls. In no time he became a patrician himself, the functional equivalent of a Rockefeller, or moderate, Republican.

For a party trying to broaden its appeal beyond the aristocracy and other wealthy voters, Macmillan was a strange pick to succeed Churchill and Eden. He was a clubman's clubman, surrounded by like-thinking moderate Conservatives in the paneled libraries and dining rooms of the all-male clubs of London's Pall Mall and St. James. Related by marriage to sixteen members of Parliament,[4] he did much of the party's "reaching out" within his own family. At one point in 1958, it was determined that of the eighty-five members of his government, thirty-five were his relatives, including seven of his nineteen cabinet members. Macmillan was even related to President John Kennedy by the marriage of Kennedy's sister Kathleen to the nephew of his wife, Dorothy.

Contrary to his sanguine, public rhetoric, privately Macmillan was gloomily pessimistic. "I think Europe is finished," he once told Labor party leader Hugh Dalton. "It is sinking."[5] "If I were a younger man, I should emigrate from Europe to the United States," where his mother, like Churchill's, had been born. His hawkish line on Suez, Macmillan said, had been an effort to halt Britain's continuing slide. Failure to confront Egyptian leader Gamal Abdel Nasser, he said, would have meant the transformation of Britain into "another Netherlands."

Macmillan had good reason to be morose. There was much to be gloomy about. Although a housing boom was underway and the economy looked superficially better, the core malignancy continued to spread. Industry was wobbly. Managers were poorly trained and too often held their jobs because of family connections. Rarely did shop floor workers have the mobility or drive to push into management. Too often, they were frozen in class-dictated patterns that discouraged climbing above one's station.

In the late 1950s, women, despite the obvious intelligence of the new Queen, played virtually no role in government or politics. Churchill had one woman, Florence Horsbrugh, in his cabinet, but Macmillan had none. He never understood women at all. His wife's nearly public affair with another Tory MP, Robert Boothby, lasted almost four decades, and the prime minister's fourth child was widely believed to have been fathered by his rival. Macmillan bottled it all up inside, turning his attention to work and the coterie of prep school graduates who surrounded him. "Mr. Attlee had three old Etonians in his cabinet," Macmillan said in 1959. "I have six. Things are twice as good under the Conservatives."

Such was the political situation in 1959 when Thatcher entered the House of Commons. The old-school, old-style old boys never rocked the boat and never expected to find a woman—especially this woman—in a position of significance. The deck was thoroughly stacked against her. Thatcher, however, was not intimidated. New to the House, she was no neophyte politically. She knew some Conservative MPs from Oxford and had since slogged through the trenches of the selection process in a skein of constituencies. She knew, if not all, a lot of tricks, including how to get noticed. On the very first day, she notified photographers in advance when the youngest MP would be arriving for her first day at Westminster. A photo of her standing next to the policeman guarding the MPs' gate made the papers the next day.

She had no problem setting up an office because she didn't have one. None of the regular members did. The twenty-five women in the then 630-seat House were expected to leave their belongings in the Lady Members' room. Thatcher moved in with a vengeance. Barbara Castle, a senior Labor party MP, was flabbergasted to discover almost immediately a row of pegs in the room filled with Thatcher's clothes and eight pairs of shoes for quick changes between debates. Thatcher worked from the corner of a desk of a secretary whom she shared with another MP in a tiny room packed with three other secretaries. It was cramped pandemonium, nothing like the luxurious private offices enjoyed by U.S. representatives. There were no private telephones; parliamentarians shared a row of phone booths. Incoming calls were shouted out and the MP would scurry to answer. Virtually all business was conducted publicly. The layout was a nightmare, but everyone except the leadership shared it and there was an unexpected advantage. In no time, everyone witnessed the incredible energy of the new member from Finchley.

The House of Commons in the stunning, sixteenth-century Parliament buildings, is tiny, a surprise to visitors who arrive expecting the Mother of Parliaments to be far plusher and more sweeping. A sixty-eight-foot–long rectangle, the actual chamber is divided by a central aisle. At the head of the aisle stands the speaker's chair and dispatch boxes at which the leaders of the Government and Opposition speak. Benches covered in green leather face each other across the aisle. Party leaders and cabinet members—"shadow cabinet" if they are members of the Opposition leadership—sit on the first row of facing benches only three yards apart. MPs without ministerial responsibility sit behind and are known as "back-benchers."

The chamber can become outrageously raucous. Far from a genteel forum for tranquil debate, the Commons is a fighting pit where the weapons are oratory, wit, contempt-laced sarcasm, a carefully honed instinct for political advantage, and an innate sense of the jugular. The speaker repeatedly shouts, "Order! Order!" in an often futile referee's effort to curtail the braying catcalls and insults flying back and forth across the divide and to impose some structure of debate onto the cacophony. Amid the howling, distinguished interjections can be heard reminding onlookers they are not at a soccer match. By tradition, members address each other with exaggerated politeness as "My Honorable Friend . . ." unless one is or has been a government minister in which case the salutation becomes "My Right Honorable Friend." The salutations are often followed by a chain of verbal abuse. Left-wing Labor MP Ken Livingstone, for example, was thrown out of the Commons for five days for describing "My Right Honorable Friend the Attorney General" as "an accomplice to murder."

Thatcher was more than ready for the rough and tumble, but her first concern was getting her maiden speech under her belt. The reception given to an MP's first speech often makes the difference between a good or a dismal start—instant acceptance or an equally quick dismissal. At the beginning of each new Parliament, back-benchers are given a chance to introduce noncontroversial legislation if the government sees fit and there is an opening on the legislative calendar. The new members conduct a lottery to determine the order of their turn. Some end up waiting interminably. Thatcher, though, was lucky.

Out of scores of new names, she drew the second slot; she would definitely get to speak early in the new session. She did not have much time to pick a topic but, after consulting the leadership, decided to introduce a bill giving the press the right to attend local government council meetings. Until then, each individual council had the right to decide whether to admit reporters, despite the fact that all were funded by the public. Thatcher's choice was not based on any great love for the press, but it did reveal an interesting combination of basic principles, research, and clever political thinking. She was prompted by a newspaper printing strike, which led to several Labor-dominated councils refusing, in a solidarity move, to allow strike-breaking reporters in to cover their meetings. This was a red flag to Thatcher, who had an antipathy to labor unions. Launching the bill in her maiden speech would give it an extra push. But she had a second motive that demonstrated just how far ahead of the game she was already: she knew that legislation and a speech promoting increased press freedom were bound to get widespread and positive press coverage.

She delivered the speech on a Friday afternoon, a time when

many private bills are scheduled because most MPs have already scattered for the weekend. This Friday, because of Thatcher's advance notices, a sizable audience of about a hundred eyed her as she rose. Typically, there was no introductory build-up. She got straight to it. "I knew the constituency of Finchley which I have the honor to represent would not wish me to do other than come straight to the point," she began. Then, without glancing at the notes in her hand, she delivered a thoroughly researched and methodical explanation of her bill. Over the next twenty-seven minutes, without a hint of nervousness—although speeches are the one thing that terrify her—she built her argument with a compelling array of data, a method that would become her trademark. Her bill would allow the press entry to meetings as a right, not a favor, and would allow reporters the necessary background information to conduct public scrutiny professionally. "I hope that MPs will consider that a paramount function of this house is to safeguard civil liberties, rather than to think that administrative convenience should take first place in law."[6]

The speech won Thatcher high praise. "Very impressive," the *Daily Telegraph*'s Bill Deedes recalled thirty years later. At the time, he called her remarks "front-bench quality" and said that they suggested "an uncanny instinct for the mood of the House which some members take years to acquire—and many never acquire at all." Not everyone was as pleased with the legislation itself, including the chairman of Finchley's Tory-dominated local council. His committee meetings, he said, would most assuredly not be open to reporters. The council declined to pass a motion congratulating Thatcher on her efforts to spearhead the bill, which did eventually pass, in amended form.

The debut was a major event for Thatcher, though there was a minor disappointment. Denis, who could have listened from the Stranger's Gallery, as the guest balcony is named, was missing again. This time, he was off on a business trip to the Middle East. Witnessing her endless hours and total devotion to work and Denis's separate life, junior staff gossiped that if he were not off with another woman he soon would be. But there is no indication that the marriage was ever in trouble. The Thatchers understood each other, and both felt strongly about maintaining their separate careers. There was no one else. They were comfortable when they were together. Neither admitted to requiring much support or attention, so the marriage continued to work.

Her conspicuous drive and the attention she commanded on the press bill caused Fleet Street, then headquarters for the national newspapers, to begin charting her progress and promoting her. The youngest woman in the House, photogenic and pegged as a comer, Margaret Thatcher drew more attention than any other woman from the very beginning. In October 1960, a London charity named her one of six women of the year, and at the luncheon marking the event, she took questions from the nearly 600 women present. Who would she like to be if she were someone else? Anna Leonowens, the English governess in *Anna and the King of Siam,* was the reply. Anna "had a sense of purpose and the perseverance to carry out this purpose. She went to Siam with a sense of purpose and, because of her, slavery was abolished." This was actually a highly romanticized version of what actually happened when the English schoolteacher arrived in what's now Thailand. Thatcher's version contained as much fiction as fact, but that did not deter her. The lesson was valid.[7]

Thatcher worked tremendously hard throughout her early years in Parliament, doing all her own research and huddling over books in the House of Commons library for hours at a time. Once in a rare display of frailty, she collapsed and was sent home to rest. She was back the next morning. Quick, thorough briefing became her trademark. She was neither a genius nor an intellectual, but she was bright. Whatever Thatcher missed in pure brainpower—and with degrees in chemistry and law, she didn't miss much—she made up in hard work. Others might be smarter, might have greater knowledge in depth, might have more experience, but no one could out-study or out-prepare her. Her years of exploring tax law were good training for skipping through thick volumes assimilating essential nuggets.

Once she had her material together, Thatcher wrote her speeches in longhand, revised them, then wrote them again on small notecards she could hold in her hand. The notes were a safeguard. By the time she had her remarks on cards, she had them committed to memory and only rarely, when she had to recite a string of figures, referred to the notes. Details tripped off her tongue, suggesting an arsenal of facts in reserve. Critics who were less well prepared were reluctant to counterattack. In these early years, Thatcher was capable of putting MPs to sleep with her statistics, but she knew how to wake them up again, sometimes unintentionally. Once in mid-barrage in a speech on pensions, an aide handed her some fresh statistics. "Gentlemen, I have the latest red hot figure," she began. As the House dissolved in hoots and catcalls, the blush rose from her neck until she stood crimson.[8]

As she established herself, Thatcher showed her strong Tory colors, but she was not a sycophant to the leadership. "She never cowered," notes Sir Clive Bossom, an early private secretary.[9] From the outset, she was more radically right than the government and never shied from pointing out where her views differed. Yet she never went so far that questions were raised about her loyalty. She voiced her opinions carefully, to have done otherwise would have meant isolation and impeded her future prospects. The parliamentary parties do not indulge rebels. The House of Commons has never, for example, accommodated the kind of freewheeling independent grandstanding allowed in the U.S. Congress. Mavericks in the Commons gain neither power nor influence.

One area where she took exception was the Macmillan government's approach to public spending. She was convinced that the Treasury kept too slack a hand on the nation's purse strings. "Having been a member of Parliament for eighteen months now, the thing which still troubles me most of all—and something which is fundamental to everything—is control of government expenditure. We are chasing after the hundreds and thousands, but tending to let the millions go by." She called for stricter accountability. "The nation must present its accounts to Parliament as a company does to its shareholders." Failure to do so would mean more waste and delays in chopping the income tax rate, an early and persistent objective. Until that was done, "it will be extremely difficult to bring down and control government expenditure and, therefore, the level of taxation is not going to be considerably reduced."[10]

Homing in on tax affairs was a natural pursuit for a tax barrister. But in addition to her tax experience, Thatcher has a compulsion about waste, another legacy of the tight-fisted Alf. (Years later, she would show the same obsession in bringing home leftovers from formal dinners, freezing and reheating them later for herself and Denis if he was around.)

As she got involved in studying the budget, another core belief surfaced: a bias for business investors over speculators. She would support tax hikes on speculative profit rather than profit created by firms actually producing something. "It is the speculators in shares we want to get at," she said, "the person who is making a business of buying and selling shares, not to hold them for their income-producing properties, but to live on the profit he makes from the transactions."[11]

When the government introduced a criminal justice bill in 1961, Thatcher used the opportunity to get her beliefs on the record. She was sketching in the details of her political philosophy. She vigorously supported legislation favoring corporal punishment, including a proposal that courts had the right to prescribe whipping with canes for offenders up to the age of seventeen. Those from seventeen to twenty-one could be beaten with birch rods. It was clear very early that the American Civil Liberties Union would not be around to recruit Margaret Thatcher. "In our desire for humanitarian reform of offenders, we have lost sight of the purpose of the criminal courts and the aims of punishment," she said emphatically. "I do not accept that all offenders guilty of the most violent crimes are necessarily mental cases." The government opposed the corporal punishment amendment, but Thatcher's rebellion—she led sixty-seven Tory MPs in a revolt—did not harm her. Six months later, she was eating lunch with her sister Muriel, a rare occurrence, when a message arrived summoning her to Downing Street and a meeting with Macmillan.

Parliament was still in summer recess, but would resume in two weeks with the Queen's traditional speech at the ceremonial state opening. Thatcher thought Macmillan intended to ask her to be one of the seconders of the Queen's remarks that are prepared by the government of the day and merely read by the monarch. But the prime minister surprised her. He offered her a job in the Ministry of Pensions and National Insurance. The post was junior, but she had been in Parliament only two years. Suddenly she was "in government" with an appointed post. She rushed back to tell her sister. She wished the first offer had not come so soon. The twins were only eight, and now, caught up in the whirlwind of a ministry, her time with them would be more limited still. But she didn't hesitate. She had little choice, she told Muriel. "When you are offered a job, you either accept it or you are out." She was in. Alf was delighted, but Beatrice had not lived to see her daughter named to a government post. She had died of cancer in December 1960, a year after Margaret had entered Parliament. Once more, Denis was not around. This time he was in Japan. Thatcher quickly wrote to tell him what had happened, but before the letter arrived, he had heard the news on the BBC's World Service radio.

CHAPTER FIVE

Thatcher, Milk Snatcher

THATCHER, NOT SURPRISINGLY, aroused mixed feelings when she arrived in 1961 at the Ministry of Pensions and National Insurance. But John Boyd-Carpenter, the minister in charge, was untroubled. A politician himself, he knew precisely what Macmillan was up to. "She was very junior, so it was quite exceptional, a bit of a gimmick," he said. "Here was a prime minister in power a few years trying to brighten up his image by appointing a good-looking woman."[1]

Sir Eric Bowyer, the ministry's chief civil servant, was incensed. Macmillan himself sat in Parliament for fourteen years before he got a government job. Thatcher had been an MP for less than two years. Not only that, she was a mother of two, lived out of town, and her husband was rarely around. She'd never be able to fill the job. "We shan't get much work out of her," Bowyer grumbled. Quickly both men discovered otherwise. As Boyd-Carpenter put it, "We could not have been more wrong." They had not anticipated her routine: sleeping four hours a night and working most of the other twenty.

Four months after arriving, she was called on in Parliament to defend the Tories for not raising pensions. It was her first address to the MPs as a member of the government. Having buried herself in homework, she argued the case with such zeal that the Commons was stunned into silence. In a forty-four-minute speech, she had gone back sixteen years to 1946 for statistics. She knew how the situation of British pensioners contrasted with those in Scandinavia in 1953. She knew how British pensions compared to West Germans' in 1959. She knew the cost of living in a nonsmoking versus a smoking home in 1951. It was just like old times trying to stump Alf around the Grantham dinner table. The Kesteven girls would have recognized the pattern as she started to hit her stride.

Poised against her and the government was the shadow minister on pensions, Richard Crossman, the ablest intellect among Labor's front-benchers. Thatcher battered him into submission. "Seeing Crossman knocked about was highly amusing," Boyd-Carpenter recalled. "It was obvious she had done her homework and he had not done his." On fact and detail, she constantly corrected him. It was the continuation of the pattern: she would never be bested on detail or outworked.[2]

She was equally diligent as she did the ministerial spadework required of any junior apprentice, culling thousands of letters inquiring about pension rights. One night, at the end of a long debate, she returned to her office to deal with mail and began ripping apart the standard responses that had been prepared for her signature by civil servants. "Have them redone," she ordered Sir Clive Bossom, her private secretary. "That bloody woman," bellowed the writer. "Her job is to sign them, not read them." Bossom chuckled at the recollection. "She's never signed anything without carefully studying it. If she doesn't like it, back it goes."[3] The anonymous writer may have been the first to call her "that bloody woman" in aggravation, but he wasn't the last; in later years, she was often referred to as "TBW." Everyone understood.

Pensions lacked the pressure of a major ministry, so Thatcher had time to explore the inner workings of government. One of the first things she learned was that civil servants tailored their advice to ministers, giving them what it was thought they wanted to hear rather than a range of options. The discovery helped ingrain Thatcher's mistrust of most bureaucrats, who she felt made more red tape than they cut. In the 1980s, Jonathan Lynn and Antony Jay parodied that tendency of the bureaucracy in a popular satirical television series called *Yes Minister* and a sequel, *Yes Prime Minister*. Thatcher, who does appreciate political wit, loved the shows, which occasionally cut close enough to actual cabinet debates to prompt questions about leaks.

While she labored away with her head down, Macmillan was about to lose his. The foundations of the empire crumbled quickly after Suez, forcing him to dismantle the superstructure. Macmillan admitted the inevitability in a 1960 speech in Cape Town that would be forever identified with him. "In the twentieth century, we have seen the awakening of national consciousness in people who have for centuries lived in dependence on some other powers. Fifteen years ago, this movement spread through Asia . . . today the same thing is happening in Africa," he said. "The wind of change is blowing through this continent and, whether we like it or not, we must all accept it and our national policies must take account of it."

The "wind of change" speech marked the next and near final stage in the retrenchment of British imperial policy. Over the next two years, Macmillan decolonized vigorously. Union Jacks fluttered down from thousands of flagpoles around the world—in Malaya, Kenya, Pakistan, Aden, Cyprus, Nigeria, Jamaica. Emigrants, preferring their old imperial administrators to uncertain futures under new national leaders, streamed out of those countries to Mother Britain. There, they irreparably shifted a largely white demographic balance that had been essentially unchanged for centuries, creating repercussions still felt in Thatcher's prime ministership.

As the empire slipped away like sand in an hourglass, so did confidence in Britain's future. Macmillan had campaigned in 1959 on the slogan "You never had it so good," attempting to capitalize on a mini-economic boom and Britons' fallacious belief that their country remained a world power. But Supermac's 79 percent approval rating in 1960 was a faded memory two years later. By then, a balance-of-payments crisis had led to a run on the pound, a jump in unemployment, and a wage freeze. Support for Macmillan plummeted to the lowest prime ministerial rating in nearly a quarter-century: since Chamberlain had sold out to Hitler. When the Tories were badly defeated in a by-election for the safe seat of Orpington, near London, the depth of the problem was revealed.

Macmillan first tried to spend his way out of trouble, a tried and true political tactic. When Chancellor of the Exchequer Selwyn Lloyd balked, he and six other cabinet ministers were dismissed in a major political bloodletting dubbed "The Night of the Long Knives." Thatcher agreed with Lloyd. Alf's grocery displayed a "no credit" sign, and Thatcher fiscal conservatism was based on the paternal maxims "Never be in debt" and "Never pay out more than you take in." Spending was anathema to Thatcher, but she kept quiet when Lloyd was under fire, realizing that he was a goner. She has a powerful sense of self-preservation and had no intention of sticking her neck out in a losing cause. Thatcher was too pragmatic to risk a quick end to her nascent career. Macmillan pushed ahead, ignoring wage guidelines to prime the pump, but nothing worked and the economy kept sliding. Disparities were still enormous. The richest 1 percent still owned 25 percent of all Britain's wealth.[4]

Two body blows sent the government to the canvas. The first involved Britain's efforts to join the Common Market, which had been organized in 1957 by six continental nations—France, West Germany, Italy, the Netherlands, Luxembourg, and Belgium. Until Suez in 1956, Britain had remained aloof from Europe, choosing to maintain its major economic relationships with the Commonwealth nations rather than building new ones with the European community. This was a strategic miscalculation of major proportions. The rationale had been that the Commonwealth nations were already producing the raw materials necessary to fuel postwar industry. Britain failed to spot the quick pace of economic development on the continent, particularly the speedy recovery of Germany and France. But the problems involved in linking up with the continent went much deeper.

"Europe," to most Britons, meant "the continent" and did not include Britain. "We are with Europe, but not of it," said Winston Churchill in 1930. "We are interested and associated, but not absorbed." Centuries of war, rivalry, monarchical marriages and divorces, different languages and cultures, and an innate sense of British superiority were the context for the sentiments behind Churchill's words. The feelings were summed up once in a tabloid headline: "Fog Shrouds Channel; Continent Isolated."

After World War II, talk of greater cooperation grew, but not integration. Britain had rejected an invitation to join a postwar European coal and steel federation, reluctant to cede even a hint of sovereignty. The idea of a European army was similarly rebuffed. "I meant it for them, not us," sniffed Churchill.[5] In 1952, then Foreign Secretary Eden said, "We know in our bones we cannot" join Europe because "Britain's story and her interests lie far beyond the continent of Europe."[6] When the same six members of the European Coal and Steel Community gathered in 1955 to organize a broader market, Britain attended only as an observer. Nor was there any interest in collaborating in a joint atomic energy project. Britain already had nuclear weapons and believed it had more to lose than gain by offering its expertise.

The Suez experience undercut Britain's stand-offishness.

America's sharp condemnation of the invasion shook the "special relationship." The idea of some link with Europe suddenly grew in appeal. Macmillan thought it made economic sense to join the Common Market, even though he shared the political and psychological reservations of his fellow Tories, who were reluctant to concede any authority to a continental supra-force. The Tories were not the only ones with doubts. Many Britons felt that throwing in their lot with the continentals was misguided. Hugh Gaitskell, who had succeeded Clement Attlee as Labor party leader, also strongly opposed joining, arguing that membership would mean "the end of Britain as an independent state." Nonetheless, by the summer of 1962 with the Commonwealth in shards and the Europeans offering at least some fragment of economic hope, Macmillan formally applied for membership. Thatcher supported him.

Macmillan had not, however, forgotten his friends and blood relatives, the Americans, and was determined to maintain the Atlantic connection. In a December 1962 meeting in Nassau with Macmillan, John Kennedy agreed to provide Britain with Polaris submarine missiles, thus ensuring that the country would remain a nuclear power. The decision reinvigorated the "special relationship" but infuriated Charles de Gaulle. The French president was still irate about Britain's cave-in to the U.S. demand for withdrawal from Suez, and despite his hospitable exile in Britain during the war, he had long fumed over Britain's Atlanticism. De Gaulle had been jealous of the close relationship between Roosevelt and Churchill and felt they had frozen him out. Once, during an argument with the leader of the Free French, Churchill lashed out, "Each time we have to choose between Europe and the open sea, we shall choose the open sea. Each time I have to choose between you and Roosevelt, I will choose Roosevelt."[7]

Churchill and Roosevelt were gone, but de Gaulle had a long memory. Three weeks after Washington and London announced the Polaris deal, de Gaulle vetoed Britain's application for membership in the European Economic Community (EEC). "One day, perhaps, England will be admitted to Europe," he sneered, "after it has detached itself from its ties with the Commonwealth and the United States." Macmillan was shattered. "All our policies, at home and abroad," he wrote in his diary, "are in ruins."[8]

There was more to come. The following summer, Macmillan was pummeled again, this time by the Profumo scandal, which erupted around the revelation that his minister of war was having an affair with a young prostitute named Christine Keeler. She was also, it turned out, sleeping with a Soviet naval attaché. At first, John Profumo, buoyed by the support of his prime minister, denied the allegations to the House of Commons. But only days later, with more details flooding the press, Profumo admitted he had lied to Parliament and resigned. Macmillan looked a fool. The government wobbled. He satisfied the barrage of calls demanding his resignation by falling ill with prostate trouble and subsequently stepping down.

Macmillan's resignation threw the party into chaos. The question of a successor loomed. Some believed the job would go to Deputy Leader Rab Butler, but Macmillan wanted his foreign secretary, the Earl of Home, a singularly undynamic former MP, to succeed him. This decision amazed almost everyone, including Home, and his unexpected ascension prompted an important question. What kind of party were the Conservatives going to be— inoffensive paternalists, once again looking back instead of forward, or more aggressive free-enterprisers?

If the question were a test, the Conservatives failed on two counts: first, by picking Home; second, by the manner in which the selection was carried out, secretly and undemocratically by an old boy network of Etonian grandees who made up the core of the party leadership. Home was a thoroughly decent man, but the epitome of an old-style, between-the-wars, Tory paternalist, hardly cut out for the modern cut and thrust. Home was an anachronism and proof that the Tories had not abandoned their recidivist tendencies.

Home renounced his title, since peers cannot sit in the House of Commons, and became Sir Alec Douglas-Home. Aware that he had no popular mandate, he called a quick election in October 1964, less than a year after taking over the party. The political landscape had changed dramatically since Macmillan had trounced Labor by one hundred seats in 1959. The economy was now quite obviously staggering, the nation was in retreat overseas, and the Labor party had a new dynamic leader named Harold Wilson.

Wilson was a legitimate new generation politician. Only forty-eight, he was less a hard-core socialist than a brilliant political streetfighter who could drive home a theme with a twist on the floor of Parliament. He promised modern leadership to bring Britain into the technological age and turned the battle into the country's first "image" election, casting himself as a brash, young technocrat battling uphill against a stuffy peer, a sixty-one-year-old heirloom from a bygone age. "After a half century of democratic advance, the whole process has ground to a halt with a fourteenth-century Earl," Wilson scoffed.[9]

When the returns came in, the Tories' one hundred-seat majority of 1959 had evaporated. Finchley returned Thatcher comfortably, though her own majority had been halved. Wilson was the new prime minister, if barely. With a majority of four, he could not be expected to hang on long without another election. The Tories did not want to be stuck again with Douglas-Home, who got the message all too clearly. In eight months, the gentle aristocrat stepped down from his position as party leader, eventually picking up a life peerage and returning to the calmer red leather benches of the House of Lords, to which he was better suited.

Before bowing out, however, he performed one act which may be his most enduring legacy. Upset by the uproar that had surrounded his own secret selection as party leader, Sir Alec revised the succession rules to make the process more open and democratic. He designed a two-tier ballot, in which a contender needed at least a 15 percent spread over his next rival to win the round. Without the spread, there would be a second ballot in which other contestants could throw their hats into the ring, and then a third if necessary, and so on until the 15 percent lead was opened up. A decade later, the new process would enable Thatcher, the darkest of dark horses, to unseat an incumbent who had no intention of stepping down.

Edward Heath, a former minister of labor and the man in charge of Britain's 1961 application for Common Market membership, succeeded Douglas-Home in the first exercise of the more open selection process. Thatcher voted for Heath. He was not a close friend, but they did have a certain amount in common. Neither was a member of the establishment. Douglas-Home, Macmillan, and Churchill were all aristocrats, but Heath was the son of a lower middle-class builder, which should have given him a closer affinity to the grocer's daughter. Both Thatcher and Heath came from backgrounds where personal advancement was believed to be the result of hard work; both were also puritanical. Both had gone to public grammar school and had graduated from Oxford. The musical Heath attended Balliol College on an organ fellowship. Nine years older than Thatcher, he had also been president of the Oxford University Conservative Association.

In a country where accents are lethal weapons or fatal targets in the class struggle, codes of origin and education that may determine success or failure, both were mocked for their non-U pronunciation and their less-than-successful attempts to posh them up. Despite a sensitive musical ear and four years amid classy accents at Balliol, Heath's effort at refining his strangled Southeast vowels had had no success at all. George Bernard Shaw, who pinpointed the English obsession with accent in *Pygmalion,* on which the musical *My Fair Lady* was based, might have been speaking to both of them when he wrote in 1912, "It is impossible for an Englishman to open his mouth without making another Englishman hate or despise him."[10] Critics of Heath and Thatcher took the observation to heart.

Both are also loners. Neither has, or had, much of a circle of friends. Heath did have a greater number of political cronies while in office, but otherwise he kept to himself. A socially awkward bachelor, he is extraordinarily uncomfortable around women— painfully shy and almost physically incapable of talking with them, a fact that would color his relationship with Thatcher. The wives of colleagues invariably describe social interaction with Heath as dreadful. Heath always solicitously inquires about the wife of Tory grandee William Whitelaw, a longtime political colleague, but refrains from speaking with her in public. Once, during a weekend at the residence of a British ambassador on the continent, the diplomat was called away and Heath was left at the residence with the ambassador's wife. They did not speak during his three-day stay. He ignored even her "good morning" greetings.

Heath can talk to men, but can be highly abrasive and arrogant even with them. Those close to him, his personal entourage, claim he can be warm and charming, but they are a small group. Edward Heath was a very odd man to be a successful politician. But Britain has long accommodated eccentrics, including Prince Charles, who talks to plants, if not his wife Princess Diana. Nor was Heath a great orator. Years after leaving office, he drew bigger crowds in the Commons than when he was prime minister. MPs packed the benches, eager to hear his venomous criticism of his successor, Mrs. Thatcher.

Although Heath and Thatcher would become bitter enemies, he was her mentor when he first took over the Conservative party. Heath's support of Thatcher, however, was not completely magnanimous. His bachelor status made it imperative that he have a woman in his cabinet. "It didn't matter who it was, he simply had to have one," one of his ministers recalled. At first there were no likely candidates, and Heath canvassed the Tory inner circle for ideas. "We are having some troubles with who should be the woman," Heath told James Prior during one such call.

Prior suggested Thatcher, but Heath had been talking to Whitelaw about her. "Willie thinks once we get Margaret we shall never get rid of her," he said.[11] Whitelaw recommended another woman named Mervyn Pike, and Heath, who knew none of the eleven Tory women MPs, took the advice and named Pike shadow social security minister. He did, however, name Thatcher to a string of junior posts, for which she expressed her gratitude.

They tolerated each other. Heath was almost completely indifferent to Thatcher, at first ignoring her at meetings. She, on the other hand, knew that despite Heath's difficult personality, the party boss held her future in his hands. So she got on with her work, trying to maintain a good professional relationship and avoiding any potentially awkward situation. Luckily, there was plenty of work for her. Few politicians ever have the chance to get so much experience so quickly. He let her remain chief opposition spokeswoman on pensions, but in 1965 also assigned her to the same post in the Department of Housing and Land. Because the Conservatives were in opposition, she had no actual power, but she was acquiring knowledge and experience. Her job, the job of all ministers in opposition, was to attack and discredit the government, constantly chipping away at their credibility. To this end, she wielded every tool: scalpel, axe, and sledgehammer.

Britain was jumping in the mid-1960s, though in superficial ways. England won the World Cup soccer championship in 1966, while the Beatles, the Rolling Stones, Mary Quant, microminis, and Carnaby Street in "swinging London" all contributed to a feeling that the country was experiencing a cultural renaissance. Harold Wilson, who seemed to epitomize the fresh spirit, was also riding high. Sensing a crest, he called a quick election in March 1966 to boost his slender majority. The party slogan, "You know Labor works," worked for Wilson. He swept back into office with a healthy majority of ninety-seven seats, enough to ensure he would not be dislodged for years.

As Wilson's position became more secure, Thatcher pressed on in the background, building up her portfolio and collecting political tickets. After the 1966 defeat, Heath switched her to the number two spot on the shadow Treasury team. The move was particularly welcome; it rescued her from the kind of "social policy" ministry where women were often confined and placed her at the center of a varsity, all-comers sector. Thatcher had no doubt that she could make something of the new position. She knew budgets lay at the very core of governance; one could not have too much experience in Treasury matters. She also liked the challenges involved in mastering budget intricacies. She felt good about her progress. In a Royal Albert Hall speech to 5,000 members of the National Union of Townswomen's Guilds, she cast down her marker. "In politics, if you want anything said, ask a man; if you want anything done, ask a woman." The women roared their approval.[12]

Thatcher used her new perch at Treasury as a steppingstone to further prominence, going back on the attack, dive-bombing the latest Labor party budget introduced by Chancellor of the Exchequer James Callaghan. In order to keep Labor's campaign pledge not to raise taxes, Callaghan had invented a euphemistic equivalent, a complicated selective tax on employers that based assessments on the type of business being operated. Thatcher found the proposal an easy target and swooped with relish. As in the pension debate, she had done her research. When she announced that her information spanned the previous twenty years, there were gasps of disbelief from the MPs. Callaghan glared at her as she pointed to what she called the plan's failings. The legislation, she noted, discriminated against working mothers who employed nannies, as she did, but who were not eligible for tax relief. "Gilbert and Sullivan should be living at this hour. This is sheer cockeyed lunacy," she remonstrated. "The chancellor needs a woman at the Treasury."

Her spirit, obvious fearlessness, and intelligence won her attention. "This one is different," said Iain Macleod, the shadow chancellor and thus her boss. "Quite exceptionally able, a first-class brain."[13] He told Heath and his colleagues that she was definitely cabinet material, then took her under his own wing. Macleod was dying, but the education he gave her before he did was invaluable.

"Iain always got the politics of any problem right," Thatcher said. "He had an instinct for how the ordinary person would react to situations and proposals. He would look at a budget in political terms first and establish what the consequences would be of a certain course of action. He believed you had to bring human nature into your calculations. If you did not get it right politically, the economics would turn out to be wrong."[14] Macleod also taught her the value of having the right specialists around. "Let them expound their arguments fully, then go away and make the decision," he told her. Thatcher adopted the routine, absorbing it as effortlessly as Macleod's other tactical lessons in the arts of the House of Commons. These included the proper timing of difficult votes, a priceless skill. "There is an art in timing clause by clause debates," Thatcher explained.[15] "Many's the time I worked up a twenty-minute speech involving great financial complexities only to be told by Iain just before I got to my feet—'you've got three minutes, not a second more.' My God, it taught me to sort out what was the chief point and get straight to it."

Day by day she loved her work at the Treasury more and more. Her ultimate goal, she decided, was to run the department as chancellor, but at the time she doubted it would be possible in her lifetime. "The Tory party will never allow a woman chancellor of the exchequer," she later told a colleague.[16]

After only twenty months at Treasury, Heath moved her again, to the Ministry of Fuel and Power. Again, the timing was propitious. The Labor government was launching a full-scale program to nationalize major industries. The steel industry was the first to be removed from the control of the private sector, and the electricity and gas industries were scheduled to follow. In addition, Thatcher's new position gave her exposure to another crucial issue. Seismic exploration of the North Sea had revealed major oil and gas deposits, deposits that would have a huge impact on Britain's economy over the next two decades. She dug into those issues, but in October 1967 Heath moved her once more. Mervyn Pike had retired, and Peter Walker, Heath's campaign manager, recommended Thatcher take her place in the shadow cabinet, the front bench. Heath concurred and brought her in as shadow minister for power. A year later she took over as shadow minister for transport, and in 1969, she was assigned to the Ministry of Education. Heath was unaware of it, but he was sowing the seeds of his own destruction. Thatcher was collecting enough experience to be dangerous.

Throughout her shuffling from one ministry to the next, Thatcher displayed a consistent right-wing voting pattern in the Commons. She opposed pro-abortion bills and any efforts to reform anti-gay legislation. Just as adamantly, she spearheaded opposition to an equal rights motion at the 1968 Tory conference. Her stance infuriated women's activists, who considered her a living example of what they stood for.

Thatcher, however, rejected all suggestions that gender had

anything to do with opportunity or success. That, she felt, was a ludicrous opinion to hold in Britain and all the more out of place in the quintessentially male Conservative party. To have presented herself as a woman MP instead of an MP who happened to be a woman almost certainly would have doomed Thatcher's ambition and prospects, but she was not just playing along with the Tory leadership. Her father had treated her as a child with ability, not as a daughter. "You get on because you have the right talents," he told her. Success was never, in Thatcher's mind, a matter of sex. Feminists, to her, wanted something given to them that they weren't willing to work for. "I am absolutely satisfied that there is nothing more you can do by changing the law to do away with discrimination," she said at a Tory conference in 1968. "I don't think there's been a great deal of discrimination against women for years."[17]

At the same conference, she delivered the annual lecture to the Conservative Political Center, an invitation that usually went to one of the party's brightest stars. She chose "What's wrong with politics?" as her topic and spent weeks on the text. She got little press, but the message was essential Thatcher. Two decades later, she continues to believe everything in it, evidence that she is a conviction politician with a constant credo.

"I believe that the great mistake of the last few years has been for the government to provide or legislate for almost everything," she said, stating the first principle of what would become "Thatcherism." "What we need now is a far greater degree of personal responsibility and decision, far more independence from the government and a comparative reduction in the role of government." Excessive reliance on government curbed individual initiative, a second essential precept. Conservatives wanted to lower taxes because of the "real belief that government intervention and control tends to reduce the role of the individual, his importance and the desirability that he should be primarily responsible for his own future."[18]

She opposed Harold Wilson's wage and income policy because she did not believe the government had any right to determine which salaries should increase or hold steady. "There is nothing wrong in people wanting larger incomes," she insisted. "It would seem a worthy objective for men and women to wish to raise the standard of living for their families and give them greater opportunities than they themselves had. I wish more people would do it. We should then have fewer saying 'the state must do it.' "

Thatcher knew she would be accused of endorsing a gospel of selfish greed, a charge that would pursue her as it does most free enterprise politicians, including Ronald Reagan and George Bush. She dismissed such criticism. "The point is that even the Good Samaritan had to have the money to help, otherwise he too would have had to pass on the other side."[19] She defended the marketplace as the natural forum for competition and enthusiastically declared herself a monetarist, advocating the government's control of the money supply, not income. The philosophy came from Alf Roberts, but Denis reinforced it. Often, late at night, he talked to her about companies battling for market share and the damage caused by excessive government intervention. Thatcher believed that her monetarist approach made perfect sense, but in the 1960s she was preaching nothing less than revolution, total opposition to postwar government policies of both the socialist Labor and paternalistic Conservative parties. It would be another decade before she could storm the socialist ramparts in earnest; the Conservatives had to get back into power first.

Their chances were improving. By 1967, Wilson, who once said "a week is a long time in politics," was in trouble. Because of mounting government spending and weak trade—the twin plagues of the postwar period—the economy was continuing to deteriorate. Wilson tried spending cuts and a six-month freeze on wage and price increases, precisely what he had vowed not to do. Everyone jumped on him, the Tories because he looked vulnerable and his own left wing because they were furious with the wage freeze. Wilson warned the Left against too vigorous a rebellion: "Every dog is allowed one bite, but a different view is taken of a dog that goes on biting."[20] The giant Trades Union Congress—Britain's equivalent of the AFL-CIO and the party's biggest single constituency—joined in the attack on his government.

Wilson's response was to prepare anti-union legislation, anathema, if not outright treason, in a party that had been founded as the political arm of the trade union movement. Labor's left wing opposed him on votes. They did not want to see the government topple, but they wanted their displeasure registered. In the midst of open warfare within his own government, a humiliated Wilson backed down and withdrew the proposals. The battle foreshadowed titanic struggles with the unions, whose leaders were considered the most powerful men in the country.

Wilson struggled through 1968 and 1969, battling strikes and the effects of a devalued pound sterling. One effect of the sliding pound was that British troops east of Suez were shipped home. Britain could no longer afford to keep them overseas. By 1970, the cheaper pound had boosted British trade and Labor had narrowed a 19 percent Tory lead in polls to only 4 percent. Bolstered by what appeared to be an improved economic climate and renewed support from his party after he increased wages for government workers, Wilson felt sufficiently confident to call an election, his third, for June 1970.

The election was a hare and tortoise affair. Wilson, the rabbit who felt cocky, jumped out to a lead he thought would hold, then cut back his campaigning. Heath was an awkward campaigner. He had none of the roguish charm of Wilson. Cold and aloof even from his associates, he appeared even colder and more aloof to voters. He did not seem real. His sexuality was confusing. Britons wondered whether he was gay or had any sex life at all. The answers seemed to be no and no. Campaign consultants toned down his image as a classical music buff and stressed his love of the sea. An interested, if not talented sailor, Heath was buffed up with a macho man-of-the-elements image.

The outcome was in doubt until the end, when it became clear that most Britons were more concerned about the economy and the influence of the unions than their leader's personality. Heath upset Wilson 46 percent to 43 percent and moved, with his grand piano, into Downing Street. Two blocks away in the House of Commons, the new prime minister had a comfortable, if not unassailable, majority of thirty seats. Thatcher went from opposition spokeswoman on education to secretary of state for education. She was not merely in government, but in the cabinet. Best of all, after eleven years in Parliament, she finally had an office of her own, a roomy corner suite on Curzon Street near Berkeley Square in the heart of Mayfair. There was also a chauffeur-driven car to shuttle her around. Instead of slacking off, the support structure inspired Thatcher to work even harder.

"Within the first ten minutes of her arrival, she uncovered two things to us: one, an innate wariness of the Civil Service, quite possibly even a distrust; and secondly, a page from an exercise book with eighteen things she wanted done that day," said Sir William Pile, permanent undersecretary at the education department and thus her top civil servant. "Now these were two actions quite unlike anything we'd come across from predecessors. Later on, we'd say that this was only the beginnings of the revelation of a character that we'd have to get used to and that we hadn't run into before."[21]

Thatcher took over the Ministry of Education at a volatile time for students and teachers. In the United States, student protests aimed at ending the Vietnam War had broken out, culminating in the student takeover of Columbia University in New York. In France, hundreds of thousands of students had taken to the streets in 1968 calling for revolutionary societal change. In China, the Cultural Revolution was underway, forcing millions of students out of school and into the streets. In Britain, as the nation's baby boomers entered the school pipeline, a furious debate raged over declining standards, the future of education, and the relationship between schooling and the perpetuation of the class system. The interest was reflected in a sharp increase in spending on education. In 1954, Britain had spent 3.2 percent of its GNP on education. By 1970, the proportion had doubled to 6.5 percent. For the first time the nation was spending more money on schools than on defense.[22]

At the heart of the debate was changing the traditional grammar and secondary school system, plus the fee-paying "public" (meaning "private") schools into a network of larger "comprehensive" schools. The overall goal was to help break down the class barriers—fortified by a school system that segregated by sex, ability, and class—that were thought to be accelerating the country's decline. For generations, students had been segregated by sex straight through adolescence. When the eight million children attending state schools reached the age of eleven, they took the "11-plus" exams, which sorted them into tracks for secondary school—often dooming countless late developers. The highest-scoring 20 percent, usually from the middle class, went on to academic "grammar schools." The duller 80 percent were sent to "secondary modern schools." Separate they were; equal they were not. Segregation by talent, and implicitly by class, was the whole point of elitist education. The best students got a terrific education, but the less talented were offered little.

The comprehensive schools were created in the late 1950s and 1960s by politicians and school officials determined to make the system fairer. Parents applied the pressure for change after seeing children who did not excel on the 11-plus exams losing any chance for top-level education. The comprehensives offered a wide variety of courses, from carpentry to Latin, in an attempt to blur the distinctions between vocational and university-prep training. Harold Wilson had pledged to abolish the 11-pluses and reorganize secondary education on the comprehensive plan. But the effort was too sudden, poorly planned, and proved in many instances to be a disastrous experiment. They were "state" schools, but run by local authorities, creating as wide a disparity in standards as the traditional grammar schools. In addition, many of the first comprehensives were too big, with huge, difficult-to-control classes. The ranks of teachers, the new social engineers, swelled. Some were not well qualified, but given union strength in the mid-1960s, the National Union of Teachers had the muscle to prevent firings. The coherence of the old school system had been shattered, but the new system was not working.

Thatcher scrapped Labor's policy of transforming schools into comprehensives, often against their will, her first day on the job. Her order was the first of the eighteen items on the handwritten list she handed Pile. She had a draft rescission order on her desk by the end of the day. "She said 'action this day' and she got it," said Pile. "We didn't stop to argue." Her rationale was that there should still be a place for top-quality select schools. "I have sometimes thought that some extreme advocates of equality would be happy if all the children were in bad schools so long as they were all equally bad," she said. Besides, no one insisted everyone live in the same kind of house, "so why shouldn't parents buy a different kind of education for their children?"

Thatcher hated the sheer size of the comprehensives, which were up to ten times the size of a traditional school. She has never liked anything big: big bureaucracies, big houses, a big entourage. "She was wary of size in itself because big bodies had a life of their own," said Pile.[23] "She couldn't actually control them as easily as she could small bodies." She also thought many of the courses taught in the comprehensives were a waste. Stick to basics and teach them well was her motto. But there was another, more personal reason for her dislike of comprehensives. She had come up through the grammar school system and appreciated its worth, including the attention paid students in small classes. She was not going to stand by as the system that had given her a way to the top was eliminated.

Where school administrators, parents, and local councilors wanted comprehensives, she concurred and went with the flow. For all her opposition in principle, she approved 95 percent of the 2,765 requests she received to change over. But if the parents balked, she tended to heed their wishes over any others in the equation. Those decisions won more attention. She was accused of elitism, of being a moss-backed right-winger determined to prevent the poor from achieving school ambitions. When she defended her approach before the highly politicized National Union of Teachers, hundreds walked out in protest. She was unfazed. She had never hidden her anti-unionist sentiments. She had always believed that unions were anti-individual. When the public outcry grew, she responded to adversity the way she always does. She lowered her head and pressed on.

The comprehensives dispute eventually receded from the headlines when Thatcher instigated another controversy that put her on the line. Heath had taken office with a pledge to cut government spending and planned to chop more than $700 million from his first budget. At Education, Thatcher had no choice but to pick up her own axe. She had turned down several budget-cutting proposals, including one to put entrance charges on libraries. Her father had considered the public library his university. She would not prevent anyone else from using it the same way, but something had to go. She decided to end the $19 million free milk program for primary schoolchildren aged seven to eleven. Since poor children would be exempt, Thatcher had a rationale. "I took the view that most parents are able to pay for milk for their children and that the job of government was to provide such things in education which they could not pay for, like new primary schools." Wilson's Labor government, she pointed out, had halted free milk to secondary schools and had met little opposition. "The important thing was to protect education and that's what we did," she said.

The explanation did her little good. The public was outraged. Opponents charged that Thatcher's cuts would lead to a tripling of the numbers of children with calcium deficiency and began to consider ways to avoid implementing the policy. When some administrators said they would use property taxes to pay for milk, the government rushed through legislation to make such moves illegal. Methyr Tydfil, a Welsh mining town, continued the free distribution for all students, saying the town was already too familiar with malnutrition and rickets. The revolt collapsed when the government, playing hardball, announced that the local councilors would be personally responsible for the $5,000 milk bill each term.

Demonstrators took to the streets throughout Britain, bellowing, "Thatcher, Milk Snatcher." She was cast in Parliament and in the press as a mother taking milk from the mouths of babes. The fact that a woman was doing this made the policy seem more unsympathetic. She was shouted down at public meetings. At one school, students refused to accept awards from her. In Liverpool, debris thrown from the audience forced her off the podium. She took refuge in the home of a local MP, whose wife asked how the appearance had gone. "Very rowdy," Thatcher replied, pulling back her blouse to reveal a huge, spreading bruise on her upper chest where she had been hit with a rock. The wife's jaw dropped.

"Did it hurt?"

"It hurt like mad," Thatcher conceded.

"What did you do?" the horrified hostess asked.

"I went on speaking. What else could I do?"

When the woman asked if she could call a doctor, Thatcher declined. "I've got two more engagements," she said. "Give me a nice, hot cup of tea."[24]

Milk wasn't the only issue on the Thatcher agenda. She also raised the price of school meals, unchanged for several years, and rejected a suggestion to renovate slum area schools, claiming the money could be better spent on new schools. A $5 million subsidy to allow private schools to cut tuitions further enraged her critics, who were fast multiplying. Whenever she rose to speak in Parliament, Labor back-benchers began a cadence: "Ditch the bitch."

The Left made her their number one target, portraying her as a hard, middle-class suburbanite, ambitious, ruthless, and unfeeling, fit only for garden parties in her Tory hats and string pearls. They called her a child hater and accused her on the floor of the House of having her children at the same time; the way most convenient for her career. The twins were taunted at school, and the criticism did not come solely from the Left. The staunchly pro-Tory *Sunday Express* called her "the Lady Nobody Loves." Britain's biggest daily paper, *The Sun*, bannered the headline "The Most Unpopular Woman in Britain" over an article that remarked: "At a time when Mr. Heath's government is desperately seeking an image of compassion and concern, Mrs. Thatcher is fast emerging as a liability."

Within the cabinet, she was unpopular. Because she headed a minor ministry, she was not part of the inner circle anyway, but the feeling against her went beyond her fringe status. Home Secretary Reginald Maudling could not stand Thatcher and repeatedly called her "that bloody woman." He, like so many others, recognized that not only was she not one of the boys, she was causing the boys trouble. They were appalled at her single-mindedness and worried about the political price that the party would pay. At cabinet meetings, where some of her critics sat, she said little. When she did speak up, it was often not what her male colleagues wanted to hear. Once, as Heath was conducting a small meeting in Number 10 to discuss the appointment of a new director of the BBC, Geoffrey Howe suggested one name. "He's got much too high an opinion of himself," Heath rebutted. Thatcher jumped in with, "But, Prime Minister, most men do." The men exchanged glances and chuckled awkwardly.[25]

Women were no more comfortable with Thatcher, who had no interest in them unless they had power, which none did. Quite a few wives of cabinet ministers, some of whom were upper class, had country houses and had been reared in privilege. They had nothing in common with the driven Thatcher and felt little but hostility toward her. At one formal Downing Street lunch, during a break in the conversation, a prominent guest wondered aloud whether there was "any truth in the rumor that Mrs. Thatcher is a woman." Thatcher, sitting nearby, heard the crack, but pretended not to. Some of her fellow ministers could not decide whether to feel bad or laugh out loud. Some did both.[26]

Despite her impersonal relationship with Heath, the prime minister, to his credit, resisted repeated suggestions to dump her. The more insistent the calls, the more determined Heath, well aware of her talent, became to keep Thatcher.

At Education, she refused to crack when the criticism mounted. "It hurt her, but she hid the hurt and would never reveal anything in public," said Pile. In private, it was different. She came home at night pale and exhausted. Over stiff whiskies with Denis, she discussed the pressure. She was particularly upset over the abuse Mark and Carol had to bear. She sometimes broke down and sobbed. "The criticism was vicious," she said later. "You have to build armor around yourself to cope."

On Christmas Eve 1970, just before midnight, she and Denis sat by their decorated tree. Underneath lay presents for the twins, a punctiliously equal number. She was in the midst of the worst six months of her life. Alf had died earlier in the year, just before she had gone into government, and she missed him terribly. Denis was consoling. "Why don't you chuck it all in?" he asked. "You don't

have to put up with this. Why go on?" Thatcher looked up. Tears
ran down her cheeks. "I'll see them in hell first," she retorted. "I
will never be driven anywhere against my will."[27]

The milk episode toughened her tremendously. She developed
a calloused, protective skin that would stand her in good stead.
Years later, she conceded that she had mishandled the situation.
She had forgotten Iain Macleod's rule of working out the politics
of an action first. At the time, chopping the milk allowance made
sense, but she probably should have done it in stages, she thought.
But, the experience had been a watershed. "The great milk furor
gave her a tremendous object lesson in the proportions of political
judgment," said a cabinet minister who served beside and under
her for years.[28] "She learned very sharply that if you're going to do
political battle, make sure first it's a big one or look to ways of
finessing it. The milk battle was not worth the frontal charge, but
it did teach her the importance of flanking maneuvers."

The milk controversy contributed to a great misunderstanding
about Thatcher—that she was only a budget cutter. Quite the contrary. She was one of the biggest spenders ever to preside over the
education ministry, an irony that her more perceptive critics would
point to later as evidence of cold-blooded expediency. She was under
orders to cut, but like all ambitious politicians, Thatcher learned
early that shrinking a department is no way to be noticed. Growth
gets attention. When she took office, education spending was at an
all-time high. Milk notwithstanding, she pushed it higher. Some
$350 million went for the rebuilding and replacing of 460 primary
schools, many of them Victorian relics. She fought for another $525
million over three years to improve technical and vocational schools
and to boost the number of nursery schools, especially in remote
areas. She fought for money to raise the school-leaving age from
fifteen to sixteen. Another campaign raised money for *Open University*, which broadcasts lectures on radio and TV and established
degree-granting correspondence courses for thousands of Britons.

Simple, basic, straightforward education—the kind of teaching
she felt she received—was her goal. Once, while visiting a primary
school, the headmaster screened a glossy film showing the children
in class, at play, and with all the amenities and equipment. At the
end, he beamed and asked for questions. Thatcher had one. "Interesting, but how do you know at the end of each week the progress
each child has made?" The headmaster blanched.

Throughout her three and a half years at Education, the only cabinet post she ever held, her style and pace remained the same: all out, no quarter. Sir Alec Douglas-Home, who was then serving as Heath's foreign secretary, came home one day and told his wife, "You know, she's got the brains of all of us put together, so we'd better look out."

She took pains to juggle career and family. Once, hosting a ministry meeting on a $50 million budget cut proposal to be tabled at a cabinet meeting the next day, she noticed it was getting dark outside. "What time is it?" she asked. Ten to five was the reply. "Oh, I must go and get some bacon." Asked what in the world she was talking about, Thatcher explained that she needed to shop for Denis's breakfast. "One of the secretaries can get it for you," said an aide solicitously, while nervously juggling the budget papers. "Oh, no, they won't know what kind he likes," she said, pushing back her chair, pulling on her coat, and leaving the room. Fifteen minutes later she was back, bacon in hand. "Now where were we?" she asked the astonished civil servants before plunging back into the columns of figures for hours.[29]

Over at Downing Street, Heath had begun his term well. He had had considerable success in transforming the image of the party. He had clearly not risen in politics as a man of property, but as a meritocrat with the paternalistic streak that characterized moderate Tories. He turned more to the right after his 1966 loss to Wilson. The Heath who came to office in 1970 was a new-age Tory. Curiously, in light of their later falling out, he was the logical precursor to Thatcher. "Stand on your own feet," was his slogan, a motto which might have been Maggie's own.

A competent manager, Heath succeeded in steering Britain into the Common Market, an objective that Macmillan had failed to accomplish. Two years into government, however, the bottom fell out of the economy when the soaring price of OPEC oil foiled his hard-line plans to trim spending. Inflation began spiraling out of control, from 5 percent to more than 16 percent. In 1973, the trade deficit soared to $5.3 billion.

Heath had come into office promising to reverse Labor's nationalization of core industries and never to introduce wage and price controls. But in 1972, his moderate instincts reasserted themselves. Worried about rising unemployment, Heath executed a tortuous U-turn, introducing an incomes policy and bailing out weak firms with massive injections of capital. The reintroduction of state control over the marketplace and industry was considered treason by right-wing Tories.

At the time, Thatcher was not among the critics of Heath's turnabout. At Education, she was spending money as fast as she could. None of her cabinet colleagues recalls her expressing any opposition to Heath's 180-degree reversal. Later, however, the Heath cave-in would be cited as the seminal turning point, the fulcrum on which Thatcher would launch her revolution. At the time, however, she stormed no barricades. She went along with it.

Troubles piled up. Strikes erupted. Engineers walked out, shutting down factories, power plants, shipyards, and newspapers. Charities issued leaflets to the elderly with instructions on how to stay warm in unheated apartments. When the coal miners, following the engineers, lead, struck, asking for a 31 percent raise, the floodgates burst. The government declared a state of emergency and instituted the SOS (Shut Off Something) program. Electric signs were shut off, darkening city centers. Thermostats were lowered to 63 degrees. When train drivers announced a ban on overtime and Sunday work, Heath put the nation on a three-day work week. Half a million workers lost jobs just before Christmas. By the end of January, 2.2 million were out of work, the worst unemployment since the Great Depression.

The Labor party called for arbitration to resolve the government's impasse with the unions. But Heath would not budge. When talks broke down, he realized he needed a new mandate and called an election in February 1974. To Heath, the election was a direct referendum on the power of the unions. "Who governs?" was the government's slogan. "Not Heath" was the answer. The election was close, and neither major party won an outright majority. Heath tried to put together a coalition government with Liberal party leader Jeremy Thorpe, but was rebuffed and soon resigned.

Wilson returned to the prime minister's office, made a higher, acceptable offer to the striking unionists, and the full working week was restored. Significantly, the cause of the problems had still not been corrected, but only covered over. For the time being. Thatcher was back on the benches of "Her Majesty's Loyal Opposition," stripped of office, staff, chauffeur, and her Education portfolio. In the postelection shakeup, she did get a new job: shadow environment minister. One more arrow for her quiver.

CHAPTER SIX

The Coup

HAROLD WILSON was prime minister again, but as the head of Britain's first minority government in more than forty years, he could scarcely govern. Labor had a four-seat edge over the Tories in the House, but had received fewer votes nationally than the Conservatives. The election was a stalemate. In June and July, the Tories and Liberals joined forces twenty-nine times to defeat union legislation sponsored by Labor. By September, a frustrated Wilson asked the Queen to dissolve the seven-month-long Parliament, the shortest of the twentieth century.

Wilson claimed to have inherited a mess from Heath—unlit streets and massive work stoppages—and to have succeeded in putting the country back to work. This was true to some extent; Wilson had made some progress. He had agreed to a $300 million pay settlement, meeting enough union demands to end the strikes that were ravaging the country. But the Conservatives argued, not unreasonably, that Labor's free spending was a short-term solution that set the stage for far worse economic problems.

The second election of 1974 was held on October 10 and gave the Labor party a forty-three-seat advantage over the Tories. When the smaller parties were added, Labor had an absolute majority of three seats. The Tories pulled in 35.8 percent of the vote, their lowest total ever. Aside from the prosperous South, a traditional Tory stronghold, the party did miserably. Tory fortunes dropped in the Midlands and the North and in Scotland and Wales. The results confirmed the need for radical restructuring, and the short-term consequences were immediate.

115

After nine years as party leader, it looked like the end of the line for Ted Heath. He had lost two elections in a row and three out of four overall, hardly a batting average to recommend a contract extension. But Heath's failure to attract voters was not his only problem. He had also made mistakes within the party. One came in the final days of the campaign, when he spoke, without approval from other party elders, of appointing a "national unity government" if elected—one in which non-Conservatives would serve. His fellow Tories were not amused, and once on the ropes, Heath had little residual support. "In the best of times, he wasn't easy, to put it mildly," said one of his closest cabinet colleagues.[1]

Heath was respected, but never loved. He did not inspire personal loyalty even when things were going well. He could not shake, nor did he bother to try, his image as a self-righteous headmaster who ran the party autocratically, taking little advice. His backbench MPs were disgruntled. Many felt their talents were unrecognized, their expertise and thinking ignored. Heath was often openly contemptuous of them, and for that matter, he was frequently insulting to his front-bench colleagues. Heath had failed to reward loyalty with honors ("gongs," as they're popularly called) such as knighthoods, which supporters expect. He had almost no backing on the right wing of the party, which was still upset by his policy U-turn in 1972. Now, as the Tories faced five more years in the wilderness, there was not much left for Heath. The sharks were circling.

The Tories have a history of swift justice toward losers, and the prevailing feeling was that Heath had had his turn. At the top level of the party, however, the old gang of centrists could see no other likely candidate, even among themselves. Several top Tories told Heath he should resign in order to be reelected by the parliamentary party. They felt he could use the mandate to counter the mounting attacks from the grass roots and back bench. If this failed, his backers were expected to support William Whitelaw, a popular centrist. The important thing, everyone stressed, was to act quickly before a serious ideological challenge arose.

Heath, stubborn as well as proud, refused. A month after the election, he informed the 1922 Committee, the organization of backbenchers, that he would not step down but would stand again. He was convinced that he had fought the past two elections on the proper grounds with the right policies. Once the postelection hysteria died down, he believed the rest of the party would realize that, too. In fact, his analysis was not far off base. Most of the moderate, nonrisk-taking Conservatives in the early 1970s had not only agreed with his U-turn and the move toward consensus it implied, but thought his wage and price policy fair.

Margaret Thatcher was not among them. But unlike such radical Tories as Enoch Powell, Nicholas Ridley, and John Biffen, she had not spoken up. No fellow cabinet member could recall her registering concern privately, though she maintains that she was deeply troubled. Her silence was probably expedient politics, another example of pragmatism and painstaking care to protect her flanks. As the head of a minor ministry, removed from the cabinet inner circle, she would have had little impact if she had tried to battle her leader in 1972. She could only hurt herself and wreck her future chances. Thatcher had voted for Heath as leader. She admired his toughness and, for the most part, his policies, but she was deeply disappointed in his performance. When he refused to do what she felt was the right thing, step down, Thatcher felt offended.[2]

But now there was no clear candidate to challenge Heath. Whitelaw had no intention of challenging the leader; too loyal, he also figured that Heath would manage another win when the party gathered. But the right wing was not in the mood to tolerate Heath another moment. They were frantic to find almost any warm body and finally decided that their best candidate would be Keith Joseph, the former minister of social services.

Joseph, a slender and intense intellectual, seems more an Oxford don than a hardball politician. But he is passionately ideological, and as an economic thinker he is tough-minded. Before the election he had criticized Heath for giving priority to full employment at the cost of holding down rising inflation. Inflation, Joseph remained convinced, was Britain's biggest problem. It simply had to be wrung out. In a speech at Preston, setting out his differences from Heath, Joseph established himself as a potential standard-bearer. Yet it was obvious to almost everyone, including himself, that he did not have the right stuff to be party leader; his style was too pedantic. His Jewishness would have also cost votes. In addition, his marriage was falling apart and one of his children was seriously ill. The fact that he was even considered as a potential candidate was a signal of the dissidents' desperation.

There were, however, reasons for his emergence. In the summer of 1974, between the two elections, Joseph had established a new party research unit called the Center for Policy Studies. The dual goal of the center was to examine ways to combat inflation (including a study of how Germany had tried to cope with hyper-inflation during the 1920s) and to analyze the best methods of minimizing government interference in the marketplace. But Joseph did not try to hide his real reason for setting up the unit, which was, he said, because "the party was going wrong."[3]

Heath had lost the little confidence that the business community held in him. Business generally was in despair. Taxation on business profit was 97 percent. Entrepreneurs were flocking out of Britain like ducks fleeing winter chill. After his 1972 turn, Heath's own reference to "the unacceptable face of capitalism" effectively destroyed any chance he might have had to restore business morale.

Unlike many of the Tories' top backers in business, Heath was not in favor of Joseph's new research center, but he could not stop it. No party funds were involved. Joseph had raised the money himself by writing to twenty businessmen and asking for pledges of £1,000 ($2,400) a year. All but two responded. One was so upset with the party's prospects that he offered £15,000 ($36,000). Once the funding was in place, Joseph appointed Thatcher vice-chairman.

Joseph had the framework for a challenge to Heath, but he was not the one for the job. "Any less likely leader of a party has seldom been seen," declared one of the nation's most senior Tories. "When Keith's name was mooted, we all roared with laughter. If that's the person who's going to challenge Ted, then we're all right."[4]

Joseph never got out of the starting blocks. Although his Preston speech had been well received, a second address destroyed any chance, however far-fetched, he might have had. Speaking in Edgbaston, near Birmingham, Joseph called for birth control for the lowest classes of society, those least able, he suggested, to care for their offspring. There was a furor, including accusations that Joseph was advocating "master race" policies. He took himself out of the running. "It was never a sensible idea. It was an illusion," he said later. "I was only running out of despair. I was flattered by the idea and was willing to be swept along. But I was a joke, a useful joke."[5]

Joseph's exit left the dissidents casting about. Thatcher, who had been approached by several back-benchers but who had supported Joseph until his exit, began to move out of the shadows.

Somebody had to stand up for a new approach, and no one was stepping forward. "We just cannot allow it," she told a friend.[6] "As a party, we must *do* something." For Heath to stay on, a tarred loser with discredited policies, would mean further deterioration of the Tories' future chances. "To deny that we failed the people is futile as well as arrogant," she declared. "Successful governments win elections. So do parties with broadly acceptable policies. We *lost*."

Thatcher was no one's first choice. "I don't think anyone at that time really thought that Margaret was a serious contender," said James Prior, who sat in Heath's cabinet as leader of the House of Commons.[7] She was, however, leading the opposition's fight against the Labor government's finance bill and doing it brilliantly. She dominated the parliamentary debate with her grasp of the nuances of the bill as well as the numbers. That was not enough to make her a candidate. What tipped the scale was that she was the *only* Conservative willing to challenge Heath.

Edward du Cann, chairman of the 1922 Committee of backbenchers, considered running. But his wife was opposed and questions were raised about some of his business connections. So du Cann pulled out before he ever really got in. The lists were closing, and with three weeks before the leadership balloting, only 2 of 276 Tory MPs eligible to vote favored Thatcher, who hadn't declared herself a candidate. Heath might be saved by default.

Thatcher was less than enthusiastic about a seemingly hopeless challenge. She still wanted to be chancellor of the exchequer, believing she'd be lucky to get that. Six months earlier, she had told a Liverpool newspaper that she thought it was impossible for a woman to reach the top. "It will be years before a woman either leads the party or becomes prime minister. I don't see it happening in my time."

She had good reason to think so. Opportunities for women had changed little in the fifteen years she had been an MP. The Queen had been on the throne nearly a quarter-century, but Britain remained a male-dominated society. Political and business decisions were made in the smoking rooms of such all-male clubs as White's and the Tories' own oasis, the Carlton Club. No woman ran a major company. Only women with family connections sat on important corporate boards. The Conservative party remained the most male of all institutions.

The "Knights of the Shires," bluebloods who shot quail and

pheasant in the autumn on thousand-acre estates, were Tories. Military men, with their cocked plumes and silver spurs, were Conservatives. Businessmen battling union bosses were Conservatives. In government, women were hardly close to the center of power. When Thatcher came to Parliament in 1959, there were only twenty-five women MPs. Now, a decade and a half later, there were twenty-seven women and only seven of those were Conservatives. Historically, those under consideration as leader had served first in one or more of the "great offices"—as foreign secretary, chancellor, or home secretary. Thatcher had not served in any of those posts. No woman had.

Within the party, there was spirited criticism of Thatcher. She was not liked, never had been. And as to loyalty? If she were now so opposed to Heath and what he stood for, why hadn't she spoken up before—or done the proper thing and resigned on principle? Those who had watched her spend heavily at Education wondered about all this budget-cutting passion. She also retained a sour odor from the "Milk Snatcher" days. Her colleagues considered her a hard worker to be sure, but hardly a champion riding forward on a white charger to rescue Britain.

Thatcher scarcely registered on the national consciousness meter. She knew nothing about foreign policy and defense. Ian Gow, a right-wing Tory who would later become a close adviser, said there were profound doubts about Thatcher. "The patricians in the party didn't like her robustly populist approach challenging the old orthodoxies. They and others wondered whether it would be possible, with the Cold War getting colder, for a woman to represent the country internationally, dealing with defense and foreign policy matters thought to be the province of men."[8]   •

Thatcher made up her mind to challenge Heath on her own. She discussed it with Denis, but not the children, who were then twenty-two. She weighed the costs. A loss would affect her career for years to come; as Ralph Waldo Emerson told Oliver Wendell Holmes, Jr., "When you strike at a king, you must kill him." She was still inclined to risk it and strike. Once she decided, she went straight to Heath to tell him, meeting him in the leader of the opposition's office in the House of Commons. What the confrontation lacked in cordiality, it made up in brevity. Lasting barely ninety seconds, the encounter was unfriendly even by Heath standards. Thatcher was not invited to sit down. Nor did Heath thank her for the courtesy of informing him. Instead, he peremptorily dismissed her, taking her challenge no more seriously than the old boys took Joseph's. Nor did anyone else. "I was chairman of the party and I didn't believe the challenge was going to happen," said Whitelaw. "None of us did."[9]

Explaining why she had decided to challenge, Thatcher wasted no time on false humility. "I saw the Tory party going much too much to the left, and there did not seem to be anyone who had the thoughts and ideas I had," she said. "It seemed to be absolutely vital for the country that I stood." Absolutely vital. Life and death. She believed in her ideas passionately and there was conviction in her delivery; this was not just a political challenge. It was the beginning of a crusade. Still, the chances of her unseating the veteran leader were slim. Britain's bookies quoted fifty-to-one odds. Then a surprising development changed Thatcher's career and the course of British history. Airey Neave adopted her.

Neave was an obscure but respected back-bencher. A short, ruddy-faced man with a big smile, he was a decorated war hero who had trained women secret agents, gaining high respect for women and their courage. Captured by the Nazis, he was the first Allied prisoner to break out of Germany's "escape-proof" prison at Colditz. Later, Neave ventured back behind enemy lines, organizing a legendary escape route for other prisoners of war. As a junior barrister at Nuremberg, he served arrest warrants on Hitler aides Rudolf Hess and Albert Speer, and after the war he wrote a well-received series of books on his experiences. Such fame helped him win entry to Parliament in 1950, the same year Thatcher first tried to win Dartford. A considerable hero, he was much tougher than he looked. Despite his background, everyone underestimated him.

Neave had no love for Ted Heath. In 1959, when he was a junior minister in the Macmillan government, he had suffered a heart attack. He reported the illness to Heath, then the government's chief whip, who told him simply, "Well, that's the end of your political career."[10]

The best part was actually just beginning. Neave recovered, but Heath never offered him a position in his government and Neave's antipathy grew. With his background in espionage, Neave knew everything going on in Parliament. As a charter member of the "anyone-but-Heath" alliance, Neave had been an early supporter of Keith Joseph. When Joseph fell by the wayside, he moved on to du Cann, for whom he rallied a support group of twenty-five

MPs. Later, he even offered to help Whitelaw challenge, but the party chairman felt committed to Heath and declined.

Neave had no problems with Thatcher, with whom he had worked as a barrister-in-training in Lincoln's Inn in London. After persuading fifteen of the twenty-five dissident back-benchers to support her, Neave signed up as her campaign manager. He had a vision about her, he said later. Calling her a "philosopher as well as a politician," Neave said she was "the first real idealist politician in a long time."[11]

Neave's vision wasn't going to get Thatcher elected, but his superb organizational ability might. He hustled her around the Commons day and night and introduced her to knots of MPs at the Members Bar and Tea Room. As Heath struggled awkwardly through lavish cocktail parties and dinners, Thatcher waged a guerrilla battle, plugging away from a borrowed office where she stationed herself to answer questions over a modest glass of claret.

Neave advised her to avoid strong policy stands, to listen well and stress the general issue of leadership. Thatcher learned fast and followed instructions. She struck an ambivalent stance on the controversial issue of Britain's entry into the Common Market, which a number of Conservatives opposed. Her views on social issues, such as abortion and capital punishment, were known to be radically right, so she took pains not to dwell on them. Generally playing down any hard ideological sentiments, she emphasized instead her willingness to listen to back-benchers if elected, a Heath failing.

As Thatcher's stock rose, so did attacks on her. She stirred up a row by suggesting that elderly people getting ready to retire should fight inflation and stretch their pensions by stocking up in advance on preservable groceries. She was doing it herself, she admitted; her own nest egg included nine pounds of sugar, six jars each of jam, marmalade, and honey, four tins of ham, two cans of tongue, one of mackerel, four of sardines, twenty tins of various fruits and vegetables, plus sheets, towels, and other items "which I know will be needed in ten to fifteen years' time." Critics accused her of hoarding. She dismissed the uproar. "They broke Keith," she said referring to Joseph's withdrawal after the social class speech. "But they won't break me."

If anything was going to break her, it was the work pace. In addition to campaigning for the leadership, Thatcher was number two in the shadow Treasury, specializing in financial legislation. With the Wilson government about to present its finance bill, she had a target that could keep her in the spotlight. By assigning her to the Treasury, Heath had inadvertently given Thatcher the launch pad from which she could destroy him. Now, the countdown was underway.

The job of passing the government's financial legislation belonged to Denis Healey, chancellor of the exchequer, and one of Labor's most impressive postwar politicians. Son of a high school principal, he had taken a first in classics at Oxford, but he was also an army veteran who had never lost the earthiness of the barracks. A brilliant pol who would later serve as defense minister, Healey possessed a theatrical, rapier wit. But he was also a broadsword specialist and the party's most formidable bully-boy. Years later he would call Thatcher "Ted Heath in drag," but when she faced him across the aisle with her extraordinary command of statistics and tax law, he had little time for sarcasm. Thatcher jousted so furiously during the December 1974 debates that the Tory back-benchers burst into cheers at her performance and journalists began tracking everything she said. Thatcher, said the *Daily Telegraph*, "has dimples of iron."

In mid-January, just after Parliament's Christmas recess and only two weeks before the Tories' first leadership ballot, Thatcher and Healey went head to head in a debate that is still recalled in Westminster. Following some withering repartee, she went for his throat, belittling him for a capital transfer tax which would be imposed on gifts, including charitable donations, and on proposed higher tax rates on inherited wealth. "You apparently do not understand the effect your tax will have on the lives of individuals, the economy, or indeed on a free society in general," she said.

Healey, who loves a fight, took off his gloves. "Mrs. Thatcher has emerged from the debate as La Pasionaria of privilege," he told the House, making a reference to Dolores Ibárruri, the Spanish Civil War's fiery Communist orator. "She has shown that she has decided to see her party tagged as the party of the rich few, and I believe she and her party will regret it."

Some might have retreated before his attack. That was Healey's intent. But Thatcher rose calmly and strode purposefully back to the dispatch box. Healey, huge bushy eyebrows bristling, glared as she took aim. She had wanted to say that Healey's remarks had not done him justice, she said, but unfortunately they had. Her opening, with the sarcastic hint of insult to come, was intended to get the listening MPs salivating, and it did. "Some chancellors are microeconomic. Some chancellors are fiscal. This one is just plain cheap," she jibed. "We on this side [of the aisle] were amazed how one could possibly get to be chancellor knowing so little about existing taxes and so little about proposals coming before Parliament. If this chancellor can be chancellor, anyone in the House of Commons could be chancellor. I had hoped the right honorable gentleman had learned a lot from this debate. Clearly he learned nothing. He might at least address himself to the practical effects because it will affect everyone, including people born as I was, with no privilege at all." The House erupted with cheers, jeers, and "Hear, hears." Thatcher had scored. She had taken on the town bully, and, though "only a woman," had sent him packing. Never before had anyone dismissed Denis Healey.

The press loved the battle. The *Daily Telegraph* weighed in again: "Reluctant though I am to risk the lady's wrath by questioning her undoubted femininity," columnist Frank Johnson wrote, "let it be said that the Tories need more men like her." Suddenly the party had a contender.

Gordon Reece, a television producer, began helping her with media contacts. He and Neave quickly set up a series of lunches with Fleet Street editors. Feminine charm, which Thatcher can turn on with impressive effect when she wants to, helped soften her straight, no-frills explanations of her populist vision and meritocratic policies. Converts soon began turning up. In a signed op-ed piece in the *Daily Telegraph*, she explained that "my kind of Tory party would make no secret of its belief in individual freedom and individual prosperity, in the maintenance of law and order, in the wide distribution of private property, in the rewards for energy, skill and thrift, in diversity of choice, in the preservation of local rights in local communities."

Lobbying of the MPs picked up. Neave and Reece improvised as they went along, borrowing American campaign strategy and television tricks. She needed 51 percent of the MPs, but instead of aiming for the minimum, the three of them decided to go for all the membership. The strategy was revolutionary; with the exception of whips rounding up votes for legislation, no one had ever lobbied the entire membership systematically.

A partial Neave head count ten days before the vote showed Thatcher with sixty-four votes, Heath with thirty-five, and Hugh Fraser, a senior back-bencher representing those who wanted neither Thatcher nor Heath, with none. Two days later, more complete numbers showed Thatcher with ninety-five, Heath with sixty-four, and Fraser with six. There were forty-three doubtfuls, twenty of whom Neave believed would go for Thatcher. Whatever happened, she was not going to be embarrassed.

Four days before the vote, Thatcher drove to Finchley and delivered a passionate defense of her thinking, addressing the accusations that she was only out to defend the rich and privileged. "You can forget all that nonsense about 'defense of privilege'—I had precious little privilege in my early years—and the suggestion that all my supporters are reactionary right-wingers. This is not a confrontation between left and right."

She also responded to criticism from within the party that she was "too hopelessly middle class" to lead the great Tory party. "If 'middle class values' include the encouragement of variety and individual choice, the provision of fair incentives and rewards for skill and hard work, the maintenance of effective barriers against the excessive power of the state, and a belief in the wide distribution of individual private property, then they are certainly what I am trying to defend." The speech was one of her most powerful. She got good press. Reporters were swarming all over her challenge by then, and the timing was perfect.

A much better television performer than Heath, Thatcher agreed to a *World in Action* program profile on the eve of the ballot, an idea that Reece had been promoting. That night, Tory MPs crowded around TV sets in the House of Commons to watch a stunning performance. In one sequence, she spoke to garbagemen at a dump, including one who stumbled over his explanation of what he collected. "Refuse?" Thatcher offered, trying to help. "And people who die," he finally added. Thatcher never missed a beat. "It is a job that has to be done and requires someone of quiet dignity to do it." The press lauded her performance. Once again, the *Telegraph* rushed in with superlatives, gushing that "she came alive as never before."[12]

She had made stunning progress. The day before the vote, Neave told her that, by his count, she had 120 supporters to Heath's 84. But newspaper polls showed up to 63 percent of the party preferred keeping Heath to bringing in Thatcher. With the exception of Keith Joseph, who supported her, the entire cabinet backed Heath.

So, when Tory MPs began trickling into Room 14 of the House of Commons on decision day, Heath had every reason to believe that his grip on the party would be extended. Peter Walker, his campaign manager, told Heath he could count on 138–144 of the 276 votes, a majority that would obviate the need for a second round.

Thatcher voted at noon, left for a working lunch, returned, and waited nervously in Airey Neave's room until the voting ended at 3:30 P.M. At 4 P.M., Edward du Cann emerged from the committee room and announced the shock result. Thatcher had 130 votes; Heath 119, Fraser 16, with 11 abstentions. Neave raced to his room. "It's good news," he blurted out. "You're ahead. There'll be a second ballot." She was astonished. In fact, it was difficult to tell who was more stunned, Heath or Thatcher. "We got it all wrong," the numbed Heath told his campaign aides. Quickly he announced he was resigning. Thatcher had fallen only nine votes short of an absolute majority, and he would not be further humiliated.

Thatcher had no sympathy for the man who had trained her. "I'll always be fond of dear Ted, but there's no sympathy in politics," she said sweetly but lethally after his exit.

Once Heath bowed out, candidates who had not stood in the first round out of loyalty rushed to take on Thatcher in the second round a week later. Her strongest opponent was Whitelaw, at fifty-six, seven years older than she. A former secretary of state for Northern Ireland, the jovial, rumpled Whitelaw, universally known as Willie, was a wealthy country squire who loved to shoot game and play golf. He was the quintessential old school, old boy Conservative. Whitelaw was, however, no empty tweed suit. He had been party chairman and an exceptionally talented MP for twenty years. His strength was as a master conciliator, a superb backstairs political operative with strong support across the whole spectrum of the party. He also had weaknesses. He was too willing to compromise, had little knowledge of economics and limited oratorical skills. He was, all in all, too ideologically centrist and, some thought, too closely identified with Heath.

Other candidates included Geoffrey Howe, the moderate former solicitor general, and MPs James Prior and John Peyton, neither of whom were expected to show much. The assumption was that they would siphon support off from Thatcher. If that happened and the second ballot was similarly inconclusive, they were expected to rally behind Whitelaw on the third.

Long before their contest, Thatcher and Whitelaw had agreed to speak to a Young Conservatives rally at Eastbourne on the south coast. Cleverly, Thatcher worked out a deal. They would not use the forum for campaigning but would instead stick to the original schedule. For Whitelaw, that meant conducting a question-and-answer session on regional development, a topic guaranteed to put his listeners to sleep, while Thatcher had clear sailing. She was scheduled to give a speech. Her torrid defense of basic Conservative ideals had the crowd on its feet cheering and gave her the next day's headlines. When the BBC's top current affairs program asked her to participate in a panel with other candidates, she refused. She had broken out of the pack.

Throughout the day of the second balloting, the 276 Conservative MPs filed again in and out of Room 14. Thatcher was fidgety. Dressed in a trim, two-piece suit accented by a pink and white tulip, she sat alone in Airey Neave's tiny, windowless office. Finally, just before 4 P.M., Neave came in. "It's all right," he told her simply. "You're leader of the opposition." She had 146 votes, 7 more than she needed, to Whitelaw's 79 and 19 each for Howe and Prior.

Tears welled in her eyes. Then, quickly regaining her self-control, she returned to business. "Thank God it is decisive," she said briskly. "We've got a lot to do. We must get down to work instantly."

CHAPTER SEVEN

Brink of Power

THERE WAS no celebrating. No champagne corks popped that afternoon in Neave's office. But the phones started ringing off the hook. One of the first calls was from Denis. As usual, he had heard the news from afar, this time by radio. Next, she scribbled a note to Willie Whitelaw. "I know how you must be feeling," she wrote, aware that she needed him and the elders. "I must talk to you. What matters above all now is the party."

Whitelaw had to decide immediately whether to go along. "Some suggested I should play hard to get and wait a few days before committing myself to serving under Margaret," Whitelaw said. But that was not his style. He decided right away that "I would serve her in any capacity she wanted, give my undivided loyalty to her as leader and that I would do my utmost to work with her."[1] His decision had major implications. Over the next decade and a half, no one served Thatcher more ably than Whitelaw, her bridge to the moderates and a talented counselor who could restrain her less temperate impulses.

Later that day, Thatcher emerged for her first news conference as leader. Winning, it quickly became apparent, had not rounded off the rough edges. Asked by a reporter to elaborate on an answer to a routine question, she snapped back: "It does not need expansion. You chaps do not like a direct answer. Men like long, rambling, waffling answers." Would she attempt to join the Carlton Club, the all-male bastion of Conservative party luminaries? She was dismissive. "I have more important matters for instant consid-

128

On October 13, 1925, Margaret Roberts was born in the spartan apartment—no running water, no indoor toilet—above her parents' grocery store.

In 1943, Margaret (*right*) was eighteen and a student at Oxford. Her father, Alf Roberts, was mayor of Grantham by then. He doted on her, while her twenty-two-year-old sister, Muriel (*left*), was closer to their mother, Beatrice.

Educated as a chemist, Margaret spent the early years after graduation working in research for a plastics firm and a food manufacturer. She never liked the work.

TWO PHOTOS: TOPHAM PICTURE LIBRARY

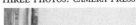

THREE PHOTOS: CAMERA PRESS

Opposite top, Margaret Thatcher has never been a great orator but, whatever the subject, is always prepared with an arsenal of facts.

Opposite center, Margaret married businessman Denis Thatcher, whose former marriage was a secret, when she was twenty-six. She surprised guests with her choice of a blue wedding dress, which she wore for years.

Opposite bottom, twins Carol and Mark have different personalities and don't get along well. Carol is warm and hardworking. Mark, known for his arrogance, is prone to trade on the family name.

Above, Labor Prime Minister James Callaghan looked smug. But Britain was tired of strikes and ready for a change when Thatcher ran against him in 1979.

Right, a cautious Thatcher waited until the verdict was clear before claiming victory number one at Conservative party headquarters. But when the final tally was in, the new prime minister was exultant.

Coming off a dramatic triumph in the Falklands, Thatcher could scarcely have lost the 1983 campaign. A strong team of old and new boys surround her, including (*left to right, back*) Norman Tebbit, Geoffrey Howe, Francis Pym, Michael Heseltine, Tom King; (*left to right, front*) William Whitelaw, Thatcher, Cecil Parkinson.

Except at state openings when Black Rod summons MPs to hear the Queen speak, the House of Commons is a raucous fighting pit where Thatcher has routinely trounced her opposition.

The Soviets first called her "the Iron Lady" and she has never given them—or anyone else—reason to change the sobriquet.

Below left, ten years older than the prime minister, Denis hates the nitty-gritty of politics and concentrates on his own business, which often takes him far from Britain. He is rarely happier, however, than when headed for the nineteenth hole.

Below right, a golf widow who doesn't mind Denis heading frequently for the course, Thatcher has few friends closer than her husband. But they have always maintained their separate lives.

TWO PHOTOS: CAMERA PRESS

Despite the good-natured grin, Thatcher is far more comfortable in the House of Commons or Downing Street than pressing the flesh on the campaign trail, a chore she barely tolerates.

Thatcher, the eighth prime minister to serve Queen Elizabeth II, is apparently the Queen's least favorite. The two women are only six months apart in age, but a world of difference separates their outlooks.

DIANA WALKER/TIME

Ronald Reagan and Thatcher formed one of the most powerful political partnerships of the postwar era, rejuvenating the "special relationship" that Churchill first forged with Franklin Roosevelt.

In December 1984, Mikhail Gorbachev was an unknown Kremlin official when Thatcher invited him to Chequers and decided she could "do business" with him. Three months later, he was running the USSR.

PETER JORDAN

DIANA WALKER/*TIME*

More comfortable with the details of foreign policy than Reagan, George Bush has a solid, but more distant, relationship with Thatcher.

Thatcher would like to go "on and on," for a fourth term at least. But when the prime minister does step down, she and Denis plan to retire to this house next to a golf course in south London's Dulwich.

CAMERA PRESS

eration," she scoffed. (The Club knew what it was about to miss and quickly dropped its gender barrier and asked her to join.)

That evening, Thatcher returned to Parliament to rejoin the debate on the Labor party's wealth equalization scheme. As she took her new place at the head of the front-bench team, MPs from both sides of the aisle rose to give her a standing ovation. She beamed. Power becomes her. She looked great and her backers told her so. "If you go on looking as attractive as you do tonight, it will be very beneficial," said Joel Barnett, the Treasury's chief secretary. It was an off-hand compliment, but one with political resonance. Thatcher never forgot it. Her appearance had long been important, but now that she was in the spotlight, it would take on even greater significance. She wanted to look good. The artful use of her femininity would become a meaningful and successful weapon in her strategic arsenal.

By the time she got home, it was past midnight. The neighborhood was mobbed. Journalists and bystanders packed the street; camera flashes lit the night. She slipped into Carol's room to say goodnight. Her mother looked brilliant, Carol thought. Happy. No more tension. Eyes glowing. Skin radiant. No lines etched in her face. She had gambled and won. At forty-nine, in politics for more than half her life, with nearly sixteen years in Parliament behind her, Margaret Thatcher was free of doubt. She knew she was right where she belonged.

The next morning she called on Heath, just after visiting a sick neighbor. There was no question that he would remain on in Parliament. Generally in Britain, politicians stay after losing or giving up a top post. She had promised him, as she had all the other leadership candidates, a shadow cabinet post if she won, but she had never specified which one she would offer him. He would not be given the shadow chancellor's job; that was certain. One of the primary reasons she challenged him had been her opposition to his economic policies. Predictions were that she'd offer him the top foreign affairs post; there was a specific precedent for that. Former Prime Minister Sir Alec Douglas-Home had returned to government as foreign secretary in Heath's own cabinet. Besides, Heath was well suited for the job. He had negotiated Britain's entry into the Common Market and had been dealing with foreign leaders throughout his four years in office. Thatcher could certainly use a hand in foreign policy. She had no international experience. At her first news conference, she had been asked her thoughts about foreign affairs and defense policy. "I am all for them," she had replied.

Heath had not yet given up his official car and driver, so Thatcher hitched a ride with a friend in an old Austin Mini to the former leader's house on the edge of Chelsea. She was not keen to have him in her cabinet, but she does not renege on promises. When they met in his study, she recalled all too well their last prickly confrontation when she revealed her challenge plans. Since both hate small talk and are worse at it than any other world-class politicians, Thatcher made no effort to be falsely amiable, but came straight to the point. "I have said publicly that I would ask you to join the shadow cabinet. Will you join us?" Heath was still in shock at his ouster. He found it incredible that it could come at the hands of a woman and was furious at her outrageous disloyalty. He did not wait to hear an offer, but turned her down.

Thatcher had anticipated his reaction, so she continued. "What are you going to do now, then?" she asked. "Stay on in the House and return to the back benches," he replied. What about the referendum on the Common Market, his baby? Britain, after finally being admitted, was awkwardly trying to decide whether it wanted to stay. He would, of course, urge it, he said. "Don't you think that would be better done from the front bench?" Thatcher asked. "No, I don't want to get bogged down in organization," he responded. "I want to be out in front as a campaigner."

She did not believe him. She wanted him inside the camp, where he could cause less damage. Lyndon Johnson had once expressed a similar strategy when asked why he didn't fire FBI Director J. Edgar Hoover. "I'd rather have him inside the tent pissing out than outside pissing in," said the earthy president. Thatcher felt the same way. Heath was, in part, staying out to keep his options open so he could rush back to the leader's job if she tripped up. Now, there was nothing else to say. They agreed not to issue a statement, and after only a few more painful seconds, Thatcher left.

For a while, she tried being nice. Two months later, they shared a platform at a meeting on the Europe campaign. Demure in her new uniform, a black dress with the double strand of pearls that would become her trademark, Thatcher was nervous. "It is with some temerity," she said gallantly, "that the pupil speaks before the master because you know more about the Common Market than anyone." Heath did not respond then, or when she later paid him a tribute in Parliament on his devotion to the EEC. For the second time, Heath glared straight ahead. His reaction won her sympathy. Many Tories were outraged at his behavior. When he later pressed his vendetta by becoming a spiteful critic, it was Heath, not Thatcher, who was seen as disloyal.

Although the feud turned venomous over the years, it was mostly one-sided. Thatcher usually ignored Heath, but he refused to speak to her, would not mention her name for years—"that woman," he called her—and took pains not to be seen near her. Taking his seat in the Commons only fifteen feet away, he would not even look at her. Initially, she was embarrassed by the antipathy, but eventually got over it. As she began asserting herself, Thatcher spoke of Heath as "yesterday's man." There were quite a few of those around, in her opinion. During her first party political broadcast, she made the point with a quip: "To yesterday's men, tomorrow's woman says hello."[2]

Thatcher still had a shadow cabinet to pick—twenty-two jobs to fill—and a party that needed restructuring. Within days of her election, she traveled to northern England and Scotland, concentrating on inner cities and industrial areas where the Tories were unpopular. Crowds, more curious than enthusiastic, turned out to see this new rarity, a woman opposition leader. Thatcher knew she had a nation to convert. The challenge was to convince an electorate that her father's age-old middle-class values were a better answer for Britain than the Labor party's welfare state with its deficit financing and income controls. Not just better. "There is no alternative," she said so often in her schoolmistressy fashion that the phrase became known simply as "TINA." The country had to learn, in her father's words, that you don't spend more than you take in to the till. People should work hard, not count on unemployment benefits. "We should back the workers, not the shirkers," she told audiences. "We need those who are going to save money, who are going to do things for themselves."

She moved quickly both publicly and privately to establish herself. U.S. Secretary of State Henry Kissinger met her at Claridges Hotel and pronounced her "quite a girl." In Parliament, she had her first run-in with Harold Wilson, who had just returned from a Kremlin meeting with General Secretary Leonid Brezhnev. Wilson was feeling pleased with himself and she wanted to prick his balloon as well as reemphasize her anti-Soviet credentials. Negotiating with the Soviets was fine as long as the contacts "never lull this house or this country into a false sense of security." Aiming an arrow straight at the chink in her new armor, Wilson's return volley dripped withering condescension. "Some of us are rather old hands at these matters," he said.

Gordon Reece thought it important for Thatcher to project warmth as well as competence. When she chopped six Heath men from her shadow cabinet soon after assuming her new position, he put her on a chatty disc jockey show instead of a serious news program. When a caller asked if she would be a good butcher if elected prime minister, her response implied that she would cut sympathetically, but would cut nonetheless. "I don't know whether I'm a good one," she replied. "I'm a reluctant one. I had a horrid day having to tell people my decisions when I could see disappointment written on their faces."

Her cabinet pruning was milder than the "Massacre" by the "Queen of the Tory Jungle" bannered in the pro-Labor *Daily Mirror*. A loyal Tory and a practical one, she kept a great many Heath supporters on. She knew the majority were loyal and would back the party until she gave them reason not to. She had reservations about some she kept, but need outweighed any immediate need for absolute fidelity.

Three Heath backers were awarded the most senior jobs. Sir Geoffrey Howe, a centrist and second ballot rival, became shadow chancellor of the exchequer. Ian Gilmour, another progressive, was named shadow home secretary, responsible for the police, immigration, and domestic order. The glamorous shadow foreign secretary job went to former Home Secretary Reginald Maudling, who disliked Thatcher but wanted the job. Whitelaw, her chief rival, became deputy leader. He promised loyalty and would prove it, but he thought his new boss was too radically right-wing and lacked sufficient compassion. Thatcher's small inner circle did not trust him a bit. "Airey and his friends were very suspicious of me," Whitelaw said. "They thought I was a Trojan horse. It took quite a while to discover that I wasn't, that I actually wanted her to succeed once she was leader. Some found that very difficult to believe."[3]

Loyal Thatcherites were also rewarded. She considered giving the shadow chancellorship to Keith Joseph but knew, even though she agreed with him, that it was politically risky to put such a radical in the top economic job. Other Tories confirmed her sense that putting Joseph in charge of the Treasury would be impolitic.

Sir Keith conceded later, though for the wrong reasons, that they were right. "I wasn't suitable," he said. "I don't have any flair."[4] Neither did Howe, who got the job, but he did have, as Britons appreciate, "a safe pair of hands."

Campaign manager Airey Neave took responsibility for policy in Northern Ireland and began putting together Thatcher's personal staff and reorganizing party headquarters at Smith Square near Parliament. There, in contrast to her measured changes in the shadow cabinet, Thatcher authorized wholesale firings with a vengeance. Out went the chairman, deputy, four vice-chairs, treasurer, and the head of research. The *Times*, no foe of Conservative prime ministers, called the carnage "the act of a downright fool." Much of the Tory establishment professed outrage, but not the public; no sooner had she finished firing people than a Gallup poll showed the Tories scampering out to a 4 percent lead over Labor, compared with a nearly 15 percent Labor lead the previous month.

The next task for the potential prime minister was to establish some international credibility, a prospect that made her nervous. Virtually everything foreign was virgin territory. She had scarcely been overseas. Until she married Denis, she had never been out of Britain. As an MP, she had spent five weeks touring the United States by train and bus on a visitors' program organized by the U.S. government, traveled to Leningrad, and attended a parliamentary conference in the Bahamas, but that was it. She had never served even in a junior position in the Foreign Office or in opposition.

Any number of political cohorts, many of them educated at private schools where language study was a requirement, could speak one or more European languages. Thatcher could not. Except for the few French words she picked up from records, she could not speak a word of another language. She had no particular interest in anything outside Britain, and even that was stretching it. Except for party conferences, she had scarcely left the south of England. For all practical purposes, she was as unfamiliar with Scotland and Northern Ireland as she was with Greece or Egypt. At heart, she was a Little Englander with an extremely narrow perspective. These gaps had to be filled in. During her first year, she made a dozen trips around Britain and several abroad, visiting France, West Germany, Luxembourg, Romania, Canada, and the United States. She was on the go so much that Harold Macmillan grumped that "she would do much better to stay at home in her garden."

The trip to the States was her most important venture. Women were hot news in the United States in the autumn of 1975; the Women's Liberation movement hit its peak in the United States that year. Instead of its traditional "Man of the Year," *Time* magazine devoted its special year-end issue to "Women of the Year." Bombarded in the land of Steinem and Friedan with questions about feminism, Thatcher made no effort to disguise her feelings.

In Chicago she was asked whether she owed at least part of her success to women's lib. "Some of us were making it long before women's lib was ever thought of," she snapped. Her sex was "something that never bothers or concerns me." She ducked behind her formidable armor. All the political leaders she had met so far, she told the audience, "just accepted me as a politician and got on with business." The women watching and listening were not going to let her off that easy. Did she prefer Mrs. or Ms.? "I am not sure I understand the significance of your question," she replied. "I am just Margaret Thatcher. You must take me as I am."[5]

She dropped any pretense of being nonpartisan, a guise most politicians adopt when traveling abroad. From bully pulpits in New York, Washington, and Chicago, she blasted Prime Minister Harold Wilson's policies. She told everyone who would listen that the Labor government in its "relentless pursuit of equality" was destroying democracy in Britain. Labor offered inequality by claiming that all should be treated the same. Thatcher's credo was closer to America's: if you work harder, you should do better. The state should not attempt to level off everyone. Consensus is for snivelers. James Callaghan, Wilson's foreign secretary, saw news reports of her visit and was irate. "When we are abroad, all of us submerge our individual party policies in the interests of the country we come from," he lectured her across the Atlantic. Nonsense, responded Maggie, as everyone called her in America. "It's not part of my job to be a propagandist for a socialist society."

She met President Gerald Ford in the Oval Office, saw Kissinger again, and talked with a number of congressmen. The trip had been marvelous. "I feel I have been accepted as a leader in the international sphere—the field in which they said I would never be accepted," she said on returning. Britons seemed to agree. New polls showed 48 percent of the country expected her to be the next prime minister, compared with only 31 percent for Wilson.

Around the world, many observers were starting to like what they saw in Thatcher, but she still had not convinced her own party.

A superb chance to rectify the situation came at the annual conference, held that year in Blackpool, a honky-tonk lower-class resort of rooming houses, game arcades, and fish-and-chip shops on the hard-scrabble West Coast. She arrived tense and anxious and became increasingly nervous as the week moved toward the nationally televised leader's speech at the final session.

Heath was there, which did not help her mood. After a hero's welcome when he reached the Victorian-era Winter Gardens Conference Center, he had no qualms about discussing the party's new leaders. Invited out by a group of journalists, Heath tore into Thatcher and Keith Joseph. They weren't Tories. They were fanatics who were going to destroy the party and country with their crazy right-wing views. As he had intended, his remarks were headlined the next morning. He put out an unconvincing denial. The result was to ratchet up the pressure on Thatcher.

By Friday she was exhausted, but refused to admit it. She had been running from caucus to fringe meeting to reception to her suite to work on her speech and had only slept a few hours since Tuesday. When Thatcher gets nervous, she gets frantic. That was happening now. She had been desperately unhappy with the initial versions of her speech. "It's not working," she complained repeatedly. "It's not right." She sent for Ronald Millar, a playwright who had written speeches for Heath.

Millar was new to Thatcher, as were almost all her top aides, but he was and would remain important. She had met him immediately after toppling Heath, when she suddenly had to deliver a long-scheduled party broadcast. Throughout her career, except at the education ministry, where she had speechwriters, Thatcher has written, in longhand, all her own material. She is not unique. In the United States, it is a rare congressman who writes his own speeches, but it is unheard of for an MP *not* to write his own remarks. As leader, though, she needed help, and with misgivings she agreed to let Millar try. Dashing off the radio speech in between scenes of a play he was rehearsing, Millar had trouble thinking of a conclusion for the five-minute text. He threw in a final quote, anonymous, but long attributed to Abraham Lincoln: "You cannot strengthen the weak by weakening the strong; you cannot help the poor by destroying the rich; you cannot help men permanently by doing for them what they could and should do for themselves."

He read her the speech aloud, a habit of his from the theater. When he finished, she said nothing and simply stared at him. Millar stared back, certain he had failed the audition. Then she reached down into her enormous handbag, extracting first a clutch purse and out of that a wallet. After an endless two minutes of her version of the Chinese box routine, she produced a tiny, yellowing piece of paper, got out of her chair, and walked over to Millar, who by then thought she had taken leave of her senses. On the tattered sheet was the same quote. "It goes wherever I go," she said, smiling at him. "Something went bing at the back of my head," said Millar later. "I knew that this woman's life and mine were somehow going to be intertwined."[6]

Millar and Thatcher worked side by side at the Blackpool conference. Millar stayed up all night writing. By late morning, the speech was strewn across the room. After a few hours sleep, Thatcher arrived in a new Tory blue outfit, hiked it up, and knelt on the floor next to him, urging him on. "I can't sit. My dress will crease and be ruined," she said, adding an urgent, "Go on, go on, go on."[7] She read a portion aloud and shook her head. "This is not me. I'm not an actress," she complained. "You have to be," he told her. "You are now a leading lady."

They scrambled to put the pages together. With a final pat of her hair, she left for the conference hall only to be stopped by a phone call. The meeting was running long. Could she wait a few more minutes. "No, no," she exploded in rage. "I'm not staying in this damned hotel room shaking with nerves another minute." The nerves stayed until she got to the floor and an elderly woman handed her a feather duster, symbol of her sweeping out the party. At the end of her introduction, Thatcher had an inspiration. She flicked the duster around the lectern and over the nose of party chairman Peter Thomas. The crowd burst into laughter. The tension broke. Thatcher relaxed and started to roll.[8]

She praised her predecessors, Churchill to Heath, who had left Blackpool so as not to hear her speak, and declared that her goal was "to overcome the country's economic and financial problems and to regain our confidence in Britain and ourselves." She explained why she had sounded so critical of Britain while she had been overseas. "It wasn't Britain I was criticizing. It was socialism. And I will go on because it is bad for Britain. Britain and socialism are not the same thing, and as long as I have health and strength, they never will be.

"Let me give you my vision," she continued. "A man's right to work as he will, to spend what he earns, to own property, to have the state as servant and not as master; these are the British inheritance." The crowd was on its feet, cheering as one. Later, when the hall was black and she was back in her suite sipping a whiskey, she turned to Airey Neave and said, "Now I am leader."

Initially, she was not a very confident leader. She had tremendous difficulty dealing with Harold Wilson on the floor of Parliament. A master at deflection, Wilson regularly dodged her head-on, top-speed, steamroller approach, frustrating Thatcher time and again. One day, called on to lead a debate, Thatcher balked. She was tired of being made the fool. If someone else led off, she would have a better feel for Wilson's strategy. Neave took her aside and explained the facts of life. "Margaret, when you're prime minister you will have to open debates quite often." She sighed, nodded, and led off.[9]

Wilson's hauteur in foreign policy debates, especially on Soviet matters, so galled Thatcher that she set out to get educated. By 1975, the United States was finally out of Vietnam and East–West relations dominated the news during her first year. The United States and Soviets launched a joint manned space shot, and heads of thirty-five nations gathered in Finland to sign the Helsinki accords, which marked the high point of detente, that short period of relaxed tension after Nixon and Brezhnev signed the SALT I nuclear arms treaty in Moscow in 1972. Despite the good feeling, a debate raged about detente, notably over whether the West had been gulled by the Soviets. In order to participate in it, she decided to learn all she could, starting with defense. Britain's experience in World War II had convinced her of the need for a strong defense, and she set out to deepen her knowledge. The research involved the kind of minute detail she loves—weaponry, plane and ship strength, troop and reserve levels; emigration policy and Soviet behavior toward dissidents.

She already had strong feelings about the Soviet Union stemming from her belief in freedom of the individual and her absolute commitment to the right to rise to the height of one's talents, neither fettered nor cosseted by the state. Socialism, particularly communism, was and is for her the very antithesis of that principle. When her research showed just how massively the Soviets had been building up their forces under Brezhnev, her visceral dislike moved up another level to specific concern.

Her first East–West speech, delivered just weeks before the signing of the Helsinki accords in 1975, when the detente buds were in fullest bloom, was the rhetorical equivalent of a sleet storm. "Detente sounds a fine word and to the extent that there has really been a relaxation in international tension, it is a fine thing," she told the Chelsea Conservative Association. "But the fact remains that throughout this decade of detente, the armed forces of the Soviet Union have increased, are increasing, and show no signs of diminishing." In January 1976, after more study, she returned to the attack, leaving no question about where she stood on Moscow. Wilson's Labor government, she said, "is dismantling our defense at a moment when the strategic threat to Britain and our allies from an expansionist power is graver than at any moment since the end of the last war." The Soviets were "ruled by a dictatorship of patient, far-seeing men who are rapidly making their country the foremost naval and military power in the world. They are not doing this solely for the sake of self-defense." The Russians, she declared, "are bent on world dominance." If the West did not wake up, then "we are destined, in their words, to end up on the scrap heap of history."

Wilson denounced the speech as emotional babbling. There was little other reaction in Britain and the remarks would have drifted off into the ether, ignored, but for one development. The Soviets went nuts. The Tass news agency labeled her "the Cold War warrior." Cartoons in *Krokodil*, the satirical newspaper, portrayed her as "the wicked witch of the West," astride a broomstick swooping over Parliament. But the best epithet of all came from *Krasnaya Zvezda, Red Star*, the Soviet army newspaper, which called Thatcher the "Iron Lady." Receiving this label was one of the best things that could have happened to her. Electorally, the "Iron Lady" tag would be a priceless winner. ("The Russians said I was an Iron Lady," she would tell audiences three years later during the 1979 campaign. "They were right. Britain needs an Iron Lady.") She boasted about her reputation at every opportunity, slamming the Soviets for "flagrantly violating" the spirit of Helsinki. Once in power, she promised, she would boost defense spending. So pleased was China with her bear bashing that Beijing immediately invited her to visit, which she did in 1977.

As she picked up steam on the foreign front, developments at home marked the beginning of the end for Harold Wilson. Unemployment had climbed to a postwar high, and public spending was out of control. Inflation hit 27 percent. Finally, just as Heath had done midway through his term, Wilson did a U-turn and announced huge spending cuts. The *Times* of London caught the crux in a headline: "So the Party's Over." But Wilson, who had just turned sixty, went further and announced his retirement, stunning his party. The wily, two-time prime minister would not be back for a third try, despite feeling, in his words, "fit as a flea." "Once I leave, I leave," he said, echoing Stanley Baldwin's 1937 words to his successor Neville Chamberlain. "I am not going to speak to the man on the bridge and I am not going to spit on the deck."

Three hours after his bombshell announcement, Wilson appeared in the Commons for question time. Facing him, Thatcher knew the occasion called for a good-natured tribute, but she found it difficult to display much affection for an opponent who had repeatedly bested her at the dispatch box. She tried, but not very hard. A partisan who considers debate in the House of Commons nothing short of war, Thatcher is a better leading lady than supporting player and is lousy at faking emotion. "In spite of our political battles, we wish you well personally in your retirement," she finally said perfunctorily. Wilson smiled and nodded.

The Tories were leading handily in polls at the time and almost certainly would have won an election if one had been held. There was, however, no requirement that an election be called. Wilson was stepping down voluntarily, and his Labor party, still holding a slim majority, would select a new party leader, who would become prime minister. Thatcher, frustrated, called for a new election, but got nowhere.

A week later, Foreign Minister James "Sunny Jim" Callaghan, the favorite, emerged from a six-man field to win the leadership and 10 Downing Street. More centrist and less tricky than Wilson, avuncular in public but often a hard-nosed bully behind the scenes, the sixty-four-year-old Callaghan had the perfect background for Labor voters. Son of a Royal Navy petty officer, he had quit school at fifteen to support his widowed mother. Entering politics through union elections, he eventually held all three "great offices of state": Chancellor, Home, and Foreign Office. By comparison with Thatcher, his experience was titanic.

In office, however, Callaghan never showed that his qualifications had taught him much. Despite his experience, his government was unimaginative. He failed to build on Wilson or address the deep-rooted economic plagues of high inflation, ever-escalating wage demands, or the weakening pound. But he could dodge and weave in Parliament. When Thatcher attacked, Callaghan countered with patronizing scorn. "Now, now little lady," he smugly goaded her across the dispatch box as she flushed. "You don't want to believe all those things you read in the newspapers about crisis and upheavals and the end of civilization as we know it. Dearie me, not at all." She was livid. Callaghan had found her hot button—withering condescension—and would keep pressing it. Naturally competitive, she was tempted to respond in kind, but knew the dangers. "As a woman leader, if I do that, the danger is it will become shrewish," she explained in a rare reference to her sex.[10] She hated to sit there and take it. Stewing was unbearably frustrating compared with the fun of regular parliamentary rough-housing.

When a currency crisis led to repeated runs on the pound and the trade gap continued to widen, the government was forced to take drastic measures. Chancellor Denis Healey canceled a trip to Asia to organize an emergency bailout from the International Monetary Fund (IMF), the kind of action usually reserved for Third World debtors. The standby IMF loan of $3.9 billion that resulted marked the limit of Britain's IMF borrowing rights and the fourth giant credit from abroad in less than a year. Only four months before, Britain had asked for and received $5.3 billion from international credit markets. Now the IMF was asking Callaghan's government to install tough austerity measures and trim the next budget by $3–$5 billion. The country was nearly bankrupt.

Labor was staggering, but Callaghan arranged a pact with the Liberals to shore up his government. Foiled again, Thatcher packed her bags and hit the road. China welcomed her with the kind of respect usually reserved for visiting heads of state, and in the United States, the new American president, Jimmy Carter, reversed his own rule and paid her special attention. In his methodical way, Carter had laid down a short-sighted rule that he would only meet visiting heads of government. Walter Mondale, his vice-president, would meet all opposition leaders. Two key Europeans—French Socialist leader François Mitterrand and Helmut Kohl, leader of Germany's Christian Democrats—had sought meetings with Carter and had been turned down. Both men, who would later lead their nations, canceled their trips.

Callaghan was Carter's best foreign friend. When the prime minister had a pinstripe suit made in which the stripes consisted of tiny "JCs," he sent material for another to the president. But Carter was a strong supporter of equal rights for women and was fascinated by the prospect of meeting the Tory leader. When Peter Jay, the British ambassador in Washington, who was Callaghan's son-in-law, lobbied Carter to meet the opposition leader, the president broke his own rule. He invited Thatcher to the Oval Office for thirty minutes and regretted it.

Jabbing her forefinger at the president, she lectured Carter on her dealings with trade unions and rejected out of hand his strongly held belief that morality should be an integral component of foreign policy. Nonsense, she sniped. "Foreign policy is simply a matter of national self-interest." Carter flushed. He said later that he found Thatcher "tough, highly opinionated, strong-willed, and cannot admit that she doesn't know something."[11] She did not think much of Carter either. She found him "mushy" and "wet," the boarding school term for soft. She understood now why Americans called Carter a wimp. She agreed with them.[12]

The U.S. trip gave her confidence a sharp boost. She loved the crowds, the enthusiasm of America, and the unrestrained applause. She felt her adrenaline racing. "The question is not whether we shall win," she told a crowd in New York, "but how large the majority will be." They roared at her feistiness, and Thatcher beamed in delight. The experience, coupled with her 1965 tour and 1975 trip, reaffirmed an innate admiration she had for Americans, if not for all their leaders, and the United States since her Oxford days.

She returned home on a personal high, but Callaghan was also looking better. The prime minister and Chancellor Healey had been forced to move to the fiscal right and had begun to cut borrowing. Wage restraints and oil revenues from the North Sea fields helped cut inflation from a 30 percent Latin American level to a more tolerable 13 percent, leading, after three nightmare years, to a fresh inflow of foreign capital. Thatcher was convinced that Callaghan was simply papering over deep economic problems. But she was too good a politician not to realize that crying wolf when the situation appeared to be improving would only hurt her. She needed a new issue.

In early 1978, she seized on an odd one—race, a sure-fire loser, a subject most politicians kept at arm's length. Until then, only right-wing maverick MP Enoch Powell and the white supremacist and fascistic National Front had dared stir up the fears of the nearly three million blacks, Indians, and Pakistanis among Britain's fifty-four million citizens. The country is proud of what it considers its instinctive racial tolerance. After all, Britain had run the empire for the most part benevolently and still presided over the multiracial Commonwealth. The kind of legalized racial discrimination that spawned the civil rights movement in the United States never existed in Britain.

However, deep pockets of racism did and do exist, not least in Parliament, which welcomed its first black MPs in 1987. The London police force has also been infamous for racial intolerance. The elite military guards units that protect the royal family remained segregated until 1988, when one young black soldier cracked the barrier at the express command of Prince Charles.

The end of empire had changed the racial makeup of Britain. Harold Macmillan vigorously promoted immigration to fill unskilled labor jobs, and Commonwealth immigration soared. Between 1959 and 1961, the influx leapfrogged almost sevenfold, from 21,000 to nearly 137,000. Soon after, the government passed legislation restricting entry to those with a British-born parent or grandparent; in other words, whites only.

In 1972, when Idi Amin expelled all resident Asians from Uganda, a Commonwealth country, Heath endorsed legislation that allowed Ugandans to enter regardless of parentage. By the mid-1970s, immigration was running at about 45,000 a year. Mosques were constructed in the shadow of cathedrals; curries replaced steak and kidney pies in some restaurants and pubs, while saris and turbans could be spotted in the most rural hinterlands.

Simultaneously, unemployment, budget cutbacks, and rising crime all focused attention on the immigrant community. Clashes escalated between whites and Asians. "Paki-bashing," the National Front called it. A Gallup poll showed 59 percent of the British public thought immigrants were "a very serious problem," and 49 percent urged the government to give immigrants money to leave.

When Thatcher spoke out in 1978, she was seizing on an issue of unquestioned appeal to blue collar workers who felt that their job security was threatened and to others who felt that their homogeneous culture was in danger of becoming diluted. She raised the race issue in a television interview after a weekend riot in Wolverhampton where 200 young blacks, provoked by a crowd of whites, retaliated by smashing shop windows and hurling bricks at police. Calling for "a clear end to immigration," Thatcher claimed that "people are really rather afraid that this country might be swamped by people of a different culture." Predicting that Britain's black and Asian population would double to 4 million by the end of the century (it stood at 3.1 million at the beginning of 1990), she said that people were frightened. "We are not in politics to ignore people's worries," she said. "We are in politics to deal with them."

Her remarks on Grenada Television's *World in Action* program set off an uproar. Labor parliamentarians called her racist. Home Secretary Merlyn Rees accused her of "making racial hatred respectable." Vilification came from all quarters. David Young, the bishop of Ripon, warned her, "You are playing a dangerous game . . . fostering emotions and feelings of prejudice, fear and hatred which can only be destructive to our society." Plenty of her own Conservatives agreed. Some felt Thatcher, if not racist herself, was dangerously right-wing and so desperate to be prime minister that she would stop at nothing. She stuck to her guns. Charges of racism were "absolute nonsense," she claimed. Not to discuss the immigration issue would have been "absolutely absurd" and irresponsible. She was riding a tiger but had a firm handhold. Within two weeks of the interview, the Tories spurted ahead eleven points in polls, from trailing Labor by two to leading by nine.

The most educational part of the fracas for Thatcher was watching her party run for cover when the heat rose. Too many, she discovered, had no guts to stand up for what had to be said and done. That they disagreed did not matter. They were "wet," or spineless, so she got tough with them, and the racial issue was only the tip of the iceberg. Ian Gilmour, her shadow home secretary, disagreed with her call for the reintroduction of the death penalty. Out he went, dispatched to the less prestigious defense ministry. Winston Churchill, grandson of the war leader, disagreed with her over continuing economic sanctions against Rhodesia. He was dumped in a flash. Honing her butcher's knife, she pulled back further from the shadow bureaucracy, drawing around her a tight, inner circle of advisers whose personal loyalty was unquestioned. The group, her first kitchen cabinet, included specialists from London's financial district and professional corporate managers and became part of her policy unit. Most were, like Thatcher, high achievers who had made it on their own without family ties, inherited wealth, or swish accents.

Urged on by their mistress, members of the inner circle loved cutting through bureaucratic red tape and delighted in scampering on end runs around her own shadow cabinet moderates. The inner circle prefiltered policy recommendations and tailored options to Thatcher's own preference before they ever came up for consideration by the larger leadership group. Internal opposition was largely quashed. It was difficult, if not impossible, for a "wet" hearing a Thatcher policy initiative for the first time to muster argument to block or modify it. The kitchen cabinet, composed of "drys," or true believers, had already anticipated potential arguments and prepared responses.

The inner circle structure offered efficiency, which Thatcher prizes, but at a price. It caused deep divisions between the ideologues and the traditional Tories. That did not bother Thatcher. She was willing to pay the price. She and her fellow drys were fine-tuning their strategy. They had decided that the best way to counter Callaghan's drift toward the political center was with a show of provocative extremism.

By early summer 1978, a general election seemed imminent. the five-year Labor mandate would not run out until October 1979, but Thatcher's personal approval had started to dip. Callaghan's advantage was his bland, reassuringly comfortable public style. Thatcher was rubbing nerves raw. She was too shrill and too rough; she lacked any softening humor. Even her hair, a sprayed semi-beehive that looked sculpted, was openly mocked as a symbol of her rigidity. Gordon Reece, anticipating an election, recommended that the Conservatives hire Britain's hottest advertising agency, Saatchi and Saatchi, to work more on the party's image and to get ready for a campaign. The company's managing director, Tim Bell, an ebullient and talented ad man with a natural instinct for high and low politics, took personal charge of the account, a watershed decision for Thatcher and the agency.

Thatcher knew almost nothing about advertising except that she needed it. She cautioned Bell, with whom she clicked immediately, about making her into someone she was not. "If you paint a picture that isn't true and I get elected, then I won't be able to do what I want because people will expect me to do something else," she told him. She had only one bit of specific advice, a lesson she had learned twenty-five years before in her first race in Dartford. Norman Dodds's posters had read "Dodds again for Dartford," but young Tories had amended them to read "Odds against Dodds again for Dartford." "Don't make posters that people can write on," she smiled with a streetfighter's glint in her eye.[13]

When Callaghan decided against the expected autumn 1978 election, he effectively put everything off until spring. Psychologically, winter is a bad time for an election in Britain, especially if it looks close. Incumbents, who get to pick the date, are judged more harshly in damp chill. The winter of 1978–79 proved to be a disaster for the government, as Britain plunged into one of its worst industrial upheavals, punctuated by a crescendo of strikes, layoffs, shortages, and closings. Truckers, railway workers, public service employees, ambulance drivers all struck in the biggest walk-out since the general strike of 1926.

Callaghan's anti-inflationary pay policy lay in tatters as unions demanded pay rises ranging from two to five times the government's 5 percent guideline. The pro-Labor *Daily Mirror* called the situation "out of control" and said "pickets have a stranglehold on our industrial life." Hospitals and schools closed. Gravediggers put down their picks and shovels. Corpses piled up in cold storages. Rubbish piled up in minimountains, blocking sidewalks, while rats scurried among the mounds. Thatcher hammered away in Parliament, but Callaghan had no solution and tried to wait out the storm. Not literally. Midwinter, he escaped the depression of what was being called "The Winter of Discontent" by flying to deliciously tropical Guadeloupe for an economic summit. He did not say it, but on his return the *Sun* newspaper headlined pointedly: "Crisis? What Crisis?" Callaghan turned testy. "We've had strikes before," he snapped. "We've come close to the brink before." His attitude rubbed many Britons wrong. Most had not been to the tropics. "The prime minister is a twit," said supermodel Twiggy.

His balancing act finally came to an end in March, when the Scottish Nationalists and the Liberals, who had been backing the government, withdrew their support. Thatcher introduced a vote of no confidence, which was preceded by a nasty crossfire that drew bad blood. "Never has our standing in the world been lower," she bellowed at Callaghan. "Britain is now a nation on the sidelines." When the motion came to a vote seven hours later, the Commons agreed there was no confidence in the government, but just barely. By a single vote, 311 to 310, Callaghan went down to defeat, the first time in fifty-five years that a government was fired for losing a vote of confidence. When the vote total was announced, the House

erupted tumultuously. Conservative MPs shouted, waved order papers, and rejoiced, but Thatcher, the picture of composure, showed
no emotion whatsoever. At home, she had a glass of champagne
with Denis. There, she admitted her excitement at the prospect of
battle. "A night like this comes once in a lifetime," she told him.
Before the champagne was finished, she called a meeting of the
shadow cabinet to plan strategy. "My troops are ready," she said.
"They've been ready for quite some time."

The next morning, as Callaghan drove to Buckingham Palace
to ask the Queen to dissolve Parliament, Thatcher indulged herself
by sleeping late, then having an unheard of breakfast in bed. Unlike
American presidential campaigns, British general elections are mer-
cifully brief, but intense. Usually, once an election is called, about
a week is spent tying up loose ends in Parliament. The campaign
itself lasts about four weeks, with election day always a Thursday.
If the incumbent loses, there is no prolonged transition. The moving
van pulls up and he's out of Downing Street the next day. The
challenger takes over immediately and the shadow cabinet members
move into their designated ministries. Continuity is provided by
civil servants who stay in place, and the government gets underway
without further interruption. Thatcher knew there would be no rest
until polling day, set for May 3, only five weeks away. Until then,
she would go full out because, though Heath had lost three of his
four elections, she knew the party would never give a woman loser
a second opportunity. "I'll only be given the chance to lose one,"
she said.[14]

Although political advertising is prohibited on television, a
restricted number of unpaid party broadcasts is allowed. Callaghan
kicked off the campaign with one of these television addresses. He
described Labor as the party of stability, whereas the Conservatives
stood for radical change. The description turned traditional party
identifications on their head, but Callaghan was correct. Labor
sought to maintain the status quo; Thatcher and her new breed of
radical Tories were the revolutionaries. She planned to open the
campaign the next day with her own TV speech. Shortly before
heading to the studio, she visited Finchley to speak with her constituents. While she was there, a call came in. A bomb had exploded
at the House of Commons. Smoke was pouring out of a car on the
ramp leading from the underground MPs' garage. Thatcher's first
thought was, "Please God, don't let it be Airey."

It was. The first MP assassinated on the grounds of Parliament since Prime Minister Spencer Perceval was murdered in 1812; Neave, sixty-three, was the shadow minister for Ulster and would have been secretary of state for Northern Ireland in Thatcher's government. The outlawed Irish Republican Army claimed responsibility for killing him with a bomb attached to the underside of his blue Vauxhall. His death was a tremendous shock to Thatcher. Neave was her mentor, her most trusted political adviser. He had made her party leader by orchestrating the victory over Heath. Without him, she would still be on the back benches, perhaps forever. More important, he was her best friend. Neave was no courtier, no putative lover, no ladies' man at all. He was a politician to the core, just like Thatcher, but he had harbored no ambitions of higher office for himself. She did not have to watch her back with Airey. He would do it for her. With him, she could stay up late, running over strategy, grinning at the latest bit of parliamentary gossip. Except for Denis, who was not interested in nitty-gritty political detail, there was no one else like that for her. And now he was dead, victim of the job that she had given him. Shattered and sobbing, she postponed her broadcast and raced to her leader's office in the House of Commons. She composed herself, went straight to her desk, and wrote a tribute. Twenty minutes later she called in speechwriter Millar, handed him the draft, and told him, "Make it better." He could not. She had struck the right tone. Carol called from Australia. Her mother described what happened, her horror and anger. "We must win now," she said. "We'll win for Airey."

She made the TV broadcast, marking out her top priority— tax cuts. But then she stopped campaigning for a week, until after Neave's funeral. When it was over, she arranged a job for his widow at party headquarters. The decision to hold off a week, in effect forsaking twenty-five percent of the campaign, was not purely emotional. Strategically, the Conservatives wanted Callaghan out front so they could attack his three years in office rather than be stuck defending some of Thatcher's more controversial policies. Tactically, Tory strategists, particularly Reece, had another concern. They worried that Thatcher's intense combativeness would grate on voters who saw and heard too much of her. Her lead in the polls ran from 6 percent to 21 percent, but they feared that if she were too provocative, she might slip quickly and perhaps irretrievably. Indeed, hope for a Thatcher stumble was a major ingredient in Labor's strategy. Largely ignored was the fact that she had actually been party leader longer than Callaghan and that despite his great ministerial experience, he was also running in his first national election.

Like boxers probing for an opening, both were uncertain about the best way to attack one another. Callaghan lashed out at her radicalism with its unknowable consequences, her anti-unionism, and her lack of experience in foreign affairs. But in the early days, he never mentioned Thatcher by name and cautioned aides not to vilify her for fear of backlash. Thatcher was also wary about mixing it up too personally. She was tempted to run a totally negative campaign, but did not want to open floodgates to a month of mud-slinging. She knew plenty of mud would be hurled at her with perhaps worse results. When Tim Bell showed her a poster portraying Callaghan as the captain of the Titanic selling tickets for the ship's next voyage, she vetoed it. A recommendation that she attack Callaghan for having two homes, an oddity among Labor's poorer working-class supporters, was immediately vetoed. "But dear, you don't understand," she said, showing her grasp of the electorate's feelings. "We want everybody to have two homes."[15]

In 1979, women made up more than half the electorate. A majority tended to vote Conservative, but it was working-class women who appreciated Thatcher's climb the most. Middle-class women found her pushy and difficult. She built on her working-class appeal by repeatedly popping into grocery stores for photo ops, buying Sunday roasts, packing them into a basket over her arm, and showing a housewife's familiarity with household prices. At one shopping mall she brandished a shopping bag crammed full of groceries in her right hand while the bag in her left hand was half empty. "The right hand holds what the pound would buy under the Tory government in 1974; the left, what it would buy under Labor today," she proclaimed. "If Labor has five more years, I would need only an envelope to carry the shopping."

The campaign was brief, but the grind exhausting. Out of the house and on the road by 7 A.M., she endured an unending series of buses, trains, planes, cars to rallies, walking tours, coffees, teas, and press conferences. She loved going to factories. She delighted in showing off her command of technical detail, all the more so in a male setting. She went to so many plants, in fact, that the *Spectator*, a sympathetic pro-Tory weekly magazine, chided her: "She has a genuine curiosity about the industrial process; it seems a pity she feels the need to satisfy it during a three-week campaign."

Most days, Denis was along beside her, sometimes frantically cutting up paragraphs of speeches, then gluing them in different order. He had more time now. The family business had been bought out in 1965, making him wealthy. He stayed on with the eventual new parent company, Burmah Oil, until 1975, when his wife became party leader and he retired to a variety of directorships—and to backing the Boss. At one farm, when Thatcher was awkwardly holding a calf for photographers, Denis notice her viselike grip on the unfortunate animal's neck. "If you're not bloody careful," he warned only half-jokingly, "you're going to have a dead calf on your hands."

She returned to Flood Street nightly, though sometimes not until 2 A.M. Food was usually left out, but at late mealtimes Thatcher pitched in to help, passing out plates, silverware, and fuss-budget style, making certain everyone had enough to eat. She rose every morning shortly after dawn. Meticulously, she packed for herself, folding each dress carefully in tissue paper. Most days, unless she was on television, she did her own makeup and hair. As the campaign wore on, to the amazement of audiences and her exhausted staff, she looked better and better. She rose earlier, stayed up later, walked faster, and talked more than anyone. Sometimes she was too tired and too excited to sleep. One night, when she'd been in bed only four hours, she said, "I couldn't get to sleep for ages, so I lay in bed and read Aristotle."

Only once did she lose her temper, in private, when party chairman Peter Thorneycroft suggested that to demonstrate party unity, she should share an appearance with Ted Heath. She exploded and stormed out of the room with such vehemence that her aides were left staring open-mouthed. Heath actually had worked hard for the Tories, if not for her, so hard that Denis Healey quipped, "It's the first time that the Ancient Mariner has ever gone to the aid of the Albatross."[16]

The election offered Britain's thirty-five million voters the broadest philosophical choice since Attlee challenged Churchill. Callaghan plumped for maintaining the welfare state, warning that a Tory victory meant more privileges for the rich and more hardship for the average family. "The welfare, prosperity, jobs, and the care of old people depend upon a Labor majority," he explained. He portrayed Thatcher's policies as divisive and threatening. Government jobs would be slashed and poor neighborhoods would become "deserts of unemployment." "The question to consider," he told voters repeatedly, "is whether we risk tearing everything up by the roots."

For her part, Thatcher made it clear that she was after nothing less than social revolution. "This election is about the future of Britain, a great country which seems to have lost its way," said the Tory manifesto, or party platform. Labor offered only "a clarion call for inertia and indolence." "Change is coming," she declared. "The slither and slide to the socialist state is going to be stopped, halted, turned back." She promised income tax cuts at every level, secret ballots in union elections to drive a wedge between members and their often more ideologically left-wing leaders, a curb on secondary picketing to prevent strikes spreading, across-the-board government spending cuts except on defense and police, replacing the nationalization of industry with privatization, and a pledge of non-interference in private industry wage negotiations. It was a free enterprise platform the likes of which had not been seen in Britain this century. "If you drain away all the resources from successful firms to help ailing firms, you will get far too few people creating wealth, far too many consuming it." The alternative to being a leader was to become "a footnote in the history books, a distant memory of an offshore island, lost in the mist of time like Camelot, remembered kindly for its noble past."

By the final week, the outcome was still in doubt. Thatcher looked and sounded like a winner. She barnstormed the country in a reconfigured bus followed by two others packed with dozens of journalists, swarms of photographers, and ten television crews, an idea borrowed from U.S. campaigns. Callaghan stuck with the old-style British method, moving about without fanfare in a leased executive jet. The press covering the Labor leader was left to their own travel devices. The predictable result: Thatcher got far more national attention. But polls still showed her early lead had shrunk dramatically. A Market and Opinion Research International (MORI) poll just days before the election said the Tories had a slender 3 percent lead. When a *Daily Mail* poll the final day put Labor out in front by 1 percent, her staff had to screw up their courage before they could break the news. First, lost in thought, she said nothing, then, "I don't think I believe that." She predicted she'd win with a majority of forty seats—comfortable, but not overwhelming. The stock market and pound, less certain, slid badly.

She spent polling day in Finchley. Thatcher had to win her

own seat if she was going to be prime minister. If she had lost Finchley, she would have been out completely even if the party won nationally. The Tories would have had to pick another leader. In early evening, she returned home to Flood Street to wait for the polls to close. Nervous, she tried to read but could not. Instead, she cleaned out her desk drawers, listening to the sound of workmen outside hammering together stands for scores of journalists beginning to clog the street.

At 10 P.M., the family returned to Finchley for the results. There, while officials counted the paper ballots by hand, she and Denis hunched over a television to listen to early returns. Once Finchley reported she had won handily, by just under 8,000 votes, Thatcher went back to London to party headquarters at Smith Square. By 1 A.M., BBC and ITN television were predicting a Conservative victory. There was, however, no significant exit polling, only a quarter of the constituencies had reported in and computer projections were still a new science, so Thatcher and Callaghan both kept quiet. Reece, smoking a huge cigar and sipping champagne, nodded at one middle-of-the-night projection that showed a Conservative majority of sixty seats.

At 4 A.M., Thatcher turned to Ronnie Millar. "If I win, have you thought of anything I might say at Downing Street?" He had. They went off alone to a quiet room. "Tell," she ordered. He pulled out a paper and, as usual, instead of handing it to her, read it aloud. The words were from St. Francis of Assisi. "Where there is discord may we bring harmony; where there is error may we bring truth; where there is doubt, may we bring faith, and where there is despair, may we bring hope." Thatcher looked at Millar. Her composure cracked. Her eyes filled with tears. "Yes," she nodded.

By 5 A.M., it was clear the Conservatives were on their way to a solid win. Callaghan had not conceded, though, so the family returned home. Flood Street was packed with well-wishers chanting, "We want Maggie" and singing the Tory campaign song, "Blue Is the Color, Maggie Is the Name." Too much noise and excitement precluded sleep. The Tories needed 318 seats to control outright the 635-seat House of Commons. By dawn, only 75 percent of the tally was in, and while it was clear she was going to get what she needed, Thatcher would not claim victory without the official word. After breakfasting on grapefruit and a boiled egg, she emerged from the house, accepted a stuffed rabbit from a child, waved to the crowd, and returned to party headquarters. There, a huge chocolate cake baked in the shape of the famous door to 10 Downing Street was wheeled in. The inscription: "Margaret Thatcher's success story."

Callaghan, in the meantime, returned to London from his Cardiff constituency and ordered his staff to remove his belongings from Downing Street. Not until that afternoon, at 2:45 P.M., did the Conservatives notch up seat 318. As soon as they did, Sunny Jim climbed into his black Daimler and drove to Buckingham Palace to submit his resignation to the Queen. Thirty minutes later, the monarch summoned Thatcher. There, as Denis waited in the anteroom, Thatcher mounted the red-carpeted staircase to the second floor for the traditional "kissing hands upon appointment." The ancient rite does not actually take place. Instead, the Queen asks whether the victor can form a government. Told yes, the Queen asked the new prime minister, her eighth in twenty-seven years on the throne, to do so. That said, the fifty-three-year-old monarch motioned the fifty-three-year-old grocer's daughter to sit down for tea and a chat that lasted forty-five minutes.

From the palace, Thatcher went straight to her new home at Number 10, less than a mile away at the other end of St. James's Park. A large crowd had gathered and, on seeing her, burst into "For She's a Jolly Good Fellow." Her family beaming beside her, Thatcher stood by the black door in the midst of a crush of reporters. "I just owe everything to my own father, I really do," she said. He had been dead nine years, but she felt as close to him then as ever. "He brought me up to believe all the things I do believe and they're just the values on which I fought the election. It's passionately interesting to me that the things which I learned in a small town, in a very modest home, are just the things that I believe won the election."

CHAPTER EIGHT

Downing Street Revolution

HER FIRST CHORES, even before moving into the upstairs apartment, were to pick a cabinet, ease misgivings about her inexperience, and allay fears that the government would lunge to the right, instantly and irrevocably. Thatcher knew there was reason to worry about a hard right swing. She had promised it. "I am not a consensus politician," she had proclaimed. "I am a conviction politician." Consensus is a code word in Britain; Thatcher was referring to the "consensus politics" of the postwar, which she hates, believing it shies from the tough decisions needed to reverse Britain's decline. Splitting the difference is not her style. Echoes of her philosophy resounded as she made her cabinet choices. "It must be a conviction government," she insisted. "As prime minister, I could not waste time having any internal arguments." So she spent her first weekend in Downing Street conducting interviews with prospects, writing thank you notes between meetings.

When she was through, the cabinet she announced offered some surprises. For all her talk about tough, like-minded ministerial colleagues, Thatcher played it safe. She picked no women. The only woman in her shadow cabinet, Sally Oppenheim, who oversaw environmental affairs, failed to make the cut. There was already one woman in the cabinet, Thatcher herself, and she did not need another. More important, she did not feel any of the eight women Tories in Parliament were qualified for a cabinet appointment. Almost all the jobs went to members of the shadow cabinet she had inherited. Overall, eighteen of the twenty-two posts were awarded to men who had served as ministers during the Heath government

153

of 1970–1974. Among the majority from the old paternalistic wing of the Conservative party was a scattering of new-direction economic pragmatists.

To keep the support of the Tory establishment and to emphasize continuity, Thatcher brought in two of the party's most senior statesmen: Lord Hailsham, seventy-one (the former Quintin Hogg, for whom she had campaigned at Oxford in 1945), as lord chancellor and Angus Maude, the sixty-six-year-old former deputy chairman of the Tory party, as paymaster general. Willie Whitelaw, who would become the spiritual successor to Airey Neave, was named home secretary.

There were reasons for appointing so many consensus moderates. She was a thoroughly untested prime minister. The men she picked all had their own parliamentary and grass-roots constituencies. Leaving them out would have caused unnecessary rancor and left them free to stymie her indefinitely. For this same reason she also brought in Peter Walker, a Heath protégé since 1965 who had managed the former prime minister's abortive effort to block Thatcher's challenge. Walker had nothing in common with Thatcher, but she knew he was bright, professional, and a top-notch communicator. He could also cause her major problems if left outside. So he joined as minister of agriculture. (And beyond all expectations was still in the cabinet more than a decade later.) She offered Heath the embassy in Washington, which would have gotten him out of town, but he recognized the offer for what it was and turned it down.

Francis Pym, another moderate, took over Defense. Lord Carrington, minister of defense under Heath and one of Britain's most skillful statesmen, took over the Foreign Office. So the Old Guard was in, though they were awarded the less controversial positions. None of those posts involved economics, where Thatcher's revolution was to be conducted. A new team, her men, would deal with inflation, government spending, taxation, and reducing the government's interference with private industry. Keith Joseph, the strongest advocate of free enterprise and minimal government intervention, was awarded the Department of Industry. The acolyte most committed to reducing govenment's involvement with industry would be in charge of promoting industry. Putting Joseph in the job, said political columnist Hugh Stephenson, "was the political equivalent of putting a monk in charge of a whorehouse."[1]

The top economics job, running the Treasury as chancellor of the exchequer, went to Geoffrey Howe, who had worked with Thatcher when she was education secretary and he was solicitor general. John Biffen, chief secretary to the Treasury, was responsible for implementing Thatcher's budget cuts. The number-three Treasury job went to Nigel Lawson, a hard-nosed financial journalist who was brilliant and arrogant. These were Maggie's front-line troops.

"Most of the cabinet did not keep Milton Friedman's works as their bedside reading," wrote Peter Riddell, political editor of the *Financial Times*. But Thatcher and her economic team did. They were monetarists, or as Keith Joseph refined the notion, believers in "monetary continence" who endorsed a tight grip on the money supply, fiscal targets, balanced budgets, and the pay-as-you-go approach to fiscal sobriety. But Friedman, the American economist whose popular book *Capitalism and Freedom* described how socialism destroyed enterprise and initiative, was not the original source of Thatcher's principal economic beliefs. Those came straight from Alf Roberts's grocery store.

Another important guru was Professor Friedrich von Hayek, the Austrian-born, British-naturalized economist whose 1944 book *The Road to Serfdom* she had read at Oxford. Hayek taught that government intervention in free markets could temporarily hold off inflation, recession, and unemployment but could not prevent or resolve them. Hayek's thinking ran counter to that of another Briton, John Maynard Keynes, perhaps the most influential economist of the twentieth century. Keynes's conviction that governments should spend to promote economic growth and maintain high employment, putting budgets into deficit if necessary, had found advocates around the world. In the United States, Franklin Roosevelt, John Kennedy, and Lyndon Johnson all embraced Keynes to justify deficit spending. Clement Attlee adopted Keynes's principles to rationalize the funding of Britain's welfare state.

Hayek was convinced that most of Keynes's intercessionary prescriptions only made things worse. A Nobel Prize winner in economics in 1974, Hayek's bottom line was that governmental fiddling, the accelerator and brake approach to fiscal management, inevitably led to disaster and, ultimately, totalitarianism. Citing the prewar German experience, he said that "the rise of Fascism and Nazism was not a reaction against the socialist trends of the preceding period, but a necessary outcome to those tendencies." The passage was heavily underlined in Thatcher's copy of *Serfdom*.

The official opening of the new Parliament came only twelve days after the election. The Queen, in ermine and the imperial state crown encrusted with rare jewels, read the speech prepared by the prime minister announcing Thatcher's legislative agenda for the upcoming session. After a pause during which she dug her glasses from her purse, the monarch began to read Thatcher's promises in an unemotional monotone that gave no hint of her own attitude toward the new prime minister and her revolutionary program:

- defense spending would increase;
- law and order would be given higher priority, with $100 million in police pay raises effective immediately;
- Britain would keep its own nuclear deterrent and also boost its contribution to NATO;
- a "full and constructive part" would be played in the Common Market, even as the government sought better membership terms;
- legislation to restrict striking picketers and limit closed shops would be introduced;
- public housing tenants would be encouraged to buy their homes from the government;
- state ownership would be reduced;
- private medical care would be encouraged;
- stiffer immigration controls would be introduced;
- the control of school systems would be taken over locally.

But the centerpiece of the package was tax reform. "By reducing the burden of direct taxation and restricting the claims of the public sector on the nation's resources," the Queen read, "my government will start to restore incentives, encourage efficiency, and create a climate in which commerce and industry can flourish."

By the time the Queen left the red-banqueted House of Lords chamber, her state carriage horses clip-cloping sedately up the Mall, the politicians were at each other's throats in the first debate of the Thatcher era. The Conservatives may have had a forty-three-seat majority, enough leeway to get any major legislation approved, but the Labor party opposition was not about to be intimidated.

"Whatever they wish to do, they will be able to get a majority," said James Callaghan, now the leader of the opposition. "The only question is whether they have the talent." Any suggestion that the Tory program could lead to more investment, productivity, and employment was, in his mind, a "delusion." Because Thatcher had predicted that her reforms would require ten years to take hold, Callaghan jibed, "We hear noises that utopia is going to have to be postponed for a day or two." Roy Hattersley, Labor's former prices minister, sniped, "All her policies turn out at the end to favor the haves at the expense of the have-nots." "You had your chance," Thatcher shot back. "Now it's our turn."

Within a month, she began putting her programs into place, beginning with Geoffrey Howe's first budget, the cornerstone of her new economic strategy. On June 12, in what for these occasions was a "brief" seventy-five-minute speech, Howe served up one of Britain's most radical budgets ever, aimed directly at rolling back socialism and chopping the handcuffs on free enterprise. Income taxes were cut by almost $12 billion. Tax rates for the highest incomes, those above $50,000, came down from 83 percent to 60 percent; the lowest tax rate dropped from 33 percent to 30 percent. The value-added tax, a sales tax, made up for some of the income tax cuts. It jumped from 8 percent and 12.5 percent to a single 15 percent rate, which was expected to push inflation, already at 17 percent, several points higher. The VAT increases added 10 cents to the price of a pint of bitter and $4,000 to the sticker of a Rolls-Royce Silver Shadow. Higher consumer taxes on cigarettes, alcohol, and gasoline were also introduced. Howe raised the prime lending rate from 12 percent to 14 percent, which strengthened the pound but made British exports more expensive and less competitive. He also announced plans to sell off $2.4 billion worth of government assets. Government spending on housing, education, energy, transport, foreign aid, and aid to cities would be slashed by $10 billion, while assistance to industry would be cut an additional $500 million. The purpose of the budget, said Howe, was "to restore incentives and make it worthwhile to work."[2]

Traditionally, chancellors get their drink of choice while presenting budgets, and Howe was sipping periodically from a stiff gin and tonic when the Commons began to erupt. "Treason!" some MPs shouted. Callaghan called the budget "unfair, unjust, inflationary, a reckless gamble." Denis Healey, the former chancellor whose policies necessitated the IMF bailout for Britain, labeled the program "a she-wolf's budget in sheep's clothing . . . a classic recipe for roaring inflation, soaring unemployment, and industrial anarchy." Trade unionists called it "a mean, diabolical budget" aimed directly at the working classes. "This will insure that the rich get richer and the poor poorer," said an infuriated Terry Duffy, head of the Engineering Workers' Union. Any hope that the unions might ease up on wage demands was gone out the window. They were enraged.

Thatcher and the cabinet knew the budget would be unpopular. "This is a severe package," conceded Biffen. "But the severity is made necessary by the situation we inherited."[3] The prime minister was worried herself that the sharp increase in VAT would increase inflation, but overall the package matched her promises and she was happy about that. She wanted no confusion about her intentions; she saw the budget as an icy shower. Shivering was inevitable, but the rescue of Britain was finally underway. As Geoffrey Howe said later, "We were signaling that the cavalry had arrived."[4]

The Tories' majority guaranteed passage of the budget unless the back bench revolted, which was not at all likely, no matter how provocative the legislation. Around the country, however, the program faced powerful resistance, and Thatcher was determined to ram it through fast. She succeeded, but the short-term price was high. The government's approval rating plunged to 41 percent, with only 33 percent supporting her handling of the economy. No postwar government had ever fallen so far so fast.

Thatcher was not disturbed, though she knew the eventual payoff would be a long time coming. Not all the Tories were as confident. Some other cabinet members, including some of the old guard, who harbored a great many private doubts about the approach, bit their tongues. "The government will not flinch from what must be done, even if the going is rough—and it could get rougher," said Carrington.

While she took the radical approach at home, continuity was the watchword in foreign affairs. During her first week in office, while wrestling with the budget, Thatcher welcomed two visiting heads of state without missing a beat. Irish Prime Minister (or taoiseach) Jack Lynch came by for a half-hour talk on Northern Ireland. She also saw Helmut Schmidt, who had offered to postpone his longstanding trip to England when the government changed. Not at all, said Thatcher, who insisted he stick to his original schedule. She had no intention of missing the chance to wine and dine the often waspish West German chancellor. She had high respect for Germany's booming economy and often cited it as a model of what she wanted to accomplish in Britain. She was also an admirer of Schmidt's powerful intellect.

Despite her admiration, she was not overwhelmed. She warned that Britain would be no "soft touch" in the European Community and also asked him to endorse her tough, anti-Soviet line on detente. "Detente is fine as long as it is a two-way street and as long as it actually happens," she said. "Detente should always be approached from a position of strength in defense." To the surprise of many, since his Social Democrats preferred a softer line on Moscow, Schmidt agreed. He had gotten along well with Callaghan, whom he called "My good friend Jim," but he seemed taken with the decisive and well-briefed Thatcher. He said she was "no soft touch" and predicted that they would get along fine.

The Schmidt meeting was a good warm-up for the two international summits on her calendar. Thatcher was particularly apprehensive about the first, in Strasbourg with the European Community. She wanted to make a good impression, but she did not intend to sit quietly like a good girl. She was determined to begin resolving Britain's perennial dispute about the amount of its contribution to the Common Market budget. In per capita income, Britain stood sixth in the ten-member Community, but because it had joined late and because of considerable anti-British sentiment on the continent, it was paying the most, almost 30 percent more than its rightful share. Thatcher found that intolerable. "The finance will simply not be there in future," she insisted.

In Strasbourg, her international team held its breath; no one knew whether she'd come out swinging or decide to feel out her fellow members first. She did not go for broke. Instead, she asked for a rate cut, but grounded her request with an impressive display of knowledge about European concerns. As always, Maggie had done her homework. She didn't get what she wanted; her whole request was deflected, but she turned the session into a personal triumph. She returned home with good reviews.

A week later, Thatcher went to Tokyo for her first economic summit with the seven Western powers—the major European countries, plus the United States, Canada, and Japan. She felt better about Tokyo than Strasbourg. Her debut had gone well, and Tokyo was scheduled to focus on ways of dealing with the oil energy crisis. Because North Sea oil was projected to make Britain energy independent by 1981, she already knew a great deal about the subject.

En route, there was one more boost to her morale, a refueling stop in Moscow.

Soviet Premier Alexei Kosygin came out on the tarmac at Vnukovo airport to greet her and then hosted a dinner in the VIP lounge with champagne and caviar. He was interested in her thoughts on the Tokyo summit, and they discussed Soviet energy, nuclear and hydroelectric power, and the world economy. Thatcher was the new kid but battled the crafty and experienced Kosygin on equal terms, trading statistic for statistic, giving away nothing and also holding back none of her grievances. She complained to the premier about Soviet aggression, the nation's military build-up, and its human rights abuses.

Kosygin was astonished. "He simply didn't believe what he saw," Foreign Secretary Carrington said. "He just stared at her, his eyes popping out on stalks."[5] When the two-hour parley was over, Kosygin nonetheless claimed he was delighted and began pressing Thatcher to make an official visit to the USSR. She was the Iron Lady and no friend, but with Beijing expressing interest in buying British Harrier jets, Moscow felt compelled to work on its relations with the newest occupant in Downing Street.

Hours later, Thatcher landed in Tokyo with an instant advantage over all her fellow heads of government. She was the only leader with an up-to-date reading on Soviet thinking. That did not impress Japan, which had no tradition of women in power, as much as Thatcher herself did. The press, fascinated by her new blonder hair, went wild. Pictures of the prime minister were plastered all over Tokyo; newspapers and magazines ran front-page and cover stories. She stood out, literally, from the male leaders. She was the junior politician attending, but because she was the only woman, she was placed out of protocol order and in the front middle of the traditional group photo. At the formal banquet, she shimmered in a stunning white gown, amid black tuxedos.[6] Thatcher always loved center stage, and this was her biggest stage so far. She felt she was right where she belonged.

Until this meeting, her fellow leaders had not known how intimidating she could be. But they learned. Her oil knowledge served her well. She knew all the details and was able to impress the other leaders and avoid getting stuck in the rancorous debates on quotas and pricing. She hit it off well again with Schmidt and even Valéry Giscard d'Estaing, the haughty French president, for whom she had done some advance planning. She had flown to Paris to meet him privately shortly after her election and complimented him on France's nuclear power program. Giscard's first impressions of her were good; later, he would come to despise her. Jimmy Carter was in Tokyo, too. He had not been happy being harangued by Thatcher when she had visited him in Washington as leader of the opposition, but at the summit the beleaguered president appreciated finding a pro-American spirit.

Internationally, Thatcher was off to a solid, but not error-free, start. Her first faux pas came in an unlikely place. On the way home from Tokyo she stopped off in Australia to see Carol and stumbled badly on a reporter's question about Rhodesia, Britain's trickiest foreign policy issue. Her response differed markedly from her government's position and set the diplomatic mandarins shaking.

The issue went back to 1965, when Ian Smith's white minority government unilaterally declared its independence from Britain. London slapped on economic sanctions as punishment. Nearly thirteen years later, just months before her election, a black majority government headed by Bishop Abel Muzorewa won a slender majority in elections and succeeded Smith. This prompted great pressure from the Conservative party's right wing, which favored recognizing Muzorewa and dropping the sanctions, which were burdening their white kith and kin in the rebel state. Thatcher agreed. She hates sanctions, not only because they are an impediment to free enterprise but because she does not think they work. She knew that their continued imposition in Rhodesia was hurting Britain economically.

But she knew nothing about Africa. Her opinions were based strictly on gut reaction and Denis's opinions. She had no interest in the nuances of various black nationalist factions battling one another. Thatcher believed that since Rhodesia had managed to hold an election and elect a black leader, it was time for Britain to recognize the country, renamed Zimbabwe, and resume business ties. She said in Australia that she doubted "very much" whether Parliament would renew the sanctions when they expired in the autumn.

Unfortunately, Muzorewa was an Uncle Tom whose election had been engineered by whites who continued to hold key positions in the new black government. The black majority's two preferred candidates, Robert Mugabe and Joshua Nkomo, pledged to continue the guerrilla war, which had already cost 20,000 lives. No black African states nor the United States, heavily involved in southern Africa during the Carter administration, would recognize Muzorewa or lift sanctions. Nor would the European Community. The Soviets backed Nkomo; the Chinese, Mugabe.

"It would have been absolutely disastrous to recognize the Muzorewa government," Lord Carrington, then foreign minister, said years later.[7] But that was Thatcher's intention. Ian Smith grinned. So did Muzorewa, who, on hearing of Thatcher's support, dug in his heels and stopped negotiating with the other black opposition. Months of hard bargaining had been swept off the table.

Two months later, July 30, 1979, Thatcher flew to her first Commonwealth conference in Lusaka, capital of Zambia, one of the front-line states, where her view on Zimbabwe was anathema. The main topic for the leaders of the forty-seven nations assembled was Zimbabwe and sanctions. Just before the meeting opened, leaders of the five black front-line states—Tanzania, Zambia, Botswana, Angola, and Mozambique—discussed presenting a united front against Thatcher's move toward Muzorewa. On the eve of her arrival, Zambian President Kenneth Kaunda denounced the British position. When Thatcher arrived the next day, the headline in the progovernment *Times of Zambia* read, "KK Lashes Thatcher."

She had been warned there might be a violent reaction to her coming. Riding down on the RAF jet, Carrington noticed her fiddling with a pair of sunglasses with oversize lenses. Because it was nighttime, the foreign secretary asked what they were for. "I am absolutely certain that when I land in Lusaka they are going to throw acid in my face," she explained.[8] Having acid thrown in her face was something Thatcher had long feared. She has never explained the origin of her concern, but for years she carried a vial of water in her purse to wash her eyes and face.

When the plane touched down, Thatcher peered from the window and saw a sea of black faces on the tarmac chanting and waving banners. The aircraft door opened and in rushed hot African air and the noise of the crowd. Thatcher stood up and strode down the aisle, leaving the glasses on her seat. "What about the glasses?" Carrington asked, hurrying to catch up. "I changed my mind. I'm damned if I'm going to let them see I'm afraid." She plunged into the melee.

The day the conference opened, oil-rich Nigeria announced it was nationalizing its British Petroleum holdings, a hint of what London could expect if it lifted sanctions. At a reception at the

British High Commission in Lusaka, an expatriate businessman encouraged her: "Don't be bullied, prime minister." "I am not bulliable," she responded. As it turned out, she was bullied, but from a different direction.

Her own advisers saved her, marshaling argument after argument to prove her wrong. Because of their advice, Thatcher turned an imminent debacle into a triumph. Switching her position, she called for a cease-fire, a new constitution, and new elections under British supervision. There was nothing short of astonishment at her new enthusiasm for bringing the Patriotic Front, the antigovernment guerrilla group, into the settlement.

What had happened? Carrington and others had fought hard and well, using her own tools, a blizzard of facts and details. And Thatcher had come around to believe that if Britain's goal was to stay off the losing side in a battle between the colonials and nationalists, then the Muzorewa–Smith government could not freeze out the Patriotic Front. She also agreed to commit British troops to monitor a cease-fire, a move no other British government had been willing to make out of fear of being dragged into an African war.

The initiative won widespread praise, even from the front-line states, where she had been denounced as a racist only days before. At the final ball, she and Kenneth Kaunda glided across the dance floor in each other's arms, smiling. The British compromise shifted the Rhodesia-Zimbabwe civil war from the battlefield to a conference table in London's Lancaster House, and eventually to elections that put Robert Mugabe in the premiership. The settlement, one of the highlights of the first term, had another significant effect: opinion about Thatcher's international skills was transformed. Black Africa was elated. Jimmy Carter was delighted that Thatcher had produced a diplomatic solution when more civil war deaths seemed the likelier outcome. U.S. admiration for Thatcher continued to grow as she resolutely sided with America on a string of issues, including the Soviet invasion of Afghanistan, the boycott of the Moscow Olympics, the Iran hostages, and Washington's call for more Allied defense spending.

At the same time, Britain's links with Europe deteriorated sharply. The Strasbourg meeting had gone well, but by the time of the second EEC summit, in Dublin, the other European leaders were gunning for Thatcher. Schmidt and Giscard, who both disliked Jimmy Carter and loathed his moralizing, thought Thatcher was getting too cozy with Washington. Her position on Allied defense increased the pressure on them to spend more. Just as de Gaulle had punished Macmillan for his Atlanticism, Thatcher was being criticized for putting too much emphasis on the trans-Atlantic "special relationship" at the expense of her European credentials.

The reasons behind Thatcher's admiration for Americans over Europeans are hardly complex. The United States, a true, loyal friend that supported Britain in World Wars I and II, has been a bulwark against communism and an indefatigable defender of the West. Almost as important is her identification with American values. Like Alf Roberts and his daughter, Americans get up early, work hard, reward merit, hate bureaucracy, prize individual freedom, and are marvelously creative. And they speak a language she understands.

All those feelings bubbled just beneath the surface in Dublin in November 1979. There was no more time to lose. "We shall judge what British interests are and we shall be resolute in defending them," she had vowed before the EEC gathering, and she defined those interests immediately. Thatcher refused to join the European Monetary System, to open British fishing areas to European fleets, or to sell North Sea oil below OPEC prices. As for Britain paying 20 percent of the EEC budget? That must be revised downward immediately.[9] "I must be absolutely clear about this. Britain cannot accept the present situation on the budget. It is demonstrably unjust. It is politically indefensible. I cannot play Sister Bountiful to the Community while my own electorate are being asked to forgo improvements in health, education, welfare, and the rest."

What she said was important, but of far more significance was the way she said it. She hollered. She shouted. She slammed her palm and ring repeatedly on the conference table. Unrelenting, she succeeded in uniting the European Community—against her. "All we are asking for is a great deal of our own money back," she insisted, banging the table for emphasis and startling the room. "I want my money."

"She certainly was adamant, persistent, and, may I say, repetitive," said Irish Prime Minister Jack Lynch. Thatcher's toughness brought comparisons with resolute male leaders, causing Giscard to remark later with a Gallic twist that he did not care for Thatcher "as a woman or as a man." At one point, while Thatcher was in full shriek, Helmut Schmidt pretended to fall asleep. Sitting up later, he told her that, if she wanted a real crisis, "you can have it here and now." He walked out in cold fury, and Dublin broke up in deadlock and bad temper. Critics, including Europhile Ted Heath, laced into Thatcher, accusing her of not knowing how to conduct government and of backing herself into an untenable negotiating position. She conceded that "patience is not one of my most obvious characteristics, but I am trying hard to learn it now."

No matter how it looked, Thatcher was not improvising. She had planned her strategy and had taken care to inform the Conservative party's Foreign Affairs Committee of her approach before she left for Dublin. She knew that Britain would not get what it wanted right away, but she was determined to get the ball rolling: there was a difference of more than $2 billion between what Britain paid the EEC and what it received in return. She would not accept the discrepancy. She would never give in.

The idea that even an enormous fight around the conference table can have a positive effect on negotiations is a central tenet of her approach. Why waste time tugging when blasting is quicker? "I'm tough because I believe in what I want to do," she says. "Negotiations are tough when someone else holds another view equally strongly, but you've got to find a way through. Sometimes I say there is *no way* I can get that through my Parliament, no way I can put that to my Parliament. Knowing I have to appear twice a week makes me much more aware of the political problems involved, but is also a great advantage over my colleagues in Europe."[10]

Thatcher has also repeatedly used this approach with Britain's trade unions. Throughout Europe, union membership was dropping during the 1970s, but not in Britain, where the proportion of unionized workers had grown from 44 percent to 53 percent. Some twelve million Britons, 22 percent of the population, were union members when she moved into Downing Street. Government and Parliament had become the victims of union power and ran the country largely according to the consent of unions, which, when disaffected, would periodically shut the nation down. Polls trying to identify the most powerful person in Britain repeatedly granted the distinction to Jack Jones, a one-time Liverpool dockworker who ran the giant Transport and General Workers' Union.

When Wilson defeated Heath in 1974, the Labor party, which had been in accord with the unions, grew disillusioned with its former allies. Barbara Castle, the talented and feisty Labor minister responsible for dealing with the unions, expressed her frustrations in her diary. "We have heaped goodies on them," she wrote in 1975, "but they have delivered nothing in return." The following year, Conservative MP Norman St John Stevas, later Thatcher's arts minister, wrote despairingly, "No government in Britain can hope to succeed today without the goodwill of the unions."

After the 1979 Winter of Discontent, even traditional Labor voters found Tory promises to crack down on unions increasingly appealing. Thatcher moved quickly to take advantage of the situation. She wanted to draw her line in the sand and to explain precisely where she stood. With inflation already looming at a terrifying 17 percent, she wanted to limit the unions' capacity to win major wage increases and hike inflation even higher. With that in mind, she instructed Employment Secretary James Prior to announce quickly the government's plan for trade union reform in July 1979. The major elements were a ban on secondary, or sympathy, picketing, which would keep strikes from spreading, an effort to break up the closed shop, and encouragement to use secret ballots in voting to limit both coercion and bloc voting.

The unions were again incensed. "A major challenge to the existing rights of workers and their unions," said Trades Union Congress TUC General Secretary Len Murray. But Thatcher was ready for a fight. "We have an absolute mandate for these proposals," she insisted during a heated House of Commons debate. "They are what the people want. . . . It is largely because of these proposals that we got more support than ever [in the May election] from members of trade unions."

In the meantime, the defeated Labor party, resigned to five years of opposition, had withdrawn into itself. Trailing the Tories at the ballot box by more than two million votes, the party had run out of intellectual steam; its prewar thinkers and sages had retired or died. By the late 1970s there were no Labor party leaders with both ideological zeal and intelligence. The trendline on socialism was down, particularly the state ownership aspect, and the pendulum was swinging again toward free enterprise. Proof was in the hundreds of thousands of trade unionists who voted for Thatcher in 1979.

When Callaghan lost to Thatcher, he was sixty-seven years old and exhausted, not least by efforts to deal with splits in his own party. Not an ideologue himself, mistrustful, in fact, of anyone driven by ideology, he was worried about Thatcher's radical conservatism, which he believed would divide the country. He knew he could not continue and did plan to step down, but first he wanted to whip the Labor party into more cohesive battle shape. The idea was nice, but unrealistic. It was not surprising that Callaghan never got the chance.

The Labor party was in a mess. Party membership had plunged, and at the local level, hard-left activists had taken over control of the party. Among the best known was Tony Benn, an aristocrat who had renounced a hereditary viscountcy, along with his full upper-class name, Anthony Wedgwood Benn. The Bennites opposed the centrist policies of moderates like Callaghan and his putative successor Healey almost as passionately as they did Thatcher's program. By the time the party gathered for its annual conference in October 1979, the battle lines had already been drawn. The fight itself was a bruiser.

Benn and the Left took the brawl straight to Callaghan, blaming him outright for Thatcher's victory. Speaker after speaker denounced the party for selling out, for replacing true, dyed-in-the-wool socialist doctrine with "watered-down Toryism." Callaghan, with some dignity, tried to defend himself. He was correct in his claim that the blame for the party's loss did not lie with the party's approach or policies as much as it did with the Winter of Discontent and the strikes. "Let's avoid party bashing among each other," he protested. "Let's have a bit of Tory bashing for a change." But nothing he said mattered much. Benn was calling for revolution, nothing less than the wholesale alteration of Britain's entire power structure. Dismantling "decaying capitalism" meant "taking on the business and banking communities," he avowed. The party even took a step in that direction, pledging to renationalize all the industries Thatcher was setting out to privatize.

Labor was about to miss a great opportunity to assail the government. After a year and a half in office, Thatcher was already in trouble at home and could have been an easy target for a united opposition. Recession loomed. Unemployment had more than doubled to rise above the psychologically painful two million mark. Inflation hit a high of 21 percent in July, while interest rates were up to 16 percent. Manufacturing, on the other hand, was down, and analysts were predicting that 7,000 firms would go under during the year. Finally, fine-tune control of the money supply, imperative if monetarism were to succeed, was totally awry—30 percent off target. Nothing was working.

"The government's entire economic strategy faces a crisis of credibility," said the *Times* of London. "The private sector, which she pledged to revitalize, is suffering while the public sector, her target for attack, is hardly affected." But instead of going after Thatcher, the Labor party trained its guns on its own members. At one point in the 1980 annual conference, fistfights between leftists and centrists broke out on live television. As the 1,250 delegates on the conference floor roared, Lena Jeger, the conference chairwoman, pounded her gavel until red-faced and shouted at the top of her voice, "This isn't a football match! We are making a spectacle of ourselves." On the sidelines, Callaghan was a spent force, powerless to halt the carnage.

Two weeks later, black and blue, Callaghan gave up the party leadership. He was the most popular political figure in Britain—leading Thatcher 47 percent to 38 percent—but he was yesterday's man in his own party. It was time for fresh vigor and new authority. The odds-on choice was Healey, who had served both as chancellor and minister of defense and was the party's most experienced man after Callaghan. But Healey, who was nonideological, was anathema to the Left and not all that easy for anyone else to deal with either. Tough and brilliant, he had made plenty of enemies along the way, bulling his way through endless party china shops.

When the leadership went to a vote, Healey was left in the dust as the party, surging left but bypassing the erratic Benn, elected Michael Foot. A sixty-seven-year-old militant socialist, Foot had been in Parliament since 1945 and had shown himself to be highly intelligent, decent, and a thoughtful debater. He was also a genuine, uncompromising radical who, for starters, opposed Britain's continued membership in the Common Market. He also wanted all nuclear missiles out of Britain and favored sending U.S. cruise missiles "back to Washington." Foot won on personality and ideology. A genial man of high integrity, he was personally popular with MPs of all political stripes in a way that Healey never could be. He had been the runner-up in 1976, when Callaghan succeeded Wilson. But his personal charm could not disguise an abysmal lack of administrative skills. Frail, with flowing white hair, thick glasses, and a rumpled tweed coat, Foot had the look of a benignly absent-minded professor from the boonies. For all his oratorical skills, he never inspired any confidence, a failing accentuated on his first day in office when he tripped in the House of Commons and broke his ankle.

Neither party was in good shape, so the political question was which was in the better position? Labor thought it had the upper hand because it had a new leader and because Thatcher was hobbled by a miserable economy. Right after his selection, polling showed Foot five points ahead of Thatcher as the preferred choice for prime minister. A Market and Opinion Research International poll found he had "rather extreme views," but was more "in touch with ordinary people" than the prime minister. Thatcher had been underrated before. She had lost no determination, but was she plugging ahead on the right course? Recession was biting deeper worldwide. Thatcher's economic policies showed no sign of taking hold and stopping the country's slide. The criticism mounted.

CHAPTER NINE

Early Doldrums

THE LABOR PARTY'S determination to commit political suicide by failing to resolve its intraparty differences and by choosing Michael Foot as leader could not have come at a better time for Maggie and her Tories. Having cut public spending and refused to bail out failing industries, Thatcher watched the unemployment figures edge upward. By February 1981, more than 2.4 million Britons were out of work, 10 percent of the job force—the worst since the Depression. When Thatcher wore a black suit one day to the House of Commons, she was asked by Labor MP William Hamilton, "Is my Right Honorable Friend dressed in black because of the unemployment figures?" The next day, in a light gray suit and white bow she stood her ground. Other governments had "cut and run" when the going got tough, but not this time. "I will not stagger from expedient to expedient," she said.[1]

Pressure mounted for Thatcher to reverse her policies, to increase taxation, and to boost public spending to cut the unemployment lines. Wilson, Heath, and Callaghan had all done it. At the two-year mark, when stresses caused by economic reform hit the system, each had executed a U-turn—which was one reason why Britain was in such difficulty. As Thatcher refused to budge, Ronald Millar wrote one of his best lines for her. "You turn if you want to. The lady's not for turning."[2] The phrase became her government's unofficial motto. The assaults in Parliament increased, but Thatcher turned scrappier. She relished the onslaught, explaining, "The adrenaline flows. They really come out fighting at me and I fight back," she said. "I stand there and think, 'Now, come on,

170

Maggie. You are wholly on your own. No one can help you.' And I love it.''[3]

Hanging tough made good headlines, but the Tories, MPs, cabinet members, and constituents were jittery. Bags of mail arrived in the constituency offices of Conservative MPs accusing her of being too rigid and unsympathetic. "Rubbish," she said when asked about her lack of compassion. "It's like a nurse looking after an ill patient. Which is the better nurse: the one who smothers the patient with sympathy and says, 'Never mind, dear. Just lie back. I'll look after you.'? Or the one who says, 'Now come on, shake out of it. I know you had an operation yesterday. It's time you put your feet to the ground and took a few steps.' Which do you think is the better nurse?"

Thatcher had no doubt about the right answer, but others wondered about her diagnosis and questioned her prescription. Protesters jammed streets chanting: "Maggie, Maggie, Maggie; Out! Out! Out!" and carrying anti-Conservative placards: "Save Jobs; Sack the Tories" and "She Must Go" and "Join Us in Fighting Her." Polls showed the Conservatives trailed Labor, with all its problems, by as much as 13 percent. Thatcher's personal approval rating slumped to 31 percent. Her own Tories began to whisper coup. Thatcher picked up the whispers but held firm. "I had no second thoughts. None," she recalled later. "I never had any doubts that our policies were right."[4]

The Labor party unwittingly threw her a lifeline. Shackled with two impossible positions—a pledge to withdraw from the EEC and to give up nuclear weapons unilaterally—Labor was split. When the party agreed to a proposal from its left wing to establish an electoral college dominated by militant unionists and radical activists, the right wing departed. The revolt had been brewing for a decade.

Three former Labor party cabinet members led the rebellion: Shirley Williams, a former education secretary, a Somerville graduate, and daughter of feminist writer Vera Brittain; David Owen, Callaghan's young, bright, but abrasive foreign secretary; and William Rodgers, Callaghan's transport minister. Former deputy party leader Roy Jenkins, back in England after four years in Brussels as president of the European Commission, joined them on the "Council for Social Democracy." Almost immediately they were dubbed "The Gang of Four," and just as quickly the vitriol from the Left burst forth. "You had better make your mind up," Michael Foot told Shirley Williams. "If you want to join another party, it is quite intolerable that you should sit here." Days later, Williams formally quit Labor, saying, "The party I loved and worked for over so many years no longer exists."

The rest followed, along with eight other moderate MPs. They formed the Social Democrats, the first significant new party in Britain since 1932, when Oswald Mosley had put together the British Union of Fascists. With 12 seats in the House of Commons, they immediately became Britain's third largest party, far behind the Conservatives with 337 seats and Labor with 255, but ahead of the Liberals, who held only 11 seats despite the fact that they had existed for more than a century and had produced Prime Ministers Gladstone and Asquith. Later, the Social Democratic party, or SDP, and the Liberals would band together in an attempt to claim the middle ground between the dominant parties.

Thatcher, who disdains centrism as the epitome of mushy compromise politics, had mixed feelings about the SDP. She agreed with Lord Hailsham that "in a confrontation with the politics of power, the soft center has always melted away."[5] She also had distinct feelings about the Gang of Four. She admires David Owen as an intelligent and articulate politician, respects his stand favoring a strong defense, and has occasionally wished he were a Conservative. She had no such feelings about Shirley Williams, whom she considered wishy-washy, a disorganized will-o'-the-wisp who skittered from issue to issue. She was equally contemptuous of Roy Jenkins, whom she considered a pompous, snotty intellectual who patronized her. Publicly, Thatcher dismissed the SDP as a variation of socialism, "wet" and rootless; privately, there was some fear that moderate Tories, the Conservatives' own "wets," would break off and join the SDP. Party chairman Lord Thorneycroft sent out a letter urging all Tories to stick with the party.

There was also a bright side. As the SDP soon merged with the Liberals, it meant the opposition was split. If a voter wearied of the Tories, he would not necessarily switch to Labor, the main opposition party. That could and would be a real advantage for the Tories in upcoming elections. On the darker side, the new centrists hurt Thatcher in the short term by magnifying her inflexibility. The SDP believed in a strong defense and opposed unilateral nuclear disarmament, but the new party's leadership also felt the government had become too stringent in its cutbacks.

Only days after the creation of the Social Democrats, Thatcher delivered her second budget. Her critics were disappointed when she pressed ahead with the revolution; those who had objected to her first, stringent budget were horrified. Heavy new excise taxes were slapped on. The price of cigarettes went up 31 cents to $1.93 a pack. Gasoline increased 44 cents per imperial gallon, while the price of scotch, the prime minister's favorite drink, leaped almost $2 a bottle. The prime rate dropped from 14 percent back down to 12 percent, but otherwise there was no good news for business. New taxes were levied on oil companies and banks. Even Howe, Thatcher's co-architect on the budget, was apologetic. "I share the disappointment everyone will feel, but I am determined to sustain firm action in the battle against inflation. To change course now would be fatal." There was no apology from Thatcher. Her goal went beyond the budget. "Economics are the method," she said. "The object is to change the soul."[6]

The opposition went wild. "A catastrophe of the first order for the British people," said Michael Foot. Some Conservatives agreed with him. Something was bound to crack. When it did, the sound was of flying Molotov cocktails, truncheons on skulls, the sirens of police, and fire trucks. There was a riot.

On a warm, April Saturday afternoon, the type when streets are filled with people tired of gray, drizzly skies of a long winter and late spring, two bobbies stopped to question a black youth in Brixton, a grimy, racially mixed neighborhood in south London where unemployment among young blacks approached 70 percent. A crowd gathered, and soon rocks, bricks, and gasoline bombs were flying. The battle raged for three days and nights between some 600 blacks, mostly West Indians, and up to 1,000 police. It ended with the arrest of 224 rioters. Some 165 police were injured; 120 buildings damaged, 9 destroyed. It had been the worst race riot in Britain's history, but Brixton residents insisted that it had little to do with race. "We are not here to hurt white people," said one. "This is about jobs and money. You can only take so much."

Brixton turned out to be a tease, a hint of more, and worse, to come. Three months later, unrest began to spread from city to city like flame on a powder trail. A wild surge of rioting, looting, and burning broke out in Liverpool, Manchester, Birmingham, and Newcastle-Upon-Tyne, as well as a dozen neighborhoods in London. "I was in Liverpool during World War II," said Liverpudlian Bill Dawson. "This seemed just the same. Buildings turned into rubble; shopkeepers sitting on their steps crying."

Thatcher appealed for an end to the violence but remained convinced that stimulating the economy would only delay better days. "Do you think we could have rejected the easy way if it had a chance of working?" she asked. "Reflation will lead to even higher unemployment and higher prices." Her obstinacy ensured a rough ride in Parliament. "You stupid woman! You stupid woman!" the beefy socialist Eric Heffer, a left-wing Liverpool MP, shouted at her during one stormy debate. Ted Heath blamed the government's economic and social policies for contributing to, if not causing, the rage. He asked how many millions more had to be unemployed before Thatcher could wring out inflation. "The impact of this [economic policy] on the social system is disastrous."

All this brought out the steel in Thatcher. Her cabinet would not attempt to address the social and economic problems behind the riots until the violence subsided, she told Parliament. Taking a sharp law and order approach, she announced that the government was preparing a new "riot act" whereby police could arrest anyone in a declared riot zone. She also declared her support for the Liverpool police's decision to tear-gas crowds. Liverpool marked the first time the gas had been used in England in a civil disorder. Thatcher was not reluctant to step up the police response even more. If water cannon and plastic or rubber bullets were needed as last resorts, she was ready. The police would get what they needed and the freedom to use it.

Her reaction to the riots was Thatcher at her worst. There was genuine despair in Britain's poor and black ghettos. The situation demanded at least an expression of understanding. There were legitimate complaints against white police brutality in black neighborhoods, particularly in London, where the Met, as the police force is known, has long had a poor reputation on racial issues. In 1981, in fact, only 286 blacks and Asians belonged to Britain's 117,000-member police force. On her various appearances and a television speech in the midst of the riots, Thatcher never mentioned the Met's racism or the bite her policies had taken out of social welfare programs. She refused to acknowledge the complexity of the issue.

Race relations are frequently blind spots for right-wing politicians, and Thatcher is no exception. She is not a racist, her 1979 immigration speech and initial Zimbabwe settlement reaction notwithstanding. She is, however, naive about race, as are countless Little Englanders from provincial towns with no ethnic minorities to speak of. Thatcher has had almost no personal contact with blacks or Asians, except for her experience with Commonwealth leaders and officials, and she has no blacks or Asians on her staff. She does admire the entrepreneurial spirit of Indian and Asian immigrants who have replaced the Alf Robertses in the nation of shopkeepers. They are meritocrats.

During the 1981 riots, Thatcher took on her national nanny role, dealing with the rioters as if they were children who had been misbehaving. This is typical Thatcher behavior. When her charges behave, Thatcher is kind, helpful, and bears no malice. But when they break the law, which is sacrosanct to her, she will crash down on the offending party with all the weight she can muster. In this case, as she saw it, the rioters had broken the rules. Period. They had to be brought into line and to demonstrate responsibility before she would consider their concerns.

When the violence escalated, she was rightly taken to task for tactlessness. "She was unable to strike the right note when a broad sense of social understanding was required," the *Times* editorialized. "The Prime Minister curiously made no serious attempt to speak to the younger generation, white or black, who make up the vast majority of the rioters." The more liberal *Guardian* newspaper warned her against "meeting violence with violence." The prime minister should recognize, the newspaper said, that "these things are the direct result of economic and interwoven social policies which pile strain on the weakest part of society." Her reaction had been more than tenacious. She had crossed into rigidity. The murmurs of dissent among her fellow Conservatives were developing into a torrent of opposition.

"The British people will not be prepared for very much longer to tolerate the worst effects of the recession if there is not a clear sign that the sacrifice will have been worthwhile," declared Defense Secretary Francis Pym. He asked the prime minister to improve job-training programs and work on reviving decrepit inner cities. Lord Thorneycroft, the party chairman, dismissed the government's assertions that the recession was over by publicly exclaiming, "There are no great signs of the economy picking up." As for the prime minister's monetarism, he argued that the government's program should not be based on "some doctrinaire economic policy." Pym and Thorneycroft were not alone. Moderates lined up in cabinet to challenge Thatcher.

Three things worried them: the continuing dismal performance of the economy; the emergence of the Social Democrats as a political threat; and the prime minister's own unwillingness to compromise and help out business by reflating. She had reluctantly agreed to provide an additional $1.3 billion for job training, but now the moderates in the party were pushing for another $1 billion to rev up the economy. A month later, they got their response.

Thatcher fired or moved all but Pym. She had said she had no time for internal argument, and she meant it. She was convinced she needed a more staunch and dependable inner circle. "Maggie's Monday Massacre" was how the pro-Tory *Sun* headlined the purge. Forty posts were affected by the shake-up. Out went Christopher Soames, Churchill's son-in-law and a legitimate Tory grandee who, Thatcher thought, was too easy on striking civil servants. Deputy Foreign Secretary Ian Gilmour, a haughty aristocrat who could not stand Thatcher and disagreed with monetarism, was given the boot, and so was Thorneycroft, an Etonian with a traditional Tory fondness for a more paternalistic party. James Prior, the employment secretary, who thought Thatcher's anti-union legislation was too harsh and should have been introduced with greater care over time, was exiled to Northern Ireland. He had been praised by Labor leader Michael Foot as "a good man who fell among monetarists."

The replacements were Maggie's men, strict loyalists, self-made men who matched her own style and image. Cecil Parkinson, a successful businessman who was the son of a railwayman, took over from Thorneycroft as head of the party. Norman Tebbit, a former airline pilot, a rigid right-winger and anti-unionist, whom Foot once described as "a semi-house-trained polecat," was named employment secretary, a signal there would be no let-up on industrial policy. Education Secretary Mark Carlisle was replaced by Keith Joseph. When more hard-liners were introduced the next day to take over the second tier of government, the Social Democrats' Shirley Williams remarked, "She has replaced the Cabinet with an echo chamber."

That was not just the view outside the party. Heath tore into the prime minister once again. "We have reached the most critical point in the Conservative party in the last sixty to seventy years," he said. Allowing unemployment to rise to three million was, in his words, "morally unjustified." Other senior figures who lacked Heath's personal bitterness also professed serious qualms about Thatcher's leadership.

By annual conference time in the fall of 1981, her approval

rating was almost through the floor, down to a humiliating 28 percent and headed toward the teens. Fewer than half the party, only 44 percent, wanted her to stay on as leader. Only 35 percent believed she could win the next election, which had to be held no later than May 1984. These were ratings lower than Chamberlain's during the appeasement crisis. In the history of modern polling, no prime minister had garnered such a low rating.

In spite of all the gloom and unrest, there were signs that something was beginning to happen. Howe saw some indicators, but in the mood of the moment was dismissed by all but the most die-hard Thatcherites as a Pollyanna. Still, union negotiations were being settled for half of what they had been; days lost to strikes were approaching a forty-year low; productivity was up almost 6 percent. Could it be that the wringing out of the economy and national psyche was working and that Thatcher's policies were starting to take hold? Or were the critics, inside and outside the party, correct? Thatcher sensed it was real, that the tide was starting to turn. But hardly anyone noticed the buds peeping up at first. It would take a dramatic confrontation on a tiny, sheep-filled archipelago 8,500 miles away to lift Thatcher out of the doldrums.

CHAPTER TEN

War in a Faraway Place

ON MARCH 19, 1982, forty Argentinians landed on South Georgia Island, part of what Britain calls the Falklands group, a treeless, gale-lashed archipelago off the coast of Argentina. Populated by 1,800 residents called "kelpers"—after the seaweed which clogs the frigid ocean—nearly 750,000 sheep and several million penguins, the islands have been British territory since 1833. Figuratively and literally, they are the last outpost of empire. Upon landing, the Argentinians identified themselves as scrap dealers and said they were there to dismantle an abandoned whaling station. In fact, they were soldiers in civilian clothes sent to gain control of the island. They sang the national anthem and hoisted the blue and white flag of Argentina, which has long claimed the islands they call the Malvinas. When London asked Buenos Aires to have the workers apply for permission to stay or to remove them, Argentina refused and got ready for battle.

The Argentine government was looking for a fight. In office only four months, President General Leopoldo Fortunato Galtieri had told his fellow junta members that he wanted to regain control of the islands before January 3, 1983, the 150th anniversary of their occupation by Britain. Galtieri proclaimed the issue a matter of honor, but it was, more accurately, an attempt to salvage his already tottering presidency. When the "scrap dealers" arrived on South Georgia, Argentina's inflation rate was 130 percent, the world's highest, and its unemployment rate the worst since World War II. As the flag went up on South Georgia, 6,000 Argentinians, already angry with the regime's violations of human rights and countless

"disappeared" citizens, were in the streets of Buenos Aires pro-
testing a spartan new economic program. Police arrested 2,000 of
them. Two weeks later, on the morning of April 2, a 2,500-man
Argentinian invasion force stormed the tiny settlement of Port Stanley, the Falklands' capital. Thousands of exuberant Argentinians
flocked to the presidential palace to applaud Galtieri.

At the time of the first reports of the invasions, 60 percent of
Britons thought the Falklands were off the west coast of Scotland.
The affair seemed a joke. When Sir Anthony Parsons, Britain's
ambassador to the United Nations, tried on April 1, the eve of the
invasion, to convince the Security Council to consider the impend-
ing attack, the members thought he was kidding. "One or two
literally thought I was playing an April Fool joke and that I wasn't
serious," Parsons said.[1] Much of the world smirked at the prospect
of a Gilbert and Sullivan battle over a sheep pasture with penguins.
Peter Sellers would have starred in the movie version, perhaps
playing both leads, a dyspeptic John Bull and a gaudy Ruritanian
dictator.[2] But before long, soldiers and sailors were dying; planes
were shot out of the sky; ships were sunk. It wasn't funny anymore.
Ten weeks later, nearly 1,000 people were dead and Margaret
Thatcher's stature had been redefined.

If Argentina had not invaded, Britain might have given the
islands back without a shot being fired. Buenos Aires had been
pressuring London about the islands for years. Shortly after taking
office, Thatcher sent Nicholas Ridley, a junior minister, to Argentina to discuss the situation. He returned with several options,
including beefing up British defense at great cost; more stalling; or
granting sovereignty to Argentina with a lease-back arrangement.
Under the last, Britain would continue to administer the islands on
behalf of the fiercely nationalistic kelpers, who are British down to
their pubs, pints of bitter, and West Country accents. Ridley and
his boss, Foreign Secretary Carrington, favored the lease-back, but
Thatcher was affronted at the suggestion that Britain might cede
sovereignty anywhere. Give up part of the national heritage? Not
on her watch.

In the fortnight between the scrap dealers' arrival and the full-
scale invasion, it was clear that serious trouble was brewing. Cables
volleyed between London and Buenos Aires, and Thatcher dispatched a nuclear submarine to the area. When intercepted Argentinian cables indicated that invasion was imminent, Thatcher
summoned the head of the navy, Sir Henry Leach, and asked,

"What can you do for us, First Sea Lord?" "I can have a full-scale task force ready within three days," he said. That was what she wanted to hear. Until then, she had only heard doubts from her army and air force chiefs. "Marvelous," she replied. "Prepare the task force."³

In the meantime, Thatcher agreed to ask the United States to try to intervene with the Argentinian junta. Thatcher told President Reagan that Britain would not escalate matters further on its own, a moot promise. Argentina's task force would reach the islands within twenty-four hours; Britain could do nothing about that. Reagan called Galtieri and was told the general was "unavailable." Two hours later, he came to the phone and the two leaders spoke through interpreters for fifty minutes. They got nowhere. Galtieri spent most of the time explaining the history of the dispute, which bored Reagan. The president offered to send an envoy of Galtieri's choice to mediate, anyone up to and including Vice President George Bush. The Argentinian leader did not respond. "Do you intend to use force?" Reagan asked. Galtieri said he felt free to use any resources available unless Britain recognized Argentinian sovereignty over the islands that day.⁴

Reagan said that Thatcher would certainly fight if an invasion took place. "I must have your assurance that there will be no landing tomorrow," Reagan pressed. Galtieri said nothing and Reagan hung up. "I spelled it out, but it didn't sound as if the message got through," the president told Secretary of State Alexander Haig. Haig passed details of the call and Reagan's gloomy assessment to British Ambassador Sir Nicholas Henderson, who was hosting the vice president for dinner. Bush had arrived saying that he might have to leave in a hurry for Argentina. When Henderson got off the phone with Haig, he told Bush, "You don't have to go to Buenos Aires. Galtieri won't talk to you."⁵

Defending the Falklands from 8,500 miles away presented an enormous military problem for London. There was, however, no question that Britain would retaliate if Argentina did invade. Allowing the junta to take over the islands without a fight would have shown Britain to be impotent. The government would have toppled. Liberal party leader David Steel pointed out that "after unsuccessful foreign ventures, prime ministers have been replaced." Enoch Powell predicted that "in the next week or so we will learn what metal the Iron Lady is made of." The Lady could read the cards as well as anyone. If she failed to act, she told her senior ministers, "my government will fall." They concurred. "We all recognized the mood of the country. We had to send the task force," Whitelaw said later. "We would not have survived the weekend as a government if we had not sent the task force."[6]

Britain's success was far from certain. The first problem was getting there and setting up a supply and communications line a third of a world away. The closest British base was Ascension Island, 4,000 miles north of the Falklands. It did not even have a harbor for ship repair. The elements would also be against Britain. The full force of the Southern Hemisphere winter, with ice and dangerous seas, would hit a blockading British fleet by late June.

Argentina's military supply line to the Falklands was only 600 miles long, and it had a well-trained air force. The quality of the army and navy was less certain, but if they were able to dig in, they would be difficult to pry out. Britain's forces had scarcely been well tested in recent years. Their last finest hour had been in World War II. Even then, for all their courage and scarlet braid, Britain had suffered horribly.

Thatcher did not waver. She was clear on the politics, but she did not gear up for battle only to keep her office. There was, yet again, a first principle at stake: the islands belonged to Britain, and Galtieri was attempting to seize them illegally. The challenge was not over a bunch of sheep pastures. It was another test of the West and of moral fiber.

Cecil Parkinson, who kept Parliament informed of the war cabinet's decisions, sensed that the heads of the military services were initially uncertain about going to war under a woman's leadership. "That evaporated very quickly," he said. "They realized she was very, very staunch."[7] The military chiefs, who regularly knelt on the floor with her in her office, poring over maps, later confirmed that. Of the entire cabinet, Thatcher was easily the most resolute. She reviewed the options with the chiefs and decided on the first punitive measures, cutting export credits and imports and freezing some $1.4 billion worth of Argentinian assets in Britain.

She also decided to hold the first Saturday session of the Commons in the twenty-six years since the Suez crisis. It was an emotional occasion. Thatcher was apprehensive. Her political situation was tenuous, the economy was a mess, her approval ratings were dreadful, and she had no residual good will to draw upon. A misstep could knock her out of office fast. She was fortunate in having several World War II veterans in her inner circle.

Thatcher put on her most determined public face, but her concern was visible. Standing at the dispatch box, she had no doubt about her decision to send a task force. "It is the government's intention to see that the islands are freed from occupation and are returned to British administration at the earliest possible moment," she told a bellicose Parliament. The islanders "are few in number, but they have the right to live in peace, to choose their own way of life, and to determine their own allegiance."

The Labor party was scathing; the government, Labor said, had been humiliated by a "tin pot dictator" and a "two-bit Mussolini." Thatcher was accused of having misjudged Argentinian intentions, failing to maintain an "over the horizon naval presence," and being unable to forestall adventurism in Buenos Aires. Criticism was not restricted to the opposition. Her own Conservatives, frustrated by the loss of Rhodesia and sensing Britain's international decline, also gave the prime minister a rough ride. Edward du Cann, a senior Tory who had been involved in the challenge to Heath, called the invasion "a humiliating day for Britain." Other Tory back-benchers bayed for blood and vengeance. They demanded the scalp of foreign minister Lord Carrington for failing to anticipate the crisis. Carrington agreed. The criticism did not bother him, but he knew it might distract the government from the campaign at hand. The right wing was after him for Rhodesia and also for the Middle East, where they thought he was anti-Israel. He knew a scapegoat was needed, and he was the obvious candidate.[8]

Thatcher's choice of Francis Pym to succeed him reflected her problems in the party. Fired the previous year from the defense ministry for opposing Thatcher's spending cuts, Pym was widely considered Thatcher's most serious rival for the leadership. Now he was back, in the most prestigious cabinet post, the one he had always wanted.

Meanwhile, in the Falklands, a tiny band of British marines who were garrisoned on the islands fought the invaders until Rex Hunt, the British governor, commanded them to lay down their arms. Hunt then left the islands, refusing to shake hands with the Argentinian general commanding the invasion. He called Hunt's snub "very ungentlemanly."

Argentina dug in. C-130s flew back and forth between mainland bases and the Port Stanley airstrip delivering food, ammunition, trucks, and more soldiers. Galtieri ordered 80,000 recently released draftees back into uniform. Eventually, 10,000 Argentinian troops would see duty on the islands. Overall, Buenos Aires could call on a seventeen-ship navy, a 130,000-man standing army, and a 20,000-strong air force. Additionally, nearly 450,000 reservists were available for call up.

One British flotilla that had been exercising off Gibraltar was en route, though there was no map of the Falklands aboard. "I didn't have a map of Fiji either, which was about as likely a destination," Fleet Commander Admiral Sir John "Sandy" Woodward said later.[9]

The aircraft carriers *Invincible* and *Hermes*, with sailors in blue and white dress uniforms lining the decks and bands playing ashore, glided out of Portsmouth harbor past *Victory*, Lord Nelson's flagship during his 1805 triumph over the French and Spanish at Trafalgar. Hundreds of British spectators, some shouting encouragement, others in tears, stood at harborside waving Union Jacks. On *Invincible* rode Prince Andrew, a twenty-two-year-old helicopter pilot, then second in line to the British throne.

Once in the Atlantic, the carriers were joined by two dozen destroyers, frigates, and support craft to form the largest armada since World War II. Far ahead of the surface ships, which would take three weeks to reach the South Atlantic, four nuclear-powered attack submarines frothed under water at speeds up to 35 mph toward the islands. In Southampton, the passenger cruise liner *Canberra* was stripped of luxury fittings and fitted with two helicopter pads, one atop a drained swimming pool. Soon to go after a similar refitting was the *Queen Elizabeth II*, pride of Britain's commercial fleet.

With the fleet at sea and the initial decision making behind her, Thatcher began to show more sure-footedness. There would be no negotiations over the islands' future until Argentina withdrew. Her new rallying cry became, "We must recover those islands." She recalled Queen Victoria's response eighty-three years previously when British troops fought uphill against the Boers in South Africa. "Failure? The possibilities do not exist," she had said. Churchill had kept the same words on his desk throughout World War II. "We must use all our professionalism, our flair, every single bit of native cunning and all our equipment," she said. "We must go calmly, quietly to succeed." Recalling Chamberlain, Pym told the House of Commons that "Britain does not appease dictators." Thatcher rejected the last of the calls for her resignation, saying, "No, now is the time for strength and resolution."

Her country agreed. One national poll found that 83 percent of Britons favored retaking the Falklands. Asked whether they should be regained through force or diplomacy, 53 percent said force was just fine. The public sentiment buoyed the Thatcher cabinet. When Defense Secretary John Nott announced the establishment of a 200-mile total exclusion zone around the islands, he added that any ships inside were fair game. "We will shoot first," he said. "We will sink them, certainly within the 200-mile radius."

Amid all the military activity, diplomacy was not ignored, but the Reagan administration found itself caught in the middle. "It's a very difficult situation because we are friends of both sides," President Reagan said initially. Washington wanted to help Britain without jeopardizing an improving relationship with Argentina. The United States looked ludicrous at first, leaving the impression that it could not choose between Britain, its closest ally, and Argentina, the Falklands aggressor, a country run by a military junta.

Behind the problem was a serious policy-making split on the U.S. side. Alexander Haig, the former NATO commander, and Secretary of Defense Caspar Weinberger were unequivocal Anglophiles. "You have trouble getting anything, just call me direct," Weinberger told British military friends repeatedly. "Whatever we've got is yours."[10]

On the other side were Jeane Kirkpatrick, the U.S. ambassador to the United Nations, and Thomas Enders, the assistant secretary of state for inter-American affairs, who oversaw U.S. policy in Latin America. They were fighting for a more even-handed U.S. approach to preserve Washington's relationships with the Southern Hemisphere. They argued that Argentina had been an important help in supporting U.S. policy against Communist guerrillas in Central America, particularly against the Sandinista regime in Nicaragua. Those efforts, Kirkpatrick argued, should not be compromised by the Falklands and a traditional affinity for Britain. U.S. embarrassment over the internal split was exacerbated when, on the day the Argentinians invaded, Kirkpatrick had dinner with Galtieri's ambassador to the United States. "We are not thrilled," said British Ambassador Henderson when he heard about the meal.[11]

The initial U.S. conclusion was that Britain could not win. Distance, logistics, the calendar, the forces—everything argued against it. In an attempt to forestall a military loss for Britain and maintain some U.S. credibility in Latin America, Reagan sent Haig on a Henry Kissinger-style shuttle mission between London and

Buenos Aires to try to negotiate for a solution. Haig, a former
Kissinger deputy with a passion for the spotlight, was eager to try.
He talked with Henderson, who told him bluntly, in an effort to
bring a quick halt to even-handedness, that American interests were
every bit as much at stake as Britain's. "If it's a question of over-
throwing frontiers and sovereignty and territorial integrity in the
American hemisphere by force, goodness knows where it could
end." As for negotiating, Henderson made it clear that Thatcher
was in no hurry. "If U.S. territory were occupied or assaulted, as
it has been, you wouldn't start negotiating until the military situation was restored. The U.S. did not sit down with Japan the day
after Pearl Harbor."[12]

Haig arrived in London worried that a British loss could be
another Suez, toppling Thatcher and crippling the nation. "I don't
have any American-approved solution in my kit bag," he said before
heading straight to Downing Street. Thatcher met him in her
second-floor study and pointed out the portrait of Wellington and
a new painting of Nelson. Her message was clear. This was the
commander-in-chief's war room; there would be no backing down.
"She was in a forceful mood, embattled, incisive, and with the right
indisputably on her side," Haig wrote later. At a steak and potatoes
working dinner, she banged the table so hard that the water glasses
shook and almost toppled. "You must never forget," she told the
U.S. secretary of state, "that Neville Chamberlain sat at this same
table in 1938 and spoke of the Czechs as a faraway people . . . a
world war and the deaths of over forty-five million people followed."
"Maybe we should ask the Falklanders how they feel about a war,"
Foreign Secretary Pym muttered. Thatcher almost jumped down
his throat.[13]

Haig raised the possibility of an international peacekeeping
force or an interim administration. Thatcher had no time for those
notions. "They're just too woolly, Al," she said. Her bottom line:
"Stop talking about American even-handedness and tell the junta
to withdraw. Only after this happens will we be prepared to talk
about the future of the islands." Haig went back to his suite at
Claridges and tossed his jacket on a chair. "Somebody get me a
drink fast," he said, pulling at the sweat spots where his shirt stuck
to his skin. "That's a hell of a tough lady."[14] He cabled Reagan
that Thatcher was not going to be headed off, that she "had the
bit in her mouth." What struck the whole U.S. team was the
strength of her convictions. She was taking a tougher line than

anyone in her war cabinet. She was not reacting to advice. She was the driving force.

After five more hours with Thatcher, Haig boarded his U.S. Air Force 707 and flew to Argentina. En route at 505 mph, he passed over the forty-five-ship British task force 30,000 feet below, steaming at 18 mph. In Buenos Aires, met by more than 15,000 flag-waving Argentinians, he proceeded directly to Casa Rosada, the presidential palace and Galtieri's office. The meeting was a disaster. "If the British want to come, let them come. We will take them on," Galtieri announced. At the same time, Argentina, which traditionally has had warm relations with Britain, was stunned by the intense British jingoism, which Thatcher was playing to the hilt. Foreign Minister Nicanor Costa Mendez seemed baffled by the depth of the emotion: "The English reaction is so absurd, so disproportionate."

The Argentinians did not want to negotiate with Haig, and he was never certain who held the negotiating power in Argentina anyway. Britain was willing to give him a chance to pull off a diplomatic solution that did not involve any loss of lives—or loss of British sovereignty. Thatcher knew that if she rejected a diplomatic effort, Britain would be clobbered by world opinion. As for Haig himself, Thatcher and the war cabinet had no regard for him. The prime minister never trusted Haig and believed he was mostly shuttling out of personal ambition. "She was certain that he was fully capable of stabbing her in the back with a middle-of-the-night deal with the Argentines for his own glory," said one of her closest aides.[15] The war cabinet also found the secretary of state inarticulate. More important, they did not think he had anything to be articulate about. How Haig had ever built up a reputation and managed to become secretary of state was beyond Thatcher and her advisers. "Haig was totally incompetent," said another prime ministerial lieutenant.[16]

Nonetheless, Thatcher knew she had to deal with him, and soon the United States began doing more. Ascension Island, the desolate, cratered way station in the South Atlantic, belonged to Britain but the airfield was under lease to the United States, which maintained a secret base there for monitoring Soviet satellites. Washington quietly returned effective control of the field to Britain. The United States filled fuel tanks and kept filling them for the British sea and air fleets. The United States did not have good intelligence satellites poised over the South Atlantic; most are aimed at the Northern Hemisphere to monitor Soviet maneuvers. Britain was reduced to scanning photos from a Landsat weather satellite, but the pictures were not very good. Neither ships nor planes showed up in the low definition shots. This reinforced the reality that Britain did not have a very clear idea at all what it was getting into. London's lack of good intelligence about Argentinian ship movements was particularly frustrating. "We got bugger all," said Chief of Defense Staff Lord Lewin later.[17] "I told my intelligence people, 'For God's sake, get someone from Paraguay down to look over the dockyard wall and send us a postcard.' "

When British commandos and marines first landed on mountainous South Georgia Island, Thatcher announced the news to Britain. "Rejoice, rejoice," the prime minister said. The next day, roars of approval greeted her in Parliament. The landing, she said, "in no way alters the government's determination to do everything possible to achieve a negotiated solution." That was disingenuous. A negotiated solution was not what she wanted at all. Such an outcome would have involved joint sovereignty, peacekeeping forces, flags of both countries. "It would have been a frightful mess," said Whitelaw[18] and Thatcher knew it, too. She was not in a negotiating mood. In fact, with the first British troops ashore, the prime minister turned more belligerent. She compared her Falklands strategy with her refusal three months before to allow a hijacked jet to take off from Stansted Airport. "That's the way to stop hijacking," she said. "Similarly, to see that an invader does not succeed is to stop further invasions and to really stand up for international law against anarchy." She was consistent; she was tough, and as London counterattacked, the nation was behind her. Her approval ratings soared to 76 percent.

A delta-winged British Vulcan bomber from Ascension Island swooped in over Port Stanley and dropped twenty-one half-ton bombs. Carrier-based Harrier jump jets followed, pounding and cratering the 4,000-foot airstrip Argentina used for the delivery of supplies. Thatcher was determined to end the conflict by mid-June, less than two months away. After that, Task Force Commander Woodward had warned, things would start to go wrong. Ships would need maintenance and would have to steam all the way to Gibraltar. Winter would settle in, along with gales off the Antarctic that would threaten thousands of troops aboard storm-tossed ships. Those considerations were foremost in her mind when the first cracks began to show in parliamentary unity. Opposition leader

Michael Foot urged the prime minister to hold off further military action and turn the war over to the United Nations for negotiation. She refused. Argentina had not complied with U.N. Security Resolution 502 to withdraw, so what was the use? She also cited the weather. "I have to keep in mind the interests of our boys who are on those warships."

Things changed on May 2, when the British submarine HMS *Conqueror*, on direct orders from London, slammed two torpedoes into the side of the 13,654-ton heavy cruiser *General Belgrano*; Argentina's second largest ship went down. Some critics questioned whether the sinking, 36 miles outside the 200-mile exclusion zone and apparently heading away, was necessary. Thatcher and the war cabinet had no doubt. The *Belgrano* had more firepower than any British ship and the capacity to sink aircraft carriers, nor had it been on a straight course. "If we had it in our sights, let it go and it had sunk a carrier, putting thousands of our lives at risk, that would have been impossible to defend," said Cecil Parkinson.[19] The Argentinian navy, according to Rear Admiral Gualter Allara, was less critical of the sinking than some Britons and called it a legitimate act, despite the fact that it took place outside the exclusion zone. "The entire South Atlantic was an operational theater for both sides," said Gualter Allara. "We, as professionals, said it was just too bad we lost the *Belgrano*."[20]

The loss of the ship and its 368 men was a huge blow to the prestige of the junta and a major psychological shock from which Argentina did not recover. The British tabloid press fanned the flames of supranationalism. "Gotcha!" bannered the *Sun* when the *Belgrano* went down. But two days later, a French-built Exocet missile fired by a Super Etendard fighter-bomber struck HMS *Sheffield*, killing 22 of the crew of 270. Thatcher was in the House of Commons when her private secretary Sir Clive Whitmore passed her a note saying the *Sheffield* had been hit and was on fire. The news devastated her. She turned ghastly pale and sat ashen-faced while Defense Minister Nott announced the news. She had always known there would be losses. Whitelaw, Lewin, and the others had warned her to steel herself for major casualties. The military chiefs had predicted privately that six to ten ships would likely be lost. This was the first.

Denis stayed up late with her, to offer support and solace. She cried, then moved to her study after midnight to write condolence notes to the families of the sailors killed on the *Sheffield*. She could not predict how the country would react to casualties. Polls showed that the nation supported the war, but Britons were not sanguine about loss of life. A MORI poll four days before the *Sheffield* was hit found that 60 percent of Britons were not prepared to lose the life of a single serviceman to defend the Falklands.

After the *Belgrano* and *Sheffield* losses, Foot renewed calls for U.N. mediation. Denis Healey questioned whether "more lives, Argentinian and British, could be lost than there are on the Falkland Islands." Robert Runcie, the archbishop of Canterbury and a former Oxford schoolmate of Thatcher's, cautioned, "It is a moral, not just political duty, to count the cost at every stage as the conflict develops." Runcie's failure to support the government unquestioningly marked the beginning of an enduring period of tension between the Church and Thatcher.

More worrisome than the domestic rumblings were signs that the resolve of Britain's supporters was cracking. Before the *Belgrano* went down, most of Britain's European partners had backed the Thatcher government by cutting trade ties to Argentina and imposing tough economic sanctions. Now, some began wavering. Ireland broke out first, insisting on U.N. mediation. Irish Defense Minister Patrick Power's statement that "obviously the British are very much the aggressors now," sent Thatcher into a rage. Dublin's reaction reinforced her natural antipathy toward the Irish, whom she considers, in large part, shiftless, sniveling, and, because of their World War II neutrality, spineless.

Bonn raised fresh doubts and, from Paris, the news was also bad. The French had been helpful when war broke out. Technicians briefed British specialists on their Exocet missile, enabling the Royal Navy and RAF to take countermeasures. Indeed, only twenty-five bombs and missiles hit British ships during the war and only eleven exploded, suggesting that the French tips had been helpful. Now President François Mitterrand's growing dismay over the widening war concerned Thatcher.

She was angry about the European wavering, but determined not to lose American support. Weinberger was a hero, speeding up deliveries of 200 Sidewinder missiles. But in order to maintain support from the White House and some international sympathy, the prime minister agreed to try diplomacy again. Politically, it was the right move at the right time. United Nations Secretary General Xavier Pérez de Cuéllar tried for three weeks, offering cease-fire plans, phased troop withdrawals, U.N. administration—basically everything Haig suggested—but neither side would concede an inch.

What finally saved the day for Britain diplomatically was Argentina's outright rejection of the U.N. proposals. Had Argentina accepted any of the suggestions, Thatcher and the war cabinet were convinced that the United States would have demanded that Britain negotiate on the basis of the new terms, as Eisenhower had done to Eden during Suez. Thatcher was delighted and relieved, therefore, when Argentina just said no. There would be no messy compromise.[21] The issue would be resolved cleanly on the battlefield.

With negotiations stalemated, winter advancing and right-wing Tories accusing her of making too many concessions, Thatcher ordered an all-out invasion. Commandos—faces blackened and wearing heavy camouflage—motored ashore, hitting beaches that were scarcely defended. They fanned out over the windswept moors. The prime minister's natural refusal to surrender to indecision or self-doubt was particularly suited to wartime leadership. She started looking and feeling better. She could sense the finale was approaching. At a Conservative party rally in Perth, Scotland, she declared. "What we have seen in the last few weeks is this ancient country rising as one nation to meet a challenge that it refuses to ignore. Perhaps we have surprised even ourselves, and I know we have surprised all those who didn't think we had it in us. . . .The springs of pride in Britain flow again."[22]

The counterattack shifted the balance in Britain's favor. By early June, the end loomed and the United States and Europe began preaching moderation. Haig urged London to be "magnanimous" in victory. Thatcher would hear none of it. Magnanimity, she said, "was not a word I use in connection with the Falklands." Giving in to "an invader, an aggressor, and a military dictator" would be "treachery or betrayal." When it was suggested that she meet Argentinian officials to discuss an end to the fighting, Thatcher refused. She was still very angry.

Her ire spilled over at home. One of her primary targets was the British Broadcasting Corporation. The prime minister was furious with the government-run and funded BBC, which had tried hard to cover the war even-handedly. Thatcher considered that almost treasonous. She wanted unquestioning support for her troops, World War II style. She was outraged when the BBC began broadcasting interviews with grieving Argentinian widows. "There are times it would seem that we and the Argentines are almost being treated as equal," she stormed, ignoring the fact that the BBC had built up its great reputation over decades by trying to avoid overt pro-British bias. Her dispute with the press about war coverage was only the start of a long-running feud with the media over what she considered to be "disloyalty."

Ten weeks after Argentina seized the islands, the 9,000 British troops encamped on the hills above Port Stanley launched an assault on the 7,500 Argentinians dug in around the tiny capital. The battle was bloody, involving hand-to-hand bayonet combat, but ended quickly. When the white flag of surrender fluttered above the town, Thatcher emerged onto Downing Street. "Today has put the Great back in Britain," she rejoiced. "This is a great vindication of everything we have done. What a night this has been for Britain."

And, she might have added, for Thatcher. In Parliament, her announcement that Argentina had surrendered brought thunderous cheers from all parties. Michael Foot rose to offer congratulations. "Perhaps there will be arguments about the origins of this matter and other questions, [but] I can understand that at this moment, the anxiety and pressures may have been relieved and I congratulate her." When she returned to Downing Street, crowds outside serenaded her with "Rule Britannia."

Thatcher was a different leader after the war. Her confidence was virtually unbounded. She dispatched former Governor Rex Hunt back to the Falklands, with symbolic plumed cap, rubbing Argentina's nose in Britain's restored colonial presence. Scarcely had the shooting stopped when she boarded an RAF jet and made the grueling twenty-three-hour flight to the Falklands to visit her troops. Mobbed by delirious kelpers, she looked regal presenting medals to servicemen. She fired an artillery piece, visited war graves, and passed shops selling photos of her, all under the eyes of cameras recording potent images for her next campaign.

She was now a successful war leader, a heroine. Far from home, against what had initially looked like considerable odds, Thatcher and her troops had decisively beaten back the forces of what were, for her, the dark side. Right, not just might, had been responsible. She had been tougher than any man involved and had remained true to basic principles. "Look at a day when you are supremely satisfied at the end. It's not a day when you lounge around doing nothing," she said. "It's when you've had everything to do and you've done it. Life isn't really just an existence. It's using all the talents with which you were born. You can only do that if you've got a government that believes that that is the purpose of life as well."[23]

Thatcher's renewed self-assurance, the attention being paid her internationally, and her new popularity at home frustrated the opposition. Foot was widely seen as too weak, too old, and too ineffectual. The Alliance was still feeling its way. In the Conservative party, opposition had been wiped out. Moderates had been effectively silenced by the Falklands victory. The right wing was so pleased by the success of her tough line that its bickering all but stopped.

Internationally, Thatcher's prestige had taken on a new dimension. No longer did she just talk like an "Iron Lady." She had proven her mettle in battle. Haig wrote later that "Britain's action in the Falklands may have marked a historic turning point in what has been a long and dangerous night of Western passivity."[24] Admirers began comparing her with a string of flattering historical figures, including Churchill, Queens Victoria and Elizabeth I, and France's Charles de Gaulle. She had done what she said she would do, and all Britain basked in pride and glory. For the first time, she had bonded herself emotionally and personally, outside politics, to the people of Britain.

The ten weeks had thoroughly altered her political situation. Practically speaking, not that much had changed. Britain still faced all the problems that threatened before Galtieri's diversion. Psychologically, however, everything was different. The mood of the country had changed as well as attitudes toward Britain. Reagan looked at Thatcher in a new light. She had played him just right, keeping the Americans on board at every critical juncture, getting priceless help.

With a diminished opposition and only eighteen months left in the five-year government, she began planning a second-term bid even as ardent supporters exulted about a third. Thatcher would not go that far, but the Falklands had transformed her chances from almost nil to a near sure thing. The first term had been one of learning hard lessons. In the second, she wanted to use that knowledge. Constantly, she told everyone who would listen that she had strong beliefs and wanted to put them into practice. She was now one of the world's best-known leaders. Her peers and counterparts, however, were not influencing her. Her ideas were still, she continued to insist, "born of the conviction which I learned in a small town by a father who had a conviction approach."

CHAPTER ELEVEN

Falklands Factor

THATCHER CONSIDERED the Falklands a personal success, a vindication of her convictions. She praised the brave boys, but underneath the tribute lay a strong sense that she had borne the struggle alone. "We fought with the support of so many throughout the world," she told a rally, "yet we also fought alone."[1] She meant the country, but it applied to her, too. She has never been one for self-deprecation or self-mockery, even when a bit of modesty, even false modesty, would have helped her. After the Falklands, she was brutally direct as always, never reluctant to acknowledge her own popularity. Asked soon afterward who would follow her, Thatcher responded cheekily but seriously, "After me? There's me."

The next challenge was to keep the wartime energy from dissipating. If the country could show its pluck in war, there was no reason not to mobilize the same drive in peacetime. The slump after World War II did not have to be repeated. And despite the lagging unemployment figures, there was definitely a reason for optimism. Indications that the economy might be improving proved accurate. During 1982, inflation dropped from 12 percent to 6 percent, budget deficits were brought into line, and the trade balance moved into healthy surplus. The shift resulted from the collapse of OPEC, the thirteen-nation oil cartel that had set high oil prices in the 1970s, and revenues from North Sea oil. The combination of the economic news and the Falklands boosted the nation's collective psyche. For the first time since Thatcher moved to Downing Street, studies found that more Britons were optimistic than pessimistic about the future. The prime minister interpreted the feeling as a sign that the country was no longer willing to be pushed around and claimed, "We have ceased to be a nation in retreat." That was her hope, her long-term goal, but was the retreat truly halted? It was too early and the signs too tenuous to be sure. What was certain, said Peter Jenkins, was that by characterizing herself and Britain as winners, the prime minister ensured that "the Falklands Factor became the Thatcher Factor."[2]

The turn of fortunes brought speculation that she would call a snap election. Her mandate did not run out until May 1984, but it is often perilous for governments to wait for term's end to call an election. In the late months of a term, they lose the maneuverability that comes from keeping the opposition guessing and off balance.

If Thatcher wanted to turn victory in the Falklands and the other good news into a new, five-year mandate, she should call an election in either June or October 1983. She preferred the second date. She was not so confident that she was ready to take the chance of losing any earlier than necessary. May had appeal because the long evenings allowed maximum campaigning, but it was shaving it close to the four-year mark, and Thatcher did not believe that the nation got full value from a government that failed to serve at least four years of a five-year term.[3] That ruled out calling the vote before May, but by early spring election fever had reached such a pitch that it was impossible to put it off until fall. In anticipation, Michael Foot had his shaggy white locks trimmed, and Thatcher, still mulling over the most opportune date, had her teeth capped, just in case.

In early May, her political advisers pushed her into a day-long strategy session at Chequers to review the bidding. They pointed out the obvious. She was in a remarkable political position, the strongest of any British leader since World War II. The MORI poll, directed by American Robert Worcester, is the Labor party's official poll and is also Britain's most reliable survey. MORI showed the Conservatives out in front by a full 15 percent with a 49 percent-to-34 percent lead over Labor, with only 15 percent for the SDP–Liberal Alliance. Other polls gave the Tories leads ranging from 11 percent to 21 percent. Inflation had slowed to 4 percent, the lowest in fifteen years, but was expected to begin rising again by fall. The unanimous advice around the table was "Go," and Thatcher, reluctantly, agreed.

Once she decided, she moved so quickly that back-bench MPs

were caught by surprise. With June 10 selected as election day, Parliament had only three days to wrap up. As a result, the government was forced to abandon some major legislation, including an awkward recommendation for 30–50 percent pay raises for MPs and cabinet members. Thatcher quickly announced that the next Parliament would consider the legislation, but that neither she nor her cabinet would accept the pay hike if passed.

It was difficult to imagine a more lopsided campaign or a bigger mismatch. The Labor party was in chaos as the campaign opened. Its forty-page manifesto, or platform, was the subject of interminable intraparty squabbling and was barely printed in time. It was clear soon after the document was released that the party would have been better off without it. Unrealistic, radical, and overly detailed, it gave the Conservatives unlimited ammunition. Entitled "The New Hope for Britain," it promised a $17 billion increase in public spending and pledged the party to cut unemployment from three million to one million, committed it to taking Britain out of the Common Market, to a nonnuclear defense (no Trident submarines or cruise missiles), to abolishing the House of Lords, to nationalizing new industries and renationalizing those privatized by the Conservatives. Labor also vowed to return power to the trade unions.

"This party promises the moon, but it would have to borrow the moon," said the *Times* of London. "Somebody else, as always, would have to pay. There is no 'new hope for Britain' in this document. There is no hope." Moderate Labor MPs were no less critical. Peter Shore, the respected shadow minister of energy, lamented that his party had written "the longest suicide note in history." Hard-line socialists were about to fly what was left of the Labor party into a mountainside.

The Conservatives were free to play it safe—and they did. Thatcher promised little and even moderated some of her more radical first-term proposals in an effort to consolidate gains though not where the trade unions were involved. She promised more controls on trade unions, including mandatory reelection of leaders every five years and putting an end to the life-long appointments that had entrenched some of the most reactionary and troublesome bosses. New legislation would ensure that strikes were called only after a secret ballot. This would prevent politicized union leaders from coercing members who wanted to work. Because the Labor party still received most of its funding from the unions, the proposed legislation was a direct challenge to those entrenched bosses with heavy political clout. Thatcher also favored more central control over the free-spending metropolitan councils of Britain's major cities, most of which were controlled by Labor.

With the Conservatives back in power, there would be more, not less, privatization. British Airways and British Telecom would go private. Britain would stay in the Common Market; pulling out would cost millions of jobs. Taxes would continue to go down, not up. As for defense, General Thatcher could not have been more enthusiastic. She reiterated her promise to upgrade the British independent nuclear deterrent by buying U.S.-built submarine-launched Trident missiles. She also pledged to deploy U.S. cruise missiles at British bases, a controversial stance in Europe at the time, but a position on which she never wavered. "The choice before the nation is stark," she said, kicking off the campaign. "Either to continue our present progress toward recovery or to follow policies more extreme and more damaging than ever put forward by any previous opposition."

Just as she had in 1979, Thatcher, having taken his measure, began campaigning a week after Foot, then quickly established dominance. Her war chest of $15 million was nearly quadruple that of Labor's $4 million, and her old campaign team was back in place. Media master Gordon Reece returned from California, where he had been promoting Occidental Petroleum's Armand Hammer, and immediately set out to soften the warrior queen's rigid facade. He convinced her to soften and lighten her hair even more and brought in more elocution trainers to tone down her voice. Photo ops presented a gentler Thatcher. One showed her in "wellies," the classic Wellington rubber boots, tramping good-naturedly across a muddy farm. Saatchi's Tim Bell again took control of the campaign's advertising. "Like your Manifesto, Comrade?" one ad inquired, going on to compare eleven points in the Communist Party Manifesto with identical positions endorsed by the Labor party.

Thatcher was so dominant and displayed such command even of the minutest details of her government that her handlers worried that she looked too much like the know-it-all of school days. Bell and Reece warned her against sounding "too headmistressy," a frequent public criticism. The prime minister was unapologetic. "I have known some very good headmistresses who have launched their pupils on wonderful careers," Thatcher told an interviewer. She had no intention of changing. "I am what I am. Yes, I do believe in certain things very strongly. Yes, my style is one of vigorous leadership. Yes, I do believe in trying to persuade people that the things I believe in are the things they should follow. I am far too old to change now." Take me or leave me, she was saying. There was no choice and she knew it.

The opposition tried to cast her as a bully, not always an inappropriate characterization. Denis Healey called her cabinet "neutered zombies" and warned that if the prime minister won big, she would be "intolerable." Roy Jenkins echoed Healey, claiming that five more years of Thatcher, "cocooned in her own self-righteousness," would inevitably divide the country. This enduring claim would form the basis of criticism of Thatcher as long as she governed.

Her campaign style was almost a photocopy of Ronald Reagan's 1980 roll over Jimmy Carter. Cecil Parkinson was the able manager, although it was difficult to imagine how anyone over the age of twelve could have botched it. Themes were meted out precisely and events meticulously planned for early in the day to make news and photo coverage easier. In a change from 1979, Thatcher was home early to Downing Street most nights, enabling her to campaign rested and refreshed. Appearances were also limited to minimize the chance of gaffes and to keep voters from hearing too much of her. Traveling again by "battle bus," complete with a well-stocked office, she crisscrossed the country, but rarely pressed the flesh. Thatcher admits to finding the physical part of campaigning "quite appalling."[4] That pleased her detectives, who were worried about the IRA. For the first time, security was an important component of a national campaign in Britain. Entry to major events and Thatcher speeches was restricted to holders of tickets handed out by local Conservative associations.

By contrast, Michael Foot's campaign was painful to observe. The Labor leader put in endless ten- and twelve-stop days, hop-scotching recklessly around the country. Waving a cane, his white hair mussed wildly, and his head bobbing to no discernible beat, he looked more life a refugee from Speakers' Corner in Hyde Park than a professional politician. He could talk without notes for hours, but not always coherently. Sometimes shouting, sometimes mumbling, frequently in the same sentence, Foot did not inspire confidence as he quoted obscure literary passages. He had an air of permanent disarray, an impression exacerbated by his lack of a real support organization. Peter Jenkins called him "a walking obituary for the Labor party." As he crawled toward the finish line, Foot's own wife, feminist author Jill Craigie, administered the coup de grace. Even if Labor won, her husband would likely step down "because it would be time to make way for a younger man," she said all too honestly.

With only days to go, Thatcher broke off campaigning and flew to Williamsburg, Virginia, to attend the annual economic summit of the Western powers. At the meeting, she defended the need for the West to deploy cruise missiles in Europe despite threats by Moscow to retaliate. The Allies backed her and praised her stewardship of Britain's economic recovery. Back in Britain, the headlines were all Thatcher. She was dealing with serious affairs of state while the opposition was struggling pettily at home. She returned exhausted but exhilarated with an unbeatable set of endorsements. "Britain is on the right track," she said; everyone knew it. "Don't turn back."

The country agreed. The *Daily Express* felt safe enough to call the election day result even before the polls opened, bannering, "Maggie Is the Man" across its front page. Hours later, proving that her 1979 upset was not a fluke, she became the first Tory in the twentieth century to win a second consecutive term. She did it with the greatest margin anyone had rolled up since 1945. She pulled down only 42 percent of the vote in the three-way race, but that translated into a huge 144-seat majority in the new 650-seat House of Commons. She admitted to rapturous supporters that the 397-209–seat spread over Labor made it "a larger victory than I dared hope for."

For Labor, however much anticipated, the result was a disaster, its worst defeat since 1918. With the exception of its base in inner London, the party captured only 3 of the 186 seats in the prosperous south of England. The Conservative base was expanding under Thatcher as traditional party loyalties broke down. Analysis showed that unskilled labor stayed with the Labor party, but not many others. The centrist Alliance, with 25 percent of the vote, almost outpolled Labor's 28 percent.

Labor, the results demonstrated, had become the party of the portion of Britain that was in decline as well as the party of the nation's minorities. Thatcher, on the other hand, had pulled in a new breed of Tory: suburban, lower middle-class, small property owners, workers who were willing to hustle and strain, people not unlike herself. The flight of the inner-city English to the suburbs, twenty-five years after the process began in the United States, was another factor in the development of this new electoral order. No longer was the Conservative party the preserve of the gentry, those who attended the right schools, those who weekended at the right country houses. These new Tories were "get on with it, man" Tories, just like Thatcher. Robert Waller, author of the *Almanac of British Politics*, said the 1983 results showed that "social changes are taking place which make the Conservatives the party of the future and Labor the party of the past."

It was 5 A.M. on June 10, 1983, by the time the vote counting, celebrating, and interviews were over. When the Thatchers returned from party headquarters to Downing Street, Carol congratulated her mother. "It's history," she said. Thatcher paused. "History, when you're making it, doesn't seem like history. You're always thinking of the next job." She flipped the switch on her bedside radio: "I wonder if there's news."[5]

CHAPTER TWELVE

War at Home

THE 1983 LANDSLIDE gave Thatcher the freedom to do what she wanted and the kind of latitude that some Tory moderates feared would lead to a doctrinaire assault. There was apprehension that social services would be destroyed, and Thatcher's critics continued to worry that the nation was being divided into haves and have-nots. Governing during the first term with a group of holdovers from Heath had grated on her; they were not, in her phrase, "one of us." Often, she felt they tried to hold her back and dilute her plans. They were not fully committed Thatcherites and were unwilling to make the sacrifices necessary to push forward her free enterprise, antisocialist crusade. Some of these fringe believers had been juggled from post to post, while others had been shuffled out. But once the June ballots were counted, her grip on the party and margin in Parliament were unassailable and the restraints were off. She could do what she wanted and with no inhibitions. So she set about packing her government with her people.

Within hours of victory, Foreign Secretary Francis Pym was summoned to Downing Street. Pym knew it was no social call. During the campaign he had ventured, on television, a cautionary observation that "landslides, on the whole, do not produce successful governments." Thatcher, angry at his impertinence, had stiffed him, saying, "I think I can handle a landslide all right." When Pym arrived, there was no beating around the bush. "Francis," she said, "I want a new foreign secretary."[1] Pym, a powerful Conservative who was her likely successor had she botched the Falklands, was out. He had performed well during that war and Thatcher knew that, but in addition to being a doubter, he was a ponderous Etonian, and she had never felt comfortable with him.

Pym left without complaint, either from himself or from other Tory moderates. His departure symbolized the Thatcherization of the party. While in the cabinet he had put his finger on some of the core questions about the prime minister that had long worried moderate Conservatives. Did she care about the whole country, or just its successful parts, just those who had worked hard, as she had, and lifted themselves up?

After he was gone, Pym picked up Thatcher's own medical analogy to demonstrate what he thought she was lacking. "If I am ill and go to my doctor," Pym said, "I hope that he will show care and concern for me. If that concern is apparent, I will much more readily accept an unpleasant cure or even the explanation that there is no cure. If it is not apparent, I will resent the cure or disbelieve the fact that there is none. I will feel that I do not matter to the doctor and therefore that the diagnosis must be unconsidered and the prescription unreliable."[2]

Pym was replaced by Sir Geoffrey Howe, who moved over from his previous post as chancellor of the exchequer. Nigel Lawson moved from minister of energy into the chancellor's slot. Willie Whitelaw was named a hereditary peer, almost perversely as he has four daughters but no male heirs to inherit his viscountcy, and moved to run the government's program in the House of Lords. Leon Brittan, a bright lawyer and Thatcher favorite despite his foppish manner, took over Whitelaw's job at the Home Office. Party chairman Cecil Parkinson was rewarded for his successful management of the campaign with the Department of Trade and Industry.

Thatcher made more than sixty changes in her government, including twelve in her twenty-one-man cabinet. She insisted that the changes did not shift the ideological balance further to the right, but that was clearly untrue. But for her continued retention of unreconstructed "wet" Peter Walker as energy secretary, the new lineup consisted entirely of men who echoed her ideas. Now the revolution could proceed.

Quite the opposite happened. Thatcher's second term began on a hesitant note, which, with few exceptions, set the tone for the next four years. She had a long way to go to wipe out socialism. The economic framework was in place along with a team set to follow her bidding, but after the cabinet shake-up she appeared to lose sight of how precisely to navigate the next stage. One problem was her health. She is remarkably robust, but that summer a rare health problem arose right after victory. Surgery to repair a detached retina in her right eye, which had bothered her during the campaign, forced her to slow her pace over the summer. It also became apparent that she was not very prepared for a second term. She had rushed into the election earlier than she wanted, and she had not taken the time to plot a second-term strategy. Labor's manifesto had been a joke, but the Tory's own platform had been cobbled together and was a bloodless document with none of the passion and overarching vision that had marked the first term.

Scandal also hit the government. "Tory chief's love child," blared the *Daily Mirror*. "I'm the father of secretary's baby," trumpeted the *Daily Express*. The chief in question was Thatcher's favorite cabinet minister, Cecil Parkinson, her campaign manager and liaison during the Falklands between the war cabinet and the rest of Parliament. Thatcher liked Parkinson because he was a committed Thatcherite, loyal to her, organized, and energetic. He was also raffishly charming with the smooth looks that she liked. No one in government played Thatcher as well as Parkinson, who, since the death of Airey Neave, had been one of her closest political confidants, one of the very few politicians invited regularly for weekends at Chequers. Parkinson knew how to jolly and cajole her, get her attention with political detail or gossip, and flatter her as a woman. (Francis Pym acknowledged that, because she had a man's mind and held a man's job, he had always treated Thatcher as a man. Pym added that his wife had told him that if he had treated Thatcher as a woman he would not have lost his job.)

Parkinson had been the cabinet's fastest-rising star, even though he was actively disliked and disparaged by the majority of his cabinet colleagues, who considered him shallow. His confirmation of his affair with his secretary meant that the prime minister, who had been thinking of naming him foreign secretary, the most senior and prestigious post after prime minister, could not offer him that reward. Otherwise, though, she decided to back him. Parkinson was hardly the first Conservative politician to be involved in a sex scandal. Indeed, the standard joke around Westminster is that Labor party scandals involve liquor, while Tories traditionally trip up on sex. Thatcher, who had few enough confidants as it was, wanted him to stay in the cabinet, all the more so since he intended to stay with his wife. "Cecil, how can I ask you to leave the cabinet because you won't leave your wife when several cabinet members

have left their wives? You've made a mistake. I'm neither con-
demning or criticizing. It's just a fact."[3]

Backing Parkinson came naturally to Thatcher and revealed
another aspect of her character: they don't make allies any more
loyal than Thatcher. She has backed colleagues accused of shoplift-
ing and homosexual cruising. She has consistently helped pals in
trouble. This behavior is part of a rarely seen Thatcher trait: her
mothering instinct. Having had little respect for her own mother,
she is anything but a traditional mother. She was not terribly maternal toward her own children, nor does she govern Britain at all
maternally. But she will mother political allies, all the more so if
they've been acting like little boys, a condition she believes lurks
barely below the surface of most men. Some of the instinct is nan-
nyish. She has, for example, while seated at the cabinet table,
ordered Chancellor of Exchequer Nigel Lawson to get his hair cut.
But she is capable of nurturing, too.

"She's your mother," says Tim Bell. "You come home having
made a fool of yourself; she puts her arms around you and says
'Well, you're a silly fool,' and gives you a cuddle." Such warmth
is never seen in public, but adds Bell, "One on one, she is spell-
binding."[4] Lord King, chairman of British Airways, one of Britain's
toughest, crustiest, and most talented bosses, is one of the least
likely executives to succumb to such charm, but he describes the
prime minister similarly. "Somehow, you end up telling her everything, good and bad, like your mother or best friend. Talking to
her when you've got a problem is like being in a confessional; you
come out feeling good even if you haven't got what you wanted."[5]
Parkinson emerged from his confessional nurtured and with his job.
He lost it a week later, when his mistress revealed more details of
the affair, including his offer to marry her, which was withdrawn
when she became pregnant.

Firing Parkinson was difficult for Thatcher. Not only had the
scandal been messy, but it involved a man she liked and was perhaps
smitten with herself. There is no evidence that Thatcher has ever
fallen off the straight and narrow, but Parkinson would have been
her kind of guy. "She's nutty about him," said a former cabinet
minister who observed the chemistry up close for years. "He's
everything she likes in a man: successful, self-made, clever, handsome, sexy, and knows how to make her feel like a woman."

Thatcher has long used her sexual chemistry. Most Britons
find her sexless—cold and aloof—and she usually is in public. But

those who have spent time with her in private have found the prime minister is no Ice Maiden. She has a powerful allure, and not just because she's dressing better. "By God, she's sexy," Joseph Luns, the former secretary general of NATO, once told a British colleague.[6] King Fahd of Saudi Arabia is reported to be a special fan, as was the late Mozambiquan President Samora Machel, who once launched himself at her in a public embrace that left both his and her aides standing in open-mouthed astonishment. French President François Mitterrand once described her as having "the eyes of Caligula, but the mouth of Marilyn Monroe." Closer to home, some cabinet ministers say Thatcher appointed the handsome Robin Leigh-Pemberton as head of the Bank of England as much for "chemistry" as out of appreciation of his leadership talents. A clever businessman, Leigh-Pemberton nonetheless told friends he was astonished at being selected. The two most favored recipients of the prime minister's feminine magnetism have been Ronald Reagan and Mikhail Gorbachev, two world-class charmers in their own right.

The loss of Parkinson was only one of the snags that plagued Thatcher's second administration. In 1984, Lawson issued a minibudget that proposed $750 million in spending cuts, but the proposal was never fully coordinated with the Defense Ministry, which had to revise spending estimates only twenty-four hours before issuing its own budgetary white paper. That's the kind of sloppiness Thatcher finds intolerable. More serious was the fact that party discipline fell apart in the House of Commons. A small majority adds cohesion to a government, particularly when it comes under siege. But Thatcher's huge, 144-seat advantage meant that Tories felt secure from external threat. As a result, they fell to squabbling among themselves, frequently challenging the prime minister's policies.

Ted Heath lead one such revolt, focusing on a government bill aimed at curtailing local councils. One of the few second-term programs with teeth, it was a plan to abolish some of the high-spending metropolitan councils. As in the United States, where Democrats dominate local and regional government, Britain's city councils are largely dominated by the Labor party. Thatcher was incensed that her national government, which provided more than half of the local council financing, had little control over how the money was actually spent. The prime minister was damned if she was going to let Labor think up costly programs for which hard-working Tories would have to pay. As far as she was concerned, the free ride was over.

Heath's frontal attack, ending five years of frigid silence, took on Thatcher for her crackdown. He blamed her for "naive and simplistic" economic policies that deepened recession and "damaged the fabric of our economy." She was cutting too sharply, he said in an outburst that reflected centrist opinion and precipitated the most embarrassing insurrection since she had become prime minister. "We can afford to care," Heath insisted. "We have never been able to afford not to."

Heath's problem, Thatcher retorted, was that he had given up when the going got tough. He had not been a sticker. She was and her goal would stay fixed. "I came to office with one deliberate intent," she said in February 1984. "To change Britain from a dependent to a self-reliant society—from a give-it-to-me to a do-it-yourself nation; to get-up-and-go instead of a sit-back-and-wait Britain."[7] The goal had not changed, but her intensity had decelerated. Media baron Rupert Murdoch articulated what many Britons were starting to think: "She has run out of puff."

In the meantime, the opposition parties accelerated. Michael Foot stepped down almost immediately after the election as Labor party leader. Tony Benn had lost his own seat and was out of the picture, unable to challenge. That was fine with Foot, who had his own successor in mind. Neil Kinnock, a copper-haired Welshman, was, at forty-one, nearly thirty years Foot's junior. An overwhelming first ballot winner at the October 1983 party conference, Kinnock swamped three heavyweight veterans and became the Labor party's youngest leader ever and its least experienced. In thirteen years in Parliament, he had never served in any government post.

Son of a coal miner and a district nurse, Kinnock considered himself a Peck's bad boy, an exuberant rebel. He had been no student and claimed to hold the record for being caned by teachers at his grammar school. He did manage to get into University College, Cardiff, where he was enthusiastic about rugby and political activism, initially in that order, though later it reversed. Academic stardom eluded him again at university. But there were compensations. He met Glenys Parry, a passionate Socialist, when she was handing out Socialist society leaflets on campus. They later married. More ideological than Kinnock (she refused his first wedding band because it was made of South African gold), she became his closest political partner.

Kinnock is Thatcher's opposite. The Labor leader likes mixing
with constituents and pressing the flesh. On the other hand, the
intellectual cut and thrust of Parliament, which Thatcher relishes,
is a burden for Kinnock. He tolerates Westminster. "The House
of Commons is like a factory," he once said. "That's where I happen
to work." With the Welsh gift of song and a knack for telling tales
and jokes—often with an edge—Kinnock is a popular after-dinner
speaker. He once brought down the house at a party conference by
singing a deep bass rendition of "Old Man River": "Dat ole man
Callaghan; he must know somethin; but he don't do nuthin."[8] In
Parliament, though, where bonhomie is less important than tightly
argued, coherent presentations, Kinnock was far less effective.

Kinnock's task was to rebuild the divided Labor party, a her-
culean effort. It wasn't clear whether he had the muscle for the job.
Those who wondered whether he had enough stature to stand up
to Thatcher cringed when, during a photo session just after his
election, he accidently tumbled fully clothed into the surf at Brighton. For those who recalled Michael Foot falling and breaking his
foot his first day as party leader, the omen was not reassuring.
There were other signals that suggested the party would not recover
its fortunes easily.

Immediately after Kinnock's victory, the party reaffirmed its
determination to jettison Britain's nuclear forces. Party activists
pushed through the policy only two days after a national poll showed
that to do so would be political suicide. According to the poll, 74
percent of all Britons, including a majority of the Labor party's
own supporters, considered the antinuke policy dangerous as well
as ill-considered. Indeed, only 24.5 percent of Britons said they
supported Labor, only 1 percent above the party's all-time low.

But with that exception, Labor was making progress. Kinnock's youth and enthusiasm brought a new energy to the party
that it badly needed. There was a new face in the Alliance as well.
David Owen, forty-five, the bright, handsome, and acerbic former
Labor foreign secretary, took over the leadership of the Social Democrats from the stuffy Roy Jenkins, sixty-two. Thatcher thought
highly of Owen's political skill and brains and once told colleagues
that he could be the next non-Tory prime minister. With the in-
clusion of the popular David Steel, also forty-five, who stayed in
place as the leader of the Liberals, Thatcher—at fifty-seven more
than a decade older than any of the new guard—was facing a fresh,
young, telegenic, and more dangerous opposition lineup.

Less than a year after Thatcher's reelection, Conservative candidates were battered in local elections. Even more ominous for the Tories was the Alliance's showing. The new party's gains came largely at the expense of the Conservatives. Tory strategists began taking a harder look at the Alliance. If the centrists merely split the opposition, that would make the political road ahead much easier for Thatcher. But if the SDP-Liberal combination hacked out a constituency in the middle and set up a coalition with a more moderate, Kinnock-led, Labor party, they could be real trouble.

Something quite different happened to give Thatcher the second-term springboard she needed. Another war broke out, this one at home. There were no bemedaled generals with gold-encrusted caps this time. This new battle pitted her against ranks of coaldust-encrusted miners from pits in the English Midlands led by a radical Marxist corporal named Arthur Scargill, head of the National Union of Mineworkers (NUM). The mineworkers were the most militant, the most difficult, the most antigovernment of all Britain's trade unionists.

If Thatcher could crack the miners, then the union movement would have to deal with her. She had already made some progress; union membership was down with the decline of manufacturing and increased automation. From 12.2 million in 1979, total union membership had dropped to 10 million by the end of 1983. Thatcher relished the chance to take on the weakened leadership. For her, a battle with Scargill and the miners offered as elemental an opportunity as the Falklands crisis, another confrontation between good and evil. She saw a chance to eliminate, once and for all, the kind of irresponsible union militancy that had brought down three of the past four governments, Tory and Labor alike.

The union problem was an old story. Antagonism had been building since the end of World War II, with lousy management also sharing the blame for the deplorable state of industrial affairs. Britain had a long history of poor management. During the halcyon days of empire, the nation set the world standard for producing superb administrators capable of preserving the status quo, but during the 1950s there were few professional managers working in Britain. Many top corporate and industrial executives owed their jobs to family connections. Contact between management and labor was scant. The class factor made mixing difficult, while the nation's basic approach to industrial production, which was to keep labor functioning at the lowest possible cost, failed to speak initiative.

By the 1960s, management had still not taken charge, so the unions, backed by Wilson's Labor government, had seized the opportunity and filled the leadership vacuum. In the absence of any significant authority, shop stewards effectively assumed managerial control of countless firms. When inflation and the oil crisis hit in the early 1970s, wages shot up, but not productivity.

Throughout the decades of labor unease, the miners had been historically the most recalcitrant union for governments. In 1974, the miners toppled Heath after a twenty-five-day coal strike. Thatcher had used this loss to dislodge him the following year. She knew the miners well. They were inefficient compared with miners on the continent, but they never stopped demanding more. As far as she was concerned, the NUM under Scargill, who took his vacations in Cuba and the Soviet Union, epitomized the rot in the British economy. Thatcher knew the miners were militant, dangerous, and that it was her duty to bring them to heel if the country was to move on. She also knew she had to pick the right moment. She had already tried once and failed.

Three years before, in 1981, 50,000 miners walked out when the government announced a program to close some mines. Thatcher, caught unprepared, backed down. This time, however, she had Ian MacGregor in the wings. MacGregor is a Scot who moved in 1940, while in his late twenties, to the United States to make his career. He was a prosperous investment banker until she lured him back to Britain in 1980 with a lucrative contract to clean up British Steel, which was losing billions. After trimming 70,000 jobs and dealing with the steel unions, MacGregor turned the company around. A tough businessman, MacGregor offers unlimited praise of Thatcher. After his experience with the prime minister while he was trying to rescue British Steel, MacGregor claimed, "Britain is the only Western democracy run by a professional."[9]

Thatcher was just as impressed by MacGregor. She wanted him to do for coal what he had done for steel. She asked him to turn around an industry that cost the government $1 billion in subsidies in 1983. The plan was not complicated. It called for closing forty inefficient pits and pensioning off 20,000 miners. But there was a hook. Thatcher knew Scargill was spoiling for a fight, so she decided to lure him into a trap. She knew he would bite anyway, despite the fact that by 1984 there was no energy shortage; despite the fact that the government had quietly stockpiled 20 million tons of coal, a five-month supply; despite the fact that spring was turning to summer and heating requirements were dropping.

As she expected, Scargill accepted the challenge when MacGregor's reforms were announced. Scargill struck the union but refused to allow a strike ballot, fearful that he could not muster the 55 percent approval required under the NUM's constitution. The move, which upset moderate miners, 40,000 of whom kept working (140,000 took to the picket lines), played right into the government's hands. "If you're afraid of democracy when you're running a union, you really should pack up and go home," said Sidney Weighell, former head of the National Union of Railwaymen. Thatcher would not have said it any differently.

Open warfare erupted between pickets and police, with bloody battles flashing nightly across the nation's television screens. By midsummer, the strike had cost more than $2 billion in lost production and the value of the pound was dropping, from $1.50 the previous year to $1.29. Pressure mounted on Thatcher to resolve the dispute, but she had a much larger purpose in mind. She had no intention of settling—ever. Like sovereignty for the Falklands, compromise with Scargill was not negotiable. Besides, she could read the signs: miners' strike funds were running low; sympathy strikes collapsed. She was not going to ease up and let them off the hook. Driven by primal rage and full-blown conviction, she planned to crush Scargill. He symbolized everything she hated.

In the end, the fight lasted fifty-one bitter weeks. By March 1985, the rank and file had streamed back to work, and the NUM called off the strike without a dent in Thatcher's resolve. In the short run, the strike had been costly: gross domestic product growth dropped from 3 percent to 2 percent; the trade surplus decreased by $2 billion, while the budget deficit jumped by the same amount. The pound slumped to an all-time low of $1.03, prompting hundreds of thousands of tourists to flood Britain for bargains.

In the longer run, the miners' strike was another historic watershed for Thatcher. The Falklands war had boosted the nation's morale, but had had no structural impact on Britain. The miners' strike did. "The strike was our Vietnam," said miner Michael Rooney.[10] Confrontational strikes, which had plagued the nation for twenty years, would not work as long as Thatcher was in Downing Street. When Ted Heath asked in 1974, "Who governs Britain?" the answer was, "The unions." A decade later, there was a different answer. The prime minister, at least this one, governed again. Her popularity soared once more. In short order, strike calls by other unions, including postal workers, railwaymen, and civil servants, all collapsed. Unions that struck or threatened to strike in the 1960s and 1970s earned huge pay and benefit hikes; by the end of the 1980s, the increases barely kept pace with inflation.

The strike result also altered the relationship between unions and management. No longer did demoralized management quake in boardrooms at the prospect of a walkout. Industry itself was changing quickly. Heavily unionized older industries, including steel and coal, were shrinking. Job expansion around the world, as well as in Britain, was coming in cleaner, higher tech industries staffed by younger, mostly white collar workers. These men and women were not interested in calls for labor solidarity or class struggle. "We're dealing with better-educated people who aren't impressed by battle metaphors and all that macho stuff," said John Edmonds, the Oxford-educated manager of the General, Municipal Boilermakers and Allied Trades Union. New union-management agreements began stressing middle-class benefits and included no-strike provisions.

The new working class was no longer the underclass traditionally represented by the Labor party. The majority of the populace, as Andre Gorz explained in *Farewell to the Working Class*, "now belongs to the post-industrial neo-proletariat." The Labor party could no longer count on representing workers. They were fair game. With the battle on for the hearts, minds, and votes of a working class on its way up, Thatcher fought hard to draw them into her ranks, courting them as aggressively as she had fought the miners. Charm could conquer as easily as force. Thatcher had learned that lesson well and she moved to consolidate her support within many groups. One group, however, failed to submit, no matter what tactics Thatcher used. The Irish Republican Army would prove to be her most formidable opponents. In October, she would learn just how far they were willing to go.

CHAPTER THIRTEEN

The Irish Question

ON OCTOBER 12, in the middle of the night, Thatcher was working in her suite at the Grand Hotel in Brighton, putting the finishing touches on her keynote speech for the 1984 party conference. It was 2:50 A.M. "Right," she sighed to chief speechwriter Ronald Millar. "That is that. Finished." She was heading for the bathroom when Robin Butler, her principal private secretary interrupted. "I know you're tired, prime minister, but there is just one more paper you must do because they want the answer tomorrow."[1]

She nodded, took the paper, and moved to an armchair by the window overlooking the rocky beach and English Channel. Suddenly, a loud blast blew out the windows and rocked the entire hotel, leaving Thatcher shaking. "There was a great whoosh of air and dust," the prime minister said later.

The explosion ripped out a thirty-five-foot-deep, fifteen-foot-wide gash in the elegant 120-year-old neo-Regency hotel where more than half her cabinet was staying. Concrete and glass crashed down into the street, and tons of rubble fell into the wood-paneled lobby, where, only hours before, hundreds of Conservative party officials had been gathered.

Millar was walking downstairs. The blast knocked him over and plunged the hotel into darkness. Party chairman John Selwyn Gummer, just outside Thatcher's door, was hurled across the corridor. Thatcher stuck her head out the door. "Is there anything I can do to help," she inquired. Gummer thought she looked alarmed, but she sounded calm. Ducking back into her suite, she sat in the dark for several moments before Millar scrambled back to the sitting

211

room clutching his shoulder. "I think that was an assassination attempt, don't you?" she asked. Geoffrey Howe's bedroom was next to Thatcher's. "Don't go in there," the prime minister snapped at the speechwriter, thinking the Howes had been blown up. But they had escaped unscathed.

In minutes, a Special Branch detective had ordered her into the bedroom. Denis, who hates party conferences and had had several drinks before retiring, had slept through the explosion. When he awakened, he and his wife sat motionless in the dark, following the instructions of the police who had seen a suspicious figure on a nearby rooftop. They thought it might be a sniper and had ordered her not to move. Thatcher never liked the dark; she hated it all the more at that moment. She felt trapped and swore that never again would she be without light.[2] The next day, she added a flashlight to the jumble in her handbag and has carried one ever since.

When the security agents gave the all clear and moved the Thatchers to the safety of Brighton's police station, she grabbed two clean blouses and two cases. One held makeup, the other her cabinet papers. Then, dressed right down to her earrings, she left the hotel with a drowsy Denis, surrounded by a cordon of detectives and uniformed police. "The conference will go on as usual," she said firmly amid the jostling. "We were very lucky."

Her escape had been very narrow. The twenty-pound gelignite bomb had exploded only thirty feet away, demolishing the bathroom where Thatcher was headed. Five people were killed, including an MP. Thirty-four were injured, including two of her senior advisers, Norman Tebbit and chief whip John Wakeham, who were trapped in the rubble for hours. Wakeham's wife was among those killed; Tebbit's wife was permanently paralyzed.

Nine hours later, in a call to a Dublin radio station, the provisional wing of the outlawed Irish Republican Army claimed responsibility, saying that their targets had been "The British cabinet and the Tory warmongers."

"Thatcher will now realize that Britain cannot occupy our country, torture our prisoners, and shoot our people in their own streets and get away with it," the caller warned, promising more violence. "Today, we were unlucky. But remember, we have only to be lucky once. You will have to be lucky always."

Thatcher, who is exceptionally brave, refused to be cowed. She took the assassination attempt as a direct personal challenge and was determined not to disrupt the conference. The IRA would get no satisfaction. When she arrived on the podium eleven hours after the explosion, her eyes were red with fatigue, but otherwise she was composed. Her hair was perfect, her makeup impeccable. The attack, she told the delegates, was "an attempt to cripple Her Majesty's democratically elected government." All attempts to destroy democracy by terrorism, she vowed, would fail. "It must be business as usual."

The attack reaffirmed Thatcher's toughness, as well as her conviction. She was determined to press her crusade against all the dark forces, including the IRA. Her declaration of war produced an uproarious, foot-stomping, eight-minute standing ovation. She looked out at the frenzy with her jaw jutting defiantly. The next day, celebrating her fifty-ninth birthday at Chequers, she dropped her veil and showed she was as frightened as anyone would have been. "This was a day I wasn't meant to see," she told the small group of well-wishers as she wept.

The bombing, which might have wiped out the British government, was the most audacious in the twenty years since the IRA had resumed its stalled battle to drive Britain from the six counties of Northern Ireland. "The Troubles," as they are known euphemistically, broke out in 1968, when Catholic activists launched a campaign for job and housing equality. They took their cue from U.S. civil rights marches of the early 1960s and the antiwar demonstrations later in the decade. In Northern Ireland, the protests began peacefully but turned violent. In 1969, when rioting broke out in Londonderry, the province's second largest city and stronghold of Catholic activism, the Royal Ulster Constabulary, was unable to keep order. British army troops were sent in to assist. The following year, the IRA began a terror campaign. Ever since, with the exception of the troubled economy, Northern Ireland has been Britain's most persistent political problem.

The internecine struggle between extremists in Northern Ireland's Catholic minority and Protestant majority has roots deep in English and Irish history. In 1171, Henry II invaded and proclaimed himself overlord of all Ireland, effectively putting an end to independent Gaelic Ireland. By 1250, most of Ireland had been overrun, but the Irish continued to struggle against the English and political domination. The Hundred Years War and the Wars of the Roses occupied the attention of English kings for a century and a half between 1338 and 1485. But at the end of the fifteenth century,

Henry VII resumed efforts to Anglicize Ireland by forbidding intermarriage and requiring the speaking of English.

In 1541, Henry VIII proclaimed himself king of Ireland, but otherwise failed to conquer the country. Not until Elizabeth I, Henry VIII's daughter by Anne Boleyn, acceded to the throne in 1558 did England try to assume full control over Ireland. Its efforts included an attempt to convert the Irish to Anglicanism by establishing the Church of Ireland. But it took Elizabeth's Protestant generals four wars to finally defeat the Catholic forces led by Hugh O'Neill and Hugh O'Donnell. The English finally took over in 1601. Among the most stubborn and troublesome fighters that the English faced were the Ulster chiefs in the north. When they were finally defeated, many of their followers fled to Catholic parts of Europe.

The Reformation intensified the national animosities. "Among the Irish, a persecuted Church fanned the resentments of a conquered people: the English were heretics, their power was illegitimate, rebellion against them lawful, their enemies were the friends of Ireland and of the Faith," wrote Máire and Conor Cruise O'Brien. "It was a vicious circle. English consciousness of these sentiments produced a feeling of insecurity: the need for security produced strong measures, thus intensifying the Irish feelings at the root of the original feeling of insecurity and creating the need for still further strong measures."[3]

In 1607, King James I, Elizabeth's successor, increased the pressure on the Irish. "You are but half subjects and therefore entitled to only half privileges," he said. He drove home his point by seizing the estates of Irish Catholic earls, some of whom had already fled, and handing out huge tracts, mostly in the north of Ireland, to English and Scottish colonizers. Over the next thirty-three years, the North was seeded with 100,000 Protestant crown loyalists.

Midway through the seventeenth century, Oliver Cromwell crushed the Irish with particular brutality. After devastating County Clare, Cromwell wrote, "There is not wood enough to hang a man, nor water enough to drown him, nor earth enough to bury him in." But the real milestone took place in 1690 near Drogheda, where English and Irish forces clashed at the Battle of the Boyne. James II, a Catholic convert seeking to regain the English throne, led an Irish army against Dutch-born King William of Orange, a Protestant. "Good King Billy's" victory made complete the Protestant domination of the North. Three centuries later, it still exists, with victors and vanquished continuing to fan old jealousies and hatreds, with parades and demonstrations that regularly erupt into violence.

English laws in the early eighteenth century which forbade Catholics from holding political office or inheriting or buying land entrenched the discrimination. The slow, complicated process of reforming those laws began during the reign of George III (1760–1820) and culminated in the Emancipation Act of 1829, which opened civil and political life to Catholics. But even then, Catholic officeholders were forced to swear allegiance to the Protestant succession, deny the temporal power of the Pope, and undertake not to weaken the Protestant establishment. (Current British law still bars Catholics from the monarchy and from several lesser offices, including regent, lord chancellor, and keeper of the great seal.)

Throughout the nineteenth century, Irish leaders, including Charles Stewart Parnell, the Protestant leader of the Catholic peasants, attempted to gain home rule for Ireland. When the home rule campaign stalled, the Irish Republican Brotherhood (IRB), forerunners of the IRA, took to the streets in an effort to win Irish independence.

In their April 1916 "Easter Rising" against the British troops, the "Black and Tans" succeeded in capturing Dublin's General Post Office and several other public buildings. The IRB's Volunteers proclaimed an independent republic and held out for a week until the soldiers shelled the post office and forced their surrender. The execution of the Rising's fifteen leaders shocked the country and led to guerrilla warfare against Britain for the next five years. Finally, in late 1921, London agreed to partition the island. The twenty-six Catholic counties of the South became the independent Republic of Ireland, while Britain retained control of the six Protestant-dominated northern counties, commonly called Ulster. For most of the next half-century, political tension eased and the two sides in the North managed to coexist relatively peacefully.

The fragile calm broke in the late 1960s with the British clampdown. Civil disobedience escalated into terrorism in 1970, when the Provisionals, or "Provos" (the bombs-and-bullets brigade of the IRA) took to the streets to battle the British "occupiers," successors of the Black and Tans so hated during the civil war. The goal of the Provos was to rekindle the glory days of Ireland's battle for independence, drive the British out, and reunite North and South.

Even old-time IRA supporters, however, were shocked by the ruth-
lessness of the Provos. Protestants and British authorities were not
their only targets. Catholics who refused to support the Provos were
subject to some of the worst brutality—kneecapping was common—the result of kangaroo court justice. Protestant militants
fought back by beefing up their own paramilitary squads and ini-
tiating terror tactics of their own.

Britain retaliated by imposing preventive detention and in-
ternment without trial, policies opposed bitterly by Catholics and
civil libertarians everywhere. The Heath government poured in
troops. From a few hundred in 1968, the garrison grew to a peak
of 22,000 by 1972. The violence escalated as well. On January 30,
1972, British troops killed thirteen demonstrators after a Catholic
rally in Londonderry. "Bloody Sunday" has been commemorated
ever since in the city, now called Derry by the Catholics because
of their hatred of the British seat of power. The massacre set the
tone for the year, the bloodiest of "The Troubles," with 274 people
killed. Altogether, from 1968 until 1990, shootings and bombings
have claimed close to 3,000 lives. Two-thirds have been civilians,
the others soldiers and police. There have been more than 30,000
injuries.

Northern Ireland is largely rural and, from the Giant's Cause-
way on the north coast to the Mourne Mountains, which crash into
the Irish Sea south of Newcastle, stunningly beautiful. But two
decades of the Troubles have had a jarring impact on the cities and
some of the most bucolic towns. Village police stations have been
surrounded by twenty-five foot walls of concrete and steel and
topped by mesh and razor wire. Mechanized surveillance cameras
scan the entrances and surrounding streets along the border between
the Ulster and the Republic, soldiers and police conduct thousands
of vehicle and driver checks daily in search of weapons and IRA
suspects and as a show of force.

In Belfast and Londonderry, troops in armored personnel carriers cruise the streets, while foot-soldier patrols zigzag through
neighborhoods. In the early years of the violence, when Britain was
interning IRA suspects without trial, women in Catholic neighborhoods, on spotting the patrols at night, would run into the streets
banging garbage can lids and yelling "Dark squads" to warn the
local men to hide.

In Belfast, scene of most of the violence, whole neighborhoods
have been redesigned with security interests in mind. Military strat-

egists have worked with civilian architects to plan new public housing tracts. Unlike the old housing areas, which were filled with alleys, secret passages, and unlimited escape routes, new projects have been built with single entrances and exits, making it easier for security forces to block them off and conduct searches. Ground between neighborhoods has been bulldozed flat into no man's lands. The most dramatic is the "Peace Line," an ugly concrete, brick, and steel wall the height of a telephone pole. Covered with graffiti like "Up the IRA" and "Kill All Papists," it separates the Protestant Shankhill from Catholic West Belfast.[4]

This war-zone planning resulted from the failure to resolve a generation of hate. British and Irish leaders have tried to break the cycle of attack and revenge reprisals through political as well as military action, but with little success. Power-sharing proposals have collapsed. Throughout, Britain has refused to pull out its troops, fearful that an IRA bloodbath would ensue. Relinquishing sovereignty was also out of the question as long as there remained a Protestant majority loyal to Britain. There seemed no logical way out.

Complicating the political situation is the psychological relationship that exists between Britain and Ireland. That relationship is complex but can be reduced to a few basic truths: (1) Ireland is tiny, with only 6 percent of the population of Britain; (2) when Britain sneezes, Ireland gets pneumonia; (3) when Ireland sneezes, Britain frequently fails even to hear it, let alone pass on a "Bless You"; (4) every issue regarding Britain is of major consequence to Ireland; and finally, (5) Britain usually reacts on Irish questions only when there is an emergency.

Thatcher's attitude toward "The Troubles" is rooted in her own strong unionist sentiment and, to a lesser extent, her childhood training as a conservative Methodist. Her attitude has also been shaped by an abhorrence of terrorism and, in particular, the painful murder of Airey Neave in March 1979. His killing instilled an absolute hatred of the IRA in her, which the Brighton bombing only intensified.

Four months after Neave's death, when she had been prime minister only three months, the IRA assassinated Lord Mountbatten near Sligo, blowing up the fishing boat of the seventy-nine-year-old war hero, diplomatic architect of India's independence, and favorite elder statesman of the royal family. That same August day, a huge bomb blew up a convoy of British soldiers patrolling in South Armagh. When a rescue helicopter appeared, a second bomb exploded, killing a total of eighteen soldiers on Ulster's bloodiest day.

Thatcher was horrified but, determined not to react overemotionally, sat first in her study and handwrote letters to the widows and families of each of the soldiers killed. Then, to demonstrate she could not be cowed, she flew to Belfast and, surrounded by Special Branch detective bodyguards and soldiers, strode the capital's streets, listening to residents' firsthand reactions to the killings. After the elaborate Westminster Abbey funeral of Mountbatten, Queen Victoria's last great-grandson, Thatcher met Irish Prime Minister Jack Lynch to discuss improving security. Lynch, who headed Fianna Fail, the Irish party with the strongest historical links to the IRA, abhorred the IRA tactics. "The present IRA bears no relation whatsoever to the IRA that existed in the early 1920s," he declared. "These men are not fighting for a United Ireland; they are maintaining the division of Ireland—the fear and bitterness that exist in the North. It is brutal and horrific gangsterism."[5]

Thatcher and Lynch ended their talks amicably enough, but neither had a solution. No one else did either. When Pope John Paul II visited Ireland a month later, he made an impassioned plea: "On my knees, I beg you to turn away from the paths of violence." The IRA rejected the entreaty, saying, "In all conscience, we believe that force is the only means of removing the evil of the British presence in Ireland."

Before 1979 was out, so was Lynch, the victim of persistent economic troubles and his close ties to London. Lynch's departure led to a period of alternating rule between two Irish leaders: Charles Haughey (elected in 1979, 1981, 1987, and 1989) and Garret FitzGerald (elected in 1980 and 1983). Haughey appalled Thatcher. "My God, this will make things ten times more difficult," said one of her cabinet ministers when Haughey replaced Lynch.[6] Haughey served in Lynch's cabinet as health and social services minister, but the two men had long disliked one another. A vastly experienced politician who had held four cabinet jobs and had served twenty-two years in the Dail, or Irish Parliament, Haughey was a strong Republican who took a more passionate view about united Ireland than the pragmatic Lynch. "I'm tinged with green, all right," he admitted after taking office. In 1970, when he served as Lynch's finance minister, Haughey was tried, and acquitted, in a Dublin court on charges of running guns to the IRA. Lynch fired him then, but Haughey, one of the most resilient politicians ever produced by Fianna Fail, was soon back in the thick of Irish governance.

Immediately after taking office as prime minister in 1979, Haughey, then fifty-four, a month older than Thatcher, declared that "the peaceful reunification of the people of Ireland is my primary political priority." The statement had the desired effect of putting his British counterpart on notice that she was dealing with a more aggressive taoiseach than Lynch.

Thatcher's and Haughey's initial relations were chilly; their attitudes about Northern Ireland at polar extremes. For Thatcher, the debate is mechanistic unless her soldiers are being blown up. She is not affected by the marshaling of historical argument as it is applied to Ireland. She has little feel for history generally and even less for Irish history. She has not read much about it and has no time to do so now. The nuances and cultural aspects of the debate have thus never been part of her ken, not the rights and wrongs of the Reformation period, nor of the civil war that resulted in partition. What matters to Thatcher is the present reality: Northern Ireland is part of the United Kingdom, and the clear majority— the 1 million Protestants of the 1.6 million Ulster residents—want to keep it that way.[7]

The terrorist aspect of the problem also matters to her. She believes that terrorists who have lost democratic elections should not be allowed to win with bombs and bullets, killing British soldiers and innocent civilians. The Queen, not the prime minister, is commander-in-chief of the armed forces, but it is Thatcher who often meets the coffins of British troops returned to England. Handkerchief in hand, she frequently has difficulty maintaining her composure. Thatcher is also convinced that IRA terrorism is part of a global problem that must be fought locally everywhere. She worries about IRA links to other terrorist groups, including those sponsored by Libya's Qaddafi, who has shipped tons of weapons and explosives into Northern Ireland. She rejects as nonsense, however, the IRA's claims of common purpose with the Palestine Liberation Organization and the African National Congress.

She revealed her strength of purpose in 1980 during the first of a series of Irish hunger strikes. The hunger strikers in the H-shaped cell blocks of Belfast's Maze prison were mostly IRA members convicted of civil crimes ranging from armed robbery to murder, but they insisted on being treated as military prisoners of war rather than as common criminals. When the Northern Ireland office, the branch of Britain's government that administers the province, refused, they refused to eat. Thatcher's attitude was that if the strikers wanted to fast to death, that was their decision. Policy would not be affected. When Cardinal Tomas O'Fiaich, primate of All Ireland, asked her to intervene, she told him to forget it.

"If these people continue with their strike, it will have no effect whatsoever," Thatcher said, calling the action merely "a ridiculous thing to do." (During a similar strike in 1972, Ted Heath's government had granted IRA prisoners political status on the recommendation of Willie Whitelaw, then Northern Ireland secretary. Thatcher was reinforced in 1980 when Whitelaw, by then home secretary and responsible for domestic security, said his earlier decision had been wrong.) The 1980 strike lasted fifty-three days before collapsing with the total capitulation of the seven strikers. Thatcher never budged.

The following year, another hunger strike hit the Maze. The leader was Bobby Sands, a tough, twenty-seven-year-old activist sentenced in 1976 to fourteen years on firearms charges. It was Sands's second stretch in the maximum security prison. He had spent three years there earlier for two armed robberies—a traditional IRA fund-raising method—and for gun possession. Sands put himself on a collision course with Thatcher in March 1981, when he vowed not to eat until he was granted political status— recognition as a POW, the freedom to wear his own clothes instead of prison garb and exemption from work. The government refused. "We do not recognize that political motives entitle people to be treated any differently from people who commit crimes for other motives," said Humphrey Atkins, a Thatcher favorite who was then Northern Ireland secretary.

That might have been that, except that four days after Sands began his fast, a Catholic MP from a constituency bordering the Irish Republic died. The IRA managed to get Sands nominated for his Westminster seat. To the dismay of the government, Sands defeated a staunch unionist to win the April 10 by-election to become a member of Parliament. Suddenly, as Sands continued to weaken on a diet of water and salt pills, the strike debate vaulted from issue to cause. Eight weeks into his fast, three members of the Irish Dail flew to Belfast to convince Sands to give up. He refused. When the three tried to see Thatcher, she turned them down. Soon after, when five British soldiers were killed in a bomb explosion, Thatcher lashed out at the strikers, saying that when the soldiers' killers were tried and convicted, "I hope no one will claim they are entitled to special privileges."

Sands soon died, as did nine others inside the Maze and fifty more outside in violence generated by the battle of wills. Pleas had flooded in from around the world for Thatcher to ease off. She never wavered. Her single-mindedness cost her support overseas, nowhere more so than in the United States. American donations to the IRA tripled after Sands's death. In New York, Prince Charles was met by anti-British demonstrations. Princess Margaret, who had caused an uproar during a visit to Chicago shortly after the Mountbatten assassination when she allegedly referred to the Irish as "pigs," canceled a planned visit. The strike had polarized public opinion, and demands for a political solution for Ulster poured in from around the world.

James Prior, who succeeded Atkins in the Northern Ireland office in 1981, launched a fresh initiative. He based his solution on the idea of power sharing in the new Ulster Assembly. Under a plan called "rolling devolution," Protestant Loyalists and Catholic Republicans would work together, gaining more power from London as they reached agreement. Despite the interest in London in reaching some kind of workable agreement, there were few Ulster hearts behind power sharing. Westminster set up a seventy-eight-seat assembly, but even before the balloting for seats began, it was clear that the divide was too wide. Catholics said they would boycott the Assembly; Protestants said they only wanted majority rule, no sharing. Thatcher herself had been cool to the whole idea. Prior resigned and the whole idea collapsed, one more failure in an endless series.

Meanwhile there was more bloodshed. In July 1982, an IRA bomb ripped through a detachment of the Queen's Household Cavalry as they trotted past Hyde Park, scattering dead and wounded men and horses in the street. Simultaneously, a bandstand in Regent's Park was demolished as the thirty-man Royal Green Jackets band was playing. The toll was ten killed and fifty-five injured. The situation was further complicated when, in the midst of the torturous process of Assembly negotiations and bombings, the Falklands War broke out and Haughey condemned British aggression. Thatcher called this an unforgivable betrayal, and relations between London and Dublin deteriorated.

For the next year, 1983, Northern Ireland festered. A Christmastime bombing in Harrods department store served as a reminder of the situation, and helped reinvigorate efforts toward a solution. In May 1984, a group of nationalist political figures from both sides of the border issued a set of recommendations for reuniting the island and for preventing further "violence, anarchy, and chaos." Contained in a document called the New Ireland Forum report, the proposals urged the establishment of a single state, with its capital in Dublin, a new nondenominational constitution, and "irrevocable guarantees for the protection and preservation of both the Unionist and Nationalist identities." The nationalists thought they had made major concessions by allowing the unionists to retain their British affiliation and by calling for a constitution that allowed complete civil and religious liberties for both sides. The report also presented two other possible solutions, the creation of a federal system with governments in both capitals sharing one president or the establishment of joint sovereignty over Northern Ireland. Ronald Reagan praised the proposals, but none of the options was acceptable to Thatcher.

A month after the Brighton bombing, Thatcher and FitzGerald held their annual summit at Chequers and discussed the Forum report. At a news conference following the meeting, Thatcher was appalling. Brighton had polished her diamond-hard resistance to compromise on Northern Ireland, and she dismissed the proposals, and FitzGerald, with the kind of imperious rudeness usually reserved for blood enemies. "I have made it clear that a unified Ireland was one solution that is out. A second solution was a confederation of two states. That is out. A third solution was joint authority. That is out—that is a derogation of sovereignty." Not only was her rejection brutal, but she had humiliated FitzGerald, one of the most decent men in international politics, a man committed to a peaceful solution. "I couldn't believe my ears when I heard her," said one of her government ministers. "It was bloody horrible."[8]

FitzGerald, who unlike Haughey admired Thatcher, was angry and embarrassed. He called her response "gratuitously offensive" and went home. But he refused to give up. Instead, he decided to take a pragmatic risk in order to resume a dialogue, postponing the age-old Irish demand for unity. FitzGerald knew that by the mid-1980s unity was no longer a rallying cry in the republic. Except idealistically, most Southerners did not want a link with the North. They knew they could not afford to police or maintain the North. Britain was spending nearly $4 billion a year on the province, an impossible sum for Ireland, one of Europe's poorest countries. But the success at the polls of Sinn Fein, the political wing of the IRA, including the election to Parliament of Sinn Fein chief Gerry Adams, convinced FitzGerald it was time to move before "the hard men" became more successful. In London, Thatcher's most loyal colleagues urged the prime minister to resume the dialogue with FitzGerald.

In part because she hoped to convince Ronald Reagan that she was trying to reach an accord with Dublin, Thatcher agreed. If she did not, she knew she would get precious little help stopping the flow of guns and money from North America to the IRA or in getting IRA suspects extradited from the United States. The decision to work with FitzGerald precipitated an intense, year-long negotiation, which culminated in the November 1985 signing of the Anglo-Irish agreement at Hillsborough Castle outside Belfast. The agreement had three important elements:

- it reaffirmed the principle that the majority must consent to any change in Northern Ireland's status and that the current majority wanted no change; if in the future, the majority wanted a united Ireland, the two governments promised to bring it about;
- it embraced the principle of devolution for a political solution, meaning the gradual transfer of power from Britain to the local authorities;
- by establishing a British-Irish body called the Intergovernmental Conference to deal with such matters as cross-border security and the administration of justice, it gave Ireland a limited, very limited, consultative say in the conduct of affairs in Northern Ireland. The binational bureaucracy marked the first time the two countries met systematically, and though there were repeated strains on the arrangement, it would continue to hold and foster cooperation.

The compromise was welcomed everywhere except by the unionists of Northern Ireland. In the United States, where some thirty million citizens claim Irish ancestry—nearly ten times the current population of the Irish Republic—the country's best-known Irishmen exulted. President Reagan called it "a great breakthrough," while Speaker of the House Thomas P. "Tip" O'Neill hailed London and Dublin for being "very courageous." (An International Fund for Ireland was established by Congress as a result of the pact; by 1990, the United States had contributed $150 million to promote job creation, investment, and human rights; other countries, an additional $30 million.)

Northern Ireland's Protestant Loyalists protested that they had been betrayed by the Hillsborough pact. The consultative role, said such leaders as the Reverend Ian Paisley, was the beginning of the total erosion of British sovereignty. "She's lying when she says they're not considering sovereignty when they give Ireland a consultative role," accused Peter Robinson of the Democratic Unionist party. "We're being cast aside and there is a deep sense of betrayal."[9] Other unionist leaders assailed the pact as part of a "monstrous conspiracy" to sell out the province to the Republic.

For the next two years, unionists tried all they could to force Thatcher to back down and disavow the pact, but she never did. Once it was in place, she hoped it would do some good toward normalizing life in the province. Then, while Ireland turned its attention to wrestling with its economy, Thatcher resumed the normal British posture toward Ireland—ignoring it as much as she could.

Fresh violence, though, was impossible to ignore. As a result of London's and Dublin's political tensions easing, the bloodshed picked up. The IRA was frustrated that chances of the British "occupation" ending any time soon had receded. From 1987 to 1989, a wave of killings ensued. Security officials blamed the bloodshed on the new political situation and the huge stockpile of weaponry collected by the IRA. The arsenal included more than ten tons of Semtex, a powerful, difficult-to-detect, Czech-made plastic explosive, a dozen or more Soviet-made SA-7 surface-to-air missiles, crates of grenades and grenade launchers, and at least fifty heavy machineguns. The weaponry arrived in three sea shipments from Libya between 1984 and 1986 and was hidden in the Irish Republic and Ulster. A fourth consignment, aboard the Panamanian-registered freighter *Eksund*, was intercepted by French agents in 1987 and disrupted the arms pipeline.

The *Eksund* seizure revealed the depth of the problem and led to a lethal round of tit-for-tat assaults. In May 1987, the British army's antiterrorist Special Air Services (SAS) regiment ambushed and wiped out an eight-man IRA team attempting to blow up a police station at Loughall. The IRA bounced back in even deadlier fashion, bombing a memorial service at Enniskillen in November, killing eleven and wounding sixty-four, most of them women and children. Britain countered in March 1988 in Gibraltar, the British-governed Rock, where an SAS squad gunned down a three-member IRA team they believed were planting a remote-control bomb.

Because the two men and a woman were unarmed and on foot when they were killed by plainclothes agents, the Gibraltar operation fixed attention on allegations that Britain had been conducting a shoot-to-kill policy against the IRA. Such charges had earlier been investigated by a widely respected police officer, John Stalker, in a case involving the 1982 killing by the Royal Ulster Constabulary (RUC) of six unarmed IRA suspects. When Stalker's confidential report concluded that senior RUC officers should be prosecuted, his seven volumes of findings were pigeon-holed. When he attempted to push ahead with his probe, Stalker himself came under investigation on what appeared to be questionable charges; allegations of "smear" and "cover-up" swirled. Suspended from his job as deputy chief constable of Manchester, Stalker was later reinstated, but having collided with nervous authorities, he retired in 1987. The controversy over shoot-to-kill was revived by the Gibraltar action and the fresh realization that the SAS had never been known to take an IRA prisoner. Whatever the case in practice, Thatcher steadfastly denied that any such "policy" existed.

Few could, or should, muster much sympathy for the IRA. Within days of the Gibraltar killings, during a funeral procession in Belfast for three other Catholics, two off-duty British army corporals blundered into the cortege; they were hauled out of their car and executed. In June 1988, the IRA blew up an army van in Lisburn, killing six soldiers. That August, a land mine exploded alongside a troop bus near Omagh, killing eight soldiers. More atrocities continued through 1989, and no one foresaw an early end to the brutality. There was no chance that the absolute impasse that existed between the Thatcher government and the IRA could ever be dissolved. Their mutual hate was too visceral and too deeply entrenched. "They don't understand the British," one of the prime minister's closest aides said, trying to explain the mutual recriminations. "The more you get up our nose, the harder we stiffen our spine." But neither has that attitude or the imbalance of forces deterred the IRA.

At the outset of the third decade of "The Troubles," the military lineup was totally one-sided. There were some 30,000 British security forces in Northern Ireland at the beginning of 1990. By contrast, security experts estimated the core IRA strength at no more than about 150 full-time activists, backed by some 800 supporters who provided intelligence and safe houses. Strength in numbers alone has never been much of a factor. Britain has been frustrated from mopping up the IRA largely because the active fighting units are so small and difficult to infiltrate. Divided into cells of only three to four volunteers, they operate independently under general policy guidelines transmitted with excruciating care via long-time, trusted confidants. They are extraordinarily resilient.

Still, the renewed violence and undiluted socialism has hurt the IRA politically. In elections in the Irish Republic in June 1989, Sinn Fein pulled down only 1.2 percent of the vote (down from 1.9 percent in 1987) and failed to win a seat in the Dail. In the 1987 British general election, Gerry Adams was reelected to Westminster, but with a reduced vote, and overall Sinn Fein won fewer than 12 percent of the Northern Ireland ballots. Declining political fortunes and heavier weapons have proven a volatile mix. As Sir John Hermon, former head of the Royal Ulster Constabulary, put it, "It's crucial for them to up the ante and keep the violence going."[10] Without the violence, they would lose what little influence they still held.

An increased number of accidental killings of innocent civilians has cost the group sympathy in its own Catholic community. Belfast's Catholic Bishop Cahal Daly has been sharply critical of what he has called the IRA's "mayhem of madness." At Sinn Fein's annual conference in 1989, Gerry Adams acknowledged that IRA "volunteers" had mistakenly killed twenty-three unarmed civilians in the previous fifteen months. Fully aware of the political cost in the community the IRA claims it wants to emancipate, he warned the killers, "You must be careful and careful again."[11] Martin McGuinness, deputy head of Sinn Fein, but whom the British security forces believed was the IRA's military commander, has also been critical of the civilian killings. "These accidents are very damaging to the armed struggle," he said in late 1988. "If they continued, they would cut into our support."[12] They did continue and they did hurt.

But if the IRA had lost support and the London–Dublin relationship had improved as a result of the Anglo-Irish accord, why at the outset of 1990 was there still no end in sight to the cycle of hate and violence? Historic hatreds have persisted, fueled by the past two decades of killings, but the economics of the situation also remained crucial.

Under Thatcher, Britain has made considerable progress in improving living conditions for the minority Catholic population, and many of the grievances that sparked the original civil rights protests have been resolved. More Catholics have been hired to fill public sector jobs, even though they still lag far behind in private industry. With a nearly static, inbred population, there has been little job turnover. Where jobs have become available, many firms, especially small ones not under government scrutiny, have resisted change. The jobs Catholics have won have been primarily unskilled. In 1989, however, the British government introduced long overdue, tougher antidiscrimination legislation, which over time should increase fair employment opportunities. Pressure from the United States to adopt the MacBride principles, a stringent affirmative action code of conduct that Britain has resisted, helped pushed the Thatcher government to enact the new laws.

New legislation notwithstanding, the economic situation in Northern Ireland was still the worst in Britain at the end of the 1980s. Unemployment in Ulster overall was officially 15 percent, but ran as high as 70 percent in some Catholic neighborhoods, more than double that in the worst Protestant areas. That continued imbalance bred frustration and fed the violence. Thatcher responded to the late 1980s killing surge by banning broadcast interviews with Sinn Fein politicians or IRA members, an attempt to deprive them of "the oxygen of publicity." The order prompted an outcry in the Catholic community, infuriated a British press already constricted by government regulations, and, at least in the short term, boosted the IRA cause.

Overall, though, the British approach has improved in the Thatcher years. It started from a low base point. With a historic legacy of arrogance and authoritarianism toward the Catholic Irish, Britain has customarily acted either slowly or with a heavy hand when advancing the cause of justice in Northern Ireland. This prime minister has been tough on the IRA for good personal and governmental reasons, but she has also moved the process forward more than Wilson, Heath, or Callaghan. Her work on the British economy has helped. London has been better able to pay for improvements in the North. That has meant that, for all the unrelenting tension and economic problems that remain, daily life for Northern Ireland's Catholics has improved. Fully 25 percent of Belfast's public housing was judged unfit for habitation in 1974; in 1989, the figure was 10 percent, the result of $2 billion spent in the capital on apartment complexes, mostly occupied by Catholics, since 1981. Building on that plus strict enforcement of the new antibias laws to restore real civil rights offered the best chance to bring dignity back to the beleaguered province, to eradicate support for the gunmen, and, after 300 tortured years, to end the killing cycles.

CHAPTER FOURTEEN

Ron and Maggie

UP AT DAWN, she works until after midnight. He strolled in at the crack of nine, wandering home at 5 P.M. or earlier. She labors through weekends and disdains vacations. He left the office some weekday afternoons to ride horses, loved to watch TV and movies at night, skipped out early Fridays, and spent more than a year of his presidency on vacation in California. She is a stickler for detail. He is a broad-brush guy. She masters briefs. He memorized lines. He would not have lasted two minutes in her cabinet, but together Margaret Thatcher and Ronald Reagan formed the most enduring political partnership of the 1980s.

Their personalities are poles apart and they sometimes irritated each other, but their beliefs are remarkably similar. They are also both savvy professionals. They knew how to use each other for individual and mutual purposes and in ways that benefited both them and their countries.

Thatcher was determined to make the pairing work, and besides, the two of them genuinely liked each other. Reagan got a kick out of being around her. At international conferences, the United States and United Kingdom usually sat next to each other. By protocol, the two heads of government are normally separated by either the foreign secretary or secretary of state. Invariably, Ronnie would switch the place cards so he could sit next to Maggie. She reciprocated with a charm that can be formidable. She made a point of standing next to him, steering him by the elbow when he needed directions, prompted him with grace in public, and protected him from the press when she thought he was floundering.

229

Thatcher and Reagan met for the first time in London in 1975, just after she became Conservative party leader. She had noticed him after his 1964 endorsement of Barry Goldwater's presidential candidacy and after her 1965 U.S. visit while he was campaigning for the California statehouse, and had kept up with some of his speeches while he was governor. (Reading articles by prominent conservatives is a regular Thatcher practice. When then U.S. Education Secretary William Bennett visited London in the mid-1980s, Thatcher quoted without notes from several of his speeches, thoroughly astonishing him.) In Reagan's case, the scheduled short appointment or drop by arranged by California friend Justin Dart stretched out to an hour and a half in the leader's office at the House of Commons. The two were struck by the similarity of their world visions. "We found great areas of agreement," Reagan said later.[1]

Both believed in the primacy of individual endeavor, unreconstructed capitalism, and the need for a strong defense against the advantage-seeking and freedom-threatening Soviets. He was confident, but also courtly, which she loves, and very good-looking. She liked that too.

They kept in touch. Reagan faded temporarily after a short, but respectable challenge to incumbent Gerald Ford in the primaries preceding the 1976 presidential race. By 1979, when Thatcher moved into Number 10, Jimmy Carter was president and Thatcher tolerated him for eighteen months. Despite their rocky first meeting, the prime minister was a faithful friend to the United States during the Carter administration because she believes, then and now, that Britain and the United States must remain staunch allies. But she did not like Carter at all. "She thought him feeble," said a cabinet minister.[2]

Thatcher was worried about the United States in 1979, concerned that the nation hadn't moved beyond its post-Vietnam slump. She looked to America as freedom's last great hope and was troubled by the nation's paroxysms of self-doubt. An introspective, hesitant United States was dangerous. The Soviets were on the move—in Angola, Southeast Asia, Central America. During Thatcher's time in Parliament, the United States had produced a skein of troubled presidencies. Kennedy had been assassinated; Johnson had been driven out over an unpopular war; Nixon was ousted in disgrace; and Ford was an unelected transitional figure. Thatcher knew that the United States needed a strong hand.

And she knew that Carter was not likely to supply it. Thatcher couldn't figure out what he believed in beyond his often repeated desire to inject a moral force into America's international relations. She found him sanctimonious, wishy-washy, and indecisive in his stop-go efforts to handle the American economy. She considered his approach to the Soviets naive and thought his human rights policies well intentioned but "wet." Carter had no purposeful vision, as far as Thatcher was concerned.[3]

She was looking for a strong American president, one with charisma who projected that strength. Carter was always compromising, seeking consensus either with Capitol Hill, foreign leaders, or the public. Then there were those horrible lapses in dignity, carrying his own suitcase, collapsing while jogging, and kissing the Queen Mother (the first time a nonfamily member had done so in more than fifty years). Thatcher was appalled when Carter remarked in public that the Queen Mother reminded him of Miss Lillian, his mother. He was trying to be a populist president but doing it all wrong. He was trying to be popular, not populist. Thatcher is a populist, trying to bring government back to the people, but she has never cared about popularity. She felt that Carter had not learned the distinction. She also thought it unfortunate that Carter was short as well as weak. With the exception of Mikhail Gorbachev, Thatcher prefers tall men. She also believes that determined and optimistic individuals with strong beliefs change history.

Reagan, 6'1" to Carter's 5'8", a charmer who likes making women feel good, was a welcome arrival. He did not kiss the Queen Mother, but he was the only foreign leader whom Thatcher regularly kissed on greeting and leaving. He was Ron and she was Margaret, but she was always cognizant that he was the president of the United States, the head of state like the monarch, as well as head of government. When the chips were down, she was always certain that she could count on the United States, but she would never take that for granted.

On matters of policy, they were blood brother and sister. No president and prime minister have ever been so close philosophically. He was a legitimate conservative, as was she. He shared her steel-willed conviction about tax cuts and a strong defense. Throughout Reagan's eight years in the White House, they were in remarkable accord. The sole major exception was Thatcher's horror at Reagan's failure to attack public spending and his inability to control the U.S. budget deficit. Periodically, like a mother scolding a child who had wasted his allowance, she would blast the United

States for not tending more scrupulously to fiscal affairs. Otherwise, they could have read each other's speeches. "She's a Reagan with brains," friends of the president said. "She's Reagan without the deficits," said British admirers.

Ideology was not their only common ground. Both came from rural towns; Dixon, Illinois, was not so different from Maggie's Grantham. Even their families had similarities. Neither the older Reagans nor the Robertses had had much formal education. Neither of the parents made it past the ninth grade. Reagan's father Jack was not a grocer, but he was a shoe salesman. Despite his alcoholism, he was a hard worker who spent much of his life laboring to own his own store, an ambition that gave his son an appreciation of entrepreneurs. In his autobiography, *Where's the Rest of Me?*, Reagan wrote that his father "never lost his conviction that the individual must stand on his own feet . . . that man's own ambition determined what happened to him."

Jack was also a strong patriot who believed in trying to do the right thing, but the family's real strength came from Reagan's mother Nelle, a cheerful hard worker, cut from the Alf Roberts mold. Thatcher liked strong men like her father; Reagan was comfortable with strong women like Nelle. He married two of them. He had little time, though, for his children. Thatcher never rejected her children the way Reagan did, but neither did she spend much time with them.

Neither Reagan nor Thatcher is a deep thinker, or a great reader of history, or an intellectual ideologue. Both trace their beliefs to the tried-and-true maxims and to their gut instincts, and both have been held in contempt by intellectuals and called shallow and narrow-minded. This is particularly unfair to Thatcher, who as a scientist and lawyer has solid academic credentials and intellectual skill. What seems to offend many about Reagan and Thatcher is their absence of self-doubt and their devotion to action over contemplation. Both Thatcher and Reagan admire doers. They don't dislike thinkers, but too much speculation makes both fidget. They both believe that almost everyone is capable of being their kind of "doer." They did not have privileged upbringings yet became successful, and they have little sympathy or understanding for those who cannot do the same. To them, failure is the result of not trying hard enough, not being willing to stand on one's own feet. That one-dimensional stance bothers many, who are offended that the disadvantaged suffer under Thatcher while the greediest prospered under Reagan. The prime minister becomes incensed by such charges; the president ignored them.

Both admired the other's tenacity. "She has the true grit of a true Brit," said Reagan.[4] She told him, "You have restored faith in the American dream." Both spread their beliefs less by speaking than preaching. The prime minister had enormous admiration for Reagan's ability to communicate his beliefs to the American people. She has had far greater difficulty doing that to her constituents. "Believing the right thing is only part of the battle," she has said. "If you cannot communicate those convictions to people, you have failed. By that measure, President Reagan has had tremendous success."[5]

Shortly after the pomp and glitter of the Reagan inauguration, Thatcher flew to Washington, the new administration's first official visitor, for the kind of open arms welcome usually reserved for a victorious general. "A kind of [John the] Baptist to Reagan's Messiah," according to Hugo Young,[6] Maggie had been out slaying socialists and mushy, consensus-driven backsliders, the same infidels Reagan would crusade against. Creating the impression that he and his cavalry had arrived to join her struggle, the president greeted Thatcher with a huge honor guard on the South Lawn of the White House. Battle streamers snapped in the breeze, while a bearskin-hatted drum major strutted. In his remarks, Reagan warned about Moscow, still led then by ailing Soviet party chief Leonid Brezhnev. "So long as our adversaries continue to arm themselves at a pace far beyond the needs of defense," the president cautioned, "so the free world must do whatever is necessary to safeguard its own security." Thatcher concurred wholeheartedly and pledged her troth. "America's successes will be our successes," she said. "Your problems will be our problems. When you look for friends, we will be there." In the Oval Office, Thatcher and Reagan talked for two hours, sealing their friendship and sampling some of the thirty-five flavors of jellybeans Reagan kept on his desk. "They may not be good for the teeth," she said, digging in gamely. "But they will be good for sugar consumption in Britain."

Thatcher proved her friendship throughout the Reagan presidency not least when she allowed him to bomb Libya from British airfields in April 1986. She supported Reagan to such an extent that critics at home found her slavishly devotional. Some called her "Reagan's poodle," all too willing to trot obediently at his heels or sit panting in his lap waiting to be fluffed.

As caricature, the symbolism makes a great drawing. As fact, the image does not hold up. For openers, anyone who has ever met or dealt with Thatcher knows that "Attila the Hen," as she is sometimes called at home, is no one's "poodle." There have also been instances in which the prime minister brought the president around to trot behind her. Thatcher only rarely turned the full force of her emotions on the president himself, but she was never reluctant to express her disagreement, forcefully if needed, to officials like Secretary of State George Shultz, one of her favorites. The relationship has been far from a one-way street for the United States. By the end of the Reagan administration, Thatcher's star in the global firmament had risen at least as high as Reagan's.

Rising European anxiety about U.S. policies contributed to the misperception that Thatcher was a presidential captive. When America projects power, the British and Europeans are apprehensive; when the United States pulls back, they still get apprehensive. A weak dollar is worrisome abroad; so is a strong dollar. Concerns that there are too many U.S. servicemen in Europe have for years been offset by fears that the United States may bring some of the troops home. Most Europeans could not comprehend America's fascination with Reagan. His likable charm, the soothing psychological effect he had on Americans, simply did not translate across the Atlantic. Many Europeans considered him a dangerous ideologue, inexperienced in world affairs and insufficiently intelligent to lead the world's greatest power. Reagan had not been in office long when those feelings were reinforced.

In December 1981, at Moscow's instigation, Polish authorities declared martial law and cracked down on the popular Solidarity trade union. The Reagan administration, in an effort to penalize Moscow and the Polish government without hurting the Polish people, responded by refusing export licenses for U.S. pipe-laying equipment to be used in the construction of a huge East–West pipeline that was to supply Siberian natural gas to Western Europe. The project originated with the oil shortages and OPEC price hikes of the 1970s, when Europe, in particular, became nervous that it relied almost entirely on the unstable Middle East for its energy needs. The Soviets, looking for hard currency, agreed to sell Europe nearly a trillion and a half cubic feet of gas a year for twenty-five years—30 percent of the continent's requirements. The Europeans would pay for construction of the $15 billion pipeline that would stretch 3,300 miles from the eastern USSR to the Czechoslovakian border. The project involved tens of thousands of jobs. Caterpillar, an American company, made the pipe-laying machines required, while other essential equipment was manufactured by European subsidiaries of U.S. firms or companies operating under American licensing.

The project had taken years to negotiate, but Reagan gave the Allies only five hours' notice of his intention to suspend all licenses. He also made his decision retroactive, which meant none of the equipment already made or in the pipeline could be shipped to the USSR. Contracts worth hundreds of millions of dollars were suddenly worthless, and thousands of European workers faced layoffs. Reagan's action threw the entire project into jeopardy. The United States, however, wasn't going to suffer. Except for worried Caterpillar employees, few other American jobs were involved. Nor did the United States have any plans to punish the Soviets directly for the Polish crackdown. Reagan refused to cancel any of the huge U.S. grain sales to the USSR. Europe was being asked to make a major sacrifice while the United States suffered no deprivation.[7]

Europeans found America's hypocrisy intolerable. So did Thatcher. She thought that the whole U.S. approach was wrong and that Reagan didn't realize that France, West Germany, and Britain—who all held huge pipeline contracts—would abandon Washington on the controversy, which they later did, leading to the embargo's collapse. No one was prepared to go along with Reagan, lose billions, and see thousands of European workers unemployed. Thatcher too wanted to punish the Communist authorities, but not by destroying European economies. "Gesture politics," she sneered.[8]

The pipeline episode helped educate Thatcher about Reagan's limitations. She realized that for all his considerable talents, the president was not very intelligent. He was a superb instinctual politician, but it was impossible to discuss issues with him in detail. That irritated her. Also troubling was the fact that he was always surrounded by aides, unlike Thatcher herself, who travels with few advisers and is capable of discussing all the issues without any help. In one "private" meeting with the president in Washington, thirteen advisers sat in the room with Reagan. Thatcher could not do anything about it there, but when George Shultz brought a note-taker to a private meeting at Chequers, she told the aide to take a walk while she and the secretary of state talked in real privacy.

"If only Reagan could have remembered substance the way he

recalled jokes," said one close Thatcher aide, his voice drifting off. The president told everyone stories, and Thatcher was no exception. She smiled and tried to tolerate them; she did not want to hurt his feelings. But when he repeated himself, she had difficulty restraining her natural impatience. During an informal dinner at the Williamsburg economic summit, Reagan started one story, "Margaret, if one of your predecessors had been a little more clever . . ." That's as far as he got. Thatcher, who had heard the line before, burst in: ". . . Yes, I know, I would have been hosting this gathering." Reagan, at first startled, then laughed and shook his head in wonder. They thought so much alike that she could finish his lines.

On her 1982 post-Falklands visit to Washington, Thatcher hoped to speak with Reagan about the pipeline. Again, he was surrounded. "They never let him out of their sights," one British official commented. Nonetheless, eventually Reagan did speak up. "It became clear almost immediately that the president did not have a clue as to the significance of the pipeline issue," said a British participant. William Clark, then Reagan's national security adviser, stood silently in his cowboy boots, while Secretary of State Alexander Haig, soon to lose his job, looked on. As a former NATO supreme commander, Haig was supposed to know Europe and understand its concerns on what to her was such a clear-cut issue. His failure to educate Reagan on the pipeline contributed to Thatcher's concerns about him during the Falklands. She concluded that Haig was an overpromoted, emotional blowhard.[9]

Appalled at the U.S. stance on the pipeline and lacking confidence in the secretary of state, Thatcher was also worried about the president. She left the meeting with her eyebrows arched. Thatcher knew she would have to work around Reagan when it came to detail. She would also look out for him. Thatcher had no doubt that Reagan needed watching over. She found him dotty in some conversations. "Not much gray matter, is there?" she wondered after one early meeting. Still, the prime minister refused to accept the obvious limitations and never criticized him personally. "She simply did not want to acknowledge that he did not have it," said a colleague. She found Reagan's deafness a considerable handicap. Sometimes, after making a point, Thatcher would look in his eyes and find them totally blank. She would repeat herself louder and watch for a flicker of recognition before moving on.

Over the years, the Ron and Maggie meetings took on a set choreography. Thatcher did almost all the talking. "On occasion, she could get very tiresome, and Reagan could barely get in a word edgewise, but for the most part, he just let her bang on," said an official who frequently sat in. "He seemed to get a kick out of watching her get all wound up." Thatcher was, despite her reservations about Reagan's attention span, impressed by the president's ability to ignore extraneous detail and find the important point in an issue.

In 1983, the invasion of Grenada put the special relationship between Thatcher and Reagan to an especially demanding test. The Caribbean island had a Marxist government but was still a member of the Commonwealth. Because it was tiny and had not been a trouble spot, no one but the tourists who loved its beaches paid much attention to it. In October 1983, however, Grenada's leader Maurice Bishop was overthrown and killed by an extreme left-wing Marxist group. Suddenly, everyone started paying attention.

Representatives of the Caribbean neighbors of Grenada quickly met in Guyana, where they split into two groups. The larger countries, backed by Britain, sought a plan to oust the Marxists. The smaller islands closer to Grenada encouraged the United States to invade, but the United States was still reeling from a suicide bombing in Beirut that had killed 241 Marines only days before. Britain knew Washington was considering invading but was repeatedly told no decision had been made. Administration officials explained that the substantial American naval presence off the island was there in case Americans had to be evacuated. Defense Secretary Caspar Weinberger, the administration's biggest Anglophile, said nothing.

Surprisingly, Thatcher's government misunderstood the Reagan fixation on communism in Central America and the Caribbean. The president felt that Jimmy Carter had let Nicaragua go Communist and was determined not to allow a similar loss. Grenada could be another Cuba and, with Nicaragua, could create the third leg of a potentially destabilizing socialist triangle close to the United States. Britain misgauged the depth of his feeling. In an economic belt-tightening measure, the Foreign Office had closed overseas posts, including those in Nicaragua and El Salvador. "Surprise, surprise," said a top British diplomat. "We closed the two little Central American places of maximum interest to our friendly, neighborhood superpower."[10]

It may not have made a difference. Two days before the United States invaded Grenada, Thatcher phoned Reagan, who had called earlier to say that the situation was serious. He was worried about the 1,000 Americans on the island, many of them students. Thatcher was calling about the meetings underway in Guyana. That was the track she was following. "Well, I'll get back to you," Reagan told her. She took that to mean that he would call before he did anything. But Thatcher was having dinner with Princess Alexandra when she learned that the Americans had invaded.

"She went ballistic," said an aide. "The angriest I've ever seen her." Back at Downing Street, she spoke to the president just after he briefed a congressional delegation and made no secret of her rage. Britain had been deliberately kept in the dark about the raid, she charged. No one had informed the Queen, Grenada's head of state. The invasion was illegal. Thatcher, a lawyer, could not for the life of her figure out the legal justification for a third party to march in and chuck out a regime it didn't like. How was the U.S. action different from the Soviet invasion of Afghanistan or the Argentinians moving into the Falklands? This kind of thing undercut the West's moral standing. She was so excited and shouting so loud that Reagan held the phone away from his ear. He apologized and explained his regret at not telling her, but he had not told Congress either. It wasn't that he didn't trust Britain or Congress, but he was afraid of leaks that might have endangered the Americans and Britons on the island.

Thatcher felt humiliated. But her reaction did not perturb Reagan. He was grinning as he described her feistiness. "She was great," he told aides. She will get over it, he added, knowing that the ends—the elimination of a nasty socialist regime—would outweigh the means with a pragmatic anticommunist like Thatcher. He was right. She was not displeased with the result. Success was the criterion, and the operation, which many thought a diversion to get the Beirut bombing news off the front pages, was an unchallenged success. "She erupted and put it behind her," said Ambassador Sir Oliver Wright. The affair did not affect their personal relationship.[11]

Britain and the Thatcher government reaped many gains from the prime minister's relationship with Reagan. In 1982, Britain was given the opportunity to upgrade its aging Polaris submarine missiles to Tridents at a bargain basement price available to no other country. Britain also picked up a $12 billion arms sale to Saudi Arabia when the United States, bowing to congressional pressure, dropped its own plans to sell the Saudis advanced jet fighters and recommended that Riyadh deal with London. Reagan also helped see to it that a variety of antitrust lawsuits aimed at British Airways were dropped. The litigation, involving trans-Atlantic pricing practices, had complicated plans to privatize the national airline.

In December 1984, after her first meeting with Mikhail Gorbachev, the prime minister flew to China and Hong Kong to sign the agreement turning the Crown Colony back to China in 1997. Already halfway around the world, she decided to return via Washington so she could talk to Reagan about two pet subjects, his Strategic Defense Initiative (SDI) and Gorbachev. Flying from Hong Kong to Hawaii, she landed at Hickham Field at 3 A.M. to refuel and decided she wanted to see Pearl Harbor. Certainly, said her military host. He would order the cars. "Don't bother," said Thatcher, motioning to the water at the west end of the airfield. "It's right over there." With that, she reached into her bottomless handbag, pulled out a flashlight, and heels clacking, led a trek across the tarmac to the water's edge, while her hosts stumbled to keep up.

Back on the plane, she did not sleep, but still emerged fresh and alert in Washington. In her wake trailed exhausted, ashen-faced assistants who could barely keep their eyes open. At 11 P.M., having been up for two days, she arrived at the British Embassy on Massachusetts Avenue. "Right, let's have a briefing meeting," she announced as her aides sagged. At midnight, she ended the briefing and asked for the following day's plan. She was to have breakfast with Vice President Bush at 9 A.M. Right, she said. Then call me at 6 A.M.; my hairdresser can come at 7 A.M., we'll have another briefing meeting at 8 A.M., and we'll go see the vice president. Until then, I'd best get to my boxes. With that, she strode up the embassy staircase to her room for two more hours of paperwork, followed by four hours' sleep.

After breakfast with Bush the next day, she helicoptered to Camp David, in Maryland's Catoctin Mountains, for her meeting with Reagan. She was worried about the president's commitment to SDI, known popularly as Star Wars, the high-tech umbrella he wanted to construct in space to defend the United States from a Soviet ballistic missile attack. In London, Gorbachev had told Thatcher how concerned the Soviets were about SDI. If Reagan went ahead with it, Gorbachev said, there would be no alternative but to match the American escalation. Thatcher was not put off by the threat. But she had found Gorbachev sensible, and she had her own doubts about Star Wars. She was a scientist and thought the idea was foolish.

By this time, Thatcher had also figured Reagan out. She believed that his lack of attention to detail could be an advantage when it came to SDI. She believed he was drifting, ill served by competing arms control factions within his own administration. It was up to her, she felt, to get Reagan back on track with a clarified position with which the rest of the Alliance could live.

As usual, she did most of the talking. For ninety minutes, with an extraordinary bluntness tolerable only because of their personal relationship, she lectured him on the demerits of Star Wars. Technologically, there were serious imperfections in the plan. Strategically, it could create a profound East–West imbalance. Politically as it related to Europe, the program could drive a wedge down the middle of the Alliance. She pleaded with Reagan not to abandon the Anti-Ballistic Missile Treaty of 1972. "The ABM treaty is of enormous value," she entreated. "It must not be cast aside."[12] She would support him on the basic in-lab research aspect of SDI, but not on advanced testing or deployment.

"Well, Margaret," the president responded calmly, "research is what this is all about." He would continue to adhere to the ABM treaty and acknowledged that it would be years before anyone had a clear idea about the applicability of the space-based defense system.

Thatcher looked relieved. In that case, she had something for him. "She reached into that handbag again and this time pulled out a goddamn communiqué, all typed up," said an incredulous American.[13] The document, quickly dubbed the Camp David accord, contained four main points: the West was not seeking nuclear superiority but balance; SDI deployment would be a matter for negotiation; the overall aim was to enhance, not undermine deterrence; arms control negotiations should keep attempting to reduce the numbers of weapons on both sides.

The president handed the paper to Robert McFarlane, his national security adviser, who nodded and passed it to Secretary of State George Shultz, who also approved. Caspar Weinberger, the harder-line defense secretary, was not at the meeting and was irate when he heard what had transpired. Before he could even be informed, Thatcher had choppered back to Washington, held a news conference, and announced the president's endorsement of the four points. She was delighted. From her vantage point, SDI was, for the foreseeable future, limited to laboratory research. Thatcher personally had nailed that down and gone as far as she could to preserve unity in the Western Alliance. She had gone around the world in six days and returned home to London in triumph in time for Christmas.

Two years later, Thatcher would race back to Washington on another rescue mission. President Reagan and Soviet General Secretary Gorbachev had met in October 1986 in Reykjavik, the capital of Iceland. Reagan had gone to Reykjavik expecting a low-key, preparatory meeting that would lead to a full summit in Washington. The president even left Nancy at home. Gorbachev surprised everyone by bringing his wife, Raisa. More important, he startled the Americans by pulling from his briefcase a major proposal calling for total nuclear disarmament within ten years.

"All nuclear weapons?" Reagan had asked quizzically. "Well, Mikhail, that's exactly what I've been talking about all along. That's what we have long wanted to do—get rid of all nuclear weapons. That's always been my goal."

"Then why don't we agree on it?" Gorbachev said.

"Suits me fine," said Reagan.[14]

There was, however, one hitch: Gorbachev insisted the nonukes deal be tied to a Reagan concession that SDI be restricted to the laboratory. That was enough to sink it. Reagan refused. Gorbachev would not budge, and the talks collapsed in disappointment and accusations of blame.

When Thatcher heard what happened, she was horrified, not by the fact that the agreement had fallen apart but that it had almost succeeded. Didn't the president know what such an agreement meant? He was cutting the ground from under the whole concept of nuclear deterrence, the entire foundation on which Western defense rested. It was just not possible to eliminate nuclear weapons. "I think a world without nuclear weapons is a dream," Thatcher said. "It's like a world without crime. You cannot disinvent knowledge, and there is always the danger that someone will have them. Therefore, there is always a need to deter that danger."

Even if it were possible to eliminate nuclear weapons, Thatcher was convinced it would be a mistake. In her mind, their deterrent factor has been the single biggest reason why there have been no wars in Europe, nuclear or conventional, since 1945. They were the best insurance policy. Besides, if all nuclear forces were removed, how would the West defend itself against the Soviet Union, which had an asymmetrically huge advantage over the West in conventional forces? The whole prospect was terrifying.

So the prime minister sprinted to Washington to explain her view. This time, Thatcher did not want to bash Reagan, who was two years older than when they had last met at Camp David. Her approach was more gentle, couched with greater care, but the goal was the same. She and Charles Powell, her top foreign policy adviser, had already explained her views to Shultz, Weinberger, and latest national security adviser, John Poindexter. They understood Thatcher's concerns about Reykjavik. Powell drafted a statement to present to the president the next day. Thatcher was doing exactly what she had pulled off two years before. If the president did not know what he was talking about, she would tell him, get him to endorse her position, then announce it in both their names.

That's exactly what happened. Back at Camp David the next morning, the paper went to Poindexter. He crossed out two words and said okay. Shultz, somewhat surprised that Thatcher had it all in writing again, looked at the statement. NATO's strategy, centered on nuclear deterrence, remained unchanged. Shultz had no problems with the wording. At the presidential cabin, the secretary of state passed the proposed statement to Reagan. He glanced at it. "That's fine with me," said Reagan. Back in Washington, Thatcher read out the statement at a news conference at the British Embassy. Here was the clarified policy. Reagan had again been rescued. Britain was still getting Trident. The Alliance was saved, no little thanks to her own personal, special relationship.

As Reagan prepared to leave the White House, he invited Thatcher to be his final state guest in November 1988, just as she had been his first. She felt lousy when she arrived, suffering from a bad cold and unhappy with Carol, who was standing in for her regular dresser. Her hair was overdone and her color was poor, but she still managed to star as First Friend amid all the glitter the outgoing Reagan administration could muster. She called Reagan's presidency "one of the greatest in America's history" and pointed out that only three British prime ministers had served throughout consecutive terms of the same president: William Pitt the Younger while George Washington was president; Lord Liverpool during the James Monroe administration; "and the third one is me." Applause echoed throughout the White House just as it would six months later in London, where she arranged for Queen Elizabeth to grant Reagan an honorary knighthood.

Within hours of leaving the White House dance floor at the end of dinner, she was cultivating the next inhabitant of the Oval Office. In praising Reagan, she never forgot to be scrupulously supportive of George Bush. How would she handle Bush? a reporter asked. "You do not handle United States' presidents," she responded with a tight smile. "You offer them your support for policies in which you both believe."

She was overjoyed that Bush defeated Michael Dukakis to win the 1988 election. Scarcely anyone in Britain knew anything about the Massachusetts governor, but Thatcher knew he was a liberal Democrat, which was enough for her. On election night, she had stayed up until 5:15 A.M. watching the results on CNN, then ducked into bed for forty-five minutes before waking and calling Bush at 6:10 A.M. London time, making certain she was the first foreign leader to congratulate him.

Thatcher likes Bush, but their relationship is very different from the one she had with Reagan. She knows him well, having courted him professionally throughout the Reagan presidency, seeing him every time she met Reagan. She knows Bush is far more alert and knowledgeable than Reagan, but she believes he lacks the former president's remarkable ability to express himself convincingly. She has never felt that he projects stature, but hopes that will develop the longer he is in office. Thatcher's biggest question mark about Bush is whether he feels strongly about anything. She and Reagan shared powerful convictions, and those were the bases of their close relationship. The prime minister is not certain that Bush has strong beliefs and worries that he may be one of those consensus, deal-cutting politicians she so suspects. She quickly put Secretary of State James Baker in that category. Thatcher does not trust Baker at all, but she is willing to give Bush the benefit of the doubt. He is a friend and an ally, but she fears he may not be "one of us." Her worst worries seemed to be realized during the president's laid back first four months in office. Nearly all decisions were put on hold while the cautious new administration conducted an extensive policy review. Thatcher was bothered.

For all his inattention to detail, Reagan had spine. Thatcher's doubts about Bush's backbone rose only weeks into his administration, when the new president caved in to demands from Bonn to hold off modernizing Europe's short-range missiles, most of which are based in West Germany, until after Germany's national elections. Thatcher, insistent that an obsolete defense is no defense, objected to the U.S. rollback, and she was worried by the speed with which the United States had capitulated. She feared that the West would succumb to the intoxicating allure of Mikhail Gorbachev's disarmament perfume and Europe would find itself denuclearized, at the mercy of a huge Soviet conventional force. She felt better at the May 1989 Brussels summit marking NATO's fortieth anniversary. She admired Bush's sweeping, creative proposals to cut troops, tanks, artillery, and planes in Europe, although she hesitated at his ambitious three-year timetable. "I think it's a little bit optimistic," she said. "It's quite optimistic. It's very optimistic."

Bush had shown he was not so cautious as to be paralyzed, a positive development in Thatcher's mind. But she planned to monitor his eagerness to compromise. Still, if the prime minister knew she did not have the same relationship with the cautious Bush that she had with her old soulmate Reagan, it remained a solid friendship, rooted in time and mutual understanding. That foundation would allow the working relationship to develop.

By fall 1989, that appeared to be happening. Aware that Thatcher would be seeing Mikhail Gorbachev in Moscow in late September, on her way home from an international meeting of conservatives in Tokyo, Bush sent her a long letter. He asked Thatcher to pass on to Gorbachev his strong reaffirmation of support for perestroika and his pledge that the United States had no intention of taking advantage of the USSR's difficulties in Eastern Europe. Thatcher was delighted at the chance to get back in the equation and gave the president a full report on Gorbachev's response when she got back to London. That kind of involvement was precisely what she hoped to maintain.

It did not bother her that Bush, more comfortable with non-English speakers than Reagan, would not construct a European policy that started and ended in London. She knew that Bush would not need her in the same way Reagan did, but she was also satisfied that she would not be frozen out. She was all the more determined to demonstrate British faithfulness as an ally. That's why she moved so quickly to endorse, within minutes of its announcement, the December 1989 U.S. invasion of Panama. Generally, though, she intended to lie back and not push Bush. He moved slowly, but deliberately. She could tolerate that. If he needed more help, the president could count on her.

It did not happen immediately. In his early months in the Oval Office, the new president's attention, when it focused on Europe, centered on West Germany. Oil was applied to the squeaky wheel, not the faithful partner. Following the NATO summit, Bush delivered the major speech of his first European tour in Germany, but then stopped in London on his way home. Just before meeting Gorbachev in Malta in December 1989, Bush invited Thatcher to Camp David. Sensitive to reports that he had ditched Thatcher in favor of new pals in Bonn, the president set about trying to reassure the prime minister that the "special relationship" was intact. Some Britons, including those who criticized her for being too close to Reagan, charged that Bush was merely going through the motions to keep Thatcher from looking like a jilted dance partner.

She had not been, but the orchestra was playing new music. Sitting down with Bush, she reveled in the welcome chance to dig into details of issues with the new president the way she never could with Reagan. She was not worried that her third U.S. president would leave her on the sidelines. She was not jealous that Bush spent time with others as well, saying, "It's quite wrong that because you have one friend, you should exclude the possibility of other friendships as well."

CHAPTER FIFTEEN

Eye of the Storm

As DOMINANT as she has been, Margaret Thatcher has also had several close calls, the kind that could have cost any prime minister the job. The Falklands War was the most obvious example, while the Brighton bomb was a different kind of close shave. But Thatcher had another narrow escape that was of little note outside Britain. The political crisis known as the Westland affair began as no more than a speck on the horizon, but grew to explosive proportions, tore the cabinet apart, and shook her government to its core. Westland was Thatcher's Watergate, her most serious political misstep, which raised the possibility that she might be forced from office. "I may not be prime minister by six o'clock tonight," she told associates on January 27, 1986.[1]

The simple origins of the episode belied its significance. The affair began as a minor financial matter, involving a single firm, the Westland Corporation, Britain's sole manufacturer of helicopters. Unlike Watergate, the Westland imbroglio did not involve anything illegal. The whole affair was really about Thatcher's style of governing: how she used, or misused, power; how she dealt with her cabinet, civil service, and personal aides; and whether her close alliance with the United States was becoming a problem for Britain.

The story began in late 1985. Westland, which was located in Somerset, had lost $140 million that year and was on the verge of financial collapse. The firm's executives began looking for a partner with deep pockets. Connecticut-based United Technologies Corp. (UTC), which had long business ties with Westland, offered to take

246

a minority share in order to give Sikorsky, its helicopter division, a foothold in Western Europe.

Several European firms had been approached, but none showed any interest in buying into Westland. Defense Minister Michael Heseltine balked at the UTC offer, however; he felt that the Connecticut firm's takeover of Westland's research and development facilities would leave Britain technologically destitute in the industry. The Westland deal, he believed, was part of a pattern that would eventually lead to a serious imbalance in the NATO alliance. Heseltine had been working closely with Weinberger, negotiating Star Wars contracts and the deployment of U.S. cruise missiles in Britain. He had grown worried that the defense relationship between the United States and Europe was nowhere near equal. The United States had all the money, was hiring the best brains, and was in danger of totally dominating the Alliance.

Heseltine argued for greater European cooperation to counterbalance the United States' technological primacy. He had had some success. Earlier that year he had played a key role in an agreement between five European countries to build jointly a jet fighter. Now, in the wake of the UTC offer, Heseltine moved to organize another continental consortium of defense contractors to bail out Westland with a European offer. The group included two British firms—British Aerospace and General Electric of Britain—West Germany's Messerschmitt-Bolkow-Blohm, Italy's Agusta, and France's Aerospatiale.

Heseltine, however, had a basic problem. Thatcher was not interested in a European consortium. She wanted the Americans. The reason, not surprisingly, was her recurring distrust of Europeans. Thatcher did not state publicly that she favored the American bid. Officially she was neutral, calling the decision a private business matter to be decided by the Westland board, which, she was privately delighted, favored the UTC offer.

Another personal reason influenced her reaction to the Westland deal—Heseltine himself. She didn't trust her defense minister. She never had. He was a maverick and, though he often agreed with her policies, was definitely not "one of us." Thatcher had been horrified when, years before, Heseltine had gone on a rampage in the House of Commons. Incensed by the singing of "The Red Flag" by Labor party members during a parliamentary debate, Heseltine shouted for quiet. When he was ignored, Heseltine scooped up the speaker's ceremonial mace and swung it around his head like a caveman about to attack a woolly mammoth. That, along with his thick, long yellow hair, earned him the nickname Tarzan.

Heseltine was a self-made millionaire, but he was far more interested in power than money. Thatcher knew it and was immediately wary. He was not a grandee, but his old-style Tory paternalism and emphasis on compassion, the "C" word it was sometimes called, made him further suspect. Finally, he was an unadulterated self-promoter and highly ambitious. As a potential rival, he had to be watched carefully. When he urged the cabinet to back the European consortium bid for Westland, Thatcher refused. He declined to fall back into line, but the prime minister, uncharacteristically uncertain of herself, failed to move authoritatively to shut him down and restore cabinet solidarity. Uninhibited, Heseltine fought a rearguard action against Thatcher for a month. It ended with him storming out of a cabinet meeting and announcing his resignation to reporters standing outside on the street. In true British fashion, the cabinet meeting continued as if nothing had happened.[2]

Instead of going away, the Westland issue escalated as Heseltine, freed of constraints, pressed forward with his own crusade, partly out of principle and partly to lay down his marker for a later leadership challenge. He charged that Thatcher was mortgaging the country's future across the Atlantic and ignoring "Britain's future as a technologically advanced country." Her pro-U.S. bias was "not a proper way to carry on government." Thatcher was livid, but did not know how to deal with her renegade former minister. In the meantime, Westland was sinking. Company officials feared that Heseltine's campaign might force UTC to retract its offer. Westland, they feared, would be stuck with a second-rate European deal or worse. It was possible that no other offer would materialize.

Heseltine charged that Leon Brittan, the minister for trade and industry, had leaned on British Aerospace to pull out of the European consortium. According to Heseltine, Brittan had warned the huge defense contractor that its U.S. sales, nearly a half billion dollars, could be jeopardized. Brittan's tangled explanation of his actions and his attempts to maintain the prime minister's neutrality defied credibility. The House of Commons echoed with calls for his resignation as the debate degenerated into a series of accusations.

Day after day Thatcher was bruised, while Brittan was savaged. Finally, in late January 1986, he resigned, becoming the designated scapegoat, when Thatcher revealed that he and her staff had approved the leaking of a letter from the solicitor general that discredited Heseltine to the press. Even her strongest supporters found the idea that Thatcher knew nothing of the leak unbelievable. Details are Thatcher's stock in trade; the idea that her closest aides would take weeks to provide her essential information when her government was being attacked was simply not credible. The case looked more like Watergate every day. Coverup had become the issue. With Heseltine gone and the devoted Brittan cut adrift, the controversy lapped ever closer to the prime minister.

"The prime minister is on trial," Labor leader Kinnock told a packed House of Commons in late January 1986. "If she will not tell the truth, she must go." Pleading has never been Thatcher's style, but she was reduced to it then. "Will the honorable gentleman not accept that there was a genuine misunderstanding?" she entreated. Her usual steely authority had disappeared, replaced by hesitancy and contrition. No, he would not. "The prime minister must come clean," Kinnock demanded. "We want the full facts and we want them now."

The only question that mattered was whether Thatcher had tried to conceal her role in the attempt to discredit Heseltine. Much of Britain believed she had, but no one could prove it. Her private office staff held firm, and in the local equivalent of executive privilege, the government refused to let the aides involved testify before the investigating committee. Thatcher escaped in the Commons when Kinnock fumbled his chance to put her away—falling to his worst instincts and ranting instead of pinning her with the right questions. Then both Heseltine and Brittan came to her rescue. Heseltine knew that if his leader was defeated on his account, his chance of succeeding her would evaporate. To that end, he stood, called her expression of regret "brave," and declared the affair over.

Brittan, back on the back benches with Heseltine, also stood to support Thatcher's explanation and took full responsibility. Their intervention rallied their reeling Tory colleagues and allowed her to win a vote of confidence easily. Interestingly though, there was a postscript to Westland, whose stockholders later backed the Sikorsky bailout package. Neither minister came back to her cabinet, but Thatcher did eventually reward Brittan with a knighthood and a secure posting to Brussels as Britain's commissioner to the Common Market. Yet she scarcely spoke to him after he resigned solely to protect her. Three years later, after his knighthood and

new job, Brittan broke his silence. Thatcher's private aides had
given him express approval to leak the letter besmirching Heseltine.
Had he said it at the time, Thatcher would probably have fallen.
But the day he made his admission, Mikhail Gorbachev visited
London and the prime minister canceled question time to talk with
the Soviet leader. With the news filled with Gorbymania, little
attention was paid to the revelation.[3]

Although she had escaped, the Westland wounds tarnished
Thatcher's image as an uncompromisingly honest leader. Almost
overnight, she looked like one more disingenuous politician. Polling
just after the final debate showed that 55 percent of Britons did not
believe her and more than half the country thought she should
resign. Even 20 percent of those calling themselves Tories urged
she step down. She would have none of it, but she had been
scarred—and scared.

She was newly vulnerable by the beginning of 1986. Her leadership style was at the root of the controversy, and her management
techniques left a lot to be desired. It was clear that at least some
of the traditionally nonpolitical Civil Service had been highly politicized during Westland. As for Thatcher herself, the unbending
determination and single-mindedness that had won her such admiration during the Falklands War and miners' strike were a dis-
advantage this time. Throughout Westland, her determination had,
more accurately, been hard-headedness; single-mindedness translated this time into a far less appealing intolerance of dissent. "She
is vulnerable to charges that her style is autocratic and that she likes
to govern with a small group of people with whom she is comfortable," said a senior aide who thoroughly supports her. "That's not
new. She's never been easy."[4]

Protests that Thatcher was too pro-American kept the Westland pot bubbling, and Westland was only one example of what
critics called her sellouts to the United States. The fact that British
firms were the single biggest buyers of U.S. companies did nothing
to mitigate the criticism. Then, when another American firm
showed up to buy another British icon just days after the Westland
saga drifted off the front pages, all hell broke loose again.

This time, General Motors was out to buy the Land Rover and
truck divisions of government-owned British Leyland (BL), the
country's largest vehicle manufacturer. For years, British Leyland
had been a financial swamp. Nationalized by Harold Wilson in 1974,
the company had cost the country billions, including $3 billion lost

in a risky expansion plan. Thatcher hated making up the losses, but with unemployment running at 13.2 percent nationally, she did not want to cut back BL's 275,000 employees. When the truck division lost $85 million in 1985, the prime minister knew something had to be done. She approached a variety of foreign automakers, and when General Motors, with the assurance that Land Rover would be included, offered $375 million, the deal seemed too good to be true. Land Rover, with its upscale jeeplike vehicles, was still profitable, but losing its market share. The company needed to retool and introduce more models. It called for more money than the government was willing to spend.

Selling to General Motors made sense. The British Leyland board liked it, for many of the same reasons that Westland favored UTC. The only drawback was that the sale meant the end of British-owned car production by the last major independent. Coming on the heels of the Westland ordeal, the humiliation was too much to bear. The sale of the truck and bus division caused little concern, but the proposed sale of Land Rover with its distinctly British associations from grouse shoots to expeditionary treks through the far reaches of what was once empire stuck in the nation's craw. "Is there nothing not for sale?" asked John Smith, the Labor party's spokesman on industrial affairs. Dale Campbell-Savours, a Labor MP, accused the government of "dropping the Union Jack and raising the Stars and Stripes over British industry."

The fact that General Motors had been making Vauxhalls in Britain for two decades before the first Land Rover was produced did not matter. What did count was image. Had Mercedes, Peugeot, or Fiat been the purchaser, the debate would have been very different. The hurdle was to avoid being embarrassed again by surrendering to the United States. A practical obstacle was fear that a cost-conscious U.S. manufacturer would cut jobs. In the West Midlands, where BL's production facilities were concentrated, higher unemployment could lead to joblessness for other British workers— Tory MPs in marginal districts.

With an election due in less than two years and support for the government sliding, popular sensitivities could be ignored only at some peril. When canvassing showed that only 19 percent of Britons thought BL should sell to the United States, the government lost its nerve and started backpedaling. General Motors was told Land Rover was no longer part of the deal. GM, having made clear that no Land Rover meant no bargain, broke off the talks. The government had been humiliated. The year 1986 was turning into a very bad one, but more bad news was to come. Again Thatcher's problem involved the United States.

On the night of April 14–15, thirteen American F-111 bombers flew from bases in Britain and, joined by a dozen A-6 attack planes launched from aircraft carriers in the Mediterranean, blasted Libya's capital city of Tripoli and the coastal city of Benghazi. Four of the F-111s aimed sixteen one-ton bombs directly at the Bab al Azizia barracks, Muammar Qaddafi's home and the command center from which he supported terrorist activity around the world.

For months, Ronald Reagan had been edging toward military action against the Libyan leader. Just after Christmas, Palestinian attacks on the Rome and Vienna airports had killed sixteen passengers. Two weeks before the raid a bomb had exploded aboard a TWA flight from Rome to Athens, killing four. Three days later, an explosion shattered a West Berlin discotheque frequented by American GIs, killing an American soldier and a Turk and injuring 230 people, including 79 Americans. Qaddafi denied involvement, but praised the killers. Washington announced that it had irrefutable proof of Libyan complicity. Reagan had already been pressuring Libya by imposing economic sanctions and moving the American fleet closer to Qaddafi's coast. After the disco attack, U.S. public opinion was white hot, the most rabid since the seizure of the hostages in Iran. The country was being shoved around by one more two-bit terrorist nation. Nonmilitary action was maddeningly ineffectual, but military measures did seem to work—or at least they made Americans, and their president, feel better. The previous October, when the United States seized four Arab terrorists who had hijacked the Italian cruise ship *Achille Lauro* and murdered an American passenger, Reagan was impressed. He had confidence that military action could be effective.

Before the attack, Reagan sent Vernon Walters, U.S. ambassador to the United Nations and veteran presidential troubleshooter, to ask the Allies to join in. France, West Germany, Spain, and Italy all said no. France and Spain even refused to allow overflights. Only Thatcher would back Reagan. She had cabled him her okay even before Walters arrived to make his pitch. She had, however, thought long and hard before agreeing. She knew she would have almost no support in cabinet. Aides determined that only Lord Hailsham, the aging lord chancellor, would back her there. She needed justification.

Three months earlier she had spoken disapprovingly of using force against Libya. "I must warn you," she told American journalists, "that I do not believe in retaliatory strikes that are against international law."[5] That was her feeling despite the fact that Britain had also been provoked repeatedly by Libya. A Libyan gunman hiding inside its embassy building on St. James's Square had shot out a window and killed a London policewoman, prompting the same kind of anti-Libyan sentiment that the killing of Leon Klinghoffer on the *Achille Lauro* produced in the United States. British authorities also had evidence that Libya had been supplying the IRA with guns and explosives. Even so, Thatcher maintained her opposition to hot pursuit. "Once you start to go across borders, I don't see an end to it," she said. "I uphold international law very firmly."

She hadn't changed her mind. She would insist that the U.S. retaliation be taken under the inherent right of self-defense spelled out in Article 51 of the United Nations Charter, a murky passage that rationalizes self-defense in broad terms, "if an armed attack occurs." Lawyers had told her not to worry. When needed, justification could be found in international law to support virtually any action.

Thatcher received specific word midway through a dinner she was hosting at Downing Street that Washington wanted to bomb Libya. Foreign Secretary Sir Geoffrey Howe and Defense Secretary George Younger happened to be there, so the three adjourned to her study to consider the request. Howe and Younger were loath to get involved. Thatcher, tougher and more eager to help Reagan if she could, leaned toward offering support, but wanted to know more. What were the targets? What guarantees were there against hitting civilian targets inadvertently? How many civilians did they expect would die? How did the United States assess the likely reaction in the other key Middle East states if it proceeded with the raid? What was the U.S. interpretation of Soviet deployment in the area? Howe and Younger recommended that Washington be forced to prove its case. The prime minister, who gave Reagan the benefit of the doubt, disagreed. She only wanted clarification, and she wanted to make certain that Washington was prepared to construct a solid case for its action under Article 51.[6]

After firing these conditions back to Washington, she decided to sleep on the request before making a final decision. As it turned out, no great debate twirled in her head. She was back in her office

by 7:15 A.M. She hadn't heard from the White House, but that
didn't matter. She had already made up her mind. "We're going
to do it," she told Charles Powell, her private secretary for foreign
and defense affairs and close adviser. "I've thought about it during
the night. It must be the right thing to do. We are their allies and
they have 350,000 troops over here. When someone needs you . . ."
her voice trailed off. The approval was typed up and cabled to
Lieutenant General Colin Powell, Downing Street's favorite of Reagan's five national security advisers. "Dear Ron," it began, signed
with the usual, "Yours ever, Margaret."

Standing alone among the European leaders, her decision
brought her condemnation at home and on the continent. Demonstrators marched in London and Thatcher was attacked scath-
ingly for exposing her countrymen to terrorist reprisal. Polls showed
that nearly 70 percent of the public felt she had erred. The Foreign
Office, known for its Arabist leanings, lined up against her. She
thought that the diplomats, as usual, were wimps.

In the House of Commons there was strong opposition, even
from the Tories. And from Labor, Kinnock accused her of being
"supine in her support for the American president." Denis Healey
called the decision "a disastrous blunder" which proved that "when
Mr. Reagan tells Mrs. Thatcher to jump, her reply is 'how high?' "
Liberal party leader David Steel accused Thatcher of turning "the
British bulldog into a Reagan poodle." "Poodlism" became a syn-
onym for "uncritical Reaganism." Her old nemesis Edward Heath
reminded the nation that he had refused Richard Nixon's request
to use British bases to resupply Israel during the 1973 Yom Kippur
War.

Thatcher is best under personal attack. In spite of her private
misgivings, she pointed out publicly that it was because of the Allies,
including Britain, that the United States kept hundreds of thousands of troops in Europe. Therefore, "It was inconceivable to me
that we should refuse United States aircraft and pilots the opportunity to defend their own people." The performance was bravura.
"A lioness in a den of Daniels," the *Times* of London called her.

There was another reason for her support of Reagan, and she
went to great pains to point it out. She reminded MPs that U.S.
aid had been vital during the Falklands crisis. "We received splen-
did support from the U.S., far beyond the call of duty," she said.
A top Whitehall official put it more bluntly: "We owed Washington
one; this evened the score." Indeed, when there were suggestions

in the press that there might be another, follow-up raid—since the Americans missed Qaddafi—British officials quickly made it clear to American diplomats and reporters that there would be no permission for a repeat performance.[7] Forget international law the next time around. She had done her bit and was paying the domestic political price for "poodlism."

The display of loyalty, against the advice of her ministers, made Thatcher an even bigger heroine in the United States, but further isolated her in Europe. That did not bother her. "Margaret," said a senior cabinet minister, "is used to being the odd person out. She seems to relish it." She did not relish the fallout at home, although she had anticipated it.

When Vernon Walters had finished his briefing before the raid, he told Thatcher, "You know, prime minister, my normal job is at the United Nations. When I go back there, I'm going into the eye of the storm."

Thatcher looked him in the eye: "General, when I go back to the British electorate, I'm going into the eye of the storm."

CHAPTER SIXTEEN

PM and HM

SIX MONTHS in age and the timeless barriers of class separate Britain's two most powerful women. Thatcher was born in October 1925, Queen Elizabeth II in April 1926. The Queen, however, has reigned since 1952. She ascended the throne twenty-seven years before Thatcher, her eighth prime minister, arrived in Downing Street. The relationship between the two intelligent and strong-willed women is complex. Though they have shared the stage for more than a decade, few details are known with certainty about their rapport because neither speaks publicly, and rarely privately, about the other. Their working relationship is professional, as it must be. But aside from the intense patriotism they share, the prime minister and Her Majesty are totally different kinds of women, with very different attitudes and approaches to British concerns.

Their styles are very different. Always perfectly coiffed and impeccably turned out, Thatcher looks more regal than the Queen, who is often content to slosh across a paddock in rubber boots and a head scarf with her beloved Corgis trailing in her wake. For many non-Britons, Thatcher, now on the best-dressed lists, has replaced the Queen as the nation's most visible symbol. When Thatcher was on a trip to Nigeria, countless onlookers believed she was the Queen. At the end of the Falklands War, Thatcher, as commander-in-chief, welcomed home the troops. The Queen, as mother, welcomed home Prince Andrew. At a massive subway fire in London, Thatcher picked her way through the buckled wreckage as firemen removed thirty-one bodies. Days later, the horror fading, several junior members of the royal family quietly visited the bereaved. No royals attended the memorial service for the 271 victims of the bomb explosion aboard Pam Am 103 above Lockerbie, Scotland, in December 1988. The prime minister visited the accident site and attended the service. Thatcher is not maternal but has assumed the role of National Mother. She is not the head of state, but in affairs of national tragedy she represents the nation with grace and dignity. As Thatcher has grown in office and become larger than life on the domestic and world stages, the Queen has shrunk.

Their power is very different. The Queen has no power per se. She cannot change the law, declare war, or even voice her political opinions publicly. As the symbol of Britain and the embodiment of continuity, she holds the power to command loyalty and to soothe the national psyche.

During her near forty years on the throne, Elizabeth has presided over enormous social change in Britain: the loss of empire and influence, the decimation of the economy, the rise of the middle class, and the abandonment of consensus government. Through it all, she has maintained her own nineteenth-century rituals—moving from castle to castle by season, attending the Royal Ascot races, opening Parliament, and sailing on her yacht *Britannia*. Yet, despite her fondness for these time-honored customs, the Queen is a thoroughly modern monarch. Since ascending the throne, she has studied all the state papers of the political parties. Because state papers are not handed on from government to government, she has a detailed sense of continuity that her transitory prime ministers, even the relatively stable Thatcher, sometimes lack. She knows all the key domestic political players. The Queen is also Britain's most experienced diplomat by far, better informed on major international issues than her most experienced foreign secretary. She knows every significant foreign leader—and most of the minor ones.

Queen Elizabeth has sharp political opinions, including strong ones about Thatcher, but to discuss them publicly could be interpreted as meddling in political affairs, which could, in the worst possible case, lead to the dissolution of the monarchy. So she refrains. She does not hesitate, however, to exercise her traditional right to advise, encourage, and warn the prime minister at their private weekly meetings. The session takes place at Buckingham Palace at 6:30 P.M. each Tuesday that Parliament sits. Held in the Queen's Audience Room, a large comfortable drawing room overlooking the palace gardens, it usually lasts about an hour. Strictly a business meeting, no refreshments are served. The Queen is direct and forthright. The prime minister, not known for her ability to listen quietly at length to the opinions of others, appreciates that and listens respectfully. Thatcher is best with people who are clear with language, including other lawyers who take a forensic approach. She gets bored when talk gets mushy. The Queen never does. Author Anthony Sampson, in a much repeated observation, once noted that those meetings "are dreaded by at least one of them."[1] That was actually truer in the prime minister's early days. Mrs. Thatcher and the Queen have arrived at a mutual respect and get along better now, although it is widely believed that the Queen finds Mrs. Thatcher the least companionable of all her prime ministers. Actually, the Queen too had some difficulty communicating with Ted Heath, but they were fairly close on issues. The Queen and Mrs. Thatcher have profound policy differences.

The Queen, as the head of the royal family, is the guardian of tradition. Thatcher is out to smash tradition and hasten the pace of change. The Queen, the first aristocrat by birth, takes her role as monarch of all her subjects, whether they be poor and disabled, rich, Tory, or Labor, very seriously. Thatcher is a meritocrat who supports the right of individuals over collectives, has no time for sluggards, and would like to eliminate the Labor party. The Queen believes there is such a thing as a national society. Thatcher has said, "There is no such thing as society."[2] To the prime minister, nations are comprised of striving individuals unrestricted by class distinctions, not artificial groups, neighborhoods, or extended families.

Their behavior is different. Both are hard-working, though no one, perhaps anywhere, works harder than Thatcher. The Queen, born to rule, has never had to claw her way to the top. She is secure with herself and her role, far more so than Thatcher, whose aggression, many close advisers say, masks insecurity. The Queen is not compulsively driven as Thatcher is. She is also far more family-oriented. The Queen loves to watch television; the long-running *Coronation Street* is a favorite. She likes to play cards and games. Cruises on *Britannia* and extended vacations at Balmoral or Sandringham castles with the grandchildren are staples on the royal calendar. All that is alien to Thatcher, who rarely relaxes with anyone other than Denis. Television bores her and she dreads games.

Their bearing is oddly confused. Reserved by nature, the Queen can be chilly but often conveys genuine warmth. Thatcher can be highly affectionate and warm, but is known for her icy control and forbidding temper. The Queen is surrounded by ladies in waiting and mistresses of the robes and lord chamberlains and all the trappings that have helped preserve the monarchy in the public eye. Thatcher has never been interested in the accoutrements of power. She disdains retinues or ranks of security agents or aides. Personal perks are minimal. If Denis goes on a business or personal trip, he drives himself to the airport. On her own overseas trips, Thatcher usually takes fewer than a dozen staff and aides. Hundreds are usually involved in a journey by a U.S. president.

Despite her penchant for economies, many Britons accuse the prime minister of trying to be more regal than the Queen. "She tries to out-Queen the Queen, but the Queen does it better," said Baroness Phillips. Critics say that Thatcher does not understand her place. That is true. Thatcher has never felt confined by "her place" or she never would have become Tory leader and prime minister. She has always wanted to give her best, which, in Britain particularly, is often seen as overreaching. Her ambition suffers because Thatcher cannot draw on the kind of easy informality that upper-class Britons associate with breeding, accent, and old money. "It's a class thing," says a noble who knows both the Queen and prime minister well. "Mrs. Thatcher doesn't have that English upper middle-class tendency toward irony and self-deprecation."[3] The Queen, on the other hand, has a keenly wry wit. "I quite agree with you, madam," she once exclaimed as her Rolls-Royce sped past a woman yelling at a splattering of royal mud. "Hmmm," said the Duke of Edinburgh, "What did she say, darling?" "She said 'Bastards!' " replied the Queen.[4]

Self-deprecation, which could take the sting out of the prime minister's leathery toughness, is hardly a Thatcher trait. Denis laughs easily at himself, but the prime minister, never willing to show an opening that might be seen as weakness, is rarely capable of doing the same. (There are, of course, exceptions. At one cabinet meeting, Thatcher announced, "We've only time for me to lose my temper and get my own way before we must adjourn.") Thatcher is not, however, adept at the gray shades of nuance that amuse the royals. Nuance is out of character for the prime minister, who has never been known for subtlety.

Thatcher's use of the royal "we" drives her critics into apoplectic spasms. "We have become a grandmother," she announced in 1989, when Mark's wife produced her first grandchild. The nation guffawed at the artifice. But few would dare to suggest personally that Thatcher is trying to assume the Queen's role. The mere idea would be unthinkable, she would say. Since childhood, she has been an ardent monarchist. She reveres the institution of the monarchy and is punctilious, some say excessively punctilious, in her treatment of the monarch. Thatcher always shows up early for her private audience with the Queen. She curtsies lower and longer than anyone, causing some royals to mock her. The prime minister gets carried away, some court observers say. "She bobs up and down like a yo-yo," sniffed one. At Christmas at Chequers, Thatcher always ensures that lunch is over in time for the Queen's broadcast holiday message. When it comes on, she insists the guests stand to watch. Once in Kenya, when local women curtsied to her, Thatcher quickly put an end to it. "That's not necessary," she said. "I'm only the prime minister."

Each year, the prime minister and Denis spend the first weekend in September with the Queen at Balmoral in Scotland. At first, Thatcher found the experience painful. A weekend in the country with aristocrats who enjoy riding, shooting, sports, and games is Thatcher's idea of torture. But her dread of the weekend receded as the two women became somewhat more comfortable with one another. The ritual of the weekend helps. Saturday morning, the Thatchers and a private secretary arrive and lunch with the Queen's top aide, her principal private secretary, Sir William Heseltine. In the afternoon a walk is arranged, followed by the Thatchers' move into the castle. Thatcher does not participate in any of the shoots that some of her predecessors enjoyed. Instead, she withdraws to work happily on her boxes. In the evening, the Queen and Prince Philip host a small, black-tie dinner. The part the prime minister hates most is the charades game the Queen sometimes enjoys after dinner. Thatcher goes rigid at the thought of making a fool of herself in front of the privately unceremonious monarch. The Queen teases her about it. At a dinner attended by six of her prime ministers, she joked of "the party games which some of you have so nobly endured at Balmoral."[5]

In addition to wry wit, the Queen has a broad sense of humor. She has appreciated prime ministers like Churchill and Harold Wilson, who knew how to jolly her. Wild slapstick can make her laugh out loud. For years, Prince Charles liked a group of comedians called the Goons, Britain's answer to the Three Stooges. There is little that Thatcher would find more horrible to contemplate than watching slapstick humor or a performance by the Goons unless it were looking on with her sovereign and trying to force a laugh. The Earl of Gowrie understood Thatcher's natural unease: "On the whole, the English upper classes know exactly how to treat monarchy, but not everyone else does."[6]

On Sunday mornings, the Thatchers join the royals for church. This is sometimes followed by a picnic. One year, the Queen and Prince Philip barbecued, then stunned the prime minister by plunging in up to their elbows to clean the dishes, beating back her entreaties to help.

Before Thatcher leaves, the Queen usually takes her to see Queen Elizabeth, the Queen Mother, for afternoon tea. Among the royals, the Queen Mother has the highest opinion of Thatcher. "The Queen Mother absolutely adores Mrs. Thatcher," said a friend of both. "Such a sensible woman," she always says. They share a natural constituency. The most popular royal, the Queen Mum has the best sense of what ordinary people like. Less elitist than her daughter the monarch, she has a nose for the mass public who constitute a large portion of Thatcher's power base. They appreciate the Queen Mum's spontaneity and lack of affectation. Her mischievous sense of humor has also endeared her to the nation. One night, alluding to the large number of homosexuals employed by the palace, the Queen Mother called down to the kitchen. "I don't know what you old queens are doing down there, but this old queen up here wants a gin and tonic."

A tolerance for homosexuals notwithstanding, the Queen Mother is a right-winger with strong views on behavior and morals and a penchant for the Victorian manners that propel Thatcher. She also has a strong sense of the importance of keeping Britain competitive. Her instincts are similar to Thatcher's own.

That is not the case with all the royals. Prince Charles, heir to the throne, has told friends for years that he thinks Mrs. Thatcher is awful. "That kind of attitude is incredibly narrow and tiresome," he has often said, criticizing her social policies and privatization schemes, which he considers relentless. He disapproves of the scaling back of welfare and urban policies, which he believed raised the levels of unemployment and despair in the inner cities in the early and mid-1980s. Prince Charles disagrees with her government-by-maxim approach and her admonitions for the nation to stand up straight and look clean and tidy. Prince Charles wants to look forward; he disdains the prime minister's 1950s virtues. For her part, the prime minister has for years considered the Prince one more bleeding heart liberal and a not very bright man who is confused about his role in life.

In recent years, however, the Prince and the prime minister, who share a guru in author–Jungian philosopher Laurens van der Post, have spent more time together and have even managed to find some common ground. In 1988, shortly after a three-hour private meeting with Charles, Thatcher made an impassioned appeal on behalf of the planet's environment, one of the Prince's favorite causes. Since then, Thatcher, the number one enemy of environmentalists for years, has spoken on a panoply of "green" issues, including the greenhouse effect. She has even hosted a 110-nation conference on the worldwide threat to the ozone layer.

The Prince has made his concessions, too, endorsing a speech Thatcher gave in Bruges in late 1988 in which she warned against Britain being subsumed in a new boundaryless Europe. Both the prince and the prime minister are committed to retaining Britain's unique characteristics. So the two may yet find themselves moving closer together.

Thatcher's relationship with the Prince is eased somewhat by the fact that he is a man. Her relationship with the Queen is complicated by the fact that the monarch is a woman. Thatcher normally feels—and often transmits—a sense of superiority to other women. She has power; they do not. She has made it against the odds; they have not. The Queen throws Thatcher off. The prime minister cannot push her around the way she does most women. "The relationship is not easy between Her Majesty and the prime minister," said one who knows both well. "Mrs. Thatcher would probably have a perfectly easy relationship with her sovereign if her sovereign had been Prince Philip."[7]

Though she would most certainly deny it, Thatcher does measure her relationship with the Queen in competitive terms. She honors and respects her monarch, but retains an acute sense of the primacy of the prime minister's role. She will listen to the monarch, but will not kowtow on public policy, the domain of the government. A few years ago, she watched on television a discussion between the Queen and then Indian Prime Minister Indira Gandhi that she felt became too political. "Down at Chequers we were not amused," said an observer of Thatcher's annoyed reaction.[8] "She shouldn't be saying that sort of thing," said Denis Thatcher. Thatcher agreed. Soon after, she stepped up her pace of visiting victims of tragedies, once the prerogative of royals. Before Mikhail Gorbachev's visit to London in 1989, there was speculation that he would invite the Queen to Moscow, the only major capital she has not seen. Prime ministerial aides squelched the suggestion immediately. Among the proffered excuses was the fact that the Bolsheviks had killed the Romanovs, the Queen's cousins, in 1918. A more realistic reason was that Thatcher was still negotiating. She liked Gorbachev, but she wanted to extract maximum concessions from the Soviets. The message was that Britain was not yet ready to reward the USSR with a royal visit. The implied veto made the Queen look ridiculous, like a student having to ask permission to go to the water fountain. The palace was indignant.

The prime minister does on occasion act on the Queen's advice. In the mid-1980s, the government was slow to devote resources for AIDS treatment and education. At a 1986 Buckingham Palace lunch, the Queen asked opposition leader Neil Kinnock whether the government was doing enough about AIDS. Kinnock did not think so. Would it help if I had a word with the prime minister? she asked. He was certain it would. I'll do that then, the Queen promised. A month later, the government set up a cabinet committee on AIDS.[9]

Thatcher and the Queen joust along the line that separates their roles, careful not to usurp the other's prerogatives, but not leaving much leeway either. When both were scheduled to speak at a memorial service for the assassinated Lord Mountbatten, they swapped speeches ahead of time as a courtesy. Thatcher much admired the informal, familial touch of the Queen's address. Her own, drafted by Lord Hailsham, was rolling Churchillian prose that made her gag. Following the Queen's lead, she chopped out all the flowery phrases and, much relieved, delivered an echo of the Queen's remarks. "They went over about equal," said a Thatcher intimate familiar with the episode. "But they otherwise would not have, a comparison the prime minister was determined to avoid. That was a real flash of the rivalry." On another occasion, the prime minister asked the palace if she and the Queen should coordinate their outfits when they were together, so they wouldn't show up in similar dress. Back came a snippy retort. No arrangements were necessary, said the palace; the Queen never noticed what anyone else wore.[10]

On the questions of what Britain needs, they are in substantial agreement. The Queen was well aware that Britain was in serious trouble when Thatcher took over. She appreciates what her prime minister has done to improve the nation's economic well-being. She also knows the prime minister acts with the best interests of Britain in mind and that they share an intense patriotism. But she still expresses concern about the long-term effects on the nation of the Thatcher revolution. "What I worry about," the Queen said recently, "is how this period will look in the history books."[11]

They disagree sharply on method. Those familiar with the Queen's thinking characterize her as a Tory "wet," a pre-Thatcher paternalist consensus-seeker. The Queen is conservative, but she is also compassionate with a vigorous sense of noblesse oblige. Had she been Thatcher, she would almost certainly have taken a softer approach and dispensed less bitter medicine in trying to engineer Britain's recovery. The Queen made little secret of her concern about the 1981 belt-tightening that led to more than one million Britons losing jobs. Like many, she worried that the forced austerity would cause a North-South split between rich and poor. Thatcher ignored her. The Queen remained worried.

The Queen made it clear during the miners' strike of 1984–1985 that she wished the government would ease up and settle. Thatcher, determined to crush the strike and its leader Arthur Scargill, ignored the advice. In 1988, when the Labor party lost a huge majority in a Scottish parliamentary seat to the Scottish Nationalist party, the Queen had the explanation. The locals had turned away from the two main parties, she said, because "they have got nothing" in the region and despair of help from Westminster.

Their biggest and most obvious difference in recent years has been over an international issue close to the Queen's heart. Thatcher and the Queen usually share a common vision in foreign affairs, but the Commonwealth is one notable exception. As the symbolic head of the Commonwealth and the actual head of state of eighteen of the forty-eight independent member states, the Queen is a passionate supporter of the association of former British colonies and dependencies. Her long reign has given the organization an underpinning it would never have had as a loose gathering of sometimes unstable nations. It is her baby.

Thatcher, on the other hand, considers the Commonwealth an outmoded relic with little clout, political or economic. "She'd much rather spend her time dealing with the summit seven (Western industrial powers) or even the (European) Community than with some of those tinpot dictators," snorted a top associate.

Their first split came shortly after Thatcher took over when the government advised the Queen against attending the 1979 Commonwealth meeting in Lusaka because of the civil war underway in adjacent Rhodesia. Queen Elizabeth would have none of it, however, and insisted on attending as planned. She arrived two days ahead of Thatcher, met all the heads of state, and thoroughly charmed Zambian President Kenneth Kaunda, who was prepared to butt heads with the prime minister over recognizing the Muzorewa regime. When Thatcher adjusted her stance and the crisis was resolved, Thatcher rightly got credit. But the Queen's skillful maneuvering behind the scenes, easing tension and paving the way toward accommodation, was essential. She was given equal credit by those involved.

The two also appear to have clashed on Thatcher's reluctance to impose economic sanctions on South Africa, an issue that bedeviled her in 1985 and 1986 and threatened to split the Commonwealth. Thatcher abhors apartheid and has given aid to front-line black states, some of them Commonwealth members, that oppose the South African government. But she is also convinced that economic sanctions do not work. She feels that they are more harmful to blacks in and outside South Africa than to the country's white minority ruling population and that sanctions would badly bruise Britain's economy with no discernible effect on South Africa's.

She also has a purely pragmatic reason for not wanting to impose sanctions. With some $18 billion invested in South Africa and an annual two-way trade worth $3 billion, Britain has more to lose than any other country.[12] Thatcher becomes incensed when harangued by smaller players. Criticism from Australia and New Zealand was swatted away like a pesky mosquito. Australia, she maintained, had only $120 million invested in South Africa, while New Zealand had "not a penny to lose." Were Britain to impose sanctions, she was certain others, Japan for example, would step in and take advantage of Britain's exit to fill their own pockets.

The prime minister and Queen's differences bubbled into public in July 1986. The catalyst was a *Sunday Times* newspaper report that the Queen was privately "dismayed" by some of the prime minister's policies, notably her refusal to consider imposing sanctions in South Africa. According to the story, which turned out to be based on off-the-record guidance from the palace's spokesman Michael Shea, the Queen was said to fear that the issue could lead to the dissolution of the Commonwealth. More generally, the paper said, "the Queen considers the prime minister's approach to be uncaring, confrontational and socially divisive."

The palace, of course, quickly denied that any such feelings were ever conveyed by anyone purporting to speak for the Queen. Not long after, the normally sure-footed Shea left his job. Yet the remarks sounded credible, and the rest of the national press began writing about a "constitutional crisis." That was not true. Neither side could have allowed it to develop into one. Downing Street labeled the *Sunday Times* story "absolute rubbish," while the palace more sedately called it "without foundation." The Queen and Thatcher said even less. Queen Elizabeth never gives interviews, and Thatcher knows how to say nothing. "I propose to follow the well-established practice of my predecessors," she told Parliament in clipped tones when asked about the brouhaha, "and not answer questions direct or indirect about the monarch."

The timing could scarcely have been worse. The story broke just as the royal family was about to display its most elegant, public face to the world at the marriage of Prince Andrew, the Queen's second son, to Sarah Ferguson in Westminster Abbey. When Thatcher was, perhaps inadvertently, assigned a partially obstructed view in the Abbey, vastly inferior to that given pop singer Elton John, the rumor mill went into overdrive.

Past slights were recalled, including the 1985 Commonwealth conference in Nassau, which centered on anti-apartheid measures. The Queen was seen on television warmly welcoming participants— until she got to Thatcher. Her face froze. Later, some saw another slap at the prime minister when the Queen personally awarded a knighthood to rock musician Bob Geldof for raising millions of dollars for African famine relief. Normally, Geldof, who is Irish, would have received his "honorary" knighthood from the foreign secretary. At another investiture, the Queen was dubbing new knights, pausing to chat briefly with each. "Who do you work for?" she asked one man about to be honored. "Mrs. Thatcher," he replied. "Oh," the Queen said, banging him on both shoulders with her sword and dismissing him without another word.[13]

After 1986, Thatcher's worst year in office, the sanctions and Commonwealth issues faded from prominence. In 1988 and 1989, the prime minister made successful visits to black Africa. She had been rigid on the sanctions issue, but had saved Britain billions and emerged in an even stronger position in Africa.

As the threat to Commonwealth unity receded, so did the worst of the splits with the Queen. When Gorbachev finally did arrive in Britain in early spring 1989 and invited the Queen to Moscow, she was delighted to accept. Thatcher smiled and said she felt "very happy and very positive" about the invitation from the Soviet leader. The Queen, whose schedule is arranged years in advance, would not be going for a while. There would be plenty of Tuesdays before then to discuss it. Not to mention more Balmoral weekends. Her latest, said Thatcher convincingly, had been "absolutely lovely."

CHAPTER SEVENTEEN

The Opposition Collapses

CONSIDERING HOW BADLY the Conservatives botched 1986, Thatcher's worst year as prime minister, it was amazing that the Labor party had not opened up a large lead over the Tories. With the Westland affair, the British Leyland fiasco, the Libyan bombing, and the prime minister's run-in with the Queen, the Conservative government had been given a nearly nonstop battering. Nor was there any good news on the margins. The economy, which had looked so positive after the Falklands, had yet to recover fully. The trade picture had improved; the deficit was under control and investment was increasing, but 3.3 million Britons remained out of work, an all-time high. Oil prices kept dropping, which cut into revenues from the North Sea fields. The value of the dollar was dropping against the pound, which made imports to Britain cheaper. But unemployment, which had tripled since she entered office, seemed an impossible hurdle for Thatcher to overcome.

The only real good news as she headed toward another election that almost certainly would be fought in 1987 was her divided opposition. Both the Labor party, the official Opposition, and the Alliance of the Liberal and Social Democratic parties, were squared off against her as they had been in 1983. The split between the opposing forces made it much more difficult to oust Thatcher, who had won both previous times without a vote majority. Also encouraging for Thatcher was the fact that both parties were divided within themselves. She needed all the help she could get.

The Alliance inadvertently helped her first. Potentially dangerous to Thatcher's Tories, the Alliance—centrist and less ideological than the two major parties—also seemed capable of draining off votes from the Labor party. Earlier in 1986, the Alliance, the so-called "nice" party, had hit 30 percent in the polls, but had dipped slightly as a result of policy differences between "the two Davids," the SDP's David Owen and the Liberals' David Steel. Both men, articulate and experienced, knew the stakes. If the Alliance were to carve out a permanent niche between the Tories on the right and Labor on the left, they would have to minimize their differences. If they didn't, the Alliance would be dead. Both main parties would savage the centrists if they discovered disunity. Neither the Liberals nor Social Democrats could prosper electorally on their own. The drawback for both parties was Britain's nonproportional representation. In the country's "first-past-the-post" electoral system, a party claims a parliamentary seat only when it wins it individually. So running up a good national vote total was irrelevant for the Alliance if it could not seize enough seats to hold the balance of power in a close election.

Owen and Steel were an odd couple. A trained medical doctor who had forsaken his practice to become an MP, Owen also quit the Labor party, where he had risen to foreign secretary at the age of thirty-six. His departure was provoked in large part by the nonnuclear defense policy adopted by the party while Michael Foot was leader. Owen felt strongly that Britain could not defend itself without nuclear weapons. The same issue had now brought him head to head with Steel and the Liberals, who wanted to give up the country's small nuclear arsenal. Owen scrambled to find some common ground to keep their differences from shattering the Alliance's surface unity.

Owen believed that the nearly obsolete, four-submarine fleet armed with nuclear Polaris missiles should be replaced with a smaller but still nuclear alternative. But he could not say that and still keep the Liberals in the Alliance. So he opted to fudge, saying that if "a European minimum deterrent," including perhaps some kind of Anglo-French nuclear collaboration, could be devised, he would put off his insistence that Britain maintain an independent deterrent. His position had a hole in it that the Soviet rocket forces could power through, and no one knew it better than Owen. But that was the farthest he could go in the interest of unity without sabotaging what he believed.

Steel acknowledged that there remained "a long way to go" to reach a defense policy acceptable to both parties. Still, he went along with the compromise, formally endorsed it, and took the hybrid to his own party conference for endorsement. He knew the murky position would displease many party members, but he had been in full control of the Liberals for ten years; he thought he could persuade the party to follow his lead. The final eight-word amendment sparked impassioned debate. After three hours of raucous wrangling, the vote was held—with miserable leadership coordination—and Steel was humiliatingly defeated. By a majority of 27 votes, out of 1,277 cast, the Liberals passed a motion which promised to take a more active role in bolstering NATO "providing that such a defense capability is nonnuclear."

The Liberals' carefully crafted pact with the SDP lay in tatters on the floor of the Eastbourne conference hall. Owen was both furious at Steel's inept handling of the vote and shocked that he could not control his party. The Band-Aid covering the Alliance's key difference had been ripped away. The rift was tailormade for Thatcher and her Tories, who had greater difficulty scoring off the usually centrist Alliance policy than Labor's more extreme socialism.

With the Alliance in the wings trying to patch its wounds, Labor stepped into the fracas. On paper, Labor looked okay. In three years at the party's helm, Neil Kinnock had beaten back much of the destructively militant left wing to revitalize it. He had scrapped some of the outmoded socialist trappings that had crippled Labor. He dropped the socialist red flag as the party's symbol and replaced it with the more ambiguous red rose. Instead of singing the Communist party's "Internationale" at the close of meetings, delegates rose and trilled the old hymn "Jerusalem."

Kinnock struck a positive chord with his attacks on Thatcher's social policies, widely perceived to be too tough on the needy, sick, and old. "There is a moral majority," he said. "It is not narrow, bigoted, self-righteous, crude; it is broad-minded and compassionate. We make our appeal to that moral majority."[1]

Kinnock lacked stature, experience, and brains, but squatting to joke and chat with the elderly, he did offer an image of warmth and compassion that Thatcher lacked. But a mistake similar to the one that paralyzed the Alliance cost him dearly. At the Labor party's annual conference in the autumn of 1986, delegates overwhelmingly reaffirmed the party's commitment to abandon Britain's nuclear deterrent. Kinnock has been a staunch unilateralist, determined to rid Britain of nuclear weapons. But most of Britain is not antinuclear. After its experiences in two world wars, Britain believes in a strong defense. Kinnock's own shadow cabinet was split on the issue. Promoting a policy of giving up the core of the country's defense was a risk. But the Labor party had given up pragmatism on defense issues when it picked Michael Foot and Neil Kinnock as the successors to James Callaghan, the last moderate Labor party leader.

A barrage of criticism—both at home and from the United States—greeted Labor's reendorsement of unilateralism. Caspar Weinberger charged that Kinnock's plan to decommission the four Polaris subs, close six U.S. nuclear bases in Britain, and bar U.S. ships carrying nuclear weapons from entering British waters could result in the dismantling of NATO. Kinnock, said Weinberger, was gambling with "the people's liberty and freedoms, the independence of Britain, and the future of Europe." Dismantling the nuclear deterrent was no less than "an invitation to attack." Richard Perle, the hawkish assistant secretary of defense who specialized in nuclear strategy, charged that Labor's policy would prevent the West from protecting Europe. When Kinnock claimed that the Weinberger and Perle criticisms did not carry the full weight of White House authority, U.S. Ambassador Charles Price II, a Reagan confidant and a diligent envoy who was on the scene, instantly countered that they were indeed speaking with the president's backing.

It was only days before Thatcher, having spotted the fatal flaw in the programs of both her opponents, took off after them. "There is now only one party in this country with an effective policy for the defense of the realm," she roared in a stem-winding keynote speech that galvanized her Tories and brought them to their feet cheering. "That party is the Conservative party." A Labor party in government would turn Britain neutralist, giving the Soviet Union "its greatest gain in forty years—and they would have got it without firing a shot." Undaunted by personal criticism, weak polls, a bomb scare, and even a sprained ankle suffered as she stumbled at the entrance of the conference hall, Thatcher had her issue. She was convinced that the Labor party had thrown away its best chance. She and her ministers would hammer away on the defense theme, staking their electoral future on the threat of communism and the preservation of trans-Atlantic ties. Norman Tebbit, the Tories' chairman and designated hatchet-man, mocked Kinnock and his troops: "Labor seems more willing to trust the invaders of

Afghanistan than Britain's allies in the defense of free Europe. The voters are not daft. They can smell a rat whether it is wrapped in a red flag or covered in roses."

Backed up by a Tory truth squad set up strictly to publicize Labor and Alliance defense statements, Thatcher's aggressiveness began to pay dividends in no time. Soon the Conservatives were back seesawing for the lead in national polls. Kinnock tried to bolster his credentials in December 1986 by traveling to the United States, but the trip backfired. The Reagan administration had no intention of helping anyone unseat the president's best international friend. The Labor leader was ignored completely; even liberal Democrats in Congress rebuffed Kinnock. He returned to Britain frustrated, the victim of headlines like "Kinnock Against the World," the banner in the left-wing *New Statesman*, which usually supports Labor. Columnist Peter Jenkins said Kinnock's policy was "unsalable, unjustifiable, unworkable and probably makes Labor unelectable." If adopted, warned NATO commander General Bernard Rogers, the strategy could lead to the withdrawal of 350,000 U.S. troops stationed in Europe.

The uproar might conceivably have died down. But on December 10, the bull-headed Kinnock—influenced by his even more rigidly ideological wife—went one step further, publishing a defense white paper that put his defense platform on the table. The ten-page document was another suicide note. It promised to decommission the four Polaris submarines, cancel plans to replace them with Trident, and banish all U.S. nuclear weapons from Britain. Britain would not pull out of NATO as France did under Charles de Gaulle in 1966. "We are not proposing to go in that direction at all," it said. Instead, Labor promised to upgrade and modernize conventional forces and weapons.

The document's reasoning was flabby. Savings from canceling the Trident program could be diverted, but even $12 billion could only finance several brigades, which would not begin to affect the conventional force balance between NATO's thirty-eight divisions and the ninety divisions manned by Warsaw Pact forces. Earlier, Labor had suggested that tank traps filled with explosives stretched across West Germany could stop a Soviet invasion. That idea had been so ridiculed that the white paper finally urged only that "manmade barriers and obstacles" be installed. The latest plan was mocked just as widely. West Germany's Social Democrats as well as the governing party, the more conservative Christian Democrats, took one look at the Kinnock white paper and rejected it out of hand. The document's call for "greater defense in depth" was, Bonn believed, a euphemism for surrendering West German territory to advancing Soviet and East bloc armies in order to defend France and Britain.

Closer to home, the *Financial Times*, the least demagogic of Britain's papers, called the Kinnock plan "palpable nonsense." Some of the Labor leader's own shadow cabinet were aghast at the proposals and tried to claim the party didn't mean it, citing Harold Wilson, who campaigned on a nonnuclear platform in the 1960s, then ignored the pledge once he got into office. Harder-line colleagues insisted Kinnock was different and meant what he said. "We won't fudge this time," promised Larry Whitty, the party's general secretary.[2]

Labor got more bad news; the economy was on the upswing. Fresh figures threatened to undercut Labor's argument that Thatcher was mismanaging the nation's finances. In October 1986, unemployment fell by 96,000, the biggest monthly decrease in fifteen years. If the trend continued, the jobless total could slip under the psychologically daunting three million barrier in time for a spring election. "The job picture is getting brighter," said Employment Minister Kenneth Clarke. "All the signs are that Britain's economy is steadily getting people back to work." Other indicators were also improved. Inflation was down to 3 percent; consumer spending was up 6 percent over 1985; manufacturing output was up 1.2 percent, the biggest quarterly jump since 1980; the trade surplus at $132 million was up after months in the red.

With a boom underway, Thatcher unleashed the powers of incumbency, loosening the taps on some of her tightest domestic policies to take advantage of the surge. For all her "Victorian virtues" and insistence that "the lady's not for turning," the prime minister proved that she is also a consummate, street-smart operator who can play hardball with the best of deal-cutters when it suits her. She handed out healthy salary boosts to public employees, local government manual workers, and firefighters. Teachers, bogged down in a sapping pay dispute for a year, settled with a hike that totaled nearly 22 percent over two years. Nigel Lawson announced a two-year $14.5 billion increase in projected public spending, the lion's share to go to education, health, and social security—all areas in which Thatcher had been sharply criticized for cutting back too severely. In rapid succession, Labor party politicians witnessed the dilution of their most potent campaign arguments.

Labor's problems multiplied when Kinnock attempted to reduce further the influence of the party's militant left wing. Moderates were delighted, but attacking the militants was not the same as getting rid of them. The effort to drive them out led to embarrassing intraparty factional fighting just as it became clear that the prime minister would soon call a general election.

The catalyst for her decision was a February 1987 by-election only four miles down the Thames from Tower Bridge in Greenwich, best known as the point from which the world's time zones are measured. In a contest to replace a long-time Labor MP who had died, early polls gave the Labor candidate a huge lead over the Alliance and Tories. But by the end of election night, Labor had lost the seat it had held for forty-two years. Thousands of Labor moderates deserted the party to protest the candidate's hard left stance. Unlike her popular predecessor, the Labor candidate Deirdre Wood supported virtually every fringe cause. She backed antinuclear protestors and gay rights. She urged that local schools sponsor Palestinian refugee camps and endorsed a plan to invite to Greenwich speakers from Sinn Fein, the outlawed IRA's political wing. She opposed Britain's continued membership in NATO, and if that were not enough, she was also obese, no boon for a candidate in an era of televised campaigns. Her appearance notwithstanding, it was her extremism that crippled her chances in what had been a safe Labor constituency.

The election focused more attention on Labor's left-wing bias. Wood's nomination revealed the party's inability to read the voters—and its disorganization. There was a hard-to-miss message in the upset. "Voters have demonstrated," said London Labor party treasurer Brian Nicholson, "that they were not prepared to vote for the lunatic fringe." Even Kinnock was forced to concede that "this was a bad result."

Conservatives referred to Wood and her ideological soul mates as the "Loony Left." Kinnock, frantic to separate them from the party mainstream, called them "the dafties." "They don't dominate the party and there's not a chance in hell they will," he insisted. But their presence was a soft, ripe target for the Thatcher team. There was no question they were badly damaging the party's prospects. In mid-January, Labor had a 5 percent lead over the Conservatives. Two months later, after the Tories targeted the defense white paper and the Loony Left, Labor woke up to find itself trailing by 6 percent. The more responsible Labor moderates, who had felt a surge of optimism over Kinnock's efforts to modernize the party, were dismayed by the suddenness of their tumble. Supporters began joining the Alliance and even the Conservatives. "There's a growing awareness among the overwhelming majority of party members," said Labor MP John Evans, "that it's time our policies and representatives reflected the views of old-fashioned working people."

The militant radicals were few in number—by most calculations less than 5 percent of the party's active members—but thanks to Britain's highly partisan, mostly Conservative newspapers, their antics gained extraordinary attention. The left-wingers, energetic on about two dozen city and town councils, represented the concerns of nonwhite, immigrant populations living in the inner cities. Some of their demands were, to put it mildly, exotic, particularly when held up to the rest of the country. In Waltham Forest in northeast London, several local schools insisted that students study a Third World language, such as Swahili or Punjabi. In east London's Newham, flags of the African National Congress, representing the black South African opposition, and SWAPO, the Namibian guerrilla group, flew over the town hall, a declaration of the town's anti-apartheid stance. Lambeth, across the Thames from parliament, twinned itself with a community in Nicaragua and a Moscow suburb. It promoted itself as a "nuclear-free zone" and had a full-time "peace and nuclear affairs officer" on the payroll.

By the time early spring 1987 rolled around, the opposition was losing its credibility. Thatcher, simultaneously broadcasting the economic news, reaped the benefits. After eight years, her programs were kicking in. Booming corporate profits and soaring consumer spending tumbled revenues into the Treasury's coffers. When it came time in mid-March for Chancellor of the Exchequer Nigel Lawson to deliver his annual budget, he had nearly $8 billion to give away. Sipping a white wine spritzer at the dispatch box, the chancellor took fifty-nine minutes to explain that the government was cutting income taxes, reducing government borrowing, and getting ready to slash interest rates. He cut the lowest tax rate from 29 percent to 27 percent and dropped other taxes, for the elderly and small companies, an additional $4 billion. Lawson also avoided irritating Britons by not raising taxes on liquor, cigarettes, or gasoline. He shrank the government's projected borrowing from $11 billion to just over $6 billion to spur corporate investment. Scarcely had he put down his text when the London stock market took off, hitting a day's record increase. The pound spurted up to $1.60, its highest level in five years.

Britain was rising from its sickbed. To be sure, there were still enormous problems. Unemployment remained above three million, but the numbers had dropped seven months in a row. The National Health Service, education, and inner cities all needed major initiatives. Britain's growth rate in spring 1987 was 3 percent, the highest in Europe and double what it had been when Thatcher came to office in 1979. If the situation held up at home and she called an election quickly, she should be unstoppable again.

First, there was some serious foreign business to attend to. Mikhail Gorbachev had invited her to Moscow. She met the Soviet party chief in the Kremlin in late March just as Kinnock was flying to Washington to try again to burnish his international credentials.

Thatcher was feeling confident and feisty again. Everything was beginning to fall into place. She was sure she would win the election, whenever she called it. Earlier talk that she might serve only two terms and then step down was quickly forgotten. She now planned to serve an entire third term, that was a certainty. And after that? Well, she was not one to count her chickens before they hatched, especially given Harold Wilson's adage that "a week is a long time in politics." But Thatcher told some friends that yes, she was thinking seriously of not only a third term but a fourth as well.

CHAPTER EIGHTEEN

Maggie and Mikhail

ONE REASON Margaret Thatcher felt so secure heading toward a third election was her powerful relationships with Ronald Reagan and Mikhail Gorbachev. The trio had a precedent in the Churchill, Roosevelt, Stalin troika, but that was a tie forged in war and Stalin was always odd man out. The second U.S.-Soviet-British triad stood on all three feet. Through luck, artful cultivation, and attention to detail, Thatcher muscled her way into what had been a duet between the superpowers. It took her a while, but it was worth it. Beefing up her ties to Gorbachev and Reagan reinforced Thatcher's world stature and reflected glory for Britain. By bringing herself into the charmed circle, Thatcher was able to ensure that Britain could cling to its all-important independent nuclear deterrent. An added reward was special status among the European allies. Once again, thanks to Thatcher's spadework, British views carried weight.

Thatcher never tried to fool herself; she never tried to pretend she was on equal footing with the superpower leaders. Nor did she attempt to become the middleman or the swing figure. A trusted partner who helped keep the sometimes fickle European alliance resolute, she always lined up with Reagan on East–West issues. But Thatcher is an honest interpreter with special skills that made her invaluable to both leaders. For Gorbachev, she was a two-way window west and an intellectual peer. Thatcher and Reagan felt the same, but Thatcher and Gorbachev talked the same, even when shouting at each other, which they did frequently.

Gorbachev considered Margaret Thatcher the toughest Western leader. But she was not a direct threat to his country, and she was the one Westerner on his wavelength who could always get through to Ronald Reagan. The fact that she was a woman brought them closer. Like Reagan, Gorbachev appreciates strong women; he married one, too. Thatcher used more than her strength and brains to win over Gorbachev. She also used every bit of feminine charm and flirtatiousness she could marshal to cement her relationship with the Soviet president.

They have a surprising amount in common. Both are lawyers. Both have science degrees. Thatcher majored in chemistry, and Gorbachev did postgraduate work in agronomy. Both came from the provinces (Gorbachev from Stavropol), were active in student politics, and rose quickly to the pinnacle of power against the odds. Thatcher, five and a half years older, was fifty-three when she became prime minister; Gorbachev turned fifty-four only days before being picked general secretary. Both were firsts: she the first woman prime minister in a male-dominated society; he the first revolutionary new Soviet leader since Lenin, a vigorous contrast to a generation of septuagenarians. Both were trying to turn around declining countries, attempting to solve serious systemic problems with little more than personal determination and courage. Both were more appreciated by foreigners than their fellow citizens.

As Thatcher got to know Gorbachev, she came to believe that the West had a genuine stake in his success. More approachable and rational than Khrushchev, yet more creative, more pragmatic, and tougher than Brezhnev, Gorbachev offers, in Thatcher's estimation, the best hope for positive change in the Soviet Union. Still, she does not want to see the West go too far or be taken in by what she contemptuously calls "airy fairy" promises. Thatcher rejected West Germany's offer to launch an aid package to help Gorbachev get his economic house in order. Her reasoning was that it was too much too soon.

Thatcher is willing to support Gorbachev only if she gets something in return—a palpably reduced threat to the West, or an improved human rights posture, for example, or a better climate for business and trade. She is willing to back joint business ventures and provide management training if the Soviets wish. But she has a reason: in the long run, an improved Russian economy could be beneficial for Britain. Something for nothing has never been a Thatcherite philosophy, in life or in a negotiation.

Gorbachev's reforms "could be reversed," Thatcher has pointed out, "if [he] does not succeed in climbing through to a rather different kind of political structure." Despite her desire to encourage him, she knows the West cannot plan a defense around a Soviet leader who may not survive politically. "If, by any chance, Mr. Gorbachev does not succeed," she said,[1] "and you've let your defenses go because you're basing your policies on hope rather than on the necessary defense of freedom, then it could be years before we climbed back to security."

Thatcher's evaluation of Gorbachev is complicated by the fact that, for all their arguments and philosophical differences, she personally likes Gorbachev a great deal. She respects his brains and courage more than those of any leader she has dealt with, a feeling that the Soviet leader seems to reciprocate. "Personal chemistry," responded Soviet spokesman Gennadi Gerasimov with a grin when asked the basis of their relationship.[2] Their chemistry was apparent from their first meeting in December 1984. Thatcher realized that this was not another old-style, stultified Soviet out of the Leonid Brezhnev school. She had, of course, briefed herself thoroughly on his background. She knew that shortly after becoming chairman of the foreign affairs commission of the Supreme Soviet in mid-1984, he had visited Italy for the funeral of Italian Communist party leader Enrico Berlinguer and impressed the Italians with his confident frankness. "You had the impression that he was very critical of the situation in the Soviet Union," said Antonio Rubbi, a Berlinguer associate. "He said there was too much centralization." Gorbachev had been similarly candid the year before on a trip to Canada. When Afghanistan was mentioned, Gorbachev said merely, "It was a mistake."[3]

These details and others such as his passion for the poetry of Pushkin and Lermontov, which he could recite (as she can recite Keats and Kipling), were all in Thatcher's briefing book that December. She sensed possibilities in the new leader, although she had hated socialism and the Soviet system from childhood. Before she met Gorbachev, Thatcher had actually had very little experience with the USSR. Several short trips failed to alter her visceral dislike and mistrust of what Ronald Reagan called the "Evil Empire." When first elected prime minister, she disapproved of everything the Soviets stood for. She had no interest in meeting or even speaking to any Soviet or Eastern bloc officials. Following the Soviet invasion of Afghanistan in December 1979, she forbade Foreign Secretary Lord Carrington to visit Moscow. "I don't want you having anything to do with those bloody Russians," she instructed.

Thatcher's breakthrough regarding Moscow did not come until sometime later, after several Soviet leaders died in quick succession. After General Secretary Yuri Andropov's death in February 1984, Thatcher began to consider the likely candidate to succeed him. Konstantin Chernenko had taken over, but it was clear that he was just a stop-gap leader, one more sickly geriatric. Her foreign policy advisers came up with three other names: Grigory Romanov, the Leningrad party boss; Viktor Grishin, head of the Moscow party organization; and Gorbachev, an agricultural specialist who was the Politburo's youngest member. Thatcher wanted to get her eyes on someone high powered. Feelers went to Moscow saying that if they'd like to send a delegation, Gorbachev or Romanov would be welcome visitors.

Gorbachev was nominated. "We knew he'd had limited exposure to the West," said a Whitehall official, "but we also knew that he was definitely different and seemed to have great potential." Thatcher was determined to invest whatever time and effort was necessary to make the meeting a success. She made a conscious decision to treat him as if he were already the new Soviet leader. As a symbol of special favor, she scheduled the talks at Chequers instead of Downing Street. It was homier, quieter, and few foreign leaders, certainly no Soviets, had ever been invited there.

From the moment he and his wife, Raisa, descended from their polished Ilyushin-62 jet at Heathrow, Britons could see that this Soviet was different. Smiling affably, he wore a well-tailored suit. Raisa, about whom little was known, was warming up for her role as Soviet first lady. She had never been on a state visit before.

The Gorbachevs dazzled the normally phlegmatic British. He alternately wisecracked and sparred his way around Parliament with the British MPs. He impressed Britons by mentioning that he had read *The Corridors of Power* by C.P. Snow and set them smiling. On a tour of the British Museum, where Karl Marx researched *Das Kapital*, he joked that "if people don't like Marx, they should blame the British Museum." He bought several suits from Gieves and Hawke, the conservative Savile Row tailors who have made military uniforms for generations of royals. But Raisa was the serious shopper. She had the British tabloids in a frenzy as she dashed around London, brandishing a gold American Express card at Harrods, buying a $1,780 pair of diamond earrings at Cartier, and skipping a trip to Karl Marx's grave to see the crown jewels at the Tower of London. Later, Thatcher would discover that Raisa was no butterfly but highly intelligent, if sometimes annoyingly outspoken.

When Gorbachev arrived for lunch at Chequers, Thatcher went out on the steps to greet him. "From the very first moment, he made a very powerful impression," said an aide who was present. "He exuded a feeling of power, of coiled energy. He had a ready smile and a flexible face, not the stern look of a Gromyko, and could make a jovial comment."

Photographers arrived. Thatcher solicitously moved everyone into position, steering Gorbachev by the elbow. Back inside there was one table for lunch. She sat him on her right, and before the food was served, the two were immersed in conversation through an interpreter. They scarcely touched the roast beef and oranges in caramel. That would become a pattern. They get too involved to eat.

After coffee, Raisa went upstairs to roam the Long Gallery with its priceless manuscripts, first editions, and handwritten letters from Napoleon. The prime minister escorted Gorbachev to the Hawtrey Room, where portraits by Constable and Reynolds gaze down from paneled walls. Instead of sitting formally at a table, they pulled up armchairs near the fireplace. Alexander Yakovlev, Moscow's ambassador to Canada when Gorbachev visited there, sprawled on the raspberry and white sofa. Foreign Ministry spokesman Leonid Zamyatin, later the Soviet ambassador to Britain, served as note-taker. The Soviet ambassador was not included. Gorbachev never referred to either of his aides. He was operating completely on his own, a signal Thatcher picked up immediately.

At the outset, Gorbachev pulled out a pile of three-by-five note cards in his own handwriting held together by a rubber band. He apologized for interrupting her Sunday afternoon. There was a Northern Caucasus proverb, he told her, that said mountain folk cannot live without guests any longer than they can live without air, but if the guests stay too long they choke. Thatcher smiled. She had plenty of time.

As he talked, he occasionally referred to the cards. Some of his notes were heavily underlined, others were circled. He announced that he was speaking with the full authority of Chernenko, but after one more early reference to the ailing Soviet party chief, Gorbachev dropped the charade and never mentioned him again. Focusing on arms control, Gorbachev anticipated an underlying Thatcher concern. He stressed that he was not trying to detach Britain from its relationship with the United States. He cited Palmerston, reminding her that he knew that "Britain has no eternal allies, only eternal interests." That was how he felt as well. Thatcher was aware that, despite his disclaimer, he was trolling bait, trying to see if he could spot an opening and drive a wedge between the British and U.S. positions. She declined to bite and let him continue.[4]

Later, they agreed there was no purpose in trying to convert one another from each other's political system. He quoted from her speeches and asked her impressions of the United States. "Tell me about these people?" Gorbachev asked. "Is President Reagan a man with whom the USSR can make progress?" Much of what he had heard about Reagan caused him concern. National Security Council documents, which at that time had just been published, showed that when the United States held a nuclear monopoly in the 1940s and 1950s, it had considered destroying several Soviet cities.

The prime minister replied that she knew Reagan well. The last thing he wanted was war. He was a passionate believer in the rights of people to be free to pursue their own lives in their own way. Reagan had been disappointed in Brezhnev's failure to negotiate during his first term, she explained. Thatcher was fascinated by Gorbachev's forthrightness. Past dealings with Soviets had always involved long opening statements followed by a reply followed by another long statement. But Gorbachev spoke briefly, twenty minutes. Her response took twelve minutes. Then they went straight to debate. She was amazed that there was no boilerplate. He was open-minded, working out some ideas dialectically, talking and arguing. He would pause to weigh what Thatcher said as she stood up periodically to toss a log on the fire.

Gorbachev was worried about SDI, the U.S. Strategic Defense Initiative, and returned to the issue again and again. Thatcher reassured him. Reagan's second term was about to begin. She thought that arms control and a reduction in East–West tension would be important to Reagan as he headed into the second half of his tenure. The previous two or three years had been stagnant for East-West affairs, but now, Thatcher believed, there was a unique opportunity for negotiation.

The talks were not all sweetness and light. Reflecting their different philosophies, there were subjects, including defense and human rights, where they disagreed vigorously. The Chequers talks launched a tradition of their sessions turning heated and argumentative. Neither gave ground as they prodded, poked, and explored each other's positions. At the same time, both reveled in the openness of the exchanges and their opponent's mastery of the subject matter. "I have never talked to any other Soviet leader at all like him," Thatcher said later, amazement creeping into her voice. "It was clear to me from the first moment that Mr. Gorbachev was from a very different generation of politicians. What was most noticeable was his tremendous self-confidence. It was a quite different experience. You don't normally enter into such a frank and outspoken debate with someone you are meeting for the first time. But we did, right from the beginning."

For three and a half hours they talked, never even taking a bathroom break, to the dismay of the note-takers. Thatcher has what aides call a royal bladder, but they hadn't known that the Soviet was similarly endowed. "You have an engagement in London," Thatcher reminded him near the three-hour mark. "It's not important," Gorbachev responded. "I much prefer to stay." When they finally emerged, they were exhausted, exhilarated, and—despite the arguments—smiling. Thatcher delivered her imprimatur. "I like Mr. Gorbachev," she said. "We can do business together." Before long, the whole world began to appreciate that Gorbachev was a man to do business with. Thatcher, however, had spotted it first, and he never forgot the early stamp of approval.

Almost immediately after their meeting, Thatcher left Britain on an around-the-world trip that took her to Beijing, Hong Kong, and Washington. She filled Reagan in on Gorbachev and left him a three-page, single-spaced summary of their Chequers meeting.

Gorbachev stayed on after she left London. Leaving Parliament one day and driving up Whitehall, he asked his motorcade to stop at Downing Street. He hadn't been there. He walked up the tiny street and stood outside Number 10, peering at the famous black door with its lion's head knocker. By the time aides inside learned he was there and raced out to invite him in, Gorbachev was driving away in his glistening, handmade, armored black Zil.

In less than three months, Konstantin Chernenko was dead, the third Soviet leader gone in twenty-eight months. Gorbachev was in charge, and no one in the West had a better feel for him than Thatcher. Her luck had come through again. She went to Moscow for the funeral, standing outside Lenin's tomb in the bitter cold with other world leaders. Next to her stood her bodyguard, Ray Parker, a towering Scotland Yard superintendent of police. His overcoat pockets bulged. Russians in the crowd nudged each other, whispering that he was obviously heavily armed. Afterward, inside the Kremlin, Thatcher beckoned Parker over, bent down, pulled off her boots, and thrust out her hands. From his pockets he produced two high-heeled shoes.

Thatcher had made the trip only to pay her respects to Gorbachev. They had an hour together, but he was accompanied by Chernenko's old aides, including veteran Foreign Minister Andrei Gromyko and Leonid Brezhnev's foreign policy adviser Andrei Alexandrov-Agentov. Not much was accomplished. Leaders from all over the world were shuttling in and out to see him. He teased her, making a point of moving her around by the arm, positioning her for the Kremlin photographers just as she had maneuvered him at Chequers. Flirting back, she told him she got the message and they both laughed, confusing aides who were not in on the joke.

Ronald Reagan had a chance to take his own measure of the new Soviet leader at summits in Geneva in 1985 and Reykjavik in 1986. The president's meetings with Gorbachev at both summits were short and general, by comparison with the Soviet's first long, detailed session with Thatcher. She was eager for a second tête-à-tête, which took place in Moscow at the end of March 1987, only two months before the British election.

Never had Thatcher prepared more intensely for a meeting. "I was nervous," she admitted. "It was far deeper than trembling because it mattered more."[5] She asked the Soviet Embassy in London for translations of every speech Gorbachev had made and spent days reading every one, annotating them in the margins. "They're very long," she sighed. "I don't think an English audience would take that kind of speech." Next, she convened at Chequers an all-day seminar with Soviet experts.

She arrived in Moscow on a gray, snowy, late-March day, wearing a stunning fur hat, accompanied by a typically tiny entourage. Gorbachev greeted her like an old friend and they got straight to business. Several of the meetings, which were held around a tiny table in the midst of a cavernous Kremlin hall, went on for more than four hours at a stretch. Little time was wasted on formal plenary sessions. The talks involved only the two leaders—who called each other "prime minister" and "general secretary"—as well as an interpreter and note-taker each. Thatcher's note-taker, Charles Powell, later said the meetings resembled "an English summer's day—thunderstorms and sunny periods." Thatcher called the exchanges "pretty intense, but never ill tempered." "There are no what I call 'diplomatic niceties' when I talk to Mr. Gorbachev,'' the prime minister explained. "We get right down to the nitty-gritty."

The stormy periods got very stormy. They hollered at each other, sometimes with their faces only inches apart. The note-takers occasionally looked over at each other with concern. Was it getting out of hand? When the tension got too high, it was Gorbachev who invariably broke it. A flareup would be soothed by an outburst of laughter. One evening, during a recess from the table, they attended the Bolshoi ballet. At intermission, over caviar, they became so involved debating the merits of East-West agricultural programs and grain silage that the second act of *Swan Lake* was delayed twenty minutes until they retook their seats. Another night, at a Kremlin banquet, they ignored other guests for two hours like lovers with eyes only for each other. They pecked at their food and spoke animatedly to each other. The body language was coquettish as it always is—they lean in, pull away, tilt heads, whisper, nod, touch arms—all the while calling each other by their formal titles. "The chemistry was quite extraordinary," acknowledged Bernard Ingham, the prime minister's spokesman. Thatcher showed up three hours late for a British Embassy lunch for Soviet intellectuals because she did not want to break off a Kremlin conversation.

Throughout the summit they disagreed almost completely on substance. A staunch believer in the idea that nuclear weapons are the West's best safeguard and that they have kept the peace in Europe since 1945, Thatcher clashed repeatedly with Gorbachev on denuclearization. Her private statements meshed perfectly with her public ones. That is common for Thatcher, but not all politicians. In a Kremlin speech she made no attempt to gloss over their differences, telling guests bluntly that "a world without nuclear weapons would be less stable and more dangerous for all of us." She also pressed forward on the human rights front, lunching with Andrei Sakharov, the symbol of the dissident movement, and breakfasting with Iosif Begun, one of the best-known Jewish refuseniks. Finally, Thatcher dominated three Soviet journalists in an aggressively bold televised interview that had Soviets admiring her candor and her own countrymen openly and proudly applauding in admiration.

In private, the talk turned again to Reagan. Gorbachev explained that his two meetings with the president had been frustrating. He was supposed to talk to Reagan, not the U.S. experts.

But Reagan knew no policy details, Gorbachev said, throwing up his hands in exasperation. His colleagues were able to speak directly to their American counterparts. They were getting a good firsthand feel for the U.S. positions. But Gorbachev was not and was hungry for more Thatcher interpretation about U.S. intentions. He would be grateful, he told her, if she would pass on his views to Washington. He valued her views. Flattering her, he said he knew he got from her the best, toughest arguments the West could provide. He could try new ideas out as well. Her consistency made her a good sounding board.

Thatcher was delighted with the role and understood Gorbachev's problem. She knew what it was like to talk to Ronald Reagan.

The Iran-Contra scandal had broken in November 1986, a month after the abortive U.S.–USSR Reykjavik summit. Thatcher was worried that Ronald Reagan seemed to be losing command. She did not tell Gorbachev, but Reagan seemed out of it, even though he still had two more years in office. She knew that he wasn't capable of responding to Gorbachev's vigorous appeals to Western public opinion. She would have to step in. She was confident that she could match Gorbachev intellectually, in expertise, and in forensic and debating skills. It was up to her to demonstrate that the West had leaders who could compete.

The Moscow visit was Thatcher's first real chance to size up Raisa, whom she presented with a first edition of Thackeray's *Vanity Fair*. It did not take her long to figure out why Nancy Reagan disliked Raisa so much. The Soviet leader's wife, who has a Ph.D., is as opinionated as she is intelligent and not at all reluctant to show off what she knows and thinks. A doctrinaire Marxist, she approaches discussions didactically, preaching and laying down the law. If she lived in Britain, one British analyst suggested, Raisa would likely be an active leader of the peace group CND, the Campaign for Nuclear Disarmament. "Not what you'd call a blushing violet, is she?" Thatcher once remarked. Raisa is neither as warm nor as thoughtful as her husband, and the prime minister soon tired of her attempts to bull her way into discussion of Western nuclear policy.

On Thatcher's last night in Moscow, the Gorbachevs hosted a small, intimate family meal—though Denis was not along—at a government guest house in the capital. Once the home of a pre-revolutionary sugar baron, the house had been the setting for meetings between Richard Nixon and Brezhnev. Thatcher thought it was Gorbachev's thoughtful effort to recreate the Chequers experience. She had been smart to give him the full treatment when he had come to Britain. In Moscow he more than repaid the favor. After dinner they wound up drinking brandy and telling stories around a roaring log fire.

Eight months later, in December 1987, Gorbachev flew to Washington to sign the INF treaty, which removed an entire class of intermediate-range missiles from Europe. En route, in a nod to Thatcher as de facto leader of Western Europe, he stopped off to brief the prime minister at Brize Norton, a nuclear RAF base near Oxford. With wind whipping the airfield to subfreezing temperatures, Thatcher stood on the tarmac without overcoat or hat to meet Gorbachev. He wore a coat and scarf and mimed shivering when he descended his plane ramp. She looked slightly strange, obviously freezing, her breath visible. The prime minister had two purposes: it was a deliberate macho display, but she also thought she looked more attractive without a coat. She was flirting.

The last notes of the "Internationale" had barely faded before the talks started. In the back of the prime minister's armored Daimler, they began gesticulating animatedly, and by the time they settled back they were right where they had broken off in Moscow eight months earlier. Gorbachev updated her on perestroika, his restructuring plan, and conceded the difficulties he was having at home. Their grilled salmon lunch was so tightly scheduled—twenty minutes—that they skipped the raspberry vacheron dessert.

By the time Gorbachev left, Thatcher was elated and worried: happy that her special relationship with Gorbachev still worked; concerned that he was outmaneuvering NATO left, right, and center. He was magnificently appealing, and Reagan was still stumbling through the worst year in his presidency. Thatcher was battling uphill against the concept of a nonnuclear Europe, which had great appeal to some Allies. "The Russian bear was easier to deal with when it looked more like a bear," she warned.[6] Gorbachev had been too successful in creating a seductive "image of reasonableness." She feared that too little attention was being paid to the Soviets' overwhelming advantage in conventional forces and chemical weapons. She was alarmed that the Soviets were again attempting to divide the Alliance, and she was more determined than ever to encourage Gorbachev on the reform front while pressing the West to hold firm on security matters. Gorbachev, she believed, would respond best when confronted by a tough bargaining stance.

After the INF treaty signing, Thatcher began to push hard for a NATO summit. She wanted to reestablish unity and reiterate and clarify NATO's nuclear defense posture. NATO, which had witnessed Reagan almost agreeing to the denuclearization of Europe at Reykjavik, had just absorbed the news of a new treaty removing the missiles the Europeans had battled to deploy only five years before. When the meeting, only the seventh leaders' summit in forty years, convened in Brussels in March 1988, Reagan was in bad shape. In delicate negotiations, the president seemed groggy. Thatcher was, as always, the protective friend at his elbow. Secretary of State George Shultz led the talks for the United States and fielded all the press questions. Asked at one point about the final communiqué, Reagan was confused as to whether or not he had seen it.

The prime minister dominated the sixteen-leader Brussels summit, though she did not get everything she wanted. She clashed with West German Chancellor Helmut Kohl over whether NATO should modernize its aging short-range missiles. Kohl said no because of the thaw in East-West relations. Germany preferred to ease up on defense. Kohl and French President François Mitterrand, a Socialist, together with such smaller nonnuclear allies as Denmark and the Netherlands, wanted to delay modernization. Thatcher took precisely the opposite tack and called for quick modernization. In the end, the leaders fudged the issue, agreeing with deliberate vagueness to keep nuclear weapons "up to date where necessary." That was better than nothing for Thatcher. The summit "stopped the rot," she said.

After his final summit with Gorbachev in Moscow in late May 1988, Reagan came through London on a last official visit. When the president left, Gorbachev dispatched his personal envoy, Oleg Grinevsky, to give Thatcher the Soviet leader's version of his meeting with Reagan. The attention delighted her. "The future is better than I have ever known," Thatcher told Russian television when asked her reaction to the U.S.-USSR summit. "I must say, anything that Mr. Gorbachev has personally promised he would do, he has done. There is a new vista, a vision of hope for us."

Gorbachev and Thatcher met for a fifth time in London in April 1989, a visit that took place in the midst of George Bush's extended policy review at the beginning of the new administration. Gorbachev, frustrated, told Thatcher of his annoyance at Bush's delay in organizing his government and formalizing his foreign policy. Gorbachev had seen President-elect Bush on his December 1988 visit to the United States, but the only high-level contact between the two nations since then had been a get-acquainted meeting in Vienna between Foreign Minister Eduard Shevardnadze and Secretary of State James Baker. "Mr. Gorbachev knows there is no foot dragging going on," Bush said as the Soviet leader arrived in Britain. But Gorbachev thought differently and told Thatcher that Bush was deliberately slowing down the momentum of arms agreements. Bush's long pause, Gorbachev suggested, was designed at least in part to derail Soviet initiatives and diminish Gorbachev's efforts. Thatcher tried to reassure him that Bush was merely being deliberate, but she saw some validity in his argument. Her own concern was that foreign policy, like nature, abhors a vacuum. With Bush on the sidelines and U.S. relations with Europe in suspended animation, Gorbachev was filling the vacuum himself.

Two months later, at the end of May 1989, Bush ended his self-imposed pause and tabled a Western arms reduction counteroffer at the NATO summit. The breather was over, and by fall the U.S.-Soviet relationship was reengaged. Bush welcomed Foreign Minister Eduard Shevardnadze to the White House in September 1989, and agreed to meet Gorbachev for their first full-fledged summit in June 1990 after a December 1989 get-together in Malta in the midst of the restructuring of Eastern Europe. In the Kremlin, Gorbachev had a visitor that same day, too. Margaret Thatcher was back in Moscow for their sixth meeting. She just happened to have with her a long message from George Bush.

CHAPTER NINETEEN

Hat Trick

IF MARGARET THATCHER'S Moscow kickoff to her third campaign in March 1987 was a tour de force, Neil Kinnock's opener was a fiasco. Snubbed by Reagan in December 1986, Kinnock had pressed hard for a March meeting with the president to balance the impact of Thatcher's Moscow trip. He knew she was bound to call an election soon with Parliament's fourth anniversary approaching in June, and he wanted to avoid getting lost in the headlines the Iron Lady was bound to get by confronting Gorbachev on her first visit to the Kremlin.

Kinnock had not met Reagan or any top administration officials during his December visit to Washington, though he had met the president before. Reagan had seen him for forty-five minutes in February 1984, four months after Kinnock took over the Labor party from Michael Foot. Three decades in age were the least of their differences. Kinnock and Reagan were ideological opposites, and the Labor leader was a vigorous opponent of Reagan's defense buildup, most notably his Star Wars campaign. Still, the two men chatted politely, and Kinnock described Reagan as "a pleasant enough chap" as he headed from the White House to the State Department for more extensive discussions with Secretary of State George Shultz. That conversation quickly degenerated into a Kinnock critique of U.S. policy in Central America,[1] as the Labor leader accused the United States of supporting "government by death squad" in El Salvador. Shultz, furious, called Kinnock "misinformed and possibly misguided." Kinnock countered that Shultz "got out of his pram" during the meeting. American listeners were

290

baffled until he explained that he meant that the secretary of state had lost his temper. Shultz later told aides Kinnock was a jerk, one of the least appealing foreign dignitaries he had ever met.

Most American presidents make a policy of meeting major opposition party leaders, and especially Britain's, because they might be running the government one day. Reagan, having ignored Kinnock on his December request for a meeting, could not duck him again. But what the president gave Kinnock that March was actually worse than no meeting at all. First, he scheduled only a thirty-minute office drop-by and then kept Kinnock waiting, cutting ten minutes from the meeting. Once Kinnock had finally made it inside the Oval Office, the president was confused, either deliberately or inadvertently, by the presence of Denis Healey, Labor's shadow foreign secretary. The president called him "Mr. Ambassador," to the chagrin of Sir Antony Acland, the distinguished British diplomat who attended in his ambassadorial capacity. After the meeting, before Kinnock could begin describing his cordial reception, the White House rushed out a frosty, contradictory statement. It said that the Labor party's unilateral disarmament policy, Kinnock's brainchild, would damage NATO and "undercut" the West's bargaining position. Kinnock had been snubbed. The British press went wild, and the Labor leader once again slunk home from Washington, humiliated.

In contrast, Thatcher's return from Moscow the following week brought forth headlines like "Maggie's Triumph." It looked like her victory over the miners, together with the improving economy and the Moscow visit, would cinch her third victory. Shortly after her return, on April 15, she held a political strategy meeting to review broad-scale election plans. She knew the second term had looked bumpy, and from time to time the government had appeared to falter. But she still had a great deal to accomplish and wanted the nation to know that she had not run out of energy.

Party chairman Norman Tebbit predicted that Kinnock would fight a "presidential election," an American-style image campaign. They expected him to fight as a personality—young, energetic, with an attractive family—representing the "caring face of socialism," not as a defender of policy. Thatcher doubted that Kinnock, who had never fought a national election, had the heft to carry off an image campaign. She found it difficult to take Kinnock seriously at all. She disliked him personally. Not only were his policies anathema to her, but she bore him none of the grudging respect that had muted her animosity toward Callaghan and Wilson.[2] To her, Kinnock was not a serious person; he was not particularly bright and did not spend much time on his homework. With the exception of twice-weekly question time in Parliament, which was required theater, she never spoke to him if she could avoid it. At the annual state opening of Parliament, when she was required to file shoulder to shoulder with him from the Commons to the House of Lords to listen to the Queen's speech, neither spoke or even exchanged glances. Both stared stonily ahead. She refused to invite him to Downing Street unless an official function made it mandatory.

British campaigns are more issue-oriented than American ones, and it was on the issues that the Tories decided to focus their attack. That made the most sense against Labor as well as against the Alliance, which seemed to be coming on strong after two by-election victories. The Alliance was a worry, but the party was split both on defense and taxation questions. Bombarding them in those areas, the Conservatives hoped, might increase the chances of exploitable rifts developing. As a backup, the Tories also dangled the possibility of a hung Parliament before the electorate. Few voters wanted that.

While mulling over the situation in late April, Thatcher received the first batch of suggested advertising from Saatchi and Saatchi, her ad veterans from the 1979 and 1983 campaigns. She loathed it. The Saatchis, who had repeated in the commercial sector their success with the Tories, were by 1987 the world's biggest ad agency. Along the way, however, they had lost Tim Bell, their political specialist, the brains behind the earlier campaigns. A charmer who cajoled and flattered Thatcher outrageously, he had been a particular favorite of the prime minister. Without Bell to reassure her, she was uncomfortable with the ads provided by the Saatchi shop. She told Maurice Saatchi she wanted more positive ad copy. She did not want to run a primarily negative campaign, which campaign professionals know works better. She wanted to brag about her successes. The Saatchis complied, and by May the campaign machine was ready to go.

Thatcher, though, was not entirely. She had had to be pushed into the 1983 election and was similarly hesitant this time, but for a different reason. She did not feel all that well. Moscow had exhausted her. An abscessed tooth plagued her, and she was nervous about party chairman Norman Tebbit.

Tebbit had not wanted the party chairman's post. He had been grieviously wounded in the Brighton bombing, which had left his wife paralyzed. His long convalescence had been interrupted by repeated operations, and his wife would always require full-time care. In charge of the Department of Trade and Industry at the time of the Brighton assassination attempt, he had been content. He had no desire to tramp the length and breadth of Britain on weekends and holidays attending party rallies and teas. He much preferred to work at his cabinet post and to stay at home where he could look after his wife. But he was the toughest hard guy in the party, an excellent cut-and-slash speaker who gave no quarter. Thatcher insisted. He finally gave in and took over in September 1985, only three months before the Westland affair. On every score, the appointment was a mistake.

Tebbit was self-made, combative, and a hard-core Conservative. He shared all these traits with Thatcher, but the relationship was never smooth. Tebbit was an abrasive loner, still filled with rage over the bombing. High strung and seething with bitterness, he seemed about to explode. No yes-man, he was never afraid to speak up when he disagreed with the prime minister, which was often. He battled her during the Westland crisis, first urging that she not jettison Defense Secretary Michael Heseltine and wondering too indiscreetly whether she might have to step down.

This caused Thatcher to realize that his appointment had been a terrible error. It dawned on her that he was after her job, but it was too late and would be too embarrassing to get rid of him. "Tebbit hates you," a political friend told her, reaffirming her own nagging fear. "If you lose, he thinks he can take over the party."[3] She had thoroughly trusted Parkinson in 1983, but whatever faith she had placed in Tebbit disappeared. Her doubts also rose about his skill as a manager. He had great instincts for the political jugular, but the prime minister doubted his organization and administrative skills. She also disliked his looks. Balding, cadaverous and with a piercing stare, Tebbit had the haunted looks of a potential ax murderer.

Despite her concerns, Thatcher felt enormous momentum pushing her toward a June election. In Parliament by early May, the MPs were pawing the floor in preparation for battle. Speaker Bernard Weatherill, barely able to control the House, noted that he sensed "an electioneering atmosphere" as he appealed for "less euphoria." The Labor party announced a new campaign slogan,

"The country's crying out for change," while Thatcher was hinting broadly that voters would have a chance "very soon" to judge her policies.

But she still needed convincing. It made no sense to call a national election until she had seen the results of the May 7 elections for local councils. More than 12,000 seats were at stake throughout England and Wales, and party professionals called the contest "the world's biggest public opinion poll." The Tories figured they could not have a better bellwether. If the results were bad, Thatcher would hold off until autumn, watch unemployment fall some more, hand out more tax cuts, and hike public spending to improve her chances.

The incumbent party often fares poorly in local voting. But this time worries about voter complacency and party defections were all for nought. The Tories gained seats. So did the Alliance. Labor was the big loser. The BBC projected that a similar vote pattern in a general election would translate into a solid Conservative win nationally. Thatcher's team gathered again the following Sunday at Chequers. In a room dominated by a portrait of Sir Robert Walpole, Britain's first prime minister, Thatcher spent two hours poring over thick computer printouts reviewing the local results. Bookies had already listed the Tories as 2–13 favorites, with Labor at 4–1 and the Alliance a 25–1 long shot. The party's private polls indicated a potential majority of 100 in the Commons, down from the 144 racked up in 1983, but a landslide nonetheless.

Thatcher was convinced. She would call the election. What she did not reveal at the Sunday strategy session was that she had dined the night before with Tim Bell, who remained one of her closest political friends. Like television guru Gordon Reece and speechwriter Ronald Millar, Bell is not an MP and is no threat to her. Because there is no possibility of future competition, Thatcher can let her hair down with him. When she asked him to review Tebbit's election strategy, which stressed targeting the Alliance, Bell was shocked.

"This is all wrong," he said.

"Why?" she asked.

"What's wrong with what we did the last time? That gave you a 144-seat majority. What's changed? We were in government then, we are now. We won a big majority then; we want another one now. We were ten points up before; we're ten points up this time. The Alliance was wobbling around the edge in 1983; it still is. Labor was in disarray; it still is. If anything, everything is better because the economic miracle is in place and you've got the miners' strike resolved in place of the Falklands. Okay, modernize, update, freshen, but someone would have to spend a long time convincing me not to do exactly what we did before."

"You mean we shouldn't do this?" the prime minister asked.

"Attacking the Alliance is madness," said Bell. "You strengthen and exaggerate their position. It's like the brand leader in the supermarket attacking the small local brand. Suddenly everybody hears about it and thinks if the big guy is attacking it, it must be really good," he replied.

"But everyone has heard of David Owen and David Steel," she said.

"That's not true," Bell retorted. "To this day, 10 percent of the population thinks Winston Churchill is still prime minister."[4]

After the strategy meeting the next day, Thatcher ordered Bell to begin adjusting the official campaign, but not to tell anyone. In the meantime, she would start the politicking. This kind of secretiveness was increasingly common in her later years as prime minister. The stealth stemmed from her private feelings about her ministers and her justifiable concern about where and when certain information is revealed. But setting up what was essentially a clandestine, back-channel political campaign was carrying furtiveness to a new level.

On May 11, she told her cabinet that the election would be held June 11, one day after the Parliament reached the four-year mark. This meant that those who elected her in 1983 would have their term's worth. With Buckingham Palace alerted and Queen Elizabeth available, Thatcher glided up the Mall in her armored Daimler for the second time to ask the monarch to dissolve Parliament. Later that day, she announced that the campaign would last a scant twenty-four days, and within minutes, the opening salvos erupted in the Commons.

"This election is about saving our country from industrial decline, social division, and the destruction of community services," said Kinnock.

"Everyone knows that Labor is unelectable and cannot win," said the SDP's Owen. "The real question is whether thoughtful voters want five more years of unbridled Thatcherism."

Thatcher seemed to think so. "I'm still bursting with energy," she said. "It's not going to be a pushover. We're ready for a fight." She did, however, reject a Kinnock challenge to a direct debate, saying it would generate "more hot air than light." When he pressed his demand, she held her ground. "You find your own platform," she jibed back. "I will not give you one." Thatcher did not waste time on small battles. She was too confident. "I would hope this is not my last election," she said. "This is only the third time of asking. I hope to go on and on." She was neither joking nor boasting. She meant it precisely as she said it. Less obvious, but just as serious, was the message to her own cabinet ministers: don't start planning the succession yet.

The party manifestos presented strikingly different images of Britain. Doom was Labor's theme. The party attempted to project a divided, joyless Britain, an "economically and socially disabled" country wallowing in Dickensian misery. Thatcher presented an entirely different vision of the nation. Her Britain had a "revived spirit and restored reputation"; her Britain could take pride in "Europe's fastest growing economy." Thatcher's campaign theme was "Power to the people," and she bolstered it with a blizzard of statistics to demonstrate that under her stewardship the number of British stockholders had nearly tripled; that the middle class increased in size from 30 percent to 50 percent of the population; that inflation had fallen from 18 percent to 4 percent.[5]

Turning her policies around was unthinkable. Instead, she promised more privatization, more choice in housing and education, more stock ownership, and better pensions. She simply would not tolerate criticism that she and her government were uncaring. "All decent people care about the sick, the unfortunate and old," she said as she blasted the whiners and hand-wringers, labeling them "moaning minnies." All they did was stand around and complain, she said.

The Alliance, as expected, took a middle line, promising more public spending than the Tories offered, but less than Labor pledged. They dodged the issue of nuclear weaponry, hoping to perpetuate the illusion of unity, but could not resist taking a shot at Labor. "On defense," said David Owen, "Labor remains a menace to its allies and the answer to the Russians' prayers." The Conservatives also fired across Labor's bow, charging that Kinnock's party "would abandon the defense policy followed by every British government, Labor or Conservative, since World War II."

No sooner was she off and running than Thatcher, surprisingly, began to stumble. Confused over her own new education policies, she seemed to suggest that state schools which chose to operate outside state control might begin charging tuition. She recovered, but conveyed the idea that she was particularly cold-hearted on education, one of the country's worst domestic problems and one of the few she has seriously mishandled. Despite a jump of 157,000 full- and part-time students entering secondary schools since 1979, government spending in real terms had dropped by 10 percent, and the schools were a mess.

The National Health Service (NHS) became the subject of the second Thatcher fumble. Asked why she went to private doctors and hospitals instead of using the NHS, Thatcher replied that private care "enables mc to go into hospital on the day I want at the time I want with the doctor I want." David Owen, a doctor himself, immediately accused her of not caring about people whose incomes did not allow such choice.

The prime minister has long been criticized for the deterioration of the health service, and she has vigorously rebutted the charges. She points out that government spending on health increased more than two and a half times during her first eight years in office. She counters arguments that health care in London has deteriorated by explaining that funding has been shifted out of the prosperous South to more needy areas. Still, complaints rightly persist. Despite the one million NHS employees—the service is Europe's biggest single employer after the Soviet Red Army—more than 700,000 people were kept waiting for surgery in the year before the election. Many hospitals were a mess, dark and filthy with ancient equipment and doctors and nurses working fourteen- and sixteen-hour shifts. The care is also highly inefficient. Operations performed on an outpatient basis in the United States can require a five-day stay in a British hospital. But Thatcher refused to throw money at the NHS, insisting that it be cleaned up and made more efficient first. The issue fanned white hot during the first rounds of her third campaign, and her remarks about her own private care made it worse.

Labor made a stunning start with its very first televised "political broadcast," one of the free TV slots allotted to each party. As the Tories had predicted, Labor's strategists concentrated almost completely on selling Kinnock, the man. The May 21 broadcast confirmed this strategy and instantly transformed the campaign. It opened with a shot of a warplane streaking through the sky. As the warplane faded into a sea gull soaring, the soundtrack segued into Labor's campaign theme, Brahms's Fourth Symphony, which introduced Neil and Glenys Kinnock walking hand in hand across a coastal cliff. The music then cut to a voice track of Kinnock explaining how the strong should help the weak. Directed by Hugh Hudson (*Chariots of Fire*), the film illustrated Kinnock's modest upbringing, featured his schools and career, and included a clip of his 1985 attack on Labor's militant left wing to demonstrate his personal toughness. Admiring comments followed from relatives and party colleagues. The Labor party was never mentioned.

American in style, the ad borrowed extensively from the Ron and Nancy school of soft-focus campaign heart-tuggers. In Britain, the ad was a breakthrough; Kinnock's personal popularity soared like the sea gull, rising an amazing 16 percent overnight. Party morale climbed, too, as the Conservatives grumped about "glossy packaging." One envious Tory MP said after the election that "the Kinnocks were packaged with professionalism and flair while most of the time we Tories seemed to lack both."

Unlike Denis Thatcher, who doggedly backed the prime minister from the shadows, Glenys Kinnock had a history of high visibility as a passionate "no nukes" campaigner. But Labor experts decided that to give her too high a profile would draw attention to the party's defense policy and lose votes. So Glenys played a carefully measured role, stumping with her husband across the marginal districts of the North, where only a few hundred votes separated Labor and Conservative candidates in the 1983 election. Glenys nodded as her husband hammered away at the themes of "throwaway towns and disposable people." She approved of her husband's portrayal of Thatcher as a latter-day Marie Antoinette, indifferent to the plight of the poor and needy.

The strategy was paying dividends, but fortunately for Thatcher, the defense policy hurdle soon sent Kinnock sprawling. In a television interview May 24 with David Frost, Kinnock, still committed to removing nuclear weapons from Britain, admitted that it would be futile for the country's conventionally armed forces to try to repel a nuclear-armed aggressor. In the event of a nuclear attack, he said, the best defense would be to employ "all the resources you have to make any occupation totally untenable." In other words, Kinnock believed in using guerrilla forces—after the conqueror had taken over.

Scenting blood, the Conservatives raced to the attack. "Britain has no ambition to live under the red flag of socialism or the white flag of surrender," said Tebbit. Soon after, Kinnock extended the blunder by declaring that a new Labor party government would decommission "within weeks" the Polaris-armed nuclear submarines that comprise the majority of Britain's independent deterrent "within weeks." "Never in the field of arms control would so much have been surrendered for so little," Thatcher mocked. Rubbing salt in the wound, the Tories rushed out hundreds of thousands of new posters, the most effective of the campaign. Over a photo of a British soldier with his hands over his head in surrender, the caption read, "Labor's policy on arms."

Others joined in the barrage of criticism. An open letter signed by 100 academics headed by Lord Blake, provost of Queen's College, Oxford, blared that "the adoption of the Labor party's defense proposals would seriously increase the likelihood of a third world war and would constitute an unacceptable risk to the security and freedom of Britain." Ronald Reagan, ignoring all protocol about interfering in other nations' electioneering, joined the fray. If Labor came to power, he said, the United States would have to persuade the new government of "the grievous error of nuclear disarmament."

As the campaign roared into high gear, the Alliance moved increasingly onto the sidelines. Its strength was the centrists who remained uncommitted to either of the larger parties. In 1983, the Alliance benefited from the pool of voters who abandoned Michael Foot and Labor but did not want to back the Conservatives. But with Kinnock waging a more formidable race than Foot, there were fewer uncommitteds. The Alliance had other problems, too.

The party's biggest flaw lay in its two-headed nature. Nobody could tell whether Steel or Owen, Tweedledee or Tweedledum as the two Davids were called, was in charge. Nor was it ever quite clear who would be prime minister if the Alliance actually got elected. Initially, they campaigned together, then split up. Often, they seemed divided on policy, including their tenuous defense compromise; and their targets never matched. Owen campaigned against Labor, while Steel aimed his shots at the Conservatives. They even appeared to differ over what to do in the event they got what they wanted—a hung Parliament in which they held the swing votes. Would they back Thatcher, who would clearly have the most seats if not a majority, or throw their support to Kinnock? That was another unanswered question.

Despite their rocky start, the Tories' polling lead held up with remarkable consistency. Throughout the month-long campaign,

Thatcher and the Conservatives maintained a 10–11 percent lead over Labor with the Alliance trailing Labor by an average of 10 percent. A rogue Gallup poll on June 3 cut the Tory lead to 4 percent and threw Conservative party headquarters into a panic. Thatcher was stunned. What was going on? She wanted to win big. In one twenty-four-hour period before other data arrived, the prime minister tried to overhaul completely her strategy and advertising for the final week.

Her dissatisfaction with the whole effort had continued through the campaign, which was taxing. She had had no chance to blow off steam, which she needs, and was getting tense. In the 1979 campaign, she sat up into the middle of the night sipping whiskey with Airey Neave. In 1983, she had done the same with Cecil Parkinson. This time, her main strategist was supposed to be Tebbit, but there was no comfortable, trusting camaraderie between them. Denis tried to soothe her, but that was not enough. To bypass Tebbit, she ran a back-channel operation instructing her old cronies Bell, Parkinson, and Reece to call her with ideas daily before 7 A.M. and after 11 P.M., which they did. Her two closest personal aides, Charles Powell and Bernard Ingham, were not, as civil servants, allowed to participate, but they often bore the brunt of her moods during prime ministerial business.

Labor's campaign had surprised Thatcher. She had not expected them to mount such a good effort. Their professionalism concerned her, especially since her own campaign was tottering with internal battles. The Saatchis were still making ads for Tebbit, but another faction was dealing with a separate advertising agency, Young & Rubicam. Bell, Reece, and Parkinson provided a third voice. Thatcher had not been able to sort out the duplication and rough edges, and the situation was sloppy. In the end, the mess did not matter.

Election day, June 11, dawned drizzly, but was bright enough for Thatcher. She not only won her third term, but—in an election that turned almost completely on her record and iron-will personality—pulled an unexpectedly huge majority of 101 seats, 43 fewer than 1983, but more than double what most Tory analysts had predicted. In several respects, the result was more impressive than either of the previous two victories. In 1979, James Callaghan's party had been sapped by trade union recalcitrance, and after five years of uninspired Labor leadership, there was solid reason to shift to the Tories even if they were led by a woman. In 1983, the incompetence of the Foot campaign combined with the post-Falklands euphoria made Thatcher unstoppable. In 1987, her task was much tougher. She had to contend with an electorate that was tiring of her and a young, vigorous opponent. Yet her triumph was overwhelming. Her 101-seat majority was the second biggest, behind her 1983 record, for any leader since 1945.

The divided opposition certainly helped. The Conservatives won with 42 percent of the vote, the same percentage they registered in 1983, while Labor and the Alliance combined for almost 54 percent. The victory confirmed the fact that given the choice between a popular leader and one they respect, Britons opt for the latter. That had been true too with Churchill, who was gruff, domineering, and difficult with colleagues. He was a bulldog, a resolute but less-than-lovable beast. Thatcher was a mongrel, a cross between a Jack Russell terrier, yipping and nagging tiresomely, and a Great Dane, high strung, fast, and dominant. Her bossiness was scarcely a factor the third time out. The campaign team did not even bother to soften any of her own rough edges. "When she first came to power, being bossy was a problem because she hadn't earned her spurs. Britons didn't like being hectored and lectured to by this headmistressy character who had yet to prove herself," said Tim Bell. "As she has become more and more successful, that manner has become less offensive. The content is overwhelming the packaging." George Younger, the former defense minister and a loyal Thatcherite, said that for all the difficult aspects of Thatcher's character, her undeniable strengths still made her the obvious choice. "Voters hang onto nurse for fear of something worse," he said.

The third straight smashing win demolished the opposition. Labor had lost three in a row under three separate leaders. Its policies were clearly unacceptable to the electorate and needed major reappraisal. David Owen identified his former party's problem succinctly: "The reason Labor has not delivered is that their policies stink." Thatcher won, he added accurately, because she represented "determined, clear, firm leadership."

Owen's own Alliance was the biggest victim, sabotaged by its ill-defined, middle-of-the-road stance. Within months of the election, the Alliance collapsed thoroughly and acrimoniously. The party that had been touted a year before as the next official opposition party lay in tatters.

None of this was obvious when Thatcher peered out the second-story window of Conservative party headquarters at 3:25 A.M. in the predawn after polling day. Beaming, she waggled three fingers for three wins at the crowd of several thousand supporters below who chanted, "Five more years." Denis stood beside her, proud as punch, while champagne corks popped. With the third consecutive win, she had passed over an invisible dividing line. No longer was she just a winner, a good politician. Now she was an historic figure.

CHAPTER TWENTY

Metal Fatigue?

THE SCOPE of the victory reinvigorated Thatcher. She had been nervous and uncharacteristically hesitant during much of the campaign. She hadn't felt well, either, but all that quickly changed. Now she was on top of the world, dominant at home, an icon everywhere else. Thatcher had no political opposition; she was the darling of the Kremlin and the White House. Both Reagan and Gorbachev sought her counsel. She was at the very peak of her mastery. Thatcher knew it and intended to use it.

She was aware that momentum had stalled during the second term. She had punished the miners and expanded privatization, but movement on domestic reforms had otherwise been disappointing. There were too many areas that still needed fixing. She was ready to rectify that. Her radical fires were blazing again. But first there were some scores to settle.

Norman Tebbit wanted to give up the party chairman's post. That was normal after an election. Thatcher's refusal to offer him another cabinet job was, however, unusual. Cut adrift, the bitter Tebbit wandered back to private life. John Biffen, leader of the House of Commons and the intellectual conscience of the cabinet, was also sacked, ending a year on thin ice. In May 1986, Biffen repeated Francis Pym's 1983 pre-election error, suggesting that the prime minister consider a "balanced ticket," meaning a less hard line, approach to the third campaign. Pym lasted a day past the second election; Biffen was dispatched the day after the third.

Freed from the constraints of government, Biffen became more publicly candid. He had become uneasy with the "Stalinist" rigidity

303

that Thatcher had imposed on cabinet debate and blasted "her desire to dance on the grave of her opponents." The grave image was not inappropriate. Thatcher has never taken many prisoners, but has dispatched most antagonists with finality. "Squashed like flies" was Biffen's description of how cabinet members felt after she was finished with them. As a result, she has driven some of Britain's best politicians from office, emasculating others who have stayed. More evidence of that appeared later in the third term, a term which was ambitious, but soured with surprising speed. Anyone who thought that with her place in history secured, Thatcher might ease up in how she treated people was wrong. She became tougher than ever. One of her closest aides attributed her style to insecurity and a need to prove herself constantly. "She's remarkably insecure," said this colleague, a strong supporter. "She's a woman in a man's world and is never entirely certain how to deal with men, so she flattens them."

Biffen was the latest squashed fly, but his vantage point as a former member of the inner circle gave his criticism extra credibility. "What I found extraordinary is how much she resents having to deal with the modest element of opposition that exists," he said. Coming from a strict Tory, a pre-Thatcher Thatcherite who was no potential rival, Biffen's criticism was remarkable; it foreshadowed rising annoyance among Tories with their leader, regardless of her success. She had become "an autocrat," he said. Berating her for "the narrowness of her social attitudes—the quite abhorrent degree of self-righteousness she exhibits in private," Biffen concluded that "her fellow East Anglian Oliver Cromwell must be her hero because she reflects much of his character."[1]

Biffen, of course, was just one more of yesterday's men to the woman that the irreverent Tory MP Julian Critchley dubbed the Conservatives' *"prima donna inter pares."*[2] Within a year, she had entered one of the worst slumps of her career, scrambling to halt a dizzying fall, but in mid-1987, Thatcher was still mistress of all she surveyed. Both the Labor and Alliance parties were struggling to avoid extinction.

The Alliance was in the worst shape. It failed even to match its 1983 showing—taking only 22 of the 650 seats in the House of Commons in 1987—primarily because the political center had evaporated. There was no need for an alternative to Thatcher and Kinnock as there had been four years before when Michael Foot had been overmatched. Additionally, the party's centrism and leadership had been poorly defined. The Alliance's postelection task was to instill shape and credibility or perish. Perish they did when the Liberals and the SDP got sidetracked and entangled over the issue of formal merger. Within two months of the election, following acrimonious debate, the Social Democrats voted to consolidate over David Owen's objections.

Owen opposed full merger, fearing that the larger Liberal party would dominate. He still strenuously disagreed with the Liberals' antinuclear policy. He was also reluctant to play second fiddle in a combined party he was unlikely to head. When the Liberals' David Steel pushed for full fusion and won, Owen stepped down and into the political backwaters. Steel stayed to shepherd the merger through, then he too moved aside. Instead of recharging the Alliance, the battle sapped what little appeal it had left. With both leaders succeeded by nonentities, the party faded into the fringe.

Kinnock remained at the Labor helm and pushed his effort to modernize the party, moderate its radical image, and institute some winning policies. Never tired of pointing out that more Britons voted against Thatcher than for her, Kinnock conceded after her third victory that a major reappraisal of Labor's strategy was required. "We need a Labor party that is attractive to a greater breadth of the public," he said, launching a far-flung study of Labor's economic, industrial, and defense policies. "The simple truth is we haven't got an economic policy," Denis Healey admitted after the 1987 loss. "Our nonnuclear policy must go," added Peter Shore, a Labor centrist. Stan Orme, the chairman of the parliamentary Labor party, warned that unless Labor moved toward the center, "we'll lose the next election and probably never govern Britain again."[3]

That fall, with the opposition regrouping and the field clear, Thatcher kicked off the most radical set of initiatives since her 1979 budget. Education, taxes, welfare, utilities, the medical and legal professions, even the system under which British brewers owned pubs—all were earmarked for major restructuring. The third term was underway in earnest.

Education was the first area to come under the government's scrutiny and scalpel. The Great Education Reform Bill, nicknamed GERBIL, was aimed at reforming the system that had operated since the Education Act of 1944 but was leaving British students ever further behind their continental counterparts. John Rae, former headmaster of Westminster, one of Britain's foremost private schools, despaired "We have possibly the worst publicly maintained education system of any developed country in the world."

Rae was not exaggerating. For the top 1 percent or so who attend the country's prestigious private schools (called "public" schools in Britain), education is superb. That, along with Oxford and Cambridge, their university-level equivalents, is the source of Britain's schooling reputation. But the country's public education is, for the most part, abysmal, a mockery of its mythic stature. Indeed, a 1988 report by the nation's Inspectors of Schools condemned one thousand of England's four thousand secondary schools as "unsatisfactory." Britain's record in sending students on to college has been among the worst in the industrialized world. Tens of thousands of sixteen-year-old "school leavers" each year enter the job market poorly educated and untrained. Only 14 percent of British high school students attend college, compared with 59 percent in the United States. The situation was one reason why Britain has had such difficulty competing internationally since the war.

Thatcher knew the system needed an overhaul, from changing primary and secondary school curricula to making universities more responsible for the way they spend the government's money. School tuition was free, but local authorities had control over the courses taught. Thatcher wanted to end that once and for all, and to establish a national curriculum. GERBIL passed in parliament to become the Education Reform Act of 1988, a revolutionary move back to basics and to greater central government control, making the system similar to the running of schools on the continent. It gave parents more say in deciding which schools their children would attend and allowed schools to opt out of local supervision and get their funding directly from central government. Other provisions instituted a three-Rs curriculum for state-funded schools, put the funding of higher education under the control of councils appointed by the central government, and wiped out tenure for university professors appointed after November 1987. The primary and secondary school proposals were less controversial than those aimed at the nation's fifty-two universities and generally won cheers. There were some complaints at the lower levels that new stress on English, math, and science would too rigidly re-create an old-fashioned curriculum. Some also feared that allowing parents to pick their children's schools could increase white flight from racially mixed districts.

The response to reforms at the university level was different.

University officials labeled the new plan "a recipe for disaster." The abolition of tenure, said Paul Cottrell of the Association of University Teachers, "will make academics easier to sack" and threaten academic freedom by forcing scholars to work according to government priorities instead of pursuing innovative research. But as Tory MP George Walden, a former minister of higher education, put it, "The higher education interests were simply incapable of reforming themselves and the government has had to take a hand." The real complaints were about greater budgetary accountability.

Thatcher's feeling was that education, like a poorly managed industry, kept expecting government to bail it out regardless of how inefficiently it operated. She felt that the university system generally, and Oxbridge in particular, was a bulwark of socialism. Professors, many of them arrogant intellectuals and leftists, sat up in their ivory towers teaching an occasional course, dithering and complaining instead of producing and getting on with it. That was not good enough for her.

She saw no reason why education should be spared the shakeup she was applying to most aspects of British society. There was nothing wrong with putting education on the same cost-conscious diet, applying market principles to a system that was not producing what the country needed to become and stay competitive. Since the early 1900s, the government had provided abundant funds to its universities. Spending on universities had increased eightfold, but the GNP had only tripled, according to Robert Jackson, her minister for higher education when the Reform Act of 1988 passed. "After the puffing up of universities and research throughout the fifties and sixties when academics said 'give us the money and no questions asked,' people were bound to start asking questions," he said.[4]

Thatcher herself had pushed for fat budgets during the early 1970s when she was education secretary, but as prime minister she was in the forefront of those asking questions. In 1981, she began cutting back spending, not in absolute funds but in the percentage of government contribution. In 1978, for example, unconditional grants from the government provided 75 percent of the university system's funds; a decade later, the figure was 55 percent. The universities screamed; *whinged* is the better British word. The lean budgets made Thatcher a hated figure on campus.

She was so hated that in 1985, Oxford had refused to award her an honorary degree. Attlee, Macmillan, Wilson, and Heath had all been awarded honorary degrees during their first year in office; Eden and Douglas-Home received theirs before becoming prime minister. All were Oxford graduates; so was Thatcher. She had been considered three times for the degree between 1979 and 1983, but each time the committee had pulled back. Two years later, when the prime minister was finally nominated, a firestorm erupted. Leading the protest were 275 dons who wrote that Thatcher's government had "done deep and systematic damage to the whole public education system in Britain, from the provision for the youngest child up to the most advanced research programs." The dons voted 738 to 319 against awarding her the degree, dishonoring the university more than the prime minister. Thatcher reacted with dignity. "If they do not wish to confer the honor, I am the last person who would wish to receive it."[5] The action reaffirmed her belief that the dons were a small-minded gaggle of short-range thinkers who neither knew nor cared how the real world operated. She would be bigger than they. She also held the purse strings to more than $4 billion in university funding and had no intention of loosening them.

The impact of her crackdown was felt quickly. By 1988, Oxford had 122 vacant teaching positions—and funds to fill only 25 slots. Two of the university's prestigious Regius chairs, established centuries ago by British kings, were unfunded and unfilled in 1989. Thousands of teachers fled Britain for richer pay packets and more modern research facilities in the United States. Cambridge philosopher Bernard Williams moved to Berkeley; so did Reading University urbanologist Peter Hall. Michael Howard, Oxford's renowned Regius professor of history, left to teach at Yale.[6]

Thatcher was unrepentant. She saw British universities suffocating under the weight of countless tenured faculty members, protected by Civil Service salary ladders, teaching irrelevant courses. Arguments that efficiency should not be the test for a great university and that arcane medieval literature courses with only a student or two helped define the best universities fell on deaf ears. That was a luxury the government could not afford. By 1990, Thatcher wanted 35 percent more science graduates and 25 percent more engineers than in 1980. She wanted students to acquire the skills that Britain needed to compete. Thatcher was willing to accept the short-term brain drain just as she accepted unemployment tripling during her first two terms, as an unfortunate necessity. The system needed wringing out. When critics claimed that universities could not be treated like factories, she asked why not. The universities had never worked to help themselves the way private U.S. universities do. Oxford's endowment, for example, is about $12 million; Harvard's, $4.5 billion. In 1988, when Oxford launched a private fund-raising drive after soliciting advice from Harvard and Princeton, no one applauded louder than Thatcher. Until then, the university had never even bothered to solicit funds from its 116,000 living graduates, some of them the most successful and richest men and women in the world.

After taking on education, Thatcher applied her free-market gospel to the National Health Service (NHS), the jewel in the welfare crown. She explained that her aim was to give hospitals and doctors greater freedom by increasing efficiency and cutting costs, but critics worried that she really wanted to privatize the system. She would have liked to, certain that it would be more efficient, but knew the country wouldn't tolerate that. When she tried to introduce private insurance, she was savaged in Parliament. Neil Kinnock called her tentative proposal "a cheap and nasty strategy from a cheap and nasty government." Thatcher pulled back, but kept fiddling with the system. Some hospitals began to rent instead of buy X-ray machines; catering and janitorial services were, in some cases, taken over by private firms. Fees for eye tests and dental exams were introduced despite polls that showed more than 90 percent of Britons opposed the charges. Trained managers replaced doctors as administrators in some hospitals.

The reforms, plus others aimed at introducing a sense of competition to increase productivity and cut waiting time for operations, made sense but worried Britons who also felt that Thatcher was trying to Americanize the system. David Owen, a doctor, warned against that. "The commercialization of health care is the primrose path down which inexorably lies American medicine—first-rate treatment for the wealthy and tenth-rate treatment for the poor." Thatcher maintained that spending on the NHS had increased 40 percent after inflation to $47 billion from 1979 to 1989. Still, complaints about service escalated along with calls for more money. Thatcher refused to be stampeded. "Pouring money in is not the answer," she said correctly. "Making the system operate better is what is needed." No matter how frequently Thatcher explained how she was trying to fix the system, she was accused of trying to destroy it to save money.

Less controversial, but no less radical, was the government's proposed deregulation of the legal system, the most sweeping change in the profession's history. At the heart of the reform was the elimination of the mandatory distinction between solicitors, who deal directly with clients, and the bewigged barristers who generally have a monopoly on presenting cases in court. Under the government's plan, another effort to induce competition to benefit consumers, all lawyers would be allowed to deal with clients and argue cases in any court after obtaining a certificate of competence. The reform would also allow lawyers to accept cases on the American model of a contingency basis, meaning no win, no fee. To prevent litigation overload, an American excess, the sums lawyers could collect would be restricted.

Lord Mackay, the lord chancellor, who is appointed by the government as Britain's chief legal officer, called the proposals "an integral part of the government's wider program to improve access to justice." Consumers endorsed the proposals, but barristers reacted strongly against what they considered the Americanization of the system and pledged to fight. "The quality of justice is threatened and the public will lose," predicted Desmond Fennell, chairman of the British Bar Association. "It will introduce an American style of justice with district attorneys, big firms of lawyers, and an enormous increase in cost and delay."

By a year into the third term, hardly a facet of British daily life had escaped Thatcher's free-market branding iron. Many areas improved, but some suffered, few more than the arts. In 1988, the chairmen of the National Gallery, British Museum, Tate Gallery, the Victoria and Albert, and the Natural Science museums appealed directly to the prime minister. They were broke. It was not a question of being unable to make acquisitions; they could not make repairs. Some paintings were being stored under plastic to keep off the rain. The Tate said it needed more than $40 million for repairs. The National Gallery claimed that its meager resources placed its art "at daily risk."[7] Thatcher wouldn't budge. The government had no money to spare and told the museums to charge admissions, set up fund-raising programs, or sell parts of their collections. Private fund-raising provides a major portion of museum and gallery support in the United States, but because the British tax system does not encourage charitable giving, the incentives for donations were not the same.

She might have made an exception or made it more attractive for the private sector to donate, but culture is a Thatcher blind spot and her government has mishandled the arts. Despite Alf's and Beatrice's efforts in Grantham or her own insistence that the twins be exposed to culture, she has never been very interested in the arts, fine or performing. The prime minister rarely visits museums or goes to a play. When she does, her favorites are the commercially successful Andrew Lloyd Webber extravaganzas. Concerts and ballet are of little interest to her and while she says she likes opera, she hardly ever attends.

The arts community generally considers her to be a philistine. "This government thinks of a subsidy as something you give to an industry that should have been closed ten years ago," said Sir Peter Hall, former director of the National Theater. "We try to get them to think of an arts subsidy as an investment, but they don't buy it. They think the arts are elitist. That's true. Excellence is elitist. But neither does this government think there are any votes in it."[8] Actor Peter Ustinov was similarly critical, as is almost everyone on the British art scene. "Thatcher's Britain may be more prosperous, but market values are not the only values."[9]

The arts weren't the only area where criticism was difficult to answer. There were other defeats in the early days of the third term that hinted at more trouble to come. In the fall of 1987, sweeping complaints about NHS funding prompted the prime minister to add more than $2 billion to the health service budget. By spring 1988, the intensity of the grumbling picked up. Intraparty criticism took on a sharper edge as Thatcher kept cutting taxes. In April, Nigel Lawson slashed the top individual tax rate from 60 percent to 40 percent, giving such a hefty boost to the disposable incomes of the rich that some of the prime minister's strongest supporters were embarrassed.

That decision only made worse a tax issue that was already highly controversial, a decision to replace local property taxes with a flat-rate poll tax on everyone over eighteen. The lump sum tax, expected to be just over $300 annually, was designed to fund local government councils, although its actual purpose was to hold them in check. Thatcher wanted to discourage town councils elected mainly by nontaxpaying voters from lavishly spending revenues collected from taxpaying homeowners and businesses. Everyone is capable, she believes; therefore everyone must contribute.

The regressive poll tax plan evoked a storm of criticism. Opponents, not a few within the Tory party, argued against a tax that required welfare recipients to pay the same as millionaires. "The fairness upon which we pride ourselves is affronted," said Michael Heseltine, the former defense secretary. When Parliament first voted on the tax in 1988, Tory rebels bolted and the government's 101-seat majority shrank to the embarrassing margin of only 25. Later, in an effort to ease the tax's passage, the government added a "safety net" which called for well-run local councils to subsidize higher-spending ones. The maladroit fallback managed to upset the few remaining supporters of a tax plan that only Thatcher herself really supported.

There was never a third-term honeymoon. The controversies over education and health service reform put a quick end to any thought that political life might get smoother the longer Thatcher stayed in Downing Street. The added tax cuts plus the furor over the poll tax increased the pressure in early 1988 and forced several more rollbacks. That spring, the nation's nearly half-million nurses and midwives were given a 15 percent pay raise worth $1.4 billion. Outrage at the realization their salaries averaged less than $12,800 led to widespread calls for a boost. At the same time, Thatcher was forced to retreat after cutting welfare benefits for the poor, elderly, and disabled. A barrage in the Commons compelled her to restore $188 million to the welfare budget. She also had to raise the eligibility ceiling on family savings for rent assistance and tax relief from $11,280 to $15,040. "We saw that what we had planned was having an unduly severe effect on some people," she explained. "We decided we had to adjust." A Tory MP gave a different explanation for her change of heart: "The constituent mailbags arrived."

The mailbags got heavier. The further Thatcher went, the more resistance she stirred up. In addition to the policies themselves, which were not easy to swallow, there were other reasons for the escalating tension.

Deputy Prime Minister William Whitelaw's retirement in January 1988 after a mild stroke was a blow from which it seemed Thatcher might never recover. By 1990, she had still not gotten over his departure. Whitelaw's retirement was a tremendous loss, bigger than Thatcher herself realized. With him gone from the cabinet, she lacked a trusted, high-ranking adviser who could restrain her most divisive inclinations. Whitelaw was no political threat to her, no challenger. He had become more an Airey Neave character, a reliable mentor, but with far better links than Neave to party centrists and the few remaining old boys. Since the departure of Peter Carrington during the Falklands War, there was no one else with Whitelaw's ability to calm Thatcher down, to get her to reexamine an issue, to smooth the bumps in the political road in Parliament or out in the country.

Another reason for the gathering of storm clouds was that Thatcher was a victim of her own success. By the spring of 1988, she'd had parliamentary majorities of more than a hundred seats for five years. She'd had no restraints. There was no Congress or Supreme Court to balance her authority. She'd had such a free hand and so much power that, combined with her unrelieved dogmatism and natural belligerence, she had become overbearing and imperious. Her current cabinet, not just dropouts like Biffen, felt she was behaving autocratically. "Pym was right," said one, recalling the former foreign secretary's admonition about landslides and good government. So was Whitelaw, who had repeatedly warned that "a large majority and a weak opposition make it much more difficult to hold the party together and govern."

Thatcher began to spend less time with her back-benchers. She was always busy, but they interpreted the slight as evidence that the prime minister was ignoring them because she didn't think she needed them. When she did meet them, she did all the talking, leaving them more disgruntled. One close associate lamented that "her transmitter is permanently on send, never on receive. It will be her downfall." The frustration of Tories who knew they would never get a government appointment under Thatcher mounted and mixed with the bile of former ministers—more than a hundred— ousted over the years. She was, however, careful not to repeat one of Edward Heath's errors. She rewarded many potential troublemakers with peerages, thus moving them out of sniping range in the House of Commons and into the Lords.

By the time she marked her tenth anniversary in power in May 1989, a rainstorm seemed to pelt the party she declined to hold. (She dismissed it as "just another working day.") Thatcher might have looked more human if she had celebrated, but at that moment there was not much call to be festive. She was in political trouble again. The economy was sagging and she was in a worse than usual midterm slump. Many Britons were fed up with her. When the Premier restaurant, on the site of the old Roberts grocery in Grantham, advertised a special meal to mark the milestone, its windows were splattered with eggs. Predictions mounted that her third term would be her last. She was besieged and bedeviled from all sides. And it would only get worse.

Nothing kept Thatcher from pressing ahead, hammering at the remaining welfare state battlements. Privatization had long been one of the government's most popular policies, but not when the water and electricity utilities were put on the block. "The sell off is becoming a turn off," said *The Economist*. "Few people are persuaded that water and electricity should be sold."[10] Polls showed that 75 percent of Britons, including many in government, opposed the sale of shares in the nation's water-supply system. "I am told there are Conservatives who support water privatization," said one Tory. "I just haven't met any." The argument against the sale was that most of the fifty-four state-run companies privatized during Thatcher's first decade—including Rolls-Royce, British Steel, Jaguar, and British Airways—operated in competitive markets and should have been run by the private sector instead of the government. But water and electricity were a different story. Water, many felt, should be free, or nearly free anyway; enough of it fell on Britain. Consumers worried about rate hikes; environmentalists about the government transferring public lands and accountability. Electricity also seemed to fall more naturally under the provenance of government. Plans to convert it were not only highly complex but involved more expensive charges. Confusion over the management of nuclear power raised still more concerns.

All the reforms were dramatic; few were popular. In the best of times they would have been difficult to implement without a considerable political cost. But the task was made more difficult by a sharp midterm economic slump. The pound, which had hit a high of $1.85 in late 1988, plunged to $1.55 in October 1989 and analysts still considered it overvalued. The trade deficit had tripled and would reach a record $3.2 billion in September 1989. Inflation had doubled since early 1988 to 8.3 percent in May 1989, the highest in Europe. To keep it from going higher, Chancellor Lawson jacked interest rates up from 7.5 percent to 15 percent, by far the highest in the West and a level last seen in Britain during the 1981 recession. The October hike pushed mortgage rates to 17 percent, all but shutting down the housing market. Because 95 percent of Britain's home mortgages float with the basic rate, council house owners felt particularly sabotaged by the rate increases, but everyone hollered for relief. Lawson, once considered Britain's economic miracle worker, became the nation's goat. The *Daily Mail*, the staunchest pro-Tory paper, labeled the one-time hero "the bankrupt chancellor" and demanded his resignation.

National dissatisfaction with the economy centered attention on one of the best known secrets in Whitehall, the persistent sharp disagreement between the prime minister and her chancellor over what to do about the economy. The two had been battling for years, and the prime minister, whose official title is First Lord of the Treasury, had refused to let Lawson run the economy. Thatcher believed that sterling's value should be maintained by market forces, not managed by the government. Lawson consistently upheld his position that intervention by manipulating interest rates, however unfortunate, was a necessary tool to avoid runaway inflation. The two also differed over whether Britain should join the European Monetary System (EMS) which keeps Western European exchange rates within a narrow band. Lawson favored EMS membership to provide a stable exchange rate, which adds certainty to government and industrial planning. Thatcher, always wary of any extranational linkage with its implicit diminution of British independent authority, repeatedly said that the time was "not yet ripe" for joining.

The EMS debate had taken on larger form as the European Community rocketed toward the economic and political integration that was scheduled to take place in 1992, a union Thatcher resisted. More competition, less regulation, free trade with Europe—all that was fine with Thatcher. What was not fine was the risk of diminished British sovereignty and the chance that the new Europe meant establishing a giant transnational bureaucracy to run it.

Her challenge to Europe began picking up steam in June 1988 when France's Jacques Delors, president of the European Commission, proclaimed that by the mid-1990s "80 percent of European economic decisions will be made in Brussels," the Community's headquarters. Thatcher, who disliked Delors both personally and for being a socialist, contemptuously dismissed the European and called his remarks "absurd" and "airy-fairy." Three months later, Delors invaded Britain. Invited to the annual conference of the Trades Union Congress, he received a standing ovation from the unions Thatcher hates when he described a "social Europe" that would preserve workers' rights.

For three weeks Thatcher stewed. Then she accepted an invitation in Delors's own backyard to stake out her ground. In a dramatic speech at the College of Europe in Bruges, she acknowledged that having her speak on Europe's future was "rather like asking Genghis Khan to speak on the virtues of peaceful coexistence." The audience chuckled, then lapsed into stunned silence as she tore into the concept of European federalism and declared war on efforts to "suppress nationhood and concentrate power at the center of a European conglomerate." She opposed the elimination of border controls because they helped keep track of terrorists and drug traffickers. She also dismissed the imposition of standard sales and excise taxes, refused to loosen Britain's tough quarantine restrictions on arriving animals, and disclaimed interest in creating a European central bank.

Her go-it-alone, pugnacious approach caused Simon Jenkins, a *Sunday Times* of London columnist, to describe Thatcher as the John McEnroe of European politicians. At home, the prime minister's nose-thumbing to Europe drew criticism, but nothing dramatic. Many working-class and lower middle-class Britons, her major constituents, share Thatcher's distrust of the continent. It was also still 1988. By 1989, the economy had slipped and new U.S. president George Bush was enthralled by West Germany. He was discovering a continent that Ronald Reagan had ignored. Suddenly, Thatcher appeared to be isolated from a Western Alliance that seemed headed for coalition without Britain. The European train was pulling out of the station and she was still on the platform. Business leaders, for years her biggest backers, began to worry that, if the economic action picked up on the continent, Thatcher's anti-Europeanism could cost London its primacy as a financial center, and cost their companies money.

Instead of reassessing, Thatcher kept up the onslaught during the run-up to the June 1989 elections to the European parliament. She opposed Community clean water standards and even regulations regarding the size of health warnings printed on cigarette packages, citing them as examples of interference in Britain's affairs. She also denounced a proposed Community charter on workers' rights as "a socialist charter, full of unnecessary controls."[11] When the results came in, it was clear that Maggie was out of step.

Before the European elections, Britain's Tories held 45 seats and Labor 32 in the 518-member European parliament, the increasingly influential legislative arm of the European Community. After the elections, the figures were exactly reversed. It was the Tories' worst showing and first nationwide defeat in Thatcher's tenure. Her aura of invincibility had been shattered. The Tories who did best were those who broke from the prime minister's Europe-bashing and endorsed the Community. "Responsibility for this abysmally negative campaign" was Thatcher's, said Peter Price, one of the Tory winners.[12] The *Sunday Telegraph*, normally a staunch supporter of the prime minister, said in an editorial that by associating herself and the Conservatives with anti-Europeanism, she had committed "a major blunder."[13]

Thatcher admitted the result was "disappointing," but dismissed it as unimportant. The balloting would have no impact on her attitude about a united Europe. The following week, the twelve European Community leaders met in Madrid and the prime minister again displayed her formidable resolve. Britain was willing to consider more "monetary cooperation," but full "monetary union" was still out. Much more "practical and pragmatic" work needed to be done first.

François Mitterrand accused her of trying to reopen "ideological debate" on questions the Community had resolved long ago. "France will not be satisfied with this fog," the French president snorted. Thatcher spurned the complaint. Among the major European leaders, she had more respect for Mitterrand, whom she considers intellectually astute but lazy, than for West German chancellor Helmut Kohl, whom she found less intelligent and politically weak. But she was not moved by either man.

She was also more and more discouraged by the evolution of the Community. Her concerns increased as the Community moved leftward, toward more socialism and control by bureaucrats—a word she spits out like an obscenity. Thatcher has not worked all those years in Britain to break down socialism, cut back the influence of bureaucrats, and get the nation's house in order just so a bunch of Europeans can wreck everything she has accomplished.

Scarcely had the leaders left Madrid than they gathered in Paris for France's bicentennial bash, a glittery festival marking the two-hundredth anniversary of the fall of the Bastille. The moment was Mitterrand's, but when interviewed, Maggie would not be denied. She belittled the French Revolution for not measuring up to the Magna Carta which predated it by five centuries. Asked whether she saw a universal message in the revolution, she responded with perfect honesty, "Pardon me for saying, but I think not. There was the terror and then Napoleon." As for "Liberty, Equality, and Fraternity, it was the Fraternity that was missing for a long time," she said.[14] She reminded Mitterrand, who barely avoided sputtering, that liberty, equality, and fraternity had figured prominently in the Ten Commandments and the Sermon on the Mount as well as at Runnymede. Then she presented the dumbfounded French president with her anniversary gift: a leather-bound copy of Dickens's novel *A Tale of Two Cities*, which contrasts France's violence during the revolution with the tranquil calm in England.[15]

The French, who dislike Thatcher in the best of times, booed and hissed her during the celebrations. Culture minister Jack Lang criticized unnamed "grinches and killjoys." Socialist Prime Minister Michel Rocard referred to "the British government's current trend toward social cruelty." Britain's tabloid press screeched back: "The Frogs Attack Maggie," said the *Sun* in a banner headline. The *Sunday Express* praised Thatcher as "the only world leader bold enough to deflate the windbaggery of the French government." By the end of the festivities, such was the state of European amity that the final banquet was canceled. Too many leaders preferred to go home.[16]

Thatcher's troubles in Madrid and France were just blips, compared with the political and economic adversity piling up at home. She was two years into her five-year term and was following her traditional pattern, on full view in 1981 and 1986, of slumping badly at the midway mark. She did not have to call an election until June 1992, but almost certainly would act in 1991, either in her favored spring or by autumn at the latest. In anticipation of a fourth try, Thatcher shook up her cabinet shortly after returning from France to give her new team two years to get into fighting shape. The intention of the shuffle, dubbed "The Night of the Long Hatpin" in memory of Macmillan's dramatic 1962 shakeup, was to project fresh vigor and it did. But unintentionally, the dismissal or shift of thirteen of twenty-two cabinet ministers was handled miserably, and left bad blood on the floor and bitter grousing within the party. Thatcher plowed unapologetically through the controversy, figuring the carnage would be forgotten by 1991. Nonetheless, the ordeal raised more questions about her judgment.

The biggest surprise was the unceremonious dumping of one of her most senior colleagues, Sir Geoffrey Howe. He had been her first chancellor of the exchequer and had served as foreign secretary for six years, but Howe had several strikes against him. At the Madrid summit, he had urged publicly that Thatcher moderate her stance on the EMS overtures. She did, slightly, but bristled and nursed a grudge. It was not the first time Howe had tried to temper her policies, particularly toward Europe, but whenever he did, it gnawed at her. More significantly, Thatcher did not share the respect that Howe's colleagues in the foreign policy community had for his abilities. They praised his negotiating skills, his thoughtfulness, caution, and experience. She, however, was tired of Howe, and considered him plodding, indecisive, and weak. He was not a Thatcher-style dynamo. Some MPs called him "Mogadon man" after a popular tranquilizer. Denis Healey once likened an attack by Howe to "being savaged by a dead sheep." Thatcher had come to rely less on Howe for foreign policy advice than on Charles Powell, her crisply direct private secretary, who enjoyed jolting her occasionally by offering options to the right of the prime minister's own natural position. Powell's status was further humiliation for the veteran foreign secretary. Powell was actually a junior diplomat on loan from the Foreign Office to Downing Street where his powerful brain, staunch loyalty, and nonthreatening role made him a Thatcher favorite. "The son she never had," insiders called the forty-six-year-old Powell.

Howe's fate was finally sealed by his failure to play down his ambition to succeed the prime minister. But Thatcher did not oust him completely. She offered him the post of Home Secretary, unfortunately already occupied by Douglas Hurd, who was furious when he heard about it just after Thatcher had reassured him that he would not be affected by the reshuffle. Howe turned it down, finally agreeing to take Whitelaw's old post as deputy prime minister, once she threw in Lawson's official weekend retreat as a deal sweetener, an act that outraged the chancellor. The deputy title sounds powerful, but is actually an honorific that depends for influence on the holder's relationship with Thatcher. Whitelaw's was good; Thatcher aides quickly made clear that Howe's was not. Adding insult to injury, Thatcher replaced Howe with John Major, a high school dropout with no experience in foreign affairs who had been in government for only two years as a junior minister in the Treasury department. Major was Thatcher's kind of guy—young, bright despite his lack of formal education, and willing to follow instructions without back talk. There was no longer any confusion over who was running British foreign policy: she was.

A few strong notes were heard over the crashing of toppled musical chairs. Christopher Patten, one of the most highly regarded younger politicians, joined the cabinet as environment secretary. The ascension of the forty-five-year-old Patten, a "wet" restored to favor after some years of near banishment, coincided with a new Thatcher interest in environmental issues that had Britons talking about "the greening of Maggie." Kenneth Baker, a smooth operator who had been running the education ministry, took over as Conservative party chairman, a sure sign that she was gearing up for electoral battle. But those solid moves could not take away the overall image that the shuffle had been botched. That feeling was reinforced when Defense Minister George Younger, a ten-year cabinet veteran, asked to be dropped. Ostensibly, the mild-mannered Younger wanted to leave to take a job as a bank director, but an aide explained there was another reason, that "he was tired of Mrs. Thatcher's strident, ideology-ridden rigidity."

The whole affair left a bitter taste and the inescapable feeling that if there had ever been much collegiality in a Thatcher government, it had long since disappeared. Maggie had angered almost everyone, rubbing raw the considerable egos of most of her senior ministers. It wouldn't take much spark to set off another explosion, but the speed with which the next blast hit Thatcher was a surprise. Only three months later, in late October 1989, Lawson abruptly resigned. The chancellor, the most senior cabinet member she had left and possibly the most intelligent, the one minister whose determination matched Thatcher's, quit following an argument over the role of one of her private advisers, Sir Alan Walters. An enthusiastic and straight-talking monetarist who had taught at Johns Hopkins University in Baltimore, Walters took on guru status during a two-year stint in Downing Street during the first term when the less confrontational Howe was chancellor. He then left government, spending much of his time in Washington, D.C., as a senior fellow at the American Enterprise Institute and as a World Bank consultant, until May 1989 when he resumed his old post. After his return, Walters and Lawson had been at odds, particularly over Lawson's persistent urging that Britain join the European Monetary System. When the press published excerpts of a Walters essay, calling the EMS a "half-baked" concept and boasting of his own "considerable influence on economic policy," Lawson exploded. Instead of tolerating Walters as Howe had endured Powell, the pricklier chancellor in effect told Thatcher "him or me." She didn't take him seriously. In the House of Commons, Neil Kinnock called on her to fire the "part-time chancellor" Walters, whom some of her own Tories called Thatcher's Rasputin. Thatcher, who would never back down to the Labor leader, responded archly that "advisers advise and ministers decide," but that wasn't enough for Lawson. Infuriated that she would not back him, he quit, handing her a "Dear Margaret" resignation letter that said, "The successful conduct of economic policy is possible only if there is—and is seen to be—full agreement between the prime minister and the chancellor of the exchequer. Recent events have confirmed that this essential requirement cannot be satisfied so long as Alan Walters remains your personal economic adviser."

She could hardly believe that Lawson had walked away. Except for Michael Heseltine, who quit over the Westland affair, ministers were fired; they didn't quit. She was embarrassed and angry, a feeling she didn't bother to disguise when she wrote him back to note that it was "a matter of particular regret that you should decide to leave before your task was complete."

Thatcher was also left with a profound political crisis. "There is now a smell of decay in the air," wrote political columnist Peter Jenkins.[17] The *Financial Times* concurred. "It is more than likely," said the newspaper, "that the behavior which drove Lawson from office may be seen in hindsight as the beginning of the end for her, too."

The new cabinet that had been introduced only two weeks before at the Conservatives' annual conference as "The Right Team for Britain's Future" was quickly reshuffled again. Convinced by senior Tories that no one could operate as chancellor unless Walters went, Thatcher belatedly fired him. John Major, who had been foreign secretary only three months, was pulled back to the Treasury to succeed Lawson. To replace Major, Thatcher called on Home Secretary Douglas Hurd, a former diplomat, who didn't mind moving this time to the most prestigious cabinet job.

These changes were not bad ones, and might even have been applauded if all had taken place neatly in July and Lawson had left under normal circumstances. There was nothing neat about Thatcher's situation, but she did have a more united and more intimidated team. No heavyweights remained; the survivors were bound to be more subservient to her own policy prescriptions. That was hardly new. Criticism that she was more isolated than ever was accurate, but meaningless. She had governed as a one-woman team for a decade with little self-doubt. Let others worry that there was no one beside her with enough stature to apply the brakes. They talked of "saving her from herself." Thatcher thought that was poppycock. This prime minister needed no saving. Asked in the wake of the Lawson imbroglio if she intended to change her style, she responded, "Certainly not. How can I change Margaret Thatcher?"

She cannot, but she did need help. She was unlikely, however, to get it within her government. Outside help saved her in both first and second terms, but there was no obvious savior on the third-term horizon. All the midterm indicators looked bad. Economists predicted with increasing frequency that recession would hit Britain in mid- to late 1990. If it did, her chances of pulling up the economy before election day would suffer, perhaps fatally. In the past, her political opposition could always be counted on to self-destruct when the going got tough. But in the early 1990, the opposition looked in the best shape it had been in years.

Neil Kinnock had made so much progress reshaping the Labor party that for the first time since Thatcher moved to Downing Street in 1979, Labor appeared a real threat. Kinnock had spent the first two years of Thatcher's third term conducting an extensive policy review. He discovered the obvious, that most Britons were not interested in supporting an old-style socialist Labor party, and this time decided to do something about it. When the party gathered in October 1989 for its annual conference under the new slogan, "Meet the Challenge, Make the Change," Kinnock made the change. He dumped the ideological baggage.

Out went commitment to unilateral disarmament; in came a call for multilaterally negotiated arms control agreements. Out went commitments to confiscatory tax policy, massive spending on social policy, and unquestioning support to labor unions; in came support for a market economy; out went pledges to renationalize enterprises privatized by Thatcher; in came a plan to return only major utilities to government control; out went doubts about European Community integration; in came a hearty endorsement for the EC's proposals for closer unity post-1992. Out went the "militant tendency" and the "loony left"; out from the National Executive Committee went Ken Livingstone, the Labor MP who symbolized the hard left.

In came an election platform cosmetically designed to take advantage of every Thatcher weakness while adopting the government's strengths. The Labor party had decided that it wanted to win for a change. Tony Benn lamented that Labor was becoming a Tory clone, that its policies were being "written by Dr. Gallup."[18] But James Callaghan, the prime minister Thatcher ousted, took a more pragmatic view: "The change was long in coming and it is welcome." National polls reflected the surge in Labor's fortunes and in early 1990 showed the party anywhere from six to twelve points ahead of Maggie's Tories.

Labor had previously squandered big midterm leads. There was certainly the possibility that, for all their improvement, they might do it again. But Kinnock had some new advantages. His biggest strength was that the opposition to the Tories was no longer divided. For the first time since 1979, the next match-up would mark a return to traditional two-party politics with the remnants of the Liberals and the Social Democrats on the sidelines. Those who opposed the Tories—a majority in the past two elections—would effectively have no choice but to vote Labor.

The changing world situation also worked to Labor's advantage. The dismantling of Eastern Europe and the Soviet empire made it more difficult to accept Thatcher's continued emphasis on a powerful defense while holding down spending on social issues. Thatcher didn't mind being out of step on Western Europe—she'd always been that—but now the stakes were changing. Missing the Europe boat the first time around in the 1950s had hurt Britain badly; the country could not afford to be left behind again in the planned 1992 integration. Nor were Bush and Gorbachev likely to be as interested in a Britain, however authoritative its leader, if it seemed to be excluding itself from the new Europe.

In Asia, China's June 1989 Tiananmen Square massacre of students and prodemocracy demonstrators created another unexpected problem for the prime minister. Thatcher reiterated after the bloodletting that Britain would still abide by its 1984 agreement with Beijing to hand Hong Kong back in 1997. Mindful of ethnic tensions at home, however, she would not allow residency rights in Britain to the 3.3 million Chinese holders of British passports in the crown colony. That prompted an uproar in Hong Kong which complained that her government was shirking its responsibilities, however faded, of empire. Under pressure, Thatcher agreed at the end of 1989 to accept 225,000 professionals, civil servants, and businesspeople, but there was no early end in sight to the debate. She had far less difficulty securing parliamentary support for a policy of forced repatriation of Vietnamese boat people who had sought refuge in Hong Kong. Thatcher's decision to send home those whom the British government did not consider genuine political refugees stirred dismay around the world. She shrugged it off, saying that the colony could not handle the influx and that other countries, including some that berated her policy, had refused to accept the refugees. The twin issues won endless headlines, but the fact remained that her anti-immigrant stance, however controversial, has never been a vote loser for Thatcher. On race as well as most foreign issues, she has always read her domestic constituents accurately, never going far wrong by playing to the Little England traits that remained deeply embedded in the nation's character.

That kind of innate strength combined with the incredible competitiveness that motivates Thatcher in a tough fight means that for all her considerable third-term troubles, few are willing to bet against her ambitious bid for a fourth consecutive term. That is because everything would have to sour for the Conservatives to lose. The mixed feelings many British voters have for their Maggie—high respect but not much love—mean she will never be able to count on victory. Such were her problems in late 1989 that there was even a brief, and ill-fated challenge to her leadership within the Tory party, the first since she had taken the party over nearly fifteen years before. Thatcher wasn't worried about losing to the little-known back-bencher Sir Anthony Meyer, but she did fear that a surge of abstentions could undermine her leadership. The threat failed to materialize and suggested that when the going got really tough, the party would continue to rally behind its only three-time winner.

Whether the country would was another question, but the Tories had an almost unassailable advantage. Their hundred-seat majority was so huge that a cataclysmic shift of the magnitude that ousted Churchill in 1945 would be needed for Labor to win in 1991 or 1992. "If we were twenty-five seats down there's no question we'd win the next election," said deputy Labor leader Roy Hattersley in 1989, "but where we're starting it's a question if we'll win or just come close."[19] Several difficulties remained for Labor. One was that the choice of the election day was up to Thatcher, and she could be counted on to put on a stunning offensive as it approached. Another was that while Kinnock had grown in his leader's job, no one would put his intellect, drive, or stature in a league even approaching Thatcher's. The fact that the majority of the seats the Tories held were virtually impregnable was another problem Labor faced. With the exception of London itself, the Conservatives held all but a handful of the seats in the prosperous south of England in 1989. The chances for significant Labor success in switching those loyalties was poor, but by no means impossible, particularly if the midterm rust on the Iron Lady turned into outright metal fatigue.

CHAPTER TWENTY-ONE

Maggie's Britain

IN THE MEMBERS' LOBBY of the House of Commons stand statues of Winston Churchill, Lloyd George, and Clement Attlee, modern Britain's political giants. Two more plinths stand empty and few doubt that one day one will bear the marble image of the Iron Lady. Like her honored predecessors, she has been a giant who has changed Britain, making it work at home and count abroad. She has broken the forty-five-year postwar consensus on the welfare state, rewritten the political rules, enlarged Britain's world role and set the nation on a new course with a new agenda. After more than a decade of doing it her way, she has made her nation into Thatcher's Britain.

Never doubting herself or her beliefs, Thatcher conducted a revolution by force of will. She arrived like the cavalry in the nick of time to pull her nation back from the brink of economic disaster and political irrelevancy. Try to imagine what Britain would be like today if she had not been around a decade ago.

Internationally, Britain mattered during the 1980s in a way that it had not since before Suez. Thatcher's moves to help end civil war in Zimbabwe had won Britain new credibility in Africa. In the Middle East, Arab leaders frustrated by the Reagan administration's lack of interest in the peace process turned to Thatcher for support. The Falklands campaign warned the world not to count out Britain militarily; it could mount a successful operation when it had to.

The United States had no stauncher friend during the 1980s. When Thatcher publicly endorsed George Bush's invasion of Panama within minutes of its start in December 1989, the president got a reminder of what the United States could expect as long as Maggie was in Downing Street. Thatcher's anti-Soviet credentials gave her a credibility comparable to Richard Nixon's after the restoration of U.S. relations with China. In 1984, she "discovered" Mikhail Gorbachev, declaring him a man the West could deal with. He has never forgotten her early stamp of approval. Britain's enhanced role in East-West relations during the decade resulted directly from Thatcher's unyielding toughness and her unique relationship with Reagan and Gorbachev.

For all her success at home and abroad, she has, of course, not solved every problem. She has even created new ones. The 1990s present tough new challenges for this prime minister. The end of the Cold War will require cold warrior Thatcher to adjust or risk being left behind as the collapsed Soviet bloc moves away from communism. Swallowing her deep-rooted reluctance to integration with Europe won't be easy either.

At home, there's plenty more to fix and she won't get it all done even if she does manage to go on and on. She wouldn't mind serving to the millennium. Such an extended run would make her Britain's longest-serving prime minister, surpassing even the eighteenth-century icons Robert Walpole and William Pitt the Younger. She'd be seventy-four then, three years younger than Ronald Reagan when he left office. But even if she doesn't win a fourth term, even if she were knocked down and out tomorrow by the famous double-decker bus, the only scenario whereby many Britons see her leaving office early, she would bequeath a considerable legacy. Her most significant accomplishment has been shattering the complacency that paralyzed Britain. She offered choices when few seemed left.

Thatcher has broken down the limitations Britons placed on themselves. During the Depression, Alf taught her to work hard on her own, never counting on help from government or anyone. She built on the lesson, demonstrating through her own fierce determination what individuals can do. Growing up in the years before World War II, watching the spread of Nazism, the pain of postwar reconstruction, and the advance of communism, she learned that the world is not an easy place. Strength is essential; a country and its people must be tough to survive, let alone prosper. After the war, Britain, tired and broke, turned soft. Yesterday's John Bull became I'm all right, Jack. Thatcher saw the deadbeats, those who thought self-improvement, growth, and profit were vulgar. She also abhorred class-conscious elitists who froze out many of the hard-driving free marketeers. Understanding the relationship between words and action, she did something about both.

Once in power, Thatcher vowed to turn the tide. For those who wanted to follow her lead, she offered opportunity and optimism.

Had it not been for the Falklands—"Two bald men fighting over a comb," said author Jorge Luis Borges—and a weak and divided opposition, Thatcher would never have had the chance to set her initiatives in place. She almost certainly would have been out of office by 1984. Instead, her uninterrupted tenure has allowed her to extend and institutionalize radical reforms.

Much that she has tried has been attempted before. She was not the first to push privatization, to adopt monetarism, to put the trade unions in a vise, or to try to destroy socialism. But the others backed down when the going got tough; Thatcher hung in, true to the moral of a rhyme she recited as a child, "It's easy to be a starter, but are you a sticker, too?" Her predecessors managed decline, relatively satisfied with the status quo. Thatcher's crusade has been directed at the status quo. She has shown that the consensus-driven politics of the postwar era were the cause, not the effect, of Britain's problems.[1]

Lord D'Abernon said, "An Englishman's mind works best when it is almost too late."[2] Thatcher recognized that it *was* almost too late. She understood that tinkering was insufficient, that a war-time effort was imperative if Britain were to avoid a slide straight into the Third World. The country was a failure, an embarrassment, given what it had been and could be again. She did not approach the mess in a genteel manner or collegially. She didn't have to. Not being one of the boys worked to her advantage. She figured out quickly that most Englishmen don't know how to deal with assertive women and took every advantage of the discovery. That helped her win the leadership of the Tories and keep challengers, within and without, off balance. Neil Kinnock has conceded that, "Mrs. Thatcher is more difficult for me to oppose because she's a woman, and I've got, however much I try to shrug it off, an innate courtesy towards women that I simply don't have towards men."[3]

Her tactics have seemed rough, in part because her opposition has been so weak. Thatcher knows the value of toughness. She has read Machiavelli, including that passage where the Prince asks, "Is

it better to be loved than feared, or the reverse? . . . One would
like to be both the one and the other, but because it is difficult to
combine them, it is far better to be feared than loved if you cannot
be both."[4] From childhood, she has rarely been liked, let alone
loved, but she has been respected. If some agree with her only out
of fear, she has no regrets.

Thatcher has skipped quick fixes and taken the long view even
when her prospects looked distinctly short-term. "I came in not to
have short-term expedients," she said. "I came in to put long-term
things right, to get the country on the right road for a prosperous
future."[5] She has put it on the right road. Britain has changed in
the most important respects. But will it stay there? Will Thatcherism outlast Thatcher?

Some aspects will. Her revolution does have the roots that
allow a future. Private ownership, now widespread in Britain, gives
citizens a stake in the nation's success. One million new owners of
council houses have a new stake in a privatized society that few
would willingly surrender—even with soaring interest rates. Reduced taxes have helped Britons at the top and bottom of the economic scale. Fine-tuning is still needed, but there is no desire for
the return of the crippling tax rates that nearly nullified investment
and growth. Thatcher has destroyed ideological socialism as an
acceptable philosophy on which modern, thriving British governments can be constructed. The renationalization of most industries,
with the exception of utilities, is unthinkable. Even the Labor party
has adopted the key elements of Thatcherism. The country is less
tough, less "dry," less Conservative than Thatcher and there does
exist a strong urge for a more caring, communal Britain, but not
one sculpted by the Labor party of the 1980s.

Those realities augur permanent change. But Thatcher herself
is a big factor in determining the extent to which Thatcherism will
outlast its creator. Does she reflect the British character or is she
such an aberration that once she is no longer nannying, prodding,
kicking, and exhorting, the country will slip back into its old ways?
"It would be tragic if Mrs. Thatcher proved to be an isolated phenomenon and that a yearning for the quiet life and soft consensus
might let post-Thatcher Britain drift," said former party chairman
Norman Tebbit.[6]

Put another way, is Maggie a real Brit, as Ronald Reagan called
her, leading the charge at the head of a reluctant but otherwise
willing British force? Or is she swimming hard upstream, beating

the current by the sheer force of her own convictions, trailed by only a small school of true believers who, once she is gone, will be swept back downriver by the real national current?

Thatcher is anything but a traditional postwar Briton. Her English provincial values and crusading free enterprise are more reminiscent of the ambitions of the political power-brokers and industrial barons of nineteenth-century Britain when the nation clawed its way to global supremacy. In that sense, Thatcher is a true Brit. The trouble lies in confusing that juggernaut Britain with the contemporary version. Thatcher would like to believe that today's Britons are like her; that they can be induced to work hard, to compete, and to strive for success. That's possible, but not likely.

Thatcher cuts across the British grain. One reason she is so respected in the United States is that she embodies American traits more than British ones. American values have profoundly influenced her character. She can act like an autocrat, but she is a democratizer. Industry, individualism, free enterprise, risk taking, directness, provincialism, anti-elitism, anti-intellectualism—all are qualities she shares more with Americans than with her fellow Britons. (Those who think she would make a good American president, however, are mistaken. She can ride roughshod within the Conservative party, but being head of state, which she is not, requires an appreciation for consensus that is anathema for Thatcher. She would constantly battle Congress and state and local governments.)

A political entrepreneur, she has taken risks to move Britain forward. Britain, however, still gets its greatest pleasure from looking back. Thatcher has stripped off the overlays of cracked paint and chintz covering Britain's past to get down to the nation's steel framework. Not only has the process been painful, but Britons are uncomfortable with the very idea of basics. They like costumes and coverup. It is no coincidence that Britain produces those talented actors and actresses. Britons are superb at creating artificial personae. Many, especially the powerful, are elliptical and complex. Thatcher is straightforward and simple. Britons constantly equivocate; Thatcher never does.

Thatcher is all about disruption and bashing institutions. "She can't bear to see an institution without hitting it with her handbag," one Tory has said. Nothing draws her ire more than consensus, a cherished notion in Britain where behavior patterns are circumscribed. Britons queue neatly and keep their voices lowered in public, part of a code of behavior designed to round off rough edges, making for greater compatibility on islands with a collective land-mass smaller than Oregon but home to nearly sixty million people.

"There is nothing so illiberal and so ill-bred as audible laughter," wrote Lord Chesterfield.[7] Delightful wit and perceptive insight, some sharply contrarian, can make conversation in Britain sparkle. More often, the basic element is caution. Most Britons don't talk about themselves, their children or family, their work, religion, or politics. That would be very public, very American. They pick safe subjects; the weather is always available. None of that is Thatcher's way. She hates small, safe talk. Nor does she hesitate to break into a hearty laugh when the mood strikes.

To supporters, Thatcher is a Hercules, a one-of-a-kind political colossus who has pushed back debilitating socialism and replaced it with high-energy free enterprise and opportunity. She has crushed the power of trade unions, eliminated the constrictions of stultifying government control, invigorated the economy, and restored Britain's standing in the world.

To critics, she is an autocrat, harsh and uncaring, who has fostered a national ethic of greed, divided the nation, destroyed its industrial capacity, and refused to recognize a future with Europe, instead, selling out to the United States.

She has already succeeded in bulldozing Attlee's welfare state. The "British disease" of trade union power run amok, uncontrollable wildcat strikes, and hidebound and cowardly management unable to make competitive decisions has been cured, in her most significant specific accomplishment. Some union reforms, such as requiring secret prestrike votes, have proven popular with workers. As a result, strikes reached their lowest level in half a century. In 1979, British industry lost thirty million workdays to strikes; in 1989, less than two million. As union influence shrank, productivity soared. In manufacturing, productivity rose 3.5 percent, the fastest rise in the world, ahead even of Japan. Output per worker has climbed more than 5 percent a year since 1980—higher than that in Japan, Germany, or the United States.

For the employed, life in Thatcher's Britain has been good. Real earnings remain low by comparison with the continent but have increased steadily since 1979. The rich have gotten richer. British tax rolls include 20,000 sterling millionaires, a fourfold increase in the past five years. Homeownership is at an all-time high.

By 1989, 68 percent of Britons owned their own home, up from 53 percent in 1979. Foreign assets of $160 billion make Britain second only to Japan as a creditor nation.

In tax policy, Thatcherism is Reaganism without the deficits. For years, some of Britain's biggest corporate and individual earners had fled the country. In her first budget, Thatcher cut top-bracket taxes of 83 percent on earned income and 98 percent on unearned to a uniform 60 percent. This began to correct the tax exile problem. By the end of her first decade, the exiles were flocking back. At the end of 1989, the top rate was 40 percent, close to the Reagan administration's 33 percent (after the addition of state and local taxes). Corporate tax reform dropped the rate for businesses from 52 percent to 35 percent and increased corporate tax revenues from $7 billion in 1979 to nearly $30 billion in 1989. The corporate ethic has changed as well. As recently as the mid-1980s, British executives came to work late, took three-hour lunches complete with cocktails, wine, and brandies, and went home early. At the beginning of the 1990s, such behavior was rare. The power breakfast had arrived in Britain, with the sixty-minute nonalcoholic lunch, and jogging.

Entrepreneurism also arrived. "If there is one thing history will give Mrs. Thatcher credit for," said John Faulds, managing director of 3i, Britain's biggest venture capital firm, "it is that she has stimulated an enterprise culture."[8] Between 1979–1990, Britain created more than a million new jobs, more than all the European Economic Community combined. During 1987 and 1988, 500 new businesses opened their doors every week. Flex-time has caught on; so have management buyouts. Corporate culture is vibrant. British Steel, which lost $4 billion in 1979, earned $265 million in 1988. ICI, Imperial Chemical Industries, made a profit of $2 billion each year in 1987, 1988, and 1989.

Executive salaries, for decades the lowest among industrialized nations, have climbed during the Thatcher years. A Labor party survey in 1989 showed that the number of company directors earning $782,000 or more had increased 40 percent over the previous year. That was misleading. In the international salary sweepstakes, Britain still ranks low, with compensation far more modest than some of the huge U.S. salary and bonus packages. Thatcher herself is no exception. She receives $82,300 a year, the same as all her Cabinet colleagues. For years, she has declined to accept the additional $19,000 allowed her as Prime Minister.

"There's a new generation over here," said John Banham,

director general of the Confederation of British Industry. In 1986 and 1987, Britain spent more than $40 billion buying foreign businesses. Foreign investors have returned the favor; foreign investment in Britain is up more than 100 percent since 1979. In Scotland, the influx of computer makers to an area outside Edinburgh called Silicon Glen has pushed computers ahead of Scotch whiskey as Scotland's biggest export.

In the south, where service industries prospered, billions of dollars flowed into Docklands, the decrepit old warehouse and wharf district lining the Thames. The East End of London, with a new inner-city airport, was transformed. The City, London's equivalent of Wall Street, boomed. Overboomed, actually, then shook itself out and settled down. A popular play, *Serious Money*, by leftist playwright Caryl Churchill, satirized the successes and foibles of the heavy trading action and played to packed houses.

Traditional British vacation destinations like Blackpool and Brighton lost favor as more affluent Britons flew abroad to Italy, Greece, and the United States. Half of Britain seemed to visit Orlando and Disney World during the 1980s. Neil Kinnock recognized the improvements. He conceded in 1987 that one reason the Labor party had to rethink its long-term strategy was because so many of its members owned second homes and vacationed in Spain.

Much of the prosperity flowered in the south, though not all. The northwest of England, parts of Scotland, and Northern Ireland improved dramatically. "There is a look of returned and growing prosperity about much of the northwest these days," the *Financial Times* said early in Thatcher's third term.[9] Prosperity increased in Manchester; downtown Glasgow was rejuvenated. Billions of pounds were poured into Belfast and Londonderry for new public housing, roads, and new employment prospects.

Thatcher's Britain also has a dark side. The number of homeless Britons climbed 38 percent between 1984 and 1989, while overall funding for public housing, according to Labor party statistics, dropped 60 percent. Nearly two million Britons, many in the decaying industrial north, went on the dole over the decade, while most of the new jobs were created in the south. Unemployment peaked at 3.2 million in 1986, but by 1990 had fallen to 1.6 million, still more than the 1.3 million unemployed whom Thatcher inherited. The unemployment problems in the Midlands and North have cost the Conservatives politically. In Scotland, one of Britain's most impoverished areas, the Tories hold only ten of seventy-two par-

liamentary seats. In Wales, another troubled area economically, the
Conservatives emerged after the 1987 election holding only eight
of thirty-eight seats.

More Britons than ever considered themselves part of the middle class, up from 33 percent to 40 percent. Robert Worcester,
director of the MORI poll, called that "the biggest change in social
class structure in a decade in the history of the country." Yet the
number of people living below the poverty line increased to an
estimated nine million, causing former Liberal party leader David
Steel to conclude that "this country is becoming increasingly divided."[10] Harold Macmillan, who became Lord Stockton, reiterated
the criticism. "It breaks my heart to see what is happening to our
country today," he said midway through the 1984–1985 miners'
strike. "The growing division between the south and the
north . . . cannot be allowed to continue."

Benjamin Disraeli, Queen Victoria's favorite prime minister,
noted the divide a century and a half ago: "two nations between
whom there is no intercourse and no sympathy; who are as ignorant
of each other's habits, thoughts, and feelings, as if they
were . . . inhabitants of different planets; who are formed by different breeding, are fed by a different food, are ordered by different
manners and are not governed by the same laws."[11] The shared
sufferings and marginal triumphs of two world wars engendered a
greater national consensus, but the divide did not disappear. Those
who blame Thatcher for rending a seamless national fabric are
mistaken, but she did not mend the tear.

Some worry about Thatcher's tendency to encroach on certain
basic freedoms, particularly dissenting speech, to avoid government
embarrassment. That concern became more pronounced in 1989
when the government pushed through a new Official Secrets Act,
updating a 1911 law on the disclosure of information that was already far more stringent than any restrictions in the United States.
Thatcher is intolerant of questions about what should fall under
the rubric of national security. Her intolerance is best represented
by her fulminations against the BBC for its interviews with Argentinian widows during the Falklands War, its attitude toward allowing the U.S. to bomb Libya from British bases, and its interviews
with suspected IRA members. Reacting to these political missteps,
the Prime Minister shook up the BBC management. Then, two
years after the Falklands War, when a senior Defense Ministry
official leaked details that raised questions about the official version

of the sinking of the *Belgrano,* he was prosecuted—unsuccessfully—under the Official Secrets Act.

The most vivid example of Thatcher's determination to ban potentially embarrassing information was the infamous *Spycatcher* case. For more than two years, from 1985 to 1987, the government sought to bar publication of *Spycatcher,* the memoirs of retired counterintelligence agent Peter Wright. Thatcher pressed the case despite the fact that virtually all of Wright's relevations—including the claim that Sir Roger Hollis, the former head of British counterintelligence, had been a Soviet mole—had been previously published with government approval. Thanks to her campaign, the book quickly became an international best seller. But in Britain it remained banned until the Law Lords, Britain's highest court, finally overturned the embargo, ruling that the government could not lock the barn after the horse had left. Thatcher was outraged by the whole affair, contending that her opposition had nothing to do with freedom of speech, but everything to do with keeping the secret service secret. Smarting from the outcome and determined to prevent a repeat, she pushed new legislation that gives the government more specific powers over some kinds of information. The full impact of this legislation is still to be felt.

Thatcher's muscle-flexing has created considerable uneasiness in Britain. Some Thatcher critics fear that such social engineering combined with a new dynamism has created a meaner and greedier society. Many Britons worry that the nation's sense of community (which traditionally helped preserve social cohesion) has eroded. There is cause for concern.

The number of societal dropouts increased. In the old industrial centers and in grim, dank council housing projects in and around cities, a growing underclass of the underprivileged was spawned. Not just the disabled, weak, elderly, or poor, these outsiders have no place in Thatcher's Britain.

Drug use increased, as it did worldwide, and along with it crime and violence. The country once prided itself on what was, for the most part, an unarmed police force. That is no longer the case. Violent crime has increased as have incidents of public violence. The urban riots of 1981 and 1985 had already shaken what for generations had been an essential serenity in Britain. One of the most dramatic indicators that something was sociologically awry was a horrifying increase in soccer violence. Soccer and violence is a commonly volatile mix worldwide, but the problem has been far worse in recent years in Britain. In 1985 in Brussels' Heysel Stadium, Liverpool fans wielding metal posts mobbed seats occupied by supporters of a Turin club, causing 39 deaths and injuring 425 people. Almost five years later, regular English teams—not Scottish, Welsh, or Northern Irish—were still banned from play on the continent. In 1988, British fans clashed with German and Dutch supporters in Düsseldorf after a European championship. The following year, ninety-five people were crushed to death when fans pressed into an overcrowded stadium in Sheffield. Analysis of the causes of soccer violence has been a growth industry in Britain. Those looking for easy explanations have blamed unemployment or the edge that Thatcher has put into British society. But the majority of those arrested in the wake of soccer violence have held jobs. If the causes are unclear, so are the solutions.

Soccer violence is just one symptom of the problems that remain in Britain, problems exacerbated by the islands' idiosyncratic social forces, by the fluctuations of the world economy, by the complicated burden of history that does and always will shape Britain's expectations of itself.

Thatcher says she will know when it's time to leave office. Many wonder if that's so; many doubt that she will ever step down voluntarily. Only weeks after her November 1989 announcement that she would probably retire after winning a fourth term, she revised her opinion. On second thought, she was prepared to lead the Conservatives into two more general elections. "I have had so many protests," she explained, ". . . by popular acclaim I am prepared to carry on."[12] It was impossible to determine how serious she was. Some Tories said that Thatcher was simply trying to avoid making herself a lame duck prematurely.

What is clear is that she lives for nothing other than to continue remaking and improving Britain according to her formula. Any other vocation pales. When she does leave Number 10, if it's not to "twang a harp" as she puts it, she will be offered the traditional peerage. It's hard to imagine her in the House of Lords on the sleepy red benches, rather than the House of Commons where she has been a fixture since 1959, her voice raised, edged with scorn, to smite down challengers. It's hard to imagine Margaret Thatcher as anything other than the mistress of Downing Street. As Norman Tebbit once asked, "What would she do if she weren't Prime Minister? One doesn't see her retiring to gardening or making marmalade." One does not.

CHAPTER TWENTY-TWO

In Her Own Words

FAMILY

"What's right for the family is right for Britain." *Sunday Express,* June 29, 1975.

"The nation is but an enlarged family." Speech to St. Lawrence Jewry, February 2, 1981.

"What is the real driving force of society? It is the desire for the individual to do the best for himself and his family. How is society improved? By millions of people resolving that they will give their children a better life than they have had themselves." Cardiff speech, April 16, 1979.

"This party is very much in favor of the family, but that does not mean arguing for every single benefit to be increased." Speech to House of Commons, January 17, 1980.

"Our grandparents and parents were brought up without trendy theories and didn't make a bad job of it." *Daily Mirror,* May 25, 1978.

"You have to tell your children what's right and wrong and you must obviously have some rules, but you don't want rules for the sake of rules and you must explain them. They ask endless questions and you need endless patience, but you have got to explain. You have got to try and give them answers. One of the big problems today is that some parents don't talk to their young children enough. Now I was lucky. I had someone in to help with the twins and I was told how important it was to talk to them. When you pick them up and bathe them, there should be a continuous round of chatting. Of course, mothers are always busy and there are a lot of pressures, but you have to try to find time to explain things." Patricia Murray, *Margaret Thatcher: A Profile*, 1980.

HOME LIFE

"There was not a lot of fun and sparkle in my life. I tried to give my children more." Speech at Grantham High School for Girls, June 6, 1980.

"I was brought up very, very seriously. I was a very serious child and we were not allowed to go out to much entertainment. Going out to a film was a very great treat." Talk at Grantham High School for Girls, June 6, 1980.

"Life wasn't to enjoy yourself, but to work and do things. Home was very small. I remember having a dream that the one thing I really wanted was to live in a nice house with more things than we had. We had not got hot water and there was an outside toilet. So when people tell me about these things, I know about them." Yorkshire TV, *Women to Women*, November 19, 1985.

"I think I was probably closer to my father, but my mother was a good woman who was always intensely practical and I learned a lot of practical stuff from her. She taught me how to cook and bake bread, how to make my own clothes and how to decorate. We always used to decorate our own home because we could never afford to have decorators in. I've always liked doing things with my hands." Patricia Murray, *Margaret Thatcher: A Profile*, 1980.

"I went to church four times on a Sunday and I owe a great deal to the church for everything in which I believe. I am very glad that I was brought up strictly." Talk at Grantham High School for Girls, June 6, 1980.

"There are times when I've been desperately unhappy and disappointed . . . knocked about a bit, as they say." *Observer*, March 16, 1969.

"There are times when I get home at night and everything has got on top of me when I shed a few tears, silently, alone. I often unwind by ironing or turning out the airing cupboard, which personally I find very relaxing." *Women's World*, September 21, 1978.

"I do not have to worry about money. It is expensive to be in politics. One has to be well-groomed and one has to entertain." *Guardian*, March 23, 1962.

"I'm romantic enough to remember the details of my marriage. Of course I had my practical side and converted my wedding dress into a dinner dress and wore it for a long time afterwards." *Daily Mail*, September 10, 1979.

"It dawned on me that this [marriage] was the biggest thing in one's life now kind of sorted out and, therefore, one turned one's mind to other things." *Times*, November 11, 1985.

"I was just lucky with Denis. Absolutely marvelous. He's always encouraged me to use one's talents. Then we had a marvelous family. Everything just came right." BBC Radio, February 1981.

"He has his rugger cronies and I have a circle of political friends. We have a life together and a life apart and I think that's very important." *Daily Mail*, May 3, 1980.

"Denis has his own life and work and that's been very important to both of us. He's not my second fiddle. He's first fiddle in his own orchestra. In fact, he's his own conductor." *Daily Express*, February 20, 1986.

"Our home is both our base and our refuge. In the evenings we just flop and talk." *News of the World*, May 4, 1980.

"I still tidy round myself at weekends, but I'm afraid I don't do much dusting. And my cooking—I used to be good—is the simple stuff now. Shepherd's pie or fling in an omelette or casserole—nothing difficult." *Daily Express*, August 13, 1980.

"Popping up to the little flat at the top of Number 10 and doing a poached egg on toast is what I like to do on weekends." Talk at Grantham High School for Girls, June 6, 1980.

ROLE OF WOMEN

"Remember that poem of Kipling's—'the female of the species is more deadly than the male'? No man is as tough as a woman in defense of his children. I think women are more interested in the long-term future than men because they are thinking about the world in which their children will live." *Daily Mail*, November 18, 1976.

"It is possible, in my view, for a woman to run a home and continue with her career provided two conditions are fulfilled. First, her husband must be in sympathy with her wish to do another job. Secondly, where there is a young family, the joint incomes of husband and wife must be sufficient to employ a first-class nanny-housekeeper to look after things in the wife's absence. The second is the key to the whole plan." *Evening News*, February 25, 1960.

"I still do the cooking myself . . . rush in, peel the vegetables, put the roast in, all before I take off my hat. There are all sorts of emergencies that women at home all day build up into mountains. But a job, outside interests, keep the emergencies fairly well in proportion." *Daily Telegraph*, March 18, 1966.

"If we couldn't afford to have resident help in the home, I would give up my career tomorrow." *Daily Telegraph*, March 12, 1968.

"I was dead lucky. Our home was in London and I always knew that I could get back if anything went wrong. That eased my mind tremendously. Had I not had a London constituency, I do not think I could have done it." *Today*, June 27, 1986.

"One does wish there were [more] women in Parliament because then one would be less conspicuous oneself. I'd like to get on with the job without being in the limelight all the time." *Sunday Express*, January 16, 1972.

"Many women have the opportunities but do not use them . . . or are too easily contented with the job that they're doing and do not necessarily make the effort to climb the tree . . . sometimes it's thought to be unfeminine. It isn't at all, you know." BBC World Service, March 2, 1984.

"I hope we shall see more and more women combining marriage and a career. Prejudice against this dual role is not confined to men. Far too often, I regret, it comes from our own sex. . . . It is possible to carry on working, taking a short leave of absence when families arrive and returning later. The idea that the family suffers is, I believe, quite mistaken. To carry on with a career stimulates the mind, provides a refreshing contact with the world outside— and so means that a wife can be a much better companion at home." *Cosmopolitan*, May 1983.

"I don't notice that I'm a woman. I regard myself as the Prime Minister." *Daily Mirror*, March 1, 1980.

On male heads of state: "They don't patronize me for being a woman. *Nobody* puts me down." *Daily Express*, August 13, 1980.

"I am absolutely satisfied that there is nothing more you can do by changing the law to do away with discrimination. After all, I don't think there's been a great deal of discrimination against women for years." Thames television, January 6, 1981.

"The battle for women's rights has been largely won. The days when they were demanded and discussed in strident tones should be gone forever. And I hope they are. I hated those strident tones you hear from some 'women's libbers.' " Speech to Institution of Electrical Engineers, July 26, 1982.

"The feminists have become far too strident and have done damage to the cause of women by making us out to be something we're not. You get on because you have the right talents." *Times*, May 10, 1978.

IMAGE

"I stand here in my red chiffon gown, my face softly made up, my hair gently waved—the Iron Lady of the western world?" *Sunday Telegraph*, February 1, 1976.

"If you saw me writing a speech at four o'clock in the morning, with my makeup gone and running my hands through my hair, you'd get a different picture." *Daily Express*, August 13, 1980.

"Denis loves bright colors, like this fuschia dress. But it's really not practical—people remember if they've seen you in pink and think you've only got one outfit." *Times*, November 17, 1986.

"Denis does like a bit of glitter." *Times*, November 17, 1986.

"I like to be made a fuss of by a lot of chaps." *Daily Mirror*, February 14, 1975.

"I am worried about my image. I'm going to change it. I'm very aware that my image is important. I'm not at all pleased with the way I look on TV. I'm going to do something about it and the first thing is my hair. I'm going in for the unkempt look." *Daily Mail*, May 4, 1976.

"I adore red, but of course I can only wear it at home or on holiday. People really do comment, you know." *Daily Telegraph*, October 5, 1964.

"I feel terribly guilty I am not wearing blue, but I am going to the television studios and the background is bright turquoise, so I have to wear brown. We girls must think about these things." *Times*, April 2, 1979.

ON GOVERNMENT

"My policies are based not on some economic theory, but on things I and millions like me were brought up with: an honest day's work for an honest day's pay; live within your means; put by a nest egg for a rainy day; pay your bills on time; support the police." *News of the World*, September 20, 1981.

"Economics is the method; the object is to change the soul." Sunday *Times*, May 5, 1981.

"I came to office with one deliberate intent: to change Britain from a dependent to a self-reliant society; from a give-it-to-me to a do-it-yourself nation; a get-up-and-go instead of a sit-back-and-wait Britain." Speech to Small Business Bureau, February 8, 1984.

"The mission of this government is much more than the promotion of economic progress. It is to renew the spirit and solidarity of the nation." Speech in Cambridge, July 6, 1979.

"What I am desperately trying to do is create one nation with everyone being a man of property or having the opportunity to be a man of property." Sunday *Times*, February 27, 1983.

"I don't believe this country wants weak government. I don't believe they want a government to be so flexible that it becomes invertebrate. I think they want a government with a bit of spine. You don't want a government of flexi-toys." *Sun*, July 9, 1985.

"This is not just a fight about national solvency. It is a fight about the very foundations of the social order. It is a crusade not merely to put a temporary block on Socialism but to stop its onward march once and for all." *Times*, October 9, 1976.

"We shall not be diverted from our course. To those waiting with bated breath for that favorite media catch-phrase, the U-turn, I have only one thing to say: you turn if you want; the Lady's not for turning." Speech to Conservative party conference, October 10, 1980.

"We don't change our tune to whoever we are talking." *Daily Express*, April 24, 1987.

"Without the strong, who would provide for the weak? When you hold back the successful you penalize those who need help." Speech to Conservative party conference, October 13, 1978.

"I am leader of the pack. What's a leader for but to lead the pack? Of course they are behind me. If they were in front of me they would be the leaders." London Weekend Television, March 4, 1980.

"Just remember this. If you are to be leader, you don't just sit back and mutter sweet nothings or listen and do nothing. That's not the essence of leadership." *Daily Mail*, May 3, 1980.

"I am painted as the greatest little dictator, which is ridiculous—you always take some consultations." *Times*, June 8, 1983.

PERSONAL QUALITIES

"I'm not hard. I'm frightfully soft. But I will not be hounded. I will not be driven anywhere against my will." *Daily Mail*, February 2, 1972.

"I'm a tough boss and I drive people. I am not the great dictator. But I do know my own mind. I do know the direction in which I want to go and I do try to influence argument with argument." *Daily Express*, February 20, 1986.

"There are two sides of me: the informal friendly me and the iron touch, the Iron Lady. But just because you have to demonstrate iron from time to time, that doesn't mean that it should show through the whole time." *Daily Mail*, May 3, 1980.

"I cry. What human being with any sensitivity wouldn't? Men cry too. There's nothing wrong with crying at the appropriate time." *Daily Mail*, September 10, 1979.

"Power does create loneliness. Other people make the easy decisions so one is left with the difficult ones." *Daily Telegraph*, March 24, 1986.

"I'm absolutely amazed when some people say I am hard or uncaring, because it is so utterly untrue. I can't say it because it's like saying 'I'm a very modest person.' Nobody believes you. But when people meet me, they say 'you're not a bit like I thought you'd be.' But you can't meet everyone, more's the pity." *Daily Express*, February 20, 1986.

"I've never had more than four or five hours' sleep. Anyway, my life is my work. Some people work to live. I live to work." *Sunday Daily Mail*, February 3, 1985.

"I don't like sugar. But I do like a thick sauce with fish and fruit with meringue on top, and chocolate sauce with ice cream. I love baked potatoes too, but only with lots of butter. You just learn not to eat too much, to take the top off a tart and scuffle around to find the fruit underneath." *Sunday Daily Mail*, February 3, 1985.

"My pleasure reading is the John le Carré kind of thing, which I love; of course, I do read biography, and some philosophy and anything in connection with the home. I love going through the house and garden magazines, seeing what these people are doing who have time and money to do it." *Times*, May 5, 1980.

"Life is infinitely more precious to me now [after the IRA Brighton bombing attack]. Something like that alters your perspective. You're not going to be worried or complain about silly niggly little things anymore." *Daily Telegraph*, November 13, 1984.

"I think astrology charts are fun, but I'm not guided by them." *Sun*, July 9, 1985.

WEALTH AND ENTERPRISE

"There are too few rich and too few profits." Speech to Conservative National Union Executive, June 13, 1975.

"The way to recovery is through profits." Speech to Conservative party conference, October 10, 1975.

"No one would have remembered the Good Samaritan if he'd only had good intentions. He had money as well." *Weekend World,* January 6, 1980.

"Unfortunately in our education system youngsters are still not given sufficient encouragement to go into industry or commerce and not told that it is a good thing to make an honest profit. They should be told that if you don't make a profit, you won't be in business very long because you haven't anything to plow back for tomorrow. You make your profit by pleasing others so you have to make it honestly." *Director,* September 1983.

"That is what capitalism is: a system that brings wealth to the many, not just to the few." Speech to a joint session of Congress, February 20, 1985.

"You cannot look after the hard-up people in society unless you are accruing enough wealth to do so. Good intentions are not enough. You do need hard cash." BBC TV, July 11, 1977.

"Most people would think it right that those who are in work should be better off than those who unfortunately cannot find work." *Hansard,* December 18, 1982.

"It is neither moral nor responsible for a government to spend beyond the nation's means—even for services which may be desirable." Speech to conference of Conservative trade unionists, November 1, 1980.

PRIVATIZATION

"When you take into public ownership a profitable industry, the profits soon disappear. The goose that laid the golden eggs goes broody. State geese are not great layers." Speech to constituents in Finchley, January 31, 1976.

THE LABOR PARTY

"To many of us it seems there is precious little difference between the policies of the Communist Party and the policies of the Labor Party." *Times*, December 12, 1980.

"What the Labor party of today wants is: housing municipalized; industry re-nationalized; the police service politicized; the judiciary radicalized; union membership dynamized and, above all and most serious of all, our defense neutralized. Never. Never in Britain." Speech to Conservative party conference, October 10, 1986.

"A Labor Britain would be a neutralist Britain. It would be the greatest gain for the Soviet Union in forty years. And they would have got it without firing a shot." Speech to Conservative party conference, October 10, 1986.

DEFENSE

"A bully has no respect for a weakling. The way to stop a bully is not to be weak. The way to stop a bully from ever being a bully is to say, 'I'm as strong as you. Anything you do to me, I can do to you.' We are going for nuclear and conventional disarmament, but we're going about it in the right way." *World This Weekend*, January 10, 1982.

"Nuclear weapons have been a deterrent to war. I therefore believe we should keep them." Speech to House of Commons, June 15, 1982.

On whether she would actually use nuclear weapons: "If necessary, yes." Speech to House of Commons, January 15, 1981.

RELATIONS WITH THE UNITED STATES

"This party is pro-American." *Times*, October 13, 1984.

"I support very much the approaches that the president is taking. As you know, I am his greatest fan." *Times*, February 18, 1985.

"We see so many things in the same way. You can speak of a real meeting of the minds. I feel no inhibitions about describing the relationship as very, very special." *Financial Times*, February 23, 1985.

"The West could have no better or braver champion [than Ronald Reagan]." Speech at Conservative party conference, October 11, 1985.

"We are very fortunate to have someone else's weapons stationed on our soil, to fight those targeted on us." *Time*, February 16, 1981.

"The Americans can rely on me absolutely in defense and in everything in which I believe." *Daily Mail*, November 7, 1983.

"The United States has no Socialist party. No Socialist party has been in power. That is why it has always been the country of last resort for every currency." *Times*, June 1, 1984.

"In the United States, you have two parties based on free enterprise, freedom and justice. Here the two main parties have two fundamentally different philosophies." *Director*, September 1983.

RELATIONS WITH THE SOVIET UNION

"The Russians are bent on world domination." *Times*, January 20, 1976.

"The threat to peace comes from Communism, which has powerful forces ready to attack anywhere. Communism waits for weakness. It leaves strength alone. Britain must therefore be strong: strong in her arms, strong in her faith, strong in her own way of life." Margaret Roberts election leaflet fighting Dartford seat, 1950.

"They put guns before butter while we put everything before guns." Speech at Kensington Town Hall, January 20, 1976.

"Every child knows the story of Little Red Riding Hood and what happened to her in her grandmother's cottage in the forest. Despite the new look of these communist parties, despite the softness of their voices, we should be on the watch for the teeth and the appetite of the wolf." *Morning Star*, May 26, 1976.

"Communism never sleeps, never changes its objectives. Nor must we." *Financial Times*, May 23, 1979.

"Me? A Cold Warrior? Well, yes—if that is how *they* wish to interpret my defense of values and freedoms fundamental to our way of life." Speech to Finchley constituents, January 31, 1976.

"Is there conscience in the Kremlin? Do they ever ask themselves what is the purpose of life? What is it all for? No. Their creed is barren of conscience, immune to the promptings of good and evil." *Times*, September 30, 1983.

"I like Mr. Gorbachev. We can do business together." Chequers, December 1984.

"If he told me he was going to do something, I would implicitly trust his word." Moscow, 1987.

SOCIALISM

"State Socialism is totally alien to the British character." *Times*, June 8, 1983.

"Socialists have always seemed to me to assume that other people were creating a world for them to distribute." *Director*, September 1983.

"Marxists get up early to defend their cause. We must get up even earlier to defend our freedom." *Daily Mail*, June 13, 1978.

"My job is to stop Britain going red." November 3, 1977.

"Let Labor's Orwellian nightmare of the left be the spur for us to dedicate with a new urgency our every ounce of moral strength to rebuild the fortunes of this free nation. If we were to fail, that freedom could be imperiled. So let us resist the blandishments of the faint-hearts; let us ignore the howls and threats of the extremists, let us stand together and do our duty and we shall not fail." Speech at Tory party conference, October 10, 1980.

"The Socialist battle cry is always the same. 'The Conservatives,' they say, 'want unemployment.' 'Conservative cuts,' they claim, 'would double or treble those out of work.' Now this is nonsense and we must recognize it as nonsense." *Times*, October 9, 1976.

"Step by step we are rolling back the frontiers of Socialism and returning power to the people." Speech to Conservative party conference, October 11, 1985.

"There are some people deeply hostile to everything I believe in because they don't want a free enterprise system. They are out to create anarchy and chaos because they don't want recovery under this system." *Sunday Times*, August 3, 1980.

"Marxism has had it." *Washington Post*, November 1988.

BRITISH PRIDE

"Wherever I go I am offered Perrier water. I get very irritated because we have a perfectly good British alternative in Malvern water." *Sun*, July 9, 1985.

LAW AND ORDER

"I personally have always supported capital punishment. I think that the vast majority of people in this country would like to see the death penalty restored. It isn't that I wish to see it used a very great deal." *Times*, April 26, 1979.

"People who go out prepared to take the lives of other people forfeit their own right to live." *Times*, October 16, 1984.

"I think the cane has a place in the training of children." *Sunday Pictorial*, July 30, 1961.

"We need more police, not less. They carry out their duties magnificently." *Hansard*, July 26, 1981.

NORTHERN IRELAND

"I understand the tragedy of Northern Ireland. It is a tragedy in which there are a few people who use the gun, murder, explosives and violence to intimidate the civilian population into surrender when they could not persuade them through the ballot box." *Times*, May 15, 1981.

TRADE UNIONS

"There are people in this country who are great destroyers; they wish to destroy the kind of free society we have. Many of these people are in unions." Thames TV, April 24, 1979.

"I do not believe that people who go on strike in this country have a legitimate cause." *Hansard,* June 17, 1982.

"There is no problem about my getting on with trade unions or trade unions getting on with me, provided we are both interested in getting a flourishing Britain." BBC TV, February 23, 1976.

IMMIGRATION

"We do not think people can go on coming in at this present rate. There should be immediate and substantial reduction in the numbers coming in." BBC TV, April 27, 1977.

"I have constantly tried to limit the flow of immigrants . . . a high proportion are young and likely to have families." Speech at House of Commons, May 5, 1981.

CRITICISM

"I have no idea why people keep attacking me. I don't think I deserve it at all." *Sunday Express*, January 1, 1972.

"The criticism has been vicious, but in the end, you have to build an armor around yourself, knowing the things they say about you aren't true. I think it's worse for Denis, having to sit back and listen to it all. When he sees me tired, he says, 'Why don't you give this job up?' My greatest strength, I think, is that come what may, I somehow cope." *Daily Mail*, February 2, 1972.

"People can be so vicious and if you pay too much attention, you get a complex about yourself. People always try to topple you, but they won't win. I read very, very little about myself. If there's a snide remark I know it could put me off for two or three hours, maybe stop me concentrating. So I don't look." *Daily Express*, August 13, 1980.

"Those people, particularly in the House [of Commons], who yelp and yawp at me every day aren't worried about my policies *failing*. That's not why they want me to change them. They're trying to knock me off those policies because they believe they will *succeed*." *Daily Mail*, May 3, 1980.

"I must say the adrenaline flows when they really come out fighting at me and I fight back and I stand there and I know: 'Now come on, Maggie, you are wholly on your own. No one can help you.' And I love it." *Times*, December 1, 1980.

THE SUCCESSION TO HER

"I hope to go on and on and on." BBC with John Cole, May, 1987.

"There will come a time when a younger person is entitled to a chance. But if I'd said that right at the beginning, they'd have said: 'Maggie's going before the fourth election. You don't know whom you're going to get.' So I suggest you do know who you're going to get. It's me!" *Daily Telegraph*, May 21, 1987.

"It has always been my strategy that we should stay in power long enough to make sure that the Labor party realizes that their policies will never result in their re-election. . . . I want to be sure that the things we have achieved are entrenched. I want to make sure that they become almost a part of the habit and custom of the British people, so deeply entrenched that they cannot be overthrown for many generations. It is not that I believe no one else is fit. It is simply that people know the way I drive and that so long as I am in Number 10, there will be no doubts." *Evening Standard*, March 17, 1987.

"I have no wish to retire at all for a very long time. I am still bursting with energy." *Daily Express*, April 24, 1987.

"Obviously at some time or other you have to hand over to someone new, fresh, young, dynamic. You do not want to cling on so they have to say: 'Who is going to tell the old girl she had better go?' " *Star*, June 25, 1986.

"I think male prime ministers will one day come back into fashion." Interview, 1987.

Notes

CHAPTER ONE: *The Inheritance*

1. Barnett, *The Collapse of British Power*, p. 72.
2. Manchester, *The Last Lion, Alone*, p. 46.
3. Heussler, *Yesterday's Rulers: The Making of the British Colonial Service* (New York: Syracuse University Press, 1963), p. 76; cited in Barnett, p. 64 n.
4. Barnett, p. 63.
5. Ibid., p. 67.
6. Dimbleby and Reynolds, *An Ocean Apart*, p. 101.
7. Manchester, p. 85.
8. Ibid.
9. Dimbleby and Reynolds, p. 129.
10. Ibid., p. 135.
11. Sked, *Britain's Decline*, p. 27.
12. Churchill, *The Second World War*, 4: 583.
13. Manchester, pp. 48–49.
14. Brzezinski, *The Grand Failure*, p. 9.
15. Childs, *Britain Since 1945*, p. 31.
16. Ibid., p. 32.
17. Ibid., p. 33.
18. Kaiser, *Cold Winter, Cold War*, p. 29.
19. Childs, p. 36.
20. Sked, p. 28.
21. Childs, p. 39.
22. Blake, *The Conservative Party from Peel to Thatcher*, pp. 263–64.
23. Childs, p. 38.

CHAPTER TWO: *Grocer's Daughter*

Thatcher's early years are well described by other authors to whom I am indebted, including Patricia Murray, Penny Junor, Allan J. Mayer, and Nicholas Wapshott and George Brock. In addition to author interviews and visits to Grantham, Oxford, and Dartford, Dixie Nichols and Brigid Forster provided extensive research for this chapter.

1. Parkhouse, *Sunday Express*, July 20, 1975.
2. Ibid.
3. Wapshott and Brock, *Thatcher*, p. 27.
4. Parkhouse.
5. Mayer, *Madam Prime Minister*, p. 30.
6. Interview with author, January 1989.
7. Ibid.
8. *Daily Telegraph*, February 5, 1975.
9. Leo Abse, *Margaret, Daughter of Beatrice*, 1989.
10. *Daily Mail*, May 25, 1989.
11. Molly Brandreth to Brigid Forster, February 1989.
12. Parkhouse.
13. Junor, *Margaret Thatcher*, p. 13.
14. Manchester, p. 604.
15. Wapshott and Brock, p. 37.
16. Ibid., p. 47.
17. Ibid., p. 40.
18. Margaret Wickstead to Brigid Forster, February 1989.
19. Wapshott and Brock, p. 40.
20. Ministry of Labor documents, 1943.
21. Parkhouse.
22. Wapshott and Brock, p. 49.
23. Mayer, p. 49.
24. Young and Sloman, *The Thatcher Phenomenon*, p. 17.
25. Ibid., p. 18.
26. Interview with author, November 1988.
27. Young and Sloman, p. 20.
28. Bawden, in *My Oxford: Recollections of 12 Oxford Graduates, 1918–1971*, edited by Ann B. Thwaite, Robson Books, 1977.
29. Junor, p. 20.
30. Dimbleby and Reynolds, p. 170.
31. Murray, *Margaret Thatcher*, p. 38.
32. Ibid.
33. Ibid.
34. Interview with author, January 1989.
35. Ibid.
36. Junor, p. 26.
37. Mayer, p. 65.
38. Ibid.
39. Junor, p. 26.

40. Interview with author, January 1989.
41. Mayer, p. 66.
42. Murray, p. 43.
43. Wapshott and Brock, p. 56.
44. Ibid., p. 57.
45. Interview with author, January 1989.

CHAPTER THREE: *Wife and Mother*

1. Junor, p. 35.
2. *The Times* (London), October 5, 1970; cited in McFadyean and Renn, *Thatcher's Reign,* p. 120.
3. Malcolm Rutherford, *Financial Times,* March 8, 1986, cited in Young, *One of Us,* p. 38.
4. *The Times* (London), October 5, 1970.
5. Gardiner, *Margaret Thatcher,* p. 46.
6. Interview with author, January 1989.
7. Interview with William Deedes, January 9, 1989.
8. Newhouse, *New Yorker,* February 10, 1986.
9. *Time,* August 14, 1989.
10. To Frank Melville, London.
11. Wapshott and Brock, p. 57.
12. Junor, p. 34.
13. Mayer, p. 71.
14. Interview with author, January 1989.
15. Ibid.
16. Ibid.
17. Ibid., also Murray, p. 48; Wapshott and Brock, p. 60.
18. Mayer, p. 71.
19. Murray, p. 49.
20. Junor, p. 36.
21. Wapshott and Brock, p. 60.
22. Young, pp. 39–40.
23. Gathorne-Hardy, Jonathan, *The Unnatural History of the Nanny* (Dial, 1973), reviewed in *Time,* August 13, 1973.
24. Junor, p. 40.
25. Interview with author, January 1989.
26. Junor, p. 49.
27. *Daily Express,* August 13, 1980.
28. Murray, p. 63.
29. Interview with author, January 1989.

CHAPTER FOUR: *Into Parliament*

1. Thomson, *Margaret Thatcher,* p. 102.
2. Childs, p. 72.

3. Jenkins, *New York Times Book Review*, March 5, 1989.
4. Childs, p. 95.
5. Jenkins, citing Macmillan biography by Alistair Horne (Macmillan, 1989).
6. Wapshott and Brock, p. 77.
7. Mayer, p. 79.
8. Ibid., p. 80.
9. Interview with author, December 1988.
10. Wapshott and Brock, p. 79.
11. Ibid., p. 80.

CHAPTER FIVE: *Thatcher, Milk Snatcher*

1. Interview with author, December 1988; also Young and Sloman, p. 23.
2. Ibid.
3. Interview with author, December 1988.
4. Childs, p. 282.
5. Dimbleby and Reynolds, pp. 222–23.
6. Ibid., p. 223.
7. Ibid., p. 259, citing Charles de Gaulle, *War Memoirs: Unity, 1942–1944* (Weidenfeld, 1956), p. 227.
8. Macmillan, *At the End of the Day*, p. 367, quoted in Dimbleby and Reynolds, p. 260.
9. Mayer, p. 84.
10. Honey, *Does Accent Matter?* p. 142; also cited in Steve Lohr, *New York Times*, January 31, 1989.
11. Interview with author, December 1988.
12. Junor, p. 69.
13. Wapshott and Brock, p. 85.
14. Geoffrey Parkhouse, unpublished Thatcher interview, 1970.
15. Ibid.
16. Young and Sloman, p. 33.
17. Thames Television, January 6, 1981, cited in McFadyean and Renn, p. 111.
18. Junor, p. 62; Wapshott and Brock, p. 270.
19. Wapshott and Brock, appendix, p. 278.
20. Foote, *A Chronology of Postwar British Politics*, p. 128.
21. Young and Sloman, p. 24.
22. Sampson, *The Changing Anatomy of Britain*, p. 114.
23. Young and Sloman, p. 26.
24. Junor, p. 72.
25. Cabinet source to author, December 1988.
26. Junor, p. 73; Wapshott and Brock, p. 97.
27. Parkhouse, unpublished.
28. Cabinet source to author, January 1989.
29. Young and Sloman, p. 22.

CHAPTER SIX: *The Coup*

1. Cabinet source to author, January 1989.
2. Interview with author, January 1989.
3. Keith Joseph to author, January 1989.
4. Party source to author, December 1988.
5. Joseph to author.
6. *Time*, February 10, 1975.
7. James Prior to author, December 1989.
8. Ian Gow to author, January 1989.
9. William Whitelaw to author, December 1988.
10. Wapshott and Brock, p. 126.
11. Murray, p. 104.
12. Cockerell, *Live from Number 10*, p. 217.

CHAPTER SEVEN: *Brink of Power*

1. Whitelaw, *The Whitelaw Memoirs*, p. 143.
2. Mayer, p. 127.
3. Whitelaw to author, December 1988.
4. Joseph to author, January 1989.
5. Wapshott and Brock, p. 157.
6. Ronald Millar to author, January 1989.
7. Junor, p. 107.
8. Ibid.
9. Ibid., p. 109.
10. Mayer, p. 141.
11. Jimmy Carter, *Keeping Faith* (Bantam, 1982), p. 113.
12. Cabinet sources to author, December–January 1988–89.
13. Tim Bell to author, December 1988.
14. Mayer, p. 174.
15. Bell.
16. *Time*, April 21, 1979.

CHAPTER EIGHT: *Downing Street Revolution*

1. Stephenson, *Mrs. Thatcher's First Year*, p. 12.
2. *Time*, June 25, 1979.
3. Ibid.
4. Geoffrey Howe to author, January 1989.
5. Lord Carrington to author, December 1988.
6. Mayer, p. 203.
7. Carrington.
8. Carrington, *Reflect on Things Past*, p. 277.
9. Stephenson, p. 89.
10. Interview with author, January 1989.

CHAPTER NINE: *Early Doldrums*

1. *Time*, February 16, 1981.
2. Millar to author, January 1989.
3. *Time*, February 16, 1981.
4. Interview with author, January 1989.
5. Sampson, p. 96.
6. *Sunday Times* (London), May 3, 1981.

CHAPTER TEN: *War in a Faraway Place*

I have relied heavily in this chapter on the extensive coverage of the ten-week war in the international editions of *Time* magazine, which, between May 10 and May 31, 1982, ran four consecutive cover stories on the Falklands. I owe special thanks for material and recollections provided by London correspondents Bonnie Angelo and Frank Melville and their counterparts in Argentina: Barry Hillenbrand, Bill McWhirter, and Gavin Scott. George Russell, formerly chief correspondent for South America, wrote many of the stories in New York and afforded unique perspective. Top editor Karsten Prager oversaw the effort with exceptional skill.

1. *Sunday Times* (London), Robert Harris book review, April 9, 1989, citing *Speaking Out*, by Michael Bilton and Peter Kosminsky (Deutsch, 1989).
2. Haig, *Caveat*, p. 266.
3. Chief of Defense Staff Lord Lewin to author, December 1988.
4. Haig, p. 265.
5. Nicholas Henderson to author, December 1988.
6. Whitelaw to author, December 1988.
7. Cecil Parkinson to author, December 1988.
8. Carrington to author, December 1988.
9. Fleet Commander Sir John Woodward to author, December 1988.
10. Cabinet sources to author, December 1988.
11. Henderson.
12. Ibid.
13. Haig, p. 272.
14. Source to author, January 1989.
15. Ministerial source to author, November–December 1989.
16. Cabinet source to author, December 1988.
17. Lewin.
18. Whitelaw.
19. Parkinson.
20. *Sunday Times* (London), citing *The Fight for the Malvinas*, by Martin Middlebrook (Viking, 1989).
21. Cabinet sources to author, December–January 1988–89.
22. Harris, *Thatcher*, p. 138.
23. *Washington Post*, cited in Wapshott and Brock, p. 255.
24. Haig, p. 297.

CHAPTER ELEVEN: *Falklands Factor*

1. Cheltenham, July 3, 1982.
2. Jenkins, *Mrs. Thatcher's Revolution*, p. 165.
3. Bernard Ingham to author, June 1987.
4. Butler and Kavanagh, *The British General Election of 1983*, p. 41.
5. Junor, p. 190.

CHAPTER TWELVE: *War at Home*

1. Pym, *The Politics of Consent*, intro.
2. Pym, p. 15.
3. Parkinson to author, December 1988.
4. Bell.
5. King to author, January 1989.
6. Cabinet source to author, November 1988.
7. *The Times* (London), February 9, 1984.
8. Harris, *The Making of Neil Kinnock*, p. 108.
9. Ian MacGregor to author, December 1988.
10. *Time*, June 3, 1985.
11. Andre Gorz, *Farewell to the Working Class* (Pluto Press, 1982), p. 74, cited in Jenkins, p. 236.

CHAPTER THIRTEEN: *The Irish Question*

1. Ronald Millar to author, January 1989.
2. Thomson, *Margaret Thatcher*, p. 187.
3. O'Brien and O'Brien, *A Concise History of Ireland*, p. 61.
4. Glenn Frankel, *Washington Post*, August 14, 1989.
5. *Time*, November 12, 1979.
6. Ministerial source to author, December 1988.
7. Cabinet and ministerial sources to author, December–January 1988–89.
8. Cabinet sources to author, November–January 1988–89.
9. Peter Robinson to author, September 1985.
10. John Hermon to author, September 1988.
11. *Time*, February 13, 1989, p. 29.
12. Martin McGuinness to author, September 1988.

CHAPTER FOURTEEN: *Ron and Maggie*

1. *National Review*, May 19, 1989.
2. Cabinet source to author, November 1988.
3. Government sources to author, April 1988.

4. *National Review.*
5. Interview with author, January 1989.
6. Young, p. 250.
7. Haig, pp. 254–55.
8. Ministerial source to author, November 1988.
9. Cabinet and government sources to author, November–December 1988.
10. Interview with author, December 1988.
11. Oliver Wright to author, January 1989.
12. Talbott, *Master of the Game*, p. 207.
13. Participant to author, January 1989.
14. Regan, *For the Record*, p. 350; Talbott, p. 325.

CHAPTER FIFTEEN: *Eye of the Storm*

1. Thatcher interview with David Frost, TV-AM, May 7, 1987.
2. Young, p. 447.
3. *Sunday Times* (London), April 9, 1989.
4. Interview with author, October 1988.
5. News conference with Association of American Correspondents in London, January 17, 1986.
6. Government sources to author, December–January 1988–89.
7. Sources to author, November–January 1988–89.

CHAPTER SIXTEEN: *PM and HM*

1. Sampson, *Changing Anatomy of Britain*, p. 6.
2. Women's Own radio, October 31, 1987.
3. Interview with author, November 1988.
4. Lacey, *Majesty*, p. 322.
5. Robert Harris, *Observer*, November 27, 1988.
6. Earl of Gowrie to author, November 1988.
7. Source to author, November 1988.
8. Source to author, December–January 1988–89.
9. Source to author, January 1989.
10. Harris.
11. Source to author.
12. *Time*, August 18, 1986.
13. Source to author, January 1989.

CHAPTER SEVENTEEN: *The Opposition Collapses*

1. *Time*, October 13, 1986.
2. Larry Whitty to author, October 1986.

CHAPTER EIGHTEEN: *Maggie and Mikhail*

1. Interview with *Washington Post*, November 28, 1988.
2. Gennady Gerasimov to author, May 1989.
3. Editors of *Time, Mikhail S. Gorbachev: An Intimate Biography*, 1988. pp. 126–27.
4. Ministerial sources to author, November–January 1988–89.
5. Carol Thatcher, *Life*, October 1987, p. 32.
6. *Time*, March 14, 1988.

CHAPTER NINETEEN: *Hat Trick*

1. Leapman, *Kinnock*, p. 79.
2. Ministerial sources to author, 1985–89.
3. Campaign source to author, December 1988.
4. Bell to author, December–January 1988–89.
5. *Time*, June 1, 1987.

CHAPTER TWENTY: *Metal Fatigue?*

1. John Biffen to author, December 1988.
2. Gerald Lubenow in *Newsweek*, January 18, 1988.
3. *Time*, October 12, 1987.
4. *Observer*, July 19, 1987.
5. Young, p. 402.
6. Donna Foote in *Newsweek*, July 17, 1989.
7. Andrew Graham Dixon in *Vanity Fair*, October 1989.
8. Sir Peter Hall, to the Association of American Correspondents in London, September 2, 1986.
9. Peter Ustinov, to the Association of American Correspondents in London, February 18, 1988.
10. *The Economist*, September 16, 1989.
11. Craig Whitney in the *New York Times*, May 23, 1989.
12. David Broder in the *Washington Post*, June 20, 1989.
13. *Sunday Telegraph*, June 18, 1989.
14. *Time*, July 24, 1989.
15. R. W. Apple, Jr., in the *New York Times*, July 17, 1989.
16. *Ibid*.
17. *The Independent*, October 27, 1989.
18. *The Economist*, October 7, 1989.
19. David Broder in the *Washington Post*, July 16, 1989.

CHAPTER TWENTY-ONE: *Maggie's Britain*

1. Skidelsky, *Thatcherism*, introduction, p. 14.
2. Barzini, *The Europeans*, p. 64 (quoting Geoffrey Madan's *Notebooks: A Selection*).
3. Young and Sloman, p. 39.
4. Anthony King in Skidelsky's *Thatcherism*, p. 56.
5. *Weekend World*, June 12, 1988.
6. Tebbit, *Upwardly Mobile*, p. 268.
7. Quoted in Barzini, p. 51.
8. *Business Week*, April 6, 1987.
9. *Financial Times*, October 29, 1987.
10. *Time*, June 22, 1987.
11. Disraeli, *Sybil: The Two Nations*, quoted in *Time*, December 24, 1984.
12. *The Times* (London), November 24, 1989.

Bibliography

Adeney, Martin and Lloyd, John. *The Miners' Strike, 1984–5: Loss Without Limit.* Routledge and Kegan Paul, 1986.

Barnett, Correlli. *The Collapse of British Power.* Alan Sutton, 1984.

Barzini, Luigi. *The Europeans.* Penguin, 1983.

Bell, David S. *The Conservative Government, 1979–84.* Croom Helm, 1985.

Blake, Robert. *The Conservative Party from Peel to Thatcher.* Methuen, 1985.

Bogdanov, Vernon and Skidelsky, Robert. *The Age of Affluence, 1951–1964.* Macmillan, 1970.

Bradshaw, Kenneth and Pring, David. *Parliament and Congress.* Constable, 1972.

Bruce-Gardyne, Jock. *Ministers and Mandarins.* Sidgwick & Jackson, 1986.

Brzezinski, Zbigniew. *The Grand Failure.* Scribners, 1989.

Burch, Martin and Moran, Michael. *British Politics.* Manchester University Press, 1987.

Butler, David and Kavanagh, Dennis. *The British General Election of 1979.* Macmillan, 1980.

———.*The British General Election of 1983.* Macmillan, 1984.

———.*The British General Election of 1987.* Macmillan, 1988.

Carrington, Peter. *Reflect on Things Past.* Collins, 1988.

Castle, Barbara. *The Castle Diaries.* Weidenfeld and Nicolson, 1980.

Chesshyre, Robert. *The Return of a Native Reporter.* Viking, 1987; gritty societal look from beyond London.

Childs, David. *Britain Since 1945.* Methuen, 1979.

Churchill, Winston S. *The Second World War.* 6 vols. Cassell, 1948–54.

Cockerell, Michael. *Live from Number 10.* Faber, 1988.

Cole, John. *The Thatcher Years.* BBC, 1987.

Coleman, Terry. *Thatcher's Britain.* Bantam, 1987.

Coleville, John. *The Fringes of Power.* Hodder and Stoughton, 1985.

Cosgrave, Patrick. *Margaret Thatcher: A Tory and Her Party.* Hutchinson, 1978.

Crick, Michael. *The March of Militant.* Faber, 1986.

Daly, Macdonald and George, Alexander. *Margaret Thatcher in Her Own Words.* Penguin, 1987.

Dimbleby, David and Reynolds, David. *An Ocean Apart.* Random House, 1988; a superb account, both scholarly and eminently readable, of the twentieth-century relationship between Britain and the United States.

Donoughue, Bernard. *Prime Minister: The Conduct of Policy Under Harold Wilson and James Callaghan 1974–79.* Jonathan Cape, 1987.

Eatwell, John. *Whatever Happened to Britain.* Duckworth/BBC, 1982.

Foot, Paul. *The Politics of Harold Wilson.* Penguin, 1968.

Foote, Geoffrey. *A Chronology of Postwar British Politics.* Croom Helm, 1988.

Gardiner, George. *Margaret Thatcher.* Kimber, 1975.

Gilmour, Ian. *Inside Right: A Study of Conservatism.* Quartet, 1977.

Haig, Alexander M., Jr. *Caveat.* Macmillan, 1984.

Hanson, A. H. and Walles, Malcolm. *Governing Britain.* Fontana/Collins, 1970.

Harris, Kenneth. *Thatcher.* Weidenfeld and Nicolson, 1988.

Harris, Robert. *The Making of Neil Kinnock.* Faber, 1984.

Hastings, Max and Jenkins, Simon. *The Battle for the Falklands.* Michael Joseph, 1986.

Henderson, Nicholas. *Channels and Tunnels.* Weidenfeld and Nicolson, 1987.

Honey, John. *Does Accent Matter?* Faber, 1989.

Howard, Anthony and West, Richard. *The Making of the Prime Minister.* Jonathan Cape, 1965.

Jenkins, Peter. *Mrs. Thatcher's Revolution.* Jonathan Cape, 1987; original and insightful writing about postwar British politics from one of that nation's preeminent commentators.

Johnson, Paul. *Modern Times.* Harper & Row, 1983.

Joseph, Keith. *Stranded on the Middle Ground.* Center for Policy Studies, 1976.

Junor, Penny. *Margaret Thatcher.* Sidgwick & Jackson, 1983; the most detailed look at Mrs. Thatcher's personal life.

Kaiser, Robert G. *Cold Winter, Cold War.* Stein and Day, 1974.

Kavanagh, Dennis. *Thatcherism and British Politics.* Oxford University Press, 1987.

Kellner, Peter and Hitchens, Christopher. *Callaghan: The Road to Number 10.* Cassell, 1976.

Kleinman, Philip. *The Saatchi and Saatchi Story.* Weidenfeld and Nicolson, 1987.

Kogan, David and Kogan, Maurice. *The Battle for the Labour Party.* Kogan Page, 1982.

Lacey, Robert. *Majesty.* Sphere Books, 1977.

Leapman, Michael. *Kinnock.* Unwin Hyman, 1987.

Lewis, Flora. *Europe.* Touchstone, 1987.

Longford, Elizabeth. *The Queen.* Ballantine, 1983.

MacGregor, Ian. *The Enemies Within.* Collins, 1986.

Manchester, William. *The Last Lion, Alone.* Little Brown, 1988.

Mayer, Allan J. *Madam Prime Minister.* Newsweek, 1979.

McFadyean, Melanie and Renn, Margaret. *Thatcher's Reign.* Chatto and Windus, 1984.

Messenger, Charles. *Northern Ireland: The Troubles.* Hamlyn, 1985.

Minogue, Kenneth and Biddiss, Michael. *Thatcherism: Personality and Politics.* Macmillan, 1987.

Murray, Patricia. *Margaret Thatcher.* W. H. Allen, 1980; good early-in-office Thatcher interviews.

Newhouse, John. "Profile: The Gamefish." *New Yorker,* February 10, 1986.

O'Brien, Máire and Conor Cruise. *A Concise History of Ireland.* Rev. ed. Thames and Hudson, 1985.

Owen, David. *Our N.H.S.* Pan, 1988.

Pearce, Edward. *Looking down on Mrs. Thatcher.* Hamish Hamilton, 1987.

Pointer, Michael and Knapp, Malcolm G. *Bygone Grantham.* 6 vols. BG Publications, 1977–87.

Prior, James. *A Balance of Power.* Hamish Hamilton, 1986.

Pym, Francis. *The Politics of Consent.* Hamish Hamilton, 1984.

Reagan, Ronald. *Where's the Rest of Me?* Karz, 1981.

Regan, Donald T. *For the Record.* Harcourt Brace Jovanovich, 1988.

Riddell, Peter. *The Thatcher Government.* Basil Blackwell, 1983.

Rose, Richard and Suleiman, Ezra N. *Presidents and Prime Ministers.* AEI Studies, 1980.

Sampson, Anthony. *The Anatomy of Britain.* Hodder and Stoughton, 1962.

———.*The Changing Anatomy of Britain.* Hodder and Stoughton, 1982; these two volumes, original and updated, are classics; required, but fascinating reading for anyone wishing to understand how Britain works.

Sked, Alan. *Britain's Decline.* Basil Blackwell, 1987.

Skidelsky, Robert. *Thatcherism.* Chatto and Windus, 1988.

Stephenson, Hugh. *Mrs. Thatcher's First Year.* Jill Norman, 1980.

Talbott, Strobe. *The Master of the Game.* Knopf, 1988.

Tebbit, Norman. *Upwardly Mobile.* Weidenfeld and Nicolson, 1988.

Thomson, Andrew. *Margaret Thatcher, The Woman Within.* WH Allen, 1989.

Thorpe, D. R. *Selwyn Lloyd.* Jonathan Cape, 1989.

Tyler, Rodney. *Campaign! The Selling of the Prime Minister.* Grafton, 1987.

Urquhart, Brian. *A Life in Peace and War.* Weidenfeld and Nicolson, 1987.

Veljanovski, Cento with Mark Bentley. *Selling the State.* Weidenfeld and Nicolson, 1987.

Walters, Alan. *Britain's Economic Renaissance.* Oxford University Press, 1986.

Wapshott, Nicholas and Brock, George. *Thatcher.* Futura, 1983; well-paced first-term detail.

Whitelaw, William. *The Whitelaw Memoirs.* Aurum Press, 1989.

Young, Hugo. *One of Us,* Macmillan, 1989; the most detailed Thatcher biography by one of Britain's most thoughtful journalists.

Young, Hugo and Sloman, Anne. *The Thatcher Phenomenon.* BBC, 1986.

Acknowledgments

To be an American journalist based in Britain is a dream assignment anytime. When news is slow, it's great; when news is hot, it's even better. My latest assignment, working in London from 1985 to 1989 as *Time*'s bureau chief, belongs in the "even better" category. Margaret Thatcher was in her prime. She surged from victory over the miners as I was arriving, roared to her third win in 1987, and notched up a decade in Downing Street as I left. She was Ronald Reagan's window on Europe and Mikhail Gorbachev's channel to the White House. Exciting times to be writing about a genuine historic figure.

One of the best parts of being assigned to Britain is the exceptional access accorded American reporters at the top levels of political and professional life. Literally hundreds of people were helpful; some are acknowledged in the text, others in the notes. Still others have requested anonymity. My debt to all of them is high and my gratitude great.

This is by no means an authorized biography, yet the Prime Minister was exceptionally generous in the time she gave me. I interviewed her at length for the book, as I had for *Time*. I traveled extensively around Britain with her, particularly during the 1987 campaign, and was one of the few non-British reporters (sometimes the only one) to accompany her overseas to the Middle East, the Soviet Union, Africa, Caribbean, and the United States. Bernard Ingham, the most talented press secretary I've encountered anywhere in twenty years of political reporting, was invaluable. So too was private secretary Charles Powell, the Prime Minister's top aide. The rest of her staff, from Downing Street doormen and telephone operators to Special Branch detectives and top campaign advisers, have without exception been gracious and helpful.

A wide circle of Mrs. Thatcher's political associates, both Tories and Opposition, were unsparing with their help. Virtually her entire Cabinet, including former members, allowed me to interview them at length. Among them, in alphabetical, not priority, order: John Biffen, leader of the House of Commons; Lord Carrington, Foreign Secretary, and NATO Secretary General; the Earl of Gowrie, Lord in waiting to the Queen, Minister of State Northern Ireland Office, and Minister for the Arts; Sir Geoffrey Howe, Chancellor of the Exchequer,

Foreign Secretary, and deputy Prime Minister; Lord Joseph, Secretary of State for Industry and of Education and Science; Tom King, Secretary of State for Northern Ireland; Cecil Parkinson, Secretary of State for Energy and Conservative party chairman; Christopher Patten, Secretary of State for the Environment; Lord Prior, Secretary of State for Employment, for Northern Ireland; Lord Pym, Foreign Secretary; Peter Walker, Secretary of State for Energy and for Wales; Lord Whitelaw, deputy Prime Minister; Lady Young, leader of the House of Lords.

Other Cabinet and senior ministers provided insights through interviews, conversations, and meetings—sometimes private, at other times in my capacity as president of the Association of American Correspondents in London—over the course of my assignment and since. Among them: Lord Boyd-Carpenter, Minister of Pensions and National Insurance; Douglas Hurd, Home Secretary; Nigel Lawson, Chancellor of the Exchequer; former Prime Minister Edward Heath; Michael Heseltine, Defense Secretary; John Major, Foreign Secretary; Nicholas Scott, Minister of State for Northern Ireland; George Younger, Defense Secretary; Norman Tebbit, Secretary of State for Employment and for Trade and Industry, also Conservative party chairman.

Britain's senior military leaders during the Falklands War were of enormous help. They included Lord Bramall, Chief of General Staff and Chief of Defense Staff; Lord Lewin, First Sea Lord and Chief of Defense Staff; Admiral Sir John Woodward, commander of the British naval task force.

Other former advisers to Mrs. Thatcher who were especially helpful included private secretary Sir Clive Bossom, parliamentary private secretary Ian Gow, and principal private secretary Sir Clive Whitmore.

Denis Thatcher declined to speak to me, holding to his established practice of not commenting to journalists. But I am grateful to Lord Deedes, one of his close friends, for helping me on family matters. My thanks also to Carla Powell, whose relationship with the family is strong and personal. There were numerous other sources for private life background who requested anonymity.

From the diplomatic community: few, if any, countries could be as rich in ambassadorial talent as Britain. Thatcher has been extraordinarily well served in the United States during the Reagan and Bush administrations by Sir Nicholas Henderson, Sir Oliver Wright, and Sir Antony Acland. All have been of immense help for my understanding of the Prime Minister's relationship with the United States and its presidents as well as being extremely hospitable personally. Lady Henderson, a former *Time* stringer herself, provided valuable additional perceptions. On the American side, Ambassador Charles Price II and Raymond Seitz, deputy chief of mission, represented the United States in Britain throughout most of the 1980s with great skill. They worked tirelessly, knew everyone of every political stripe, and were very generous in sharing their knowledge.

One of the Prime Minister's greatest accomplishments has been the reinvigoration of the British business community. Some of the businessmen who gave me priceless amounts of time included: Rupert Hambro of Hambros Bank; Lord King of British Airways; Sir Ian MacGregor of British Steel and British Coal; and Lord Hanson and Sir Gordon White of Hanson plc.

Thatcher's image- and wordmeisters are a delightful as well as talented and successful group. Thank you Tim Bell, Sir Ronald Millar, and Sir Gordon Reece for details of Mrs. Thatcher's three campaigns, as well as other insights.

A note about the royal family. Over the years, I have met and spoken to the Queen, Prince Philip, Prince Charles, Princess Anne, and the Queen Mother. The Queen gives no interviews and none of the others was interviewed as such specifically for this book. All, however, provided greater understanding, particularly for Chapter 16, "HM and PM." In addition, some provided substantive information for which I am grateful.

Opposition political figures in Britain have never been reluctant to offer their thoughts about the Prime Minister. Labor leader Neil Kinnock was an exception, declining to see me for this book. He did talk to me on other occasions during my assignment. I also watched him closely in the House of Commons and traveled with him during the 1987 campaign. Other members of the Labor team were more forthcoming. My thanks to Roy Hattersley, deputy leader; Denis Healey, Defense Secretary, Chancellor of the Exchequer, shadow Foreign Secretary; Peter Shore, Secretary of State for Trade, for the Environment; John Smith, shadow chancellor. David Owen, leader of the Social Democrats, was helpful repeatedly. Liberal party leader David Steel let me be the sole reporter accompanying him aboard his private jet during one leg of the 1987 campaign and analyzed succinctly, if optimistically, Tory vulnerabilities.

No one writes a book alone. In addition to sources I've mentioned, many others helped me.

Liz Nickson inspired this undertaking. A fine writer with a great eye and ear, she is part of every page.

Jennifer and Peter Blaker, with remarkable kindness, literally opened their home to the Ogdens, allowing us to experience Britain and know Britons in a way no other visitor in my experience has. Their hospitality was extraordinary. Julia Langdon, then of the *Daily Mirror*, now of the *Sunday Telegraph*, and Geoffrey Parkhouse, of the *Glasgow Herald*, are veteran stars of the parliamentary lobby who brought me into the inner circles of Westminster journalism and the top levels of political life with unfailing generosity. They also provided guidance on the manuscript. Frank Melville, my *Time* colleague, has an unrivaled network of political, military, and diplomatic contacts built up over a career of reporting from London. His friends include some of the most powerful and influential figures in Britain. He shared them all.

Others added knowledge and simply made my British experience more worthwhile: Babs and John Cleese, Fleur Cowles and Tom Montague Meyer, Paige and Garret Cowley, Mary and Tony MacIntosh, Francoise and Christopher Meyer, Sybil and Peter Pagnamenta, Sara and Nick Ross, Jenny and Peter Shaw, Peggy and Ian Strachan. Dixie Nichols and Bob Reiss gave me a valuable insider's view of Grantham. Susan and Howell Raines provided special support. Ray Moseley, a friend and veteran *Chicago Tribune* correspondent, offered valuable manuscript advice.

This book emerges directly from my reporting for *Time*, where some of its contents appeared. Managing editor Henry Muller and chief of correspondents John Stacks supported this effort and were generous in the leeway they allowed me while I tried to combine my careers as book author and magazine writer. That holds true also for my Washington bureau chief, Stan Cloud.

Special thanks to my London *Time* colleagues: Peter Jordan, who has photographed the Prime Minister with skill for most of her years in office and was a great companion on many of her trips; Sahm Doherty-Sefton, an old friend from many foreign capitals who, I am grateful, was in London at the right time to do photo research; Brigid Forster, who helped with some interviewing and, with Mick Brunton, assisted with research; Valerie Miller, who administered the bureau with equanimity during my frequent absences; Anne Constable and Helen Gibson, fine correspondents who, week after week, bore extra work on my behalf. Special thanks to Bonnie Angelo, my predecessor, who reported Mrs. Thatcher's first six years in office for *Time*. Her work was so thorough and her contacts so wideranging that her path-clearing made my work far easier.

Alice Mayhew, my editor at Simon and Schuster, is widely considered the best in the business. I appreciate why. Her sense of politics, people, and history is superb and guided her eye and pen unerringly over—and over—this manuscript. She sculpts ideas and language with exceptional precision and honesty.

George Hodgman, her associate, is a talented editor and was my partner for the day-to-day heavy lifting of writing and polishing. His skill and motivation made my time in the editing trenches more joy than endurance test.

Mort Janklow, my agent, believed in this book from the start and managed its path with his usual great skill. Alan Gelfuso, as always, kept me on track.

Finally, a word about my family. My father, Mike, got me into this writing business. He was right—it's not easy, but it beats everything else.

My wife, Deedy, and children, Michael and Margaret, bore the brunt of the burdens and disruptions over the course of this project, not least of which was an international move midway. They endured it all with grace, love, understanding, and constant encouragement. Full partners, they've made the work worth doing. This is their book too.

February 1990
Washington, D.C.

Index